Paris
2008

Selection of
restaurants & **hotels**

Commitments

This Guide was created at the turn of the century and will last at least as long. This foreword to the very first edition of the MICHELIN Guide, written in 1900, has become famous over the years and the Guide has lived up to the prediction. It is read across the world and the key to its popularity is the consistency of its commitment to its readers, which is based on the following promises.

THE MICHELIN GUIDE'S COMMITMENTS

→ Anonymous inspections

Our inspectors make regular and anonymous visits to hotels and restaurants to gauge the quality of products and services offered to an ordinary customer. They settle their own bill and may then introduce themselves and ask for more information about the establishment. Our readers' comments are also a valuable source of information, which we can then follow up with a visit of our own.

→ Independence

Our choice of establishments is a completely independent one, made for the benefit of our readers alone. The decisions to be taken are discussed around the table by the inspectors and the editor. The most important awards are decided at a European level. Inclusion in the Guide is completely free of charge.

→ Selection and choice

The Guide offers a selection of the best hotels and restaurants in every category of comfort and price. This is only possible because all the inspectors rigorously apply the same methods.

→ Annual updates

All the practical information, the classifications and awards are revised and updated every single year to give the most reliable information possible.

→ Consistency

The criteria for the classifications are the same in every country covered by the Michelin Guide.

→ ...And our aim

to do everything possible to make travel, holidays and eating out a pleasure, as part of Michelin's ongoing commitment to improving mobility.

Dear reader

*P*aris doesn't stand still…and neither does its Michelin Guide! A new look for 2008, with a more user-friendly layout, gives you a taste of that incredible vitality in its text and illustrations. The aim of course is to make you want to try out the carefully chosen restaurants and to stay in one of the hand-picked hotels.

Our selection – since we don't claim to be exhaustive – is based on the same criteria as always: the quality of the welcome, the service and the cooking. The range of restaurants included in the guide is intended to be wide enough to satisfy all tastes. Without succumbing to fashion or abandoning our principles, we have tried to present a broad sample of starred restaurants, gourmet bistros, brasseries and different kinds of cuisine from around the world.

While Michelin stars continue to be awarded to the best restaurants, they are not our only sign of distinction. Establishments serving good food at affordable prices are highlighted with a "Bib Gourmand".

The 60 hotels in the guide are classified in a similar manner, divided into categories reflecting all the various prices and levels of comfort found in Paris. From prestigious luxury hotels to more modest – but charming – establishments, the importance of a warm welcome and good service is never forgotten.

We hope that this new guide will help you to appreciate the many culinary facets of Paris and that your journey through its pages will be one to savour.

Consult the Michelin Guide at www.viamichelin.com
and write to us at : leguidemichelin-france@fr.michelin.com

Contents

X. Richer / MICHELIN

How to use this guide

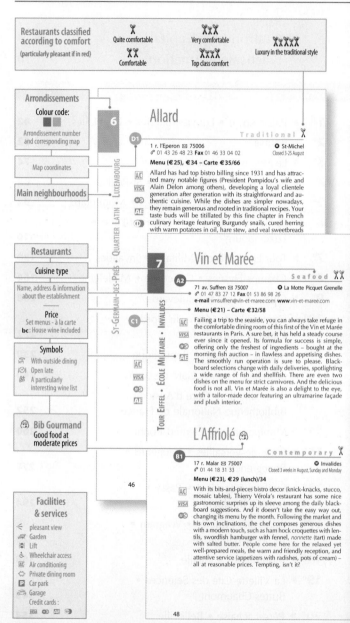

Restaurants classified according to comfort (particularly pleasant if in red)	✗ Quite comfortable	✗✗✗ Very comfortable	
	✗✗ Comfortable	✗✗✗✗ Top class comfort	✗✗✗✗✗ Luxury in the traditional style

Arrondissements

Colour code:

Arrondissement number and corresponding map

Map coordinates

Main neighbourhoods

ST-GERMAIN-DES-PRÉS · QUARTIER LATIN · LUXEMBOURG

6

Allard

Traditional ✗

D1

1 r. l'Eperon ✉ 75006   ● St-Michel
℘ 01 43 26 48 23 **Fax** 01 46 33 04 02   Closed 3-25 August

Menu (€25), €34 – Carte €35/66

AC / VISA / AE / ①

Allard has had top bistro billing since 1931 and has attracted many notable figures (President Pompidou's wife and Alain Delon among others), developing a loyal clientele generation after generation with its straightforward and authentic cuisine. While the dishes are simpler nowadays, they remain generous and rooted in traditional recipes. Your taste buds will be titillated by this fine chapter in French culinary heritage featuring Burgundy snails, cured herring with warm potatoes in oil, hare stew, and veal sweetbreads

Restaurants

Cuisine type

Name, address & information about the establishment

Price
Set menus - a la carte
bc: House wine included

Symbols
🌳 With outside dining
🕐 Open late
🍷 A particularly interesting wine list

🛞 **Bib Gourmand**
Good food at moderate prices

7

Vin et Marée

Seafood ✗✗

A2

71 av. Suffren ✉ 75007   ● La Motte Picquet Grenelle
℘ 01 47 83 27 12 **Fax** 01 53 86 98 26
e-mail vmsuffren@vin-et-maree.com **www**.vin-et-maree.com

Menu (€21) – Carte €32/58

AC / VISA / ◑◑ / AE

Failing a trip to the seaside, you can always take refuge in the comfortable dining room of this first of the Vin et Marée restaurants in Paris. A sure bet, it has held a steady course ever since it opened. Its formula for success is simple, offering only the freshest of ingredients – bought at the morning fish auction – in flawless and appetising dishes. The smoothly run operation is sure to please. Blackboard selections change with daily deliveries, spotlighting a wide range of fish and shellfish. There are even two dishes on the menu for strict carnivores. And the delicious food is not all. Vin et Marée is also a delight to the eye, with a tailor-made decor featuring an ultramarine façade and plush interior.

TOUR EIFFEL · ÉCOLE MILITAIRE · INVALIDES

C1

AC / VISA / ◑◑ / AE

L'Affriolé 🛞

Contemporary ✗

B1

17 r. Malar ✉ 75007   ● Invalides
℘ 01 44 18 31 33   Closed 3 weeks in August, Sunday and Monday

Menu (€23), €29 (lunch)/34

AC / VISA / ◑◑

With its bits-and-pieces bistro decor (knick-knacks, stucco, mosaic tables), Thierry Vérola's restaurant has some nice gastronomic surprises up its sleeve among the daily blackboard suggestions. And it doesn't take the easy way out, changing its menu by the month. Following the market and his own inclinations, the chef composes generous dishes with a modern touch, such as ham hock croquettes with lentils, swordfish hamburger with fennel, *nonnette* (tart) made with salted butter. People come here for the relaxed yet well-prepared meals, the warm and friendly reception, and attentive service (appetizers with radishes, pots of cream) – all at reasonable prices. Tempting, isn't it?

46

48

Facilities & services

🔭 pleasant view
🌿 Garden
🛗 Lift
♿ Wheelchair access
AC Air conditioning
⟷ Private dining room
🅿 Car park
🚗 Garage
Credit cards :
VISA ◑◑ AE ①

Hotels classified according to comfort
(particularly pleasant if in red)

🏠 Quite comfortable

🏠 Comfortable

🏠🏠 Very comfortable

🏠🏠 Top class comfort

🏠🏠🏠🏠 Luxury in the traditional style

| Hotels | Locating on the map | Ⓜ Metro station |

Symbols

39 rm Number of rooms
☲ Breakfast included
♦/♦♦ Prices for a single / double room
⑩ With restaurant
⌂ Quiet hotel
⊡ Swimming pool
❀ Spa
✕ Tennis
ℒ₄ Exercise room
▮ Lift
✆ WIFI
⊡ Satellite TV
⌸ Equipped conference room

Daniel

B2 🏠🏠

8 r. Frédéric Bastiat   Ⓜ St-Philippe du Roule
☒ 75008
✆ 01 42 56 17 00 **Fax** 01 42 56 17 01
e-mail danielparis@relaischateaux.com **www**.hoteldanielparis.com

22 rm – ♦€350/490 ♦♦€410/490, ☲€32 – 4 suites

egant Daniel has the charm of a town-
d between the Champs-Élysées and rue
Honoré. Since reopening in September
ft from Tarfa Salam, it feels a bit like
cave. Here, Eastern and Western aes-
combined in a well-conceived blend of
litan marriage of motifs and materials.
l to be real antique buffs, which is quite
ration mixing carpets from Kazakhstan,
ninese wallpaper, toile de Jouy fabrics,
lots of cushions, ebony furniture from
n ceramics (in the bathrooms), Syrian
atters from Turkey. You can savour this
atmosphere in a corner of the lounge
. Comfortably settled in, you will forget
dream of journeys to distant places.

TOUR EIFFEL • ÉCOLE MILITAIRE • INVALIDES

CHAMPS-ÉLYSÉES • CONCORDE • MADELEINE ▶ Plan page 166

7

8

51

Aida ✿

C3

Japanese ✕

1 r. Pierre Leroux ☒ 75007   Ⓜ Vaneau
✆ 01 43 06 14 18   Closed 5-25 August, February holidays, Tuesday lunch,
Fax 01 43 06 14 18   Saturday lunch, Sunday lunch and Monday
www.aidaparis.com   Dinner only – Number of covers limited, pre-book

Menu €90/160 – Carte €87/200

The white façade of this small Japanese restaurant blends
in so well with the urban landscape that you could easily
walk right by without even noticing it. But don't! Hidden
inside is a secret which is jealously kept by informed gourmets – a delicious Japanese establishment. The ultra-zen,
subdued interior is a chic, welcome change of scenery. You
can choose between the red lacquer counter (to be in the
first row, across from the huge hot plates) or in the private
room. The menu features refined cutting-edge cuisine, a
blend of Japanese and French. A lovely marriage of lobster, chateaubriand and calf sweetbreads with teppan-yaki
– which gets the better of sushi here – and Burgundies
passionately chosen by the chef, an expert œnologist.

First Course	Main Course	Dessert
• Pot au feu japonais.	• Huîtres sautées au beurre d'algues sur lit de cresson.	• Glace vanille et crème de marron à la truffe.
• Sashimi.	• Chateaubriant cuit au teppanyaki.	• Sorbet maison.

Map
Neighbourhoods
Arrondissement

Stars for good cooking
✿

From ✿✿✿ to ✿
...and the sample menu.

49

Paris, Gastronomic Capital

Even in these days of global tastes and revolutions in cooking Paris' coveted title is still legitimate. Yet, paradoxically, there is no typically Parisian cuisine. Contrary to cooking styles from the country – with a timeless quality from being rooted in a certain terroir – Parisian cuisine can't be reduced to one strict definition. Paris is an exception, with a gastronomic tradition that has always been fed by exchanges from all the different regions of France – and the rest of the world. Indeed, its culinary arts have been shaped by many different influences, customs and ingredients from other places – the Romans in the days of Gaul, the Orient in the Middle Ages, Italy during the Renaissance, America, Asia, and so on. Originally known for its rich cereals, fruits, vegetables and spicy dishes made with white wine and vinegar, Parisian cuisine has never stopped importing new flavours. No wonder it boasts the world's largest market at Rungis. A melting pot of cultures and heritage, it has always stood for diversity without renouncing its own identity, which took shape in the 17C under Louis XIV. The capital became the hub of France, and gastronomy was a symbol of its importance – an instrument of prestige and an art involving great skill. It was a time of ceremonial banquets, service à la française and royal or princely chefs who published treatises codifying this "science de la gueule" (according to Rabelais). The craze for French culinary methods was launched!

RESTAURANTS, A PARISIAN INVENTION

Paris can pride itself on having invented something that conquered the entire world –restaurants. These stylish places, where women were admitted, first appeared in 1765 and were the antithesis of the usual – and often unsavoury – inns and taverns. They offered people a place to have a decent meal outside their home thanks to an important innovation: custom-made meals at any hour at a fixed price and at individual tables. Restaurants were an immediate success, although their exact origin remains unclear. Some attribute their invention to Boulanger, others to Chantoiseau (they may in fact have been the same person). One thing is sure – its initial vocation was dietary before becoming dedicated to delicious food. Parisian restaurants opened up next to the salons, cafés and card game clubs near the Palais Royal, multiplying in number during the pe-

J. Lehmann / STOCKFOOD/STUDIO X

riod from 1770-90. They were an indirect consequence of the Revolution, which forced chefs who had worked for the aristocrats to set up their own businesses and take haute cuisine "into the street". But restaurants didn't become truly democratic until the working-class bouillons and brasseries were created during the 3rd Republic.

THE SURPRISE ELEMENT

People are always on the lookout for novelty in Paris, where fashions come and go. Spices were a fashionable symbol of riches in the Middle Ages, while butter sauces were in vogue in the 17C and lighter food was preferred during the Age of Enlightenment. After that the fashion favoured various types of cuisine – bourgeoise, décorative (Antonin Carême), de palace (Escoffier), régionale – and "nouvelle" cuisine in the 1970s. And where do things stand today? Nowadays, Parisian cuisine is exploding in different directions rather than embracing any one trend. It values authenticity, exoticism, experimentation and reinterpreting the past. It has connections with the jewellery business, is involved in the arts, and is much talked-about in the media. In short, it is free – and full of life.

Practical Information Paris

If you need to get to the airport, book a taxi or buy theatre tickets in Paris between gourmet meals, this practical information section will make it all much easier.

ARRIVAL/DEPARTURE

→ By air

www.aeroportsdeparis.fr
Information on daily flights: 0 892 56 39 50.
Roissy-Charles-de-Gaulle Airport, 01 48 62 12 12.
CDGVAL Metro, free 24hr shuttle service between terminals, car parks, TGV and RER stations.
By taxi, allow between 30 min and 1hr for the trip to/from Paris.
By RER B (Châtelet): 30 min.
By Roissybus (Opéra): 50-60 min.
Noctiliens (night bus): n°120/121 (Châtelet) and n°140 (Gare de l'Est): allow 1hr.
Autocars Air France: n°2 (Porte Maillot, Étoile): 45 min and n°4 (Gare de Lyon, Gare Montparnasse): 50 min
Orly Airport, 01 49 75 52 52.
By taxi, allow 20 to 30 min.
Orlybus (Denfert-Rochereau): 30 min.
Noctiliens n°31 (Gare de Lyon) and n°120 (Châtelet): 30 min.
Autocars Air France: n°1 (Invalides, Gare Montparnasse): 35 min.
Useful to know, Navette Aéroport Paris (06 24 22 42 50 or www.navette-aeroport.fr) provides collective taxi-type transport from your home (Paris and suburbs) to the airports. Other companies also operate out of Beauvais-Tillé Airport (08 92 68 20 66).

→ By train

www.sncf.fr
Gare de Lyon: trains from southeast France, Italy and Switzerland.
Gare d'Austerlitz: southwest France and Spain.
Gare du Nord: United Kingdom, Belgium, the Netherlands.
Gare de l'Est: eastern France and Germany.
Gare Montparnasse: western France.

WHEN TO COME TO PARIS

There are always large crowds in Paris during the end of the year holidays, at Easter and on 14 July. We recommend

---

▶ Discount Tickets!

www.ticketac.com lists all the shows on in Paris and offers tickets at reduced prices. There are also ticket stands at Madeleine and the Montparnasse Tower Esplanade, where you can buy theatre tickets for the same day at half price (mainly for privately run theatres).

▶ FAIRS AND SHOWS

Salon International de l'Agriculture, Porte de Versailles, 23 February-2 March.

Foire de Paris, Porte de Versailles, 30 April-12 May.

Salon du Livre, Porte de Versailles, 14-19 March.

Mondial de l'Automobile, Porte de Versailles, 4-19 October.

booking well in advance if you plan on coming then. Certain important events – such as fairs and shows – also tend to create traffic jams in the city.

→ Getting Around Paris

The excellent public transport system in Paris and its suburbs (the Transilien) combines underground and buses (RATP) and railway networks (SNCF), and operates 7 days a week. Inside Paris, the underground and tramway lines are extremely practical and reliable (line T3 goes to the Parc des Expositions at Porte de Versailles). Noctiliens buses operate at night. Times, tickets and itineraries can be found at www.ratp.fr and www.transilien.com.

→ Taxi!

Taxis can be hailed in the street – taxis for hire have a white light on the roof – or called from a taxi stand. A surcharge of about 10 % is applied after 7pm (night rate).

Taxis Bleus, 0 891 701 010 (0.23 €/mn)

Alpha Taxis, 01 45 85 85 85

Taxis G7, 01 47 39 47 39

Taxis G-Space, 01 47 39 01 39

→ By Car

What about driving in Paris? Why not – as long as you are patient and careful about avoiding rush hour and checking traffic updates at: www.viamichelin.fr, www.sytadin.tm.fr. or on your mobile phone at: http://wap.sytadin.gouv.fr, www.bison-fute.equipement.gouv.fr or www.infotrafic.com.

Don't forget to buy a Paris-Carte, the best way to pay for parking on the street (Monéo cards are also accepted). They can be bought from tobacco shops and at some news stands (10€ or 30€).

Car parks: www.infoparking.com (public car parks) or www.parkingsdeparis.com (hard copy also available).

For Breakdowns: SOS Dépannage 24hr service, 01 47 07 99 99 (66 bd Auguste-Blanqui, 13th arrondissement).

If your car is towed: Pré-Fourrière, Préfecture de Police, 01 53 71 53 71.

→ By Bicycle

Sport or transport? Cycling combines the two and is a great way to get around

Paris, especially with Vélib', the new self-service bicycle rental system. For a modest sum, you can borrow a bicycle from one of the many stations set up all over town, and drop it off at another one. For more information, see www.velib.paris.fr (01 30 79 79 30).

LIVING IN PARIS

→ News

Newspaper stalls: along with the national dailies and magazines, a number of other titles offer news about cultural activities in the capital, such as l'Officiel des Spectacles, Pariscope and the Nouvel Observateur's Paris-Île-de-France and Télérama's Sortir supplements.

Radio: several local stations broadcast in Paris in addition to nationwide radios, including FIP (105.1 FM, with traffic updates every 15-30 min).

Television: in addition to the Hertzian and cable stations, Paris Première broadcasts various programmes about life in Paris, such as Paris Dernière – perfect for finding out about those "in" places.

▶ *NO SMOKING !*

It's a done deal! Since 1st January 2008, the "no-smoking law" is valid for all public places, including cafés. No more cigarettes at the bar – and no more clouds of smoke either.

→ Museums and Monuments

As a rule, national museums are closed on Tuesdays and those of the City of Paris on Mondays. In addition, most of the major museums stay open until 9:30pm at least once a week (daily except Tuesdays for the Centre Georges-Pompidou).

You can save time and jump the queue with a Museum and Monument Pass (1, 3 or 5 days); you may also book tickets for the Louvre and many other museums (TicketNet, Fnac, department stores, etc.). The RATP-Louvre combined ticket (on sale in tourist offices and at the Eiffel Tower) offers priority access to permanent collections.

Office du Tourisme et des Congrès de Paris, 0 892 68 30 00 or www.parisinfo.com

Office du Tourisme de Paris-Île-de-France, 01 56 89 38 00 or www.pidf.com

→ Sight-seeing

Open Tour (double-decker bus), 01 42 66 56 56 or www.paris-opentour.com

Balabus (main sights in the capital), 08 92 68 77 14 or www.ratp.fr

Batobus (Compagnie des Bateaux-Mouches; you can get on and off at every stop), 0825 05 01 01 or www.batobus.com

Bateaux parisiens, 0 825 01 01 01

▶ HEALTH

Police, ☎ 17

Fire brigade, ☎ 18

Medical emergencies - Samu, ☎ 15

SOS Doctors, ☎ 01 47 07 77 77.

Anti-poison Centre (Fernand-Vidal Hospital), ☎ 01 40 05 48 48

Dental emergencies, ☎ 01 43 37 51 00

24 hour chemists: 84 av. des Champs-Élysées (galerie les Champs), 8e, ☎ 01 45 62 02 41 - 6 pl. Clichy, 9e, ☎ 01 48 74 65 18 - 6 pl. Félix-Eboué, 12e, ☎ 01 43 43 19 03

▶ OTHER USEFUL TELEPHONE NUMBERS

Lost and found, ☎ 0 821 00 25 25

Loss/theft Visa card (7j/7, 24h/24), ☎ 0 892 705 705

Loss/theft American Express card (7j/7, 24h/24), ☎ 01 47 77 72 00

24 hour babysitting: Baybichou, ☎ 01 43 13 33 23

Louvre Post Office (2 rue du Louvre - open 24h/24), ☎ 01 40 28 76 00

→ Entertainment

Paris offers a wide and eclectic range of entertainment possibilities, from the most legendary stages to the tiniest halls, and every evening the "city of light" raises the curtain on a dizzying array of theatre, opera, ballet and concert performances. Among the more well-known are the Opéra-Bastille, Opéra National de Paris Palais Garnier, Salle Pleyel, Casino de Paris, Cigale, Bataclan, Palais des Congrès de Paris, New Morning, Élysée-Montmartre, Zenith de Paris, Olympia, Crazy-Horse, Folies Bergère, Lido, Moulin Rouge, etc.

→ Shopping

Paris shops are usually open from Monday to Saturday, from 9am to 7pm (and on Sundays in some tourist areas). Gourmet shops are often closed on Mondays, but are open on Sunday mornings. Most of the big department stores close late (9:30pm) once a week.

Every week there are nearly 70 lively street and covered markets in Paris. For days and times, see www.paris.fr, the arrondissement town hall web sites and the Bureau du Commerce (01 42 76 70 14).

→ Eating

While the traditional brasserie remains the icon of Parisian restaurants (see index), the capital is teeming with establishments of all levels of comfort and every type of cuisine. In this guide we provide a list of the best restaurants in each price category.

Late night dining: see the restaurants under "It's Open!".

Where **to eat**

Fred / PHOTONONSTOP

Restaurants from A to Z

▶ *HOW TO USE THIS GUIDE...*

"Couverts" 🍴🍴🍴 *and stars* ❀ *stand for different things. "Couverts" indicate the level of comfort and service, whereas stars denote the best establishments in each category.*

❀ *Bib Gourmand: good food at moderate prices.*

N *...as in new, to help you identify restaurants with recently awarded stars and Bib Gourmands.*

🍴🍴🍴 *Red "couverts" indicate a particularly pleasant establishment that is one of our favourites.*

Where to eat

Where **to eat**

Where to eat

Where to eat

Restaurants by arrondissement

Where **to eat** ▶ by arrondissement

Where to eat ▶ by arrondissement

Where to eat ▶ by arrondissement

23

18th arrondissement

19th arrondissement

20th arrondissement

Where **to eat** ▶ by arrondissement

Starred establishments

'*A good restaurant in its category'- 'Excellent cooking, worth a detour' – 'Exceptional cuisine, worth a special journey': the mere definition of one, two and three stars says it all. Or nearly all. This has been the case ever since Michelin decided, several decades ago, to mark out the best restaurants by attributing stars - known to some as macaroons because of their resemblance - for quality cuisine.*

If we accept the principle that "only one type of cooking exists: good cooking," restaurants with a range of culinary styles can strive to obtain the awards given by Michelin inspectors; those anonymous explorers with oft-used cutlery and finely-tuned taste buds. What criteria are used? It is always about the quality of the ingredients, the mastery of the cooking and the flavours, the consistency, and the personal touches that make up the presentation.

It's important to remember, too, that the number of stars visible in the Michelin sky varies from one year to the next, and that some of the chefs who are at this moment approaching our constellation - known as the 'Rising Stars'- may at some time in the future, if they continue on the same trajectory, shine just as brightly.

Given the number of varied and ever-changing gourmet temptations one will find here, Paris occupies a special place among the gastronomic capitals. Have you appreciated a great restaurant or discovered a new talent? Do you agree with our choices or are you sceptical of our judgements? Do not hesitate to let us know: our readers' letters are always very much appreciated.

$$\text{❀ ❀ ❀}$$

Exceptional cuisine : worth a special journey !

One always eats extremely well here, sometimes superbly.

Alain Ducasse au Plaza Athénée 8e	XxXxX	168
L'Ambroisie 4e	XxxX	86
Arpège 7e	XxX	134
Astrance 16e	XxX	301
Guy Savoy 17e	XxxX	324
Ledoyen 8e	XxXxX	175
Le Meurice 1er	XxXxX	47
Pierre Gagnaire 8e	XxxX	172
Pré Catelan 16e	XxxX	299

Where **to eat** ▶ Starred establishments

27

Bib Gourmands
& moderately priced

Restaurants with set-price menus for less than 35€

Restaurant		Page
Montefiori 17ᵉ	X	337
Le Mûrier 15ᵉ	X	289
Nabuchodonosor 7ᵉ	X	159
New Jawad 7ᵉ	XX	143
L'Œnothèque 9ᵉ **N**	X ☺	218
L'Office 9ᵉ	X	218
L'Ordonnance 14ᵉ	X	272
Oscar 16ᵉ	X	316
Les Oudayas 5ᵉ	X	106
L'Ourcine 13ᵉ	X	258
Papilles 5ᵉ **N**	X ☺	107
Pasco 7ᵉ	X	160
Pataquès 12ᵉ	X	249
Le Pétel 15ᵉ	X	290
Petit Marguery 13ᵉ	XX	256
La Petite Sirène de Copenhague 9ᵉ	X ☺	219
Port Alma 16ᵉ	XXX	302
Le Pré Cadet 9ᵉ	X ☺	219
P'tit Troquet 7ᵉ	X ☺	161
Radis Roses 9ᵉ	X	220
Rech 17ᵉ	XX	331
La Régalade 14ᵉ	X ☺	273
Relais des Buttes 19ᵉ	XX	352
Riboulingue 5ᵉ	X ☺	108
Romain 9ᵉ	XX	215
La Rotonde 6ᵉ	X ☺	127
Sa Mi In 7ᵉ	X	162
Le Saint Amour 2ᵉ	X	73
Severo 14ᵉ	X ☺	274
Shin Jung 8ᵉ	X	206
Le Soleil 7ᵉ	X	162
Le Soufflé 1ᵉʳ	XX	56
La Soupière 17ᵉ	X ☺	338
Spring 9ᵉ	X ☺	221
Stéphane Martin 15ᵉ	X ☺	290
Sukhothaï 13ᵉ	X	258
La Table d'Erica 6ᵉ	X	127
Table des Oliviers 17ᵉ	X	338
Le Temps au Temps 11ᵉ	X ☺	237
Terminus Nord 10ᵉ	XX	226
Thierry Burlot "Le Quinze" 15ᵉ	XX ☺	284
Toi 8ᵉ	X	207
Le Troquet 15ᵉ	X ☺	291
Urbane 10ᵉ **N**	X ☺	229
Vaudeville 2ᵉ	XX	69
Les Vendanges 14ᵉ	XX	268
Village d'Ung et Li Lam 8ᵉ	XX	198
Villaret 11ᵉ	X	238
Villa Victoria 9ᵉ	X	221
Yanasé 15ᵉ	X	292
Yugaraj 6ᵉ	XX	121

Outdoor dining

Where **to eat** ▶ Outdoor dining

For business

Where **to eat** ▶ For business

31

Restaurants with private dining-rooms

Brasseries

Au Pied de Cochon 1er	✗✗	53	La Gauloise 15e	✗✗	283
Ballon des Ternes 17e	✗✗	329	Marty 5e	✗✗	100
Bofinger 4e	✗✗	88	La Rotonde 6e	✗⊛	127
La Coupole 14e	✗✗	266	Terminus Nord 10e	✗✗	226
Le Dôme 14e	✗x✗	265	Vaudeville 2e	✗✗	69
Gallopin 2e	✗✗	69			

Bistros

L'A.O.C. 5e	✗	101	Chez Georges 2e	✗	71
Afaria 15e **N**	✗⊛	284	Chez Georges 17e	✗✗	329
Allard 6e	✗	122	Chez Léon 17e	✗✗	327
Astier 11e	✗	235	Chez René 5e	✗	103
Au Bascou 3e	✗	78	Le Comptoir 6e	✗	123
Au Moulin à Vent 5e	✗	102	Fontaine de Mars 7e	✗	154
Aux Lyonnais 2e	✗⊛	71	Georgette 9e	✗	216
L'Avant Goût 13e	✗	257	Le Grand Pan 15e **N**	✗⊛	288
Le Bélisaire 15e	✗⊛	285	Joséphine		
Benoit 4e	✗✗✿	87	"Chez Dumonet" 6e	✗	125
Le Bistrot			Le Clou 17e	✗	336
de L'Alycastre 6e	✗	123	Léo Le Lion 7e	✗	156
Bistrot de Paris 7e	✗	151	Louis Vins 5e	✗	105
Le Bistrot des Soupirs			Moissonnier 5e	✗	106
"Chez les On" 20e	✗	358	Oscar 16e	✗	316
Bistrot St-Honoré 1er	✗	58	Oudino 7e	✗	160
Buisson Ardent 5e	✗⊛	102	Pierrot 2e	✗	73
Café Constant 7e **N**	✗⊛	152	P'tit Troquet 7e	✗⊛	161
Caves Petrissans 17e	✗⊛	335	Quincy 12e	✗	250
Chez Casimir 10e	✗	227	La Régalade 14e	✗⊛	273
Chez Cécile			Villaret 11e	✗	238
la Ferme des Mathurins 8e	✗	202	Villa Victoria 9e	✗	221

Cuisine from France...

Andouillette

À La Bonne Table 14ᵉ	✗	269
Au Petit Riche 9ᵉ	✗✗	212
La Biche au Bois 12ᵉ	✗	246
Bistrot de Paris 7ᵉ	✗	151
Bistrot St-Honoré 1ᵉʳ	✗	58
Chez Georges 2ᵉ	✗	71
Fontaine de Mars 7ᵉ	✗	154
Georgette 9ᵉ	✗	216
Joséphine "Chez Dumonet" 6ᵉ	✗	125
La Marlotte 6ᵉ	✗	126
Moissonnier 5ᵉ	✗	106
Le Vaudeville 2ᵉ	✗✗	69

Boudin

L'A.O.C. 5ᵉ	✗	101
Au Bascou 3ᵉ	✗	78
L'Auberge Aveyronnaise 12ᵉ	✗	246
D'Chez Eux 7ᵉ	✗✗	141
Fontaine de Mars 7ᵉ	✗	154
La Marlotte 6ᵉ	✗	126
Moissonnier 5ᵉ	✗	106

Bouillabaisse

Le Dôme 14ᵉ	✗✗✗	265
Marius 16ᵉ	✗✗	312
Méditerranée 6ᵉ	✗✗	120

Cassoulet

Benoit 4ᵉ	✗✗❀	87
D'Chez Eux 7ᵉ	✗✗	141
Maison Courtine 14ᵉ	✗✗❀	267
Quincy 12ᵉ	✗	250
Le Sarladais 8ᵉ	✗✗	194
Le Violon d'Ingres 7ᵉ	✗✗❀	147

Choucroute

Ballon des Ternes 17ᵉ	✗✗	329
Bofinger 4ᵉ	✗✗	88
La Coupole 14ᵉ	✗✗	266
Mon Vieil Ami 4ᵉ	✗	91
Terminus Nord 10ᵉ	✗✗	226

Confit

L'A.O.C. 5ᵉ	✗	101
Auberge Etchegorry 13ᵉ	✗	257
Au Bascou 3ᵉ	✗	78
Au Clair de la Lune 18ᵉ	✗✗	344
Chez Jacky 13ᵉ	✗✗	256
Chez René 5ᵉ	✗	103
D'Chez Eux 7ᵉ	✗✗	141
Fontaine de Mars 7ᵉ	✗	154
Joséphine "Chez Dumonet" 6ᵉ	✗	125
Lescure 1ᵉʳ	✗	60
Louis Vins 5ᵉ	✗	105
Pierrot 2ᵉ	✗	73
Le Salardais 8ᵉ	✗✗	194

Coq au vin

Allard 6ᵉ	✗	122
Au Moulin à Vent 5ᵉ	✗	102
La Biche au Bois 12ᵉ	✗	246
Chez René 5ᵉ	✗	103
Moissonnier 5ᵉ	✗	106
Quincy 12ᵉ	✗	250

Seafood

Au Pied de Cochon 1ᵉʳ	✗✗	53
Ballon des Ternes 17ᵉ	✗✗	329
Le Bistrot de Marius 8ᵉ	✗	200
Bistrot du Dôme 4ᵉ	✗	89
Bistrot du Dôme 14ᵉ	✗	271
Bofinger 4ᵉ	✗✗	88
La Coupole 14ᵉ	✗✗	266
Dessirier 17ᵉ	✗✗	327
Le Divellec 7ᵉ	✗✗✗❀	135
Le Dôme 14ᵉ	✗✗✗	265
Le Duc 14ᵉ	✗✗✗	265
L'Écaille de la Fontaine 2ᵉ	✗	72
L'Espadon Bleu 6ᵉ	✗	124
Les Fables de la Fontaine 7ᵉ	✗❀	155
Gallopin 2ᵉ	✗✗	69

Goumard 1er	✕✕✕✕✿	49
L'Huîtrier 17e	✕	337
La Luna 8e	✕✕	190
Marius et Janette 8e	✕✕	191
Marty 5e	✕✕	100
Méditerranée 6e	✕✕	120
Pétrus 17e	✕✕✕	326
Port Alma 16e	✕✕✕	302
Prunier 16e	✕✕✕	305
La Rotonde 6e	✕☺	127
Terminus Nord 10e	✕✕	226
35 ° Ouest 7e	✕	163
Vin et Marée 7e	✕✕	145
Vin et Marée 11e	✕✕	234
Vin et Marée 14e	✕✕	269

Escargots

Allard 6e	✕	122
Au Moulin à Vent 5e	✕	102
Au Petit Riche 9e	✕✕	212
Ballon des Ternes 17e	✕✕	329
Benoit 4e	✕✕✿	87
Gallopin 2e	✕✕	69
Bistrot St-Honoré 1er	✕	58
Vaudeville 2e	✕✕	69

Cheese

Montparnasse'25 14e	✕✕✕✕	264

Grills

L'A.O.C. 5e	✕	101
Au Pied de Cochon 1er	✕✕	53

Bistrot St-Honoré 1er	✕	58
Bofinger 4e	✕✕	88
La Coupole 14e	✕✕	266
Fermette		
Marbeuf 1900 8e	✕✕	189
Gallopin 2e	✕✕	69
Joséphine		
"Chez Dumonet" 6e	✕	125
La Maison de L'Aubrac 8e	✕	204
Rôtisserie d'en Face 6e	✕	126
Terminus Nord 10e	✕✕	226

Soufflés

L'Amuse Bouche 14e	✕	270
Cigale Récamier 7e	✕✕	139
Le Soufflé 1er	✕✕	56

Calf's head

Au Petit Riche 9e	✕✕	212
Au Poulbot Gourmet 18e	✕✕	345
Benoit 4e	✕✕✿	87
Chez Jacky 13e	✕✕	256
Dominique Bouchet 8e	✕✿	205
Marty 5e	✕✕	100
Le Mesturet 2e	✕	72
Stella Maris 8e	✕✕✕✿	185
Vaudeville 2e	✕✕	69
Le Violon d'Ingres 7e	✕✕✿	147

Tripe

L'Auberge Aveyronnaise 12e	✕	246
Quincy 12e	✕	250
Ribouldingue 5e	✕☺	108

...and from around the world

Antilles, Réunion, Seychelles

Coco de Mer 5ᵉ	✗	104
La Table de Babette 16ᵉ	✗✗	314
La Table d'Erica 6ᵉ	✗	127

Belgian

Graindorge 17ᵉ	✗✗ ☺	328

Chinese, Thai Vietnamese

Baan Boran 1ᵉʳ	✗	57
Banyan 15ᵉ	✗	285
Erawan 15ᵉ	✗✗	282
Kim Anh 15ᵉ	✗	289
Le Lys d'Or 12ᵉ	✗	248
Mme Shawn 10ᵉ	✗	228
Sukhothaï 13ᵉ	✗	258
Tang 16ᵉ	✗✗	315
Thiou 7ᵉ	✗✗	144
Tsé Yang 16ᵉ	✗✗	305
Village d'Ung et Li Lam 8ᵉ	✗✗	198

Greek

Cristina's Tapas by Mavrommatis 1ᵉʳ	✗	59
Les Délices d'Aphrodite 5ᵉ	✗	104
Mavrommatis 5ᵉ	✗✗	101

Indian

Indra 8ᵉ	✗✗✗	182
Jodhpur Palace 12ᵉ	✗	248
New Jawad 7ᵉ	✗✗	143
Ratn 8ᵉ	✗✗	193
Yugaraj 6ᵉ	✗✗	121

Italian

Al Dente 7ᵉ	✗	148
Bocconi 8ᵉ	✗	201
Conti 16ᵉ	✗✗	311
Delizie d'Uggiano 1ᵉʳ	✗✗	53
Dell Orto 9ᵉ	✗	216
L'Enoteca 4ᵉ	✗	90
Fontanarosa 15ᵉ	✗✗	282
Giulio Rebellato 16ᵉ	✗✗	312
I Golosi 9ᵉ	✗	217
Montefiori 17ᵉ	✗	337
L'Osteria 4ᵉ	✗	92
Le Perron 7ᵉ	✗	161
Romain 9ᵉ	✗✗	215
Sormani 17ᵉ	✗✗✗	326
Le Stresa 8ᵉ	✗✗	196
Le Vinci 16ᵉ	✗✗	315

Japanese

Aida 7ᵉ	✗ ✿	149
Azabu 6ᵉ	✗	122
Benkay 15ᵉ	✗✗✗	280
Hanawa 8ᵉ	✗✗	190
Isami 4ᵉ	✗	91
Kaï 1ᵉʳ	✗	59
Kinugawa 1ᵉʳ	✗✗	54
Miyako 7ᵉ	✗	158
Momoka 9ᵉ	✗	217
Yanasé 15ᵉ	✗	292
Yen 6ᵉ	✗	128

Korean

Sa Mi In 7ᵉ	✗	162
Shin Jung 8ᵉ	✗	206

Lebanese

Al Ajami 8ᵉ	✗✗	183
Pavillon Noura 16ᵉ	✗✗	313

North-African

Caroubier 15ᵉ	✗✗ ☺	280
El Mansour 8ᵉ	✗✗✗	180

It's open !

Restaurants open on Saturday and Sunday

Al Ajami 8ᵉ	✗✗	183
Alcazar 6ᵉ	✗✗	119
Allard 6ᵉ	✗	122
Ambassade d'Auvergne 3ᵉ	✗✗ 🟤	78
L'Appart' 8ᵉ	✗	198
Astier 11ᵉ	✗	235
L'Atelier de Joël Robuchon 7ᵉ **N**	✗ ✿✿	150
L'Auberge Aveyronnaise 12ᵉ	✗	246
Au Pied de Cochon 1ᵉʳ	✗✗	53
Ballon des Ternes 17ᵉ	✗✗	329
Banyan 15ᵉ	✗	285
Benkay 15ᵉ	✗✗✗	280
Benoit 4ᵉ	✗✗ ✿	87
Le Bistrot de Marius 8ᵉ	✗	200
Bistrot du Dôme 4ᵉ	✗	89
Bofinger 4ᵉ	✗✗	88
Le Bristol 8ᵉ	✗✗✗✗ ✿✿	171
Café de l'Alma 7ᵉ	✗	152
Café de la Paix 9ᵉ	✗✗✗	212
Caroubier 15ᵉ	✗✗ 🟤	280
Chez Georges 17ᵉ	✗✗	329
Le "Cinq" 8ᵉ	✗✗✗✗ ✿✿✿	173
Le Comptoir 6ᵉ	✗	123
La Coupole 14ᵉ	✗✗	266
Les Délices d'Aphrodite 5ᵉ	✗	104
Devez 8ᵉ	✗	204
Drouant 2ᵉ	✗✗✗	67
L'Enoteca 4ᵉ	✗	90
L'Équitable 5ᵉ	✗✗	100
L'Espadon 1ᵉʳ	✗✗✗✗✗ ✿✿	46
L'Esplanade 7ᵉ	✗✗	141
Les Fables de La Fontaine 7ᵉ	✗ ✿	155
Fermette Marbeuf 1900 8ᵉ	✗✗	189
Le Fin Gourmet 4ᵉ	✗	90
Fontaine de Mars 7ᵉ	✗	154
Fontanarosa 15ᵉ	✗✗	282
Fouquet's 8ᵉ	✗✗✗	180
Gallopin 2ᵉ	✗✗	69
La Gauloise 15ᵉ	✗✗	283
Giulio Rebellato 16ᵉ	✗✗	312
Goumard 1ᵉʳ	✗✗✗✗ ✿	49
La Grande Cascade 16ᵉ	✗✗✗✗ ✿	298
Il Vino d'Enrico Bernardo 7ᵉ **N**	✗✗ ✿	142
Jodhpur Palace 12ᵉ	✗	248
Le Jules Verne 7ᵉ	✗✗✗	136
Kim Anh 15ᵉ	✗	289
Lhassa 5ᵉ	✗	105
Louis Vins 5ᵉ	✗	105
Le Lys d'Or 12ᵉ	✗	248
La Maison de Charly 17ᵉ	✗✗	328
La Maison de L'Aubrac 8ᵉ	✗	204
Marius et Janette 8ᵉ	✗✗	191
Market 8ᵉ	✗✗	191
Marty 5ᵉ	✗✗	100
Méditerranée 6ᵉ	✗✗	120
Le Mesturet 2ᵉ	✗	72
Mme Shawn 10ᵉ	✗	228
Mon Vieil Ami 4ᵉ	✗	91
Le Moulin de la Galette 18ᵉ	✗✗	346
New Jawad 7ᵉ	✗✗	143
Les Ombres 7ᵉ	✗✗	143
L'Orangerie 4ᵉ	✗✗	89
Les Oudayas 5ᵉ	✗	106
Pasco 7ᵉ	✗	160
Pavillon Noura 16ᵉ	✗✗	313
Petit Pontoise 5ᵉ	✗	107
Pétrus 17ᵉ	✗✗✗	326
Pinxo 1ᵉʳ	✗✗	55
Le Pur' Grill 2ᵉ **N**	✗✗✗ ✿	68
404 3ᵉ	✗	80
Ratn 8ᵉ	✗✗	193
Le Relais Plaza 8ᵉ	✗✗	193
La Rotonde 6ᵉ	✗ 🟤	127
Senderens 8ᵉ	✗✗✗ ✿✿	184
La Table de Joël Robuchon 16ᵉ	✗✗✗ ✿✿	307
Terminus Nord 10ᵉ	✗✗	226
Timgad 17ᵉ	✗✗	332
Toi 8ᵉ	✗	207
La Tour d'Argent 5ᵉ	✗✗✗✗ ✿	98
Tsé Yang 16ᵉ	✗✗	305

Vaudeville 2e	XX	69
Vin et Marée 7e	XX	145
Vin et Marée 11e	XX	234
Vin et Marée 14e	XX	269
Yugaraj 6e	XX	121

Restaurants open in July and August

A Beauvilliers 18e	XXX	344
Al Ajami 8e	XX	183
Alcazar 6e	XX	119
Ambassade d'Auvergne 3e	XX ⊛	78
L'Appart' 8e	X	198
Arpège 7e	XXX ✿✿	134
Astier 11e	X	235
L'Atelier Berger 1er	X	57
L'Atelier de Joël Robuchon 7e N	X ✿✿	150
Auberge Etchegorry 13e	X	257
Au Petit Riche 9e	XX	212
Au Pied de Cochon 1er	XX	53
L'Avant Goût 13e	X	257
Azabu 6e	X	122
Baan Boran 1er	X	57
Ballon des Ternes 17e	XX	329
Benkay 15e	XXX	280
Bistro d'Hubert 15e	X	286
Bistrot Niel 17e	X	332
Le Bistrot de Marius 8e	X	200
Bistrot St-Honoré 1er	X	58
Bocconi 8e	X	201
Bofinger 4e	XX	88
Le Bristol 8e	XXXXX ✿✿	171
Café Constant 7e N	X ⊛	152
Café de l'Alma 7e	X	152
Café de la Paix 9e	XXX	212
Chez Casimir 10e	X	227
Chez Georges 17e	XX	329
Chez les Anges 7e	XX ⊛	139
Cigale Récamier 7e	XX	139
Le "Cinq" 8e	XXXXX ✿✿	173
Les Cocottes 7e	X	154
Le Comptoir 6e	X	123
La Coupole 14e	XX	266
Cristal Room Baccarat 16e	XX	311
Cristina's Tapas by Mavrommatis 1er	X	59
La Cuisine 7e	XX	140
Les Délices d'Aphrodite 5e	X	104
Devez 8e	X	204
La Dînée 15e	XX	281
Le Dôme 14e	XXX	265
Drouant 2e	XXX	67
El Mansour 8e	XXX	180
L'Espadon 1er	XXXXX ✿	46
L'Esplanade 7e	XX	141
Les Fables de La Fontaine 7e	X ✿	155
Fermette Marbeuf 1900 8e	XX	189
Fontaine de Mars 7e	X	154
Fontanarosa 15e	XX	282
Fouquet's 8e	XXX	180
Gallopin 2e	XX	69
La Gauloise 15e	XX	283
Goumard 1er	XXX ✿	49
La Grande Cascade 16e	XXXX ✿	298
Hélène Darroze- La Salle à Manger 6e	XXX ✿✿	114
Il Vino d'Enrico Bernardo 7e N	XX ✿	142
Indra 8e	XXX	182
Le Janissaire 12e	XX	244
Jodhpur Palace 12e	X	248
Joséphine "Chez Dumonet" 6e	X	125
Le Jules Verne 7e	XXX	136
Kinugawa 1er	XX	54
Laurent 8e	XXXX ✿	177
Lhassa 5e	X	105
Louis Vins 5e	X	105
Le Lys d'Or 12e	X	248
Maison Blanche (La) 8e	XXX	182
La Maison de L'Aubrac 8e	X	204
Market 8e	XX	191
Marty 5e	XX	100
Meating 17e	XX	331
Méditerranée 6e	XX	120
Le Mesturet 2e	X	72
Mme Shawn 10e	X	228
Le Moulin de la Galette 18e	XX	346
New Jawad 7e	XX	143
Les Ombres 7e	XX	143
Les Oudayas 5e	X	106
L'Oulette 12e	XXX	244
L'Ourcine 13e	X	258
Palais Royal 1er	XX	54
Pasco 7e	X	160
Pataquès 12e	X	249

Where to eat ▶ It's open!

Restaurants serving after midnight

Palais-Royal · Louvre Tuileries · Les Halles

The 1st arrondissement, a narrow rectangle that hugs the right bank of the Seine, reveals two aspects of Paris: to the east, the Halles district, the former "Belly of Paris" that was home to the capital's wholesale market but is still a busy shopping and working-class area, and the Louvre to the west, once the seat of power and still one of the smartest districts of the capital.

A ROYAL STROLL

Who can remain insensitive to the majesty of the perspective that runs from the Cour Carrée of the **Louvre** to the Arc de Triomphe on the **Place de l'Étoile,** especially at night when the city's illuminations light up the Champs-Élysées? The obelisk, straight as a gold-tipped pencil, marks the centre. To the east, it is bordered by the green Tuileries gardens, dotted with sculptures by Maillol and Rodin, which lead to the Louvre museum. An outstanding cultural and tourist attraction, the former palace never empties and patience is required before you can see the Mona Lisa's smile for yourself.

However the Café Marly, set in the museum itself and popular with the Parisian jet-set and tourists alike, is perfect for a break. Take a seat under the arcades and enjoy the view of the glass pyramid.

Alternatively, make your way to the peaceful walled gardens of the **Palais Royal,** another fa-vourite with Parisians. Gourmets also flock here because beneath the arcades, in between two top fashion designers, is the **Grand Véfour,** a historic and starred establishment popular with Cocteau, Colette and Sartre.

JEWELS AND GADGETS

As they make their way towards the Comédie Française, visitors to the Louvre gradually mingle with the man in the street and then with wealthy foreign tourists on shopping sprees in the capital's luxury shops. Along **rue Saint-Honoré** elite fashion designers rub shoulders with the "haute couture" of chocolate and further on, **place Vendôme** is the exclusive bastion of the top jewellery houses and luxury hotels. The contrast with **rue de Rivoli**'s arcades, more focused on plastic replicas of the Eiffel tower, is striking. However the street is also home to Angelina's, a chic tea-room reputed to serve the best Mont-Blanc and the most delicious hot chocolate in Paris.

Further north, the lovely glass and steel edifice on **Marché Saint-Honoré** stands in the heart of a small business district rich in good restaurants. Alternatively, head for the mythical Hemingway bar of the **Ritz,** a much-loved haunt of the author and sample one of his favourite pure malt whiskies in the lap of luxury… for just the price of a glass!

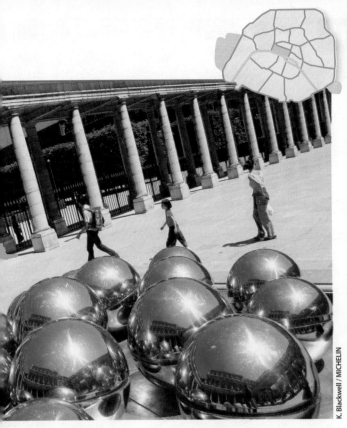

K. Blackwell / MICHELIN

AROUND MIDNIGHT

Eastbound, the scenery changes with the impressive **Forum des Halles,** built on the site of the massive iron halls designed by Baltard that used to house the main marketplace of Paris. Now the realm of retail chain stores, the area resembles an immense human ant-hive, constantly fed by arrivals from the gigantic underground metro and RER station, **Châtelet-les Halles.** At peak hours, it is almost impracticable and even a tad disreputable in the evenings. However jazz lovers are not put off as they make their way to the vaulted cellars along **rue des Lombards** and **rue de la Ferronnerie,** guided by familiar trumpet, piano and saxophone melodies. If in need of sustenance, head for the Pied de Cochon that has been catering to hungry night-birds 24 hours a day since 1946.

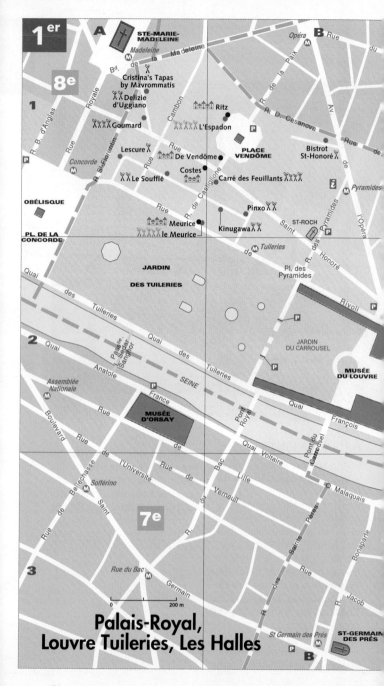

Palais-Royal,
Louvre Tuileries, Les Halles

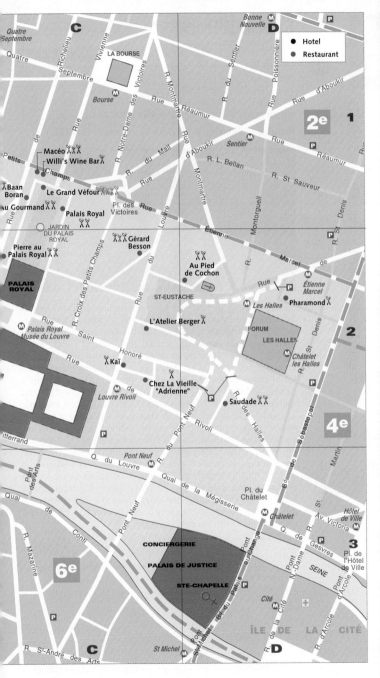

Hotel
Restaurant

Quatre Septembre

LA BOURSE

2e

1

Macéo
Willi's Wine Bar
Champs
Baan Boran
Le Grand Véfour
au Gourmand
Palais Royal
JARDIN DU PALAIS ROYAL
Pierre au Palais Royal

Pl. des Victoires

Gérard Besson

Au Pied de Cochon

Étienne Marcel

Pharamond

PALAIS ROYAL

ST-EUSTACHE

Les Halles

Palais Royal Musée du Louvre

L'Atelier Berger

FORUM LES HALLES

2

Kaï

Châtelet les Halles

Chez La Vieille "Adrienne"

Louvre Rivoli

Saudade

4e

Mitterrand

Pont des Arts

Pont Neuf

Q. du Louvre

Quai de la Mégisserie

Pl. du Châtelet

Châtelet

Hôtel de Ville

6e

Quai

R. Mazarine

CONCIERGERIE

PALAIS DE JUSTICE

STE-CHAPELLE

SEINE

3

Pl. de l'Hôtel de Ville

Av. Victoria

Q. de Gesvres

Cité

ÎLE DE LA CITÉ

R. St-André des Arts

St Michel

C

D

L'Espadon ✿

Traditional XXXXX

B1

Hôtel Ritz,   Ⓜ Opéra
15 pl. Vendôme ✉ 75001
✆ 01 43 16 30 80 **Fax** 01 43 16 33 75
e-mail espadon@ritzparis.com **www**.ritzparis.com

Menu €75 (lunch), €170/305 bi – Carte €134/217

L'Espadon

"Good cooking is the basis for true happiness." These words from Auguste Escoffier should give you an idea of the importance of gastronomy here. Escoffier, the Ritz's first chef – and a friend of César Ritz who created this Parisian luxury hotel in 1898 – raised cooking to new heights as a symbol of the French art of living. That philosophy has been carried on by César's son Charles Ritz, an avid fisherman (thus the restaurant's name), and chef Michel Roth, winner of the Bocuse d'Or and Meilleur Ouvrier de France awards. Apart from a short interlude at Lasserre, Roth has been in charge of the kitchen here for twenty years, upholding the grand tradition begun by the inventor of the Peach Melba and Poire Belle Hélène. The appetising menu is matched by some fabulous vintage wines. The same commitment to perfection is evident in the excellent service and the magnificent décor blending classical elegance with a profusion of refined details, including giltwork, velvet, and a huge trompe l'œil ceiling depicting a blue sky. Not to mention the summer garden, a charming haven of peace. A prestigious establishment with exceptional food.

First Course

- Homard breton et vinaigrette de cardamome, riviera aux amandes fraîches.
- Belons au sabayon gratiné et mousseline d'épinards.

Main Course

- Tronçon de turbot rôti à la fleur de sel, gnocchi au parmesan.
- Noix de ris de veau doré, jus perlé et pommes soufflées.

Dessert

- Millefeuille tradition Ritz.
- Chocolat soufflé, crème glacée à la pistache.

le Meurice ✿✿✿

Innovative 🍴🍴🍴🍴

A1

Hôtel Le Meurice,
228 r. Rivoli ✉ 75001
☎ 01 44 58 10 55
Fax 01 44 58 10 76
e-mail restaurant@lemeurice.com **www**.lemeurice.com

Ⓜ Tuileries
Closed 26 July-24 August, 14 February-1st
March, Saturday and Sunday

Menu €90 (lunch)/220 – Carte €164/292

A/C

VISA

MC

AE

le Meurice

It didn't take long for Yannick Alleno to reach the top of his profession. At barely forty, he has already enjoyed an impressive career brimming with awards and fine restaurants, in particular Le Meurice, the luxury hotel where he was chef de partie in 1992 and now runs the kitchen with a master's touch. Alléno is bold, ambitious and a perfectionist, leaving nothing to chance, and his brilliant and accomplished style is also highly creative. His cooking is constantly renewed, highlighting changing ingredients and seasons, in a passionate quest to codify and update Parisian gastronomy according to current tastes. His entire staff works in the same spirit of hospitality and impeccable savoir-faire. Waiters with silver platters whirl around the gilded dining room right out of Versailles, featuring a high ceiling painted with cherubs, crystal chandeliers, antique mirrors, a mosaic floor dating from 1907 and a view over the Tuileries Gardens. Positively royal!

First Course

- Chaud-froid de sole à la duxelles de champignons.
- Foie gras de canard simplement poché au vin de Chambertin.

Main Course

- Turbot cuisiné aux algues et au foie gras de canard.
- Noix de ris de veau rôtie (autumn-winter).

Dessert

- Crème mascarpone à la réglisse, coque caramel, madeleines tièdes au citron.
- Tuile croustillante fourrée d'une ganache tendre, quenelles glacées à la menthe.

Carré des Feuillants ✿ ✿

B1

Traditional XXXX

14 r. Castiglione ⊠ 75001   Ⓜ Tuileries
✆ 01 42 86 82 82   Closed August, Saturday and Sunday
Fax 01 42 86 07 71
e-mail carredesfeuillants@orange.fr **www**.carredesfeuillants.fr

Menu €65 (lunch)/165 (dinner) – Carte €127/159

Carré des Feuillants

Finding a restaurant where the atmosphere and culinary style are a perfect match is rare. The Carré des Feuillants has clearly achieved that osmosis with great subtlety. The first impression at this former convent (built during the reign of Henri IV) is one of precision and control – there's nothing exuberant or demonstratively impulsive here. The decor by painter-sculptor Alberto Bali – a friend of Alain Dutournier, and who also designed Pinxo – is made up of pure lines and natural materials that exude contemporary elegance. The serene setting is matched by impeccable service and cuisine of the same calibre. The food is inventive and full of flavour, highlighting the chef's generosity and roots in the Landes region. The threefold composition of the dishes – "foundation, accompanying vegetable and revelation" – brings out the best in the ingredients. The cellar boasts some real treasures.

First Course

- Gelée d'écrevisses, foie gras et ris de veau.
- Cuisses de grenouilles épicées, blé cassé, écume de roquette et cresson, girolles en tempura (été-automne).

Main Course

- Tendron fondant de veau de lait, cèpes, artichauts violets.
- Tronçons de Saint-Pierre ficelés de pommes de terre et caviar (winter).

Dessert

- Chocolat noir du Vénézuela, douce chicorée et suave moka.
- Envie de vacherin, grosses framboises, meringue légère au yuzu, crème fermière mascavo (summer).

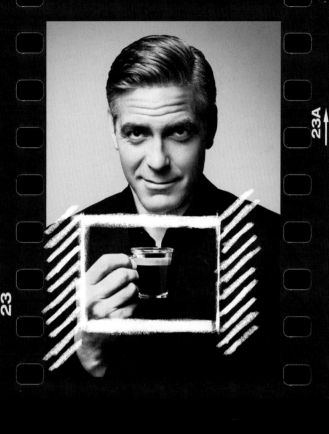

Nespresso. What else ?

Coffee, body and soul

Innovation has good prospects whenever it is cleaner, safer and more efficient.

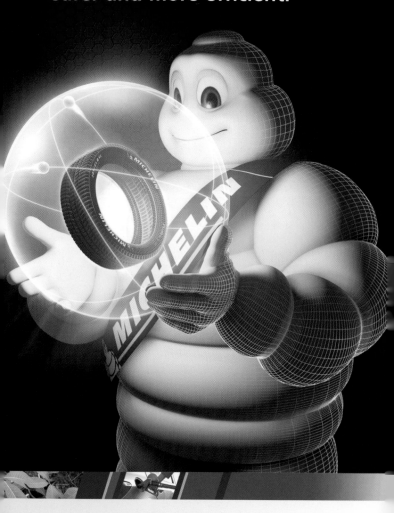

The MICHELIN Energy green tyre lasts 25% longer*.
It also provides fuel savings of 2 to 3%
while reducing CO_2 emissions.

* on average compared to competing tyres in the same category.

MICHELIN
A better way forward

Goumard ✿

A1

9 r. Duphot ✉ 75001   **Ⓜ** Madeleine
☎ 01 42 60 36 07 **Fax** 01 42 60 04 54
e-mail goumard.philippe@wanadoo.fr **www**.goumard.com

Menu €46/60 bi (lunch) – Carte €75/127

A/C
⟷
☞
VISA
Ⓜ©
AE
Ⓞ
✿

Youpi la création

Goumard is not the only name to have been associated with this establishment, which is over a hundred years old and an institution among Parisian seafood restaurants. The original Maison Prunier (dating from 1872) was already famous for its fish and oysters, and seafood still reigns here. The current owner, Philippe Dubois, accompanied by chef Olivier Guyon, has admirably upheld the tradition and continued to attract many prominent figures. The classic and cosy decor has preserved Majorelle's Art Nouveau look (from 1904) featuring oak panelling, an engraved glass façade by Labouret, lighting fixtures and inlay work by Lalique, not to mention the "listed" restrooms (a must-see). In addition to the two upstairs dining rooms decorated with Surrealist paintings and the two private *salons*, there are also two bars, the "Sextant" and a champagne bar with over 170 varieties of bubbly.

First Course
- Saumon fumé entier de Norvège, tranché à la main.
- Fleur de courgette farcie de chair de tourteau, jus à l'orange sanguine (May-October).

Main Course
- Bar de ligne rôti, poêlée d'artichaut poivrade et crevettes grises (May-October).
- Homard bleu rôti, cocotte de blettes et tronçons de macaroni

Dessert
- Sorbet au cacao amer, allumettes feuilletées au chocolat.
- Mangue et onctueux citron vert, biscuit noisette-coco.

Le Grand Véfour ✿ ✿

Classical 𝕏𝕏𝕏𝕏

C1

17 r. Beaujolais ✉ 75001
☎ 01 42 96 56 27
Fax 01 42 86 80 71
e-mail grand.vefour@wanadoo.fr
www.grand-vefour.com

🚇 **Palais Royal**
Closed 28 April-4 May, 28 July-25 August,
24 December-1st January, Friday dinner,
Saturday and Sunday

Menu €88 (lunch)/268 – Carte €194/235

A/C

VISA
MC
AE
DC

Le Grand Véfour

Illustrious patrons of the former "Café de Chartres" over the past two centuries include Lamartine, Victor Hugo, Napoleon and Josephine, and Sartre. The oldest restaurant in Paris (1784-85), known for romantic rendez-vous, revolutionaries and intellectuals, has had its ups and downs (fires, closings, etc.) as it has passed from one owner to another. The legend began in 1820 with Jean Véfour, after whom the restaurant was named. Several wars later, in 1948, Raymond Oliver took over, returning it to its former glory and earning its first stars, upheld by Guy Martin. That's the history of Le Grand Véfour in a nutshell. The unique setting, a listed monument, has been restored to its original state. The magnificent Directoire dining rooms giving onto the Palais Royal garden boast mirrored walls, crystal chandeliers, giltwork and canvases depicting scenes from antiquity. Like an artist who finds inspiration in travel and painting, the atypical chef "sketches" his cuisine with colours, shapes and textures, creating dishes that find the perfect balance between tradition and modernity.

First Course

- Ravioles de foie gras à l'émulsion de crème truffée.
- Tourteau et sucrine dans une fine gelée au persil plat, condiment de pâtissons jaunes.

Main Course

- Pigeon Prince Rainier III.
- Daurade poêlée, jus persil-gingembre, champignons et tofu.

Dessert

- Palet noisette et chocolat au lait, glace au caramel brun et sel de Guérande.
- Fine tranche de pain de Gênes et poire dans une mascarpone.

Gérard Besson ✿

C2

Traditional 🍴🍴🍴

5 r. Coq Héron ✉ 75001
📞 01 42 33 14 74
Fax 01 42 33 85 71
e-mail gerard.besson4@libertysurf.fr
www.gerardbesson.com

Ⓜ Louvre Rivoli
Closed 26 July-18 August, Monday lunch,
Saturday lunch and Sunday

Menu (€48), €120/125 – Carte €113/157

A/C
VISA
MC
AE

Gérard Besson

Gérard Besson is a timeless place, rooted since 1978 in this neighbourhood only a stone's throw from the Place des Victoires and the old Les Halles marketplace. The establishment has held up well over the years, avoiding the temptation to follow fashions – except of course for the facelift a few years ago to brighten things up. The decor is cosy and elegant, like a tastefully designed house but with a new touch of modernity – cream-coloured tones in the spacious dining room, still lifes, intimate alcoves, and fabrics with bucolic motifs.Chef Besson's remarkably consistent cooking celebrates the fine tradition and ingredients from his native Bresse region. This is a place where you can enjoy reconnecting with the reassuring "classics" that are rarely found elsewhere. The menu also spotlights seasonal dishes, including truffles, spring vegetables, summer herbs and game in autumn – a highpoint for this chef who is an avid hunter. All paired with perfect wines.

First Course
- Homard bleu en fricassée "Georges Garin", macaroni à la duxelles.
- Vol-au-vent de ris d'agneau braisés.

Main Course
- Gibier (late September-late December).
- Truffes melanosporum (January-March).

Dessert
- Fenouil confit, glace à la vanille de Tahiti.
- Millefeuille cristalisé praliné-noisette, glace caramel.

Macéo

C1

15 r. Petits-Champs ⊠ 75001 **Ⓜ** Bourse
𝓒 01 42 97 53 85 Closed 2-17 August, Saturday lunch and Sunday
Fax 01 47 03 36 93
e-mail info@maceorestaurant.com **www**.maceorestaurant.com

Menu (€ 27), € 30/49 – Carte € 52/76

When he took over this restaurant founded in 1880, Mark Williamson treated himself to a superb place full of history –both in its Second Empire decor redesigned with a chic contemporary spirit and in the personalities who have frequented it such as Colette and Eisenhower. Renamed Macéo, the place has remained a favourite of celebrities. Thierry Bourdonnais' cuisine reinvents the classics using seasonal ingredients in dishes such as saddle of hare with raisins, lentil and foie gras vinaigrette, gingerbread macaroons and pepper sorbet. There is also an asparagus menu (in season), a 100% vegetarian "green menu" and an incomparable cellar – a passion of the proprietor's, who also owns Willi's Wine Bar – featuring 250 wines from around the world.

Au Gourmand

C1

⊠ 75001 **Ⓜ** Pyramides
𝓒 01 42 96 22 19 Closed August, Saturday lunch,
Fax 01 42 96 05 72 Monday lunch, Sunday and public holidays
www.augourmand.fr

Menu € 30 (weekday lunch)/36

Au Gourmand, act I: owners Christophe Courgeau (chef) and Hervé de Libouton (maître d'hôtel) move to a larger space on the Right Bank after the success of their restaurant in the 6th arrondissement. Au Gourmand, act II: more or less the same restaurant! It is a treat to taste the updated traditional cuisine (with an ''all vegetable'' menu featuring ingredients from famed market gardener Joël Thiébault), the sophisticated service, expert advice and ample wine list. Only the decor has changed (and may do so again) – a rococo theatrical style from the former Tartufo, with mirrors, a trompe-l'œil bookcase and a fresco. So there's still time, even if you missed the 1st act!

Au Pied de Cochon

Brasserie XX

D2

6 r. Coquillière ✉ 75001
📞 01 40 13 77 00
Fax 01 40 13 77 09
e-mail pieddecochon@blanc.net
www.pieddecochon.com

Ⓜ Châtelet-Les Halles

Menu (€20), €24 – Carte €28/75

This is truly a historic monument. Need we introduce the Blanc Brothers' indispensable brasserie, a bastion in Les Halles where diners can feast cheerfully day and night? Tourists and night owls know it well. The former admire its typically Parisian Belle Epoque decor, while the latter enjoy a good bowl of onion soup before going home to bed. "*Canaille*" dishes are featured here, exemplified by the "Tentation Saint-Antoine", a gargantuan ode to pork (grilled feet, ears, snout and tails or braised ribs). Shellfish platters are another speciality. Attractive new formulas and menus await you at lunchtime and after midnight.

Delizie d'Uggiano

Italian XX

A1

18 r. Duphot ✉ 75001
📞 01 40 15 06 69
Fax 01 40 15 03 90
e-mail losapiog@wanadoo.fr **www**.delizieduggiano.com

Ⓜ Madeleine
Closed 5-20 August, Saturday lunch and Sunday

Menu €89 bi – Carte €49/102

This very Italian establishment celebrates its Tuscan origins, paying a loving tribute to the Uggiano estate. You can see that it was originally a wine and olive oil shop from the gold-ochre decor – in the style of a deluxe trattoria – with a personal touch in the form of ceramics and bottles on display in the window. The shop is still there, sandwiched between the restaurant upstairs and the vaulted 16C cellar (tastings and meals are held for groups). The cuisine pulls out all the stops, using only the best ingredients in dishes such as antipasti, risotto, loin of veal Milanese, pasta, and a few truffle specialities in season. The prices tend to be rather high, but the service is perfect. Think of it as a place for special occasions.

Kinugawa

B1

9 r. Mont Thabor ✉ 75001
✆ 01 42 60 65 07
Fax 01 42 60 45 21
e-mail higashiuchi.kinugawa@free.fr

Ⓜ Tuileries
Closed 24 December-6 January and Sunday

Menu € 30 (weekday lunch), € 75/125 – Carte € 31/83

A/C

VISA

MC

AE

Ⓓ

The art of making sushi holds no secrets for the *sushiya* here, who has mastered the ingredients and is uncompromising about their quality and freshness. But these divine mouthfuls – prepared before your very eyes at the ground floor bar – are only a glimpse of his talent. Tempura, soba, *suimonos* (soups and egg dishes) and *nikoutoris* (meat and poultry), each one more delicious than the last, round out the choices at this establishment, a worthy ambassador of Japan in the capital. Regulars – businessmen and celebrities – are fond of the two upstairs dining rooms, as serene, delicate and refined as a Hokusai print.

Palais Royal

C1

110 Galerie de Valois – Jardin du
Palais Royal ✉ 75001
✆ 01 40 20 00 27
Fax 01 40 20 00 82
e-mail palaisrest@aol.com **www**.restaurantdupalaisroyal.com

Ⓜ Bourse
Closed 21 December-
1st January and Sunday

Carte € 45/76

A/C

VISA

MC

AE

Ⓓ

A dream location in the Palais-Royal with its arcades and beautiful garden. In summer the terrace is set up there : an idyllic spot. In winter there is a lovely view from the large picture window in the dining room. The atmosphere is intimate, with an Art Deco look, mirrors, modern paintings, photographs of Colette (who lived just above here), candle-light dinners, and enthusiastic service. Bruno Hees' cuisine oscillates between tradition and seasonal dishes, including lobster and porcini mushroom cappuccino, *buisson d'escargots*, raw sea bass with olive oil and parmesan, chestnut *millefeuille* and "*Paris-Brest et retour*".

Pierre au Palais Royal

Contemporary ✗✗

C2

10 r. Richelieu ✉ 75001
✆ 01 42 96 09 17
Fax 01 42 96 26 40
e-mail pierreaupalaisroyal@wanadoo.fr

Ⓜ **Palais Royal**
Closed August,
Saturday lunch and Sunday

Menu (€ 33), € 39

A/C

VISA

ⓂⒸ

AE

What's new at Pierre au Palais Royal? Everything, since the successful takeover by Éric Sertour (new chef, new decor, new feel). This institution has been totally redesigned in black and white - chic and discreet without affectation. Witness the Bigorre ham on the chopping block, indicating the food's Southwestern slant, and the very friendly welcome. The owner is more than happy to advise you on the wines and comment on the dishes prepared by Pascal Bataillé, including *rillons de joue de bœuf, boudin noir d'Iparla au piment d'Espelette et chorizo* (spicy black pudding),*sablé breton* (shortbread) with salted caramel ice cream and candied orange. As an added bonus, there is a late seating for the theatre crowd.

Pinxo

Innovative ✗✗

B1

Hôtel Renaissance Paris Vendôme,
9 r. Alger ✉ 75001
✆ 01 40 20 72 00 **Fax** 01 40 20 72 02
www.pinxo.fr

Ⓜ **Tuileries**
Closed 5-25 August

Menu (€ 32 bi) – Carte € 38/57

A/C

VISA

ⓂⒸ

AE

The kitchen is on display in the centre of the room – bordered by a fine granite bar – in this highly fashionable, black-and-white minimalist decor (the least you expect for a restaurant at the Hôtel Renaissance Paris Vendôme). The menu features succulent tapas-style sweet and savoury creations which the chic clientele has fun eating with their fingers or picking off their neighbour's plate.This is the latest concept from Alain Dutournier, a new form of gourmet sharing! Under the impulse of this Landais and lover of Spain, the friendly staff at Pinxo proposes sautéed *chipirons*, royal crab in a vegetable roll, *blidas* of chocolate, coconut and pistachio tiramisu, perfectly presented in three portions for you to mix to your heart's content.

Saudade

D2

34 r. Bourdonnais ⊠ 75001　　　　　　　　**M** Pont Neuf
✆ 01 42 36 30 71 **Fax** 01 42 36 30 71　　　Closed Sunday
www.restaurantsaudade.com

Menu € 22 (weekday lunch) – Carte € 28/49

AC
VISA
MC
AE

There's nothing sad about this Saudade! But it is a powerful remedy against homesickness, with fado music playing in the background and large gulps of old Port. For three generations – Fernando Moura took over in 1979 – this "embassy" of Portugal has confirmed its reputation for authenticity and local flavour, all with great modesty in the discreet façade and dining rooms tastefully decorated with azulejos tiles. Maria de Fatima, the guardian of tradition, has no equal in preparing pork with clams, *caldo verde* (cabbage soup), and *arroz doce* (rice pudding with cinnamon), not to mention cod, the national dish, grilled, pan-fried, au gratin, breaded, and deep-fried. Music-lovers will enjoy the live music on the first Tuesday of every month.

Le Soufflé

A1

36 r. Mont-Thabor ⊠ 75001　　　　　　　　**M** Tuileries
✆ 01 42 60 27 19　　　Closed 3-24 August, 15 February-1st March,
Fax 01 42 60 54 98　　　　　Sunday and public holidays
e-mail c_rigaud@club-internet.fr

Menu (€ 24 bi), € 30/40 – Carte € 36/58

AC
VISA
MC
AE

This restaurant devoted to soufflés ought to be puffed up with pride! Especially since this French speciality is becoming rather scarce. Here, it is made in many forms and for all tastes: savoury (cheese, tomato, avocado, morels, roquefort and walnuts, foie gras, chicken) or sweet (coffee, Grand Marnier, berries). We recommend the set menu for the single-minded; others may opt for more traditional dishes as an alternative. This unique establishment, over thirty years old, is not just a curiosity; it is also a charming and stylish place which delights a large clientele ranging from businessmen to Japanese tourists on a spree near Place de la Concorde. Remember to book.

L'Atelier Berger

Contemporary ✗

C2

49 r. Berger ✉ 75001   **Ⓜ** Louvre Rivoli
✆ 01 40 28 00 00   Closed Saturday lunchtime and Sunday
Fax 01 40 28 10 65
e-mail atelierberger@wanadoo.fr
www.restaurant-atelierberger.com

Menu € 36/65 – Carte € 36/47

Three places in one! To diversify the gourmet experience, L'Atelier Berger has multiplied the number of spaces and kinds of ambiance. The trail starts at the infinitely cosy bar, where you can snack on cold meats, cheese and bistro dishes. Then there's the English club-style smoking lounge, where you can enjoy fine cigars and spirits (well-stocked cellar). Lastly, the warm contemporary restaurant upstairs, where you can taste the creations of Franco-Norwegian chef Jean Christiansen, who trained in some great establishments. The cuisine with Nordic and sunny southern influences features some fine specialities, including herring "from back home" marinated with spices, red tuna tartare with ginger, and recipes using Havana tobacco leaves.

Baan Boran

Thai ✗

C1

43 r. Montpensier ✉ 75001   **Ⓜ** Palais Royal
✆ 01 40 15 90 45   Closed Saturday lunchtime and Sunday
Fax 01 40 15 90 45
e-mail baan.boran@orange.fr **www**.baan-boran.com

Menu € 14,50 (lunch)/45 (dinner) – Carte € 26/40

With its naive paintings and orchids, the yellow and red exotic contemporary decor at Baan Boran is neither overdone nor trendy. The Thai cuisine is prepared by two women, from central and northern Thailand, busy cooking in their woks. The more or less spicy (depending on your taste), light and vegetarian dishes are made with age-old *savoir-faire*. Soup, *tom yam khung* (shrimp with lemon grass), sautéed chicken in sesame oil and basil, beef curry with coconut milk, sticky rice, mango soup, etc. Enticing aromas waft into the dining room. At last the dishes are served on bamboo place settings by the charming staff in traditional dress. The journey is about to commence.

Bistrot St-Honoré

Bistro ✗

10 r. Gomboust ✉ 75001   **Ⓜ** Pyramides
✆ 01 42 61 77 78   Closed 24 December-2 January and Sunday
Fax 01 42 61 74 10
e-mail bistrotsthonore@orange.fr

Menu € 28 – Carte € 30/70

VISA
Ⓜ©
ᴁ
🅰️

Fresh frogs' legs, snails, _œufs en meurette_ (poached eggs in red wine sauce) and _veau sauce vigneronne en cocotte_ (veal cooked in a red wine reduction) – all these great Burgundy specialities await you at this establishment next to the Place du Marché-St-Honoré. These authentic and invigorating dishes share the limelight with the daily specialities on the blackboard. The carefully selected wines in the cellar pay tribute to the region's vineyards. With its ham and _rosette_ sausages hanging from the ceiling, and quintessentially old Paris decor (zinc bar, wooden chairs and tables), this convivial bistro oozes charm. Detective novel writer Frédéric Dard was a regular here and wrote about its fun-loving spirit in several of his books.

Chez La Vieille "Adrienne"

Terroir ✗

1 r. Bailleul ✉ 75001   **Ⓜ** Louvre Rivoli
✆ 01 42 60 15 78   Closed 1st-21 August,
Fax 01 42 33 85 71   Saturday and Sunday – Pre-book

Menu € 25 (lunch) – Carte € 37/52

VISA
Ⓜ©
ᴁ

Adrienne has left the kitchen but her "old" establishment – housed in a 16C residence – is still favoured by longstanding fans. Yannick Guepin (formerly with Gérard Besson) has just taken over under the watchful gaze of the ex-proprietress (the tiny room is dotted with black-and-white photographs of her). The good old-fashioned cooking has lightened up, but the "basics" still get high marks, including calf's liver, kidneys, beef with carrots, stew, _blanquette de veau à l'ancienne_, baba au rhum and _crème caramel_, sprinkled with a few Corsican dishes. The polished bistro, lace curtains and counter top with dishes of the day haven't changed a bit. This is tradition with a capital "T"!

Cristina's Tapas by Mavrommatis

A1

Greek ✗

18 r.Duphot ✉ 75001
✆ 01 42 97 53 04
Fax 01 42 97 52 37
www.mavrommatis.com

Ⓜ Madeleine
Closed Monday dinner, Tuesday dinner,
Wednesday dinner and Sunday

Menu €21/29 – Carte €33/47

VISA
MC

First came the book with the reassuring title: "Ma cuisine pour femmes au bord de la crise de nerfs" (Cooking for Women on the Verge of a Nervous Breakdown). Prompted by its success, author Cristina Egal decided to open a tapas bar – a live demonstration of her clever cooking skills – and the grilled sardines, *pimientos del piquillo*, *tortillas* and other spirited snacks made her reputation. Then the Mavrommatis brothers joined in to flesh out the menu with Greek, Cypriot, Italian and North African specialities. In short, this is a blend of Mediterranean flavours to be sampled at the bar, in the cellar or in the modern room upstairs.

Kaï

C2

Japanese ✗

✉ 75001
✆ 01 40 15 01 99

Ⓜ Louvre Rivoli
Closed 31 March-7 April, 4-25 August,
Sunday lunch and Monday

Menu €38 (lunch), €65/110 – Carte €45/73

A/C

VISA
MC
AE

Healthy, different, exotic - food from Japan has become all the rage in Paris, and Japanese restaurants have been popping up all over town. Kai is a particularly enjoyable and authentic one that will delight all those who need to watch their waistline but are inclined towards a bit of indulging. Traditional specialities are presented in a minimalist setting decorated with wood, bamboo and paintings. The sushi is succulent, and the risotto of lobster and red mullet with garlic sets the scene for the *Dengaku*, a delicious charcoal-grilled aubergine with miso sauce, or the *Tonkatsu*, breaded pork escalopes with seaweed and sweet-and-sour sauce. Pierre Hermé's irresistible desserts are the one French exception on the menu.

Lescure

7 r. Mondovi ✉ 75001
☎ 01 42 60 18 91

Ⓜ Concorde
Closed August, Christmas holidays,
Saturday and Sunday

Menu €23 – Carte €21/29

Lescure, located on a street behind the American Embassy, is the kind of place that improves with age, like a good wine. It has been handed down from father to son since it was first opened in 1919, and the owners, from the Corrèze region, have a faithful following of friends who have passed the word on. The old country inn look is a great drawing card with its rustic tables – and no more than thirty place settings. Cured meats and braids of onion and garlic hang from the ceiling. Copious, mouth-watering dishes from the Limousin region are featured, as well as beef bourguignon, stuffed *poule au pot* (boiled stuffed chicken with vegetables), and for dessert, *fondant aux trois chocolats*. Exceptionally friendly staff.

Pharamond

✉ 75001
☎ 01 40 28 45 18

Ⓜ Châtelet-Les Halles
Closed 5-25 August, February school holidays,
Sunday and Monday

Carte €42/87

Pharamond hasn't stopped serving its famous speciality, *tripes à la mode de Caen*, since 1832. This classic dish, served on a copper chafing dish, sets the tone at this *canaille* establishment, an institution during the heyday of Les Halles. Don't expect modern or trendy cuisine here. The chef, Sylvain Lebardier, prefers to stick to the bistro repertoire celebrating Norman and Parisian traditions (*andouilles de Vire*, rack of lamb with sautéed potatoes, honey-covered *charlotte*). The decor is not exactly ground-breaking, but it is timeless, remaining faithful to its 100% turn-of-the-century style. In good weather, they set up tables under the trees on the terrace.

Willi's Wine Bar

Bistro ✗

C1

13 r. Petits-Champs ✉ 75001
✆ 01 42 61 05 09
Fax 01 47 03 36 93
e-mail info@williswinebar.com **www**.williswinebar.com

Ⓜ Bourse
Closed 9-24 August and Sunday

Menu (€20), €25 (lunch)/34 – Carte approx. €35

VISA
MC
🐾

More than a wine bar, this is an exceptional cellar which also has an art gallery! Born out of Englishman Mark Williamson's passion for œnology, Willi's Wine Bar has been a model since 1980. Behind its cask-shaped façade, three hundred vintages (with a clear preference for Côtes du Rhône) are available on the – almost encyclopedic – wine list, or by the glass. Other "collectors" bottles are on display in this very British décor. Chef François Yon cooks up simple Mediterranean-style dishes, served with no fuss at the bar or in the dining room, to accompany this worship of Bacchus. Have a look at the Bottle Art Collection, a series of posters commissioned every year from a contemporary artist, illustrating the remarkable nature of the place.

THE STRONGMEN OF LES HALLES

Not everyone could be a "Strongman of Les Halles". You had to be French, have fulfilled your military service, have a basic diploma (certificat d'études), be at least 1.67m tall and be able to carry a 200kg load for 60 metres. These "supermen" carried merchandise from carts – left outside the market – to sales points in the "Belly of Paris". Their distinctive feature was a wide hat topped by a lead disk to stabilize the heavy loads on their heads. All the coming and going was a sight to see! In the 2nd half of the 20C they became municipal employees, their job changed and then disappeared completely when the market was transferred to Rungis.

Bourse

Wedged in between the Palais Royal, Opéra and boulevard de Sébastopol, the second arrondissement is both the smallest and least populated of Paris. However don't be mistaken: deeply rooted in the heart of the capital, it is home to a genuine hive of commercial activity around which an often surprising mosaic of atmospheres and décors has grown up.

FROM FINANCIAL MARKETPLACES...

The Bourse district owes its name to the famous Palais Brogniard, a pompous neo-classical edifice, home, until only a short time ago, to the Paris Stock Exchange. Now closed, the temple of French finance has nonetheless retained a faithful network of devotees and the ostentatious marks of its industrious and merchant traditions are still visible in the corporate headquarters of the many banks and financial and credit institutions in the neighbourhood as well as in the streets that teem with executives and luxury cars during working hours.

A few steps away, the Sentier district – the manufacturing face of this "economic forum" – reveals the same thriving entrepreneurial spirit and its narrow streets are often blocked by delivery vans and wholesale goods. Even though the clothing workshops,

the core of Parisian fashion, are gradually giving way to young IT start-ups, the neighbourhood continues to overflow with little establishments that are perfect for a quick meal between two appointments.

... TO VEGETABLE MARKETS

The former effervescence is in striking contrast to the almost provincial charm of the Montorgueil district. Its largely pedestrian streets are lined in traditional fruit and vegetable stalls and subtly old-fashioned cafés where the locals plonk down their basket between shops for a cup of coffee.

The neighbourhood also hides countless covered galleries whose high glass and metal roofs are typical of the 19C. In between rue d'Aboukir and rue Saint-Denis in particular, don't miss the Passage du Caire (1798) whose original décor is still intact and which is home to dozens of tiny shops selling lithographs and to a highly singular population of models for shop windows, intended for the textile trade just next door in the Sentier.

HIGH-CLASS ELEGANCE

The setting and the class moves markedly upmarket between rue de la Paix, headquarters of in-

B. Gardel / HEMIS.FR

ternational calibre jewellers and place des Victoires, a stylish royal square encircled by high fashion designers. The atmosphere is decidedly plush, if not luxurious. An impression further reinforced by the refined architecture of the buildings, a succession of elegant façades of all styles and all periods. From the medieval tower of Jean sans Peur on rue Etienne Marcel to the lofty glass and steel merchant buildings on rue Réaumur, every era of Parisian history is represented.

BISTROS!

Few Parisians actually live in the second arrondissement, so bound up as it is in the world of trade and industry, but the traffic is nonetheless often at a standstill due to its central location and the appeal of its shops. So take your time and stop at one of the many traditional old bistros and admire their zinc-covered counters, walls lined in mirrors and comfortable upholstered bench seating as you sample good wholesome dishes.

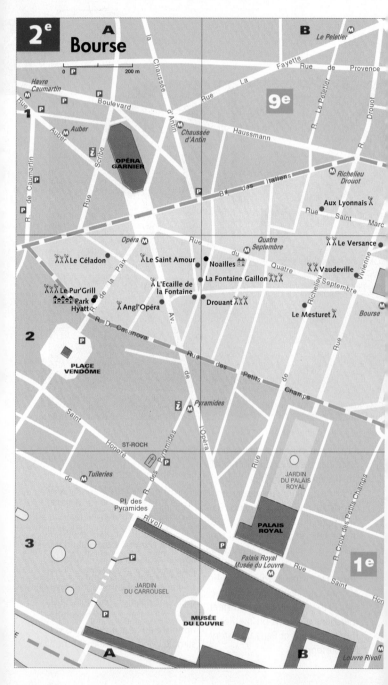

2e
Bourse

A · B

Le Peletier

Rue · de · Provence

9e

Havre Caumartin

Boulevard

Auber

Chaussée d'Antin

Haussmann

Bd · des · Italiens

Richelieu Drouot

OPÉRA GARNIER

Aux Lyonnais ✕

Rue · Saint · Marc

Opéra Ⓜ

Rue · du

Quatre Septembre Ⓜ

✕✕ Le Versance ●

✕✕✕ Le Céladon

✕ Le Saint Amour ● Noailles 🏛

Quatre

✕✕ Vaudeville

La Fontaine Gaillon ✕✕✕

✕ L'Ecaille de la Fontaine

Drouant ✕✕✕

✕✕✕ Le Pur'Grill

Park Hyatt ●

R. · de · la · Paix

✕ Angl'Opéra

Av.

Le Mesturet ✕

Bourse Ⓜ

PLACE VENDÔME

R. · De · Casanova

Rue · des · Petits · Champs

de

Saint

Pyramides Ⓜ

Honoré

ST-ROCH

de Ⓜ Tuileries

Pl. des Pyramides

Rivoli

JARDIN DU PALAIS ROYAL

PALAIS ROYAL

1e

JARDIN DU CARROUSEL

Palais Royal Musée du Louvre Ⓜ

Rue · Saint

Hon

MUSÉE DU LOUVRE

A · B

Louvre Rivoli

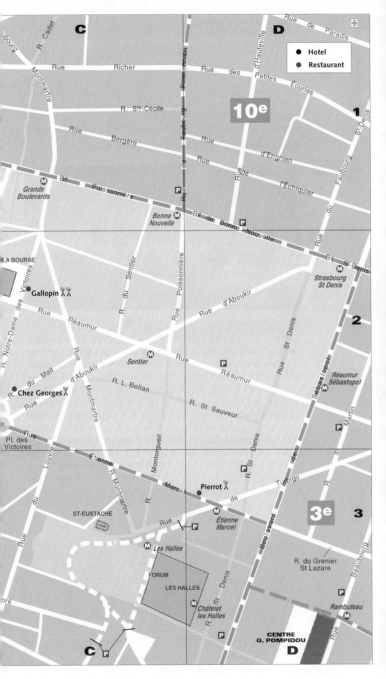

Le Céladon ✿

A2

Hôtel Westminster,
15 r. Daunou ✉ 75002
📞 01 47 03 40 42
Fax 01 42 61 33 78
e-mail christophemoisand@leceladon.com **www.**leceladon.com

Ⓜ **Opéra**
Closed August,
Saturday and Sunday

Menu € 48 (lunch), € 72 bi/110 – Carte € 82/111

A/C

VISA

Ⓜ©

ΑΕ

Ⓞ

Le Céladon

There's nothing showy or trendy about Le Céladon, the subtle and refined restaurant at the Hotel Westminster, halfway between Place Vendôme and the Opéra Garnier. On the contrary, Pierre-Yves Rochon's neo-classical decor with a hint of the Orient (damask wall hangings, Chinese porcelain vases and bookcases) exudes a feeling of luxury without ostentation, celebrating the house's emblematic colour, celadon green. A meal in this plush and intimate atmosphere is a delightful experience, like taking a journey to some faraway place. Christophe Moisand (formerly at the Relais de Sèvres and the Meurice) produces creative and masterful dishes, full of delicate flavours, combining classicism and modernity, while Richard Rahard ensures some excellent wine pairings.

First Course	*Main Course*	*Dessert*
• Pâté froid de lapin de garenne (15 sept. au 15 janv.).	• Langoustines bretonnes en tempura au carry.	• Soufflé chaud au chocolat guanaja, glace au pain d'épice.
• Crabe royal à la crème d'avocat, eau de tomate à la verveine.	• Saint-Pierre de petit bateau masqué de pousses de moutarde, "cru et cuit" de légumes niçois aux olives.	• Ananas effeuillé au sorbet de pamplemousse, "rocher coco" et miel basilic.

Drouant

B2

Traditional XXX

16 pl. Gaillon ✉ 75002   Ⓜ Quatre Septembre
✆ 01 42 65 15 16 **Fax** 01 49 24 02 15
e-mail reservations@drouant.com **www**.drouant.com

Menu € 42 (weekday lunch)/67 – Carte € 40/87

Antoine Westermann has breathed new life into Drouant, the restaurant on Place Gaillon where the Goncourt Academy awards its yearly prize. His ambition was to turn this legendary place into the latest chic brasserie where people meet to exchange ideas over a festive meal. The sleek new decor is muted yet luminous, with well-balanced proportions. Dark furniture offsets the light walls decorated with photographs; the Ruhlmann staircase leads up to a pleasant loft space; the bar area is adorned with gold; and the private dining rooms have retained their classic style. A fine setting for the expressive cuisine featuring top-quality seasonal produce (vegetables, truffles, foie gras, oysters, etc.).

La Fontaine Gaillon

A2

Seafood XXX

pl. Gaillon ✉ 75002   Ⓜ Quatre Septembre
✆ 01 47 42 63 22   Closed 9 August-1st September,
Fax 01 47 42 82 84   Saturday and Sunday
www.la-fontaine-gaillon.com

Menu € 41 (lunch) – Carte € 48/64

Everyone has been talking about this restaurant ever since Gérard Depardieu took over. But that isn't the most convincing asset possessed by this fine townhouse built in 1672 by Jules Hardouin-Mansart. The main event is the well-prepared cuisine by Laurent Audiot, formerly of Marius et Jeannette, featuring seafood, classics of French gastronomy with a twist, and daily inspirations based on market produce. Then there is the cellar, which takes an interest in small-scale producers and wines from sunny places (Morocco, Sicily, etc.). Lastly, there are the stylish, intimate dining rooms with their wood panelling, period furniture and fine paintings, not to mention the extremely pleasant "Provençal" terrace coiled around the fountain.

Le Pur' Grill ✿

Contemporary XXX

A2

Hôtel Park Hyatt,
5 r. Paix ✉ 75002
☎ 01 58 71 10 60

Ⓜ Opéra
Closed August – Dinner only

Menu € 125/300 bi – Carte € 92/225

VISA
Ⓜ©
AE
Ⓞ

The Park Hyatt now has two contemporary restaurants: Les Orchidées for lunch, and the more hushed Le Pur'Grill for dinner, a setting that befits this hotel on the rue de la Paix where luxury is all about refinement, modernity and discretion. The decor by Ed Tuttle creates an atmosphere that is both comfortable and spectacular – an unconditional success. Everything has been designed to combine magnificence and intimacy, from the range of light and dark tones and the soft indirect lighting to the space itself, a vast rotunda topped by a dome and surrounded by a colonnade with a large padded banquette – electrified by the kitchen performance in full swing. The chef orchestrating it all is Jean-François Rouquette (Taillevent, le Crillon, la Cantine des Gourmets, les Muses), who has found a setting to match his masterful talents. His attractive menu is founded on simplicity, excellent ingredients and a dash of fantasy, as in his ephemeral Fleur menu.

First Course

- Salade de homard breton et avocat, vinaigrette au yuzu.
- Vapeur d'escargots petits gris, radis rouge et raifort.

Main Course

- Pièce de bœuf Wagyu grillé au sarment de vigne, beignets d'artichauts poivrade farcis au pissalat.
- Déclinaison d'agneau de l'Aveyron, haricots coco, chorizo et romarin.

Dessert

- Figue 'O' Cassis, glace au shizo.
- Choco Tag, chutney banane/galanga et épine vinette.

Gallopin

  Brasserie ✗✗

C2

40 r. N.-D.-des-Victoires ✉ 75002   **Ⓜ** Bourse
☎ 01 42 36 45 38 **Fax** 01 42 36 10 32
e-mail administration@brasseriegallopin.com
www.brasseriegallopin.com

Menu (€ 20), € 28/34 bi – Carte € 28/76

Ⓐ/ⓒ
⟨⟩
VISA
Ⓜⓒ
ⒶⒺ
Ⓞ

The name comes from a certain Monsieur Gallopin, who
opened his first business here in 1876 and invented the
famous silver-plated beer mugs of the same name. Since
then, many *galopins* (urchins) have stood at its bar. Arletty
and Raimu were once regulars; nowadays many businessmen come to enjoy the lovely decor with its venerable bar,
wood panelling, gleaming copperware, mirrors, mouldings
and, above all, its superb 1900s glass roof (in the Belle
Epoque room). The menu features simple but reliable brasserie fare such as *foie gras de canard* (duck foie gras), *andouillette* sausages, seafood platters, sole (grilled or meunière),
and *pièce de bœuf.* With the relaxed service and atmosphere
here you'll enjoy every sip of beer – and the rest too!

Vaudeville

  Brasserie ✗✗

B2

29 r. Vivienne ✉ 75002   **Ⓜ** Bourse
☎ 01 40 20 04 62 **Fax** 01 40 20 14 35
www.vaudevilleparis.com

Menu (€ 21), € 24 (weekdays)/31 – Carte € 33/69

VISA
Ⓜⓒ
ⒶⒺ
Ⓞ

Businessmen and journalists come here for lunch (the Stock
Exchange and Agence France Presse are nearby). But in the
evenings it is filled with the lively theatre crowd. Art Deco
furnishings begin to sparkle, decibels rise and ever-smiling
waiters slalom from table to table. No doubt about it, the
Vaudeville knows its part by heart – that of a true Parisian
brasserie! Featured "On the Boards" are all the classics of
the genre, highlighted by house specialities such as *Tranche
de morue grille* (grilled slice of cod) and *purée de pommes de
terre au jus de truffe* (mashed potatoes with truffle juice). You
can order from a set menu or à la carte, and there is even a
late supper for theatre-goers. The terrace is a nice bonus in
fine weather.

Le Versance

B2

16 r. Feydeau ✉ 75002   **Ⓜ** Bourse
   01 45 08 00 08   Closed August, 24 December-2 January,
Fax 01 45 08 47 99   Saturday lunch, Sunday and Monday
e-mail contact@leversance.fr
www.leversance.fr

Menu (€ 32 bi), € 38 bi – Carte € 46/68

A/C
VISA
M/C
AE

Luxe, calme et volupté (comfort, calm and bliss) – the expression is rather hackneyed; but in this case it corresponds to reality. Le Versance is truly a gem – tasteful and elegant, classic and modern with its clean lines and grey-and-white tones. Period beams and stained glass, tables dressed to the nines, prim and proper professional waiters, smoking lounge, and serene ambiance. This is a masterstroke for Samuel Cavagnis, and his first restaurant. In the kitchen this young globe-trotter sticks with French flavours. This return to his roots is illustrated by the nicely named dishes, such as *raviole de potiron au sirop d'érable* (pumpkin ravioli with maple syrup), and *poire coing aux épices et châtaignes* (quince pear with spices and chestnuts).

Angl'Opéra

A2

Hôtel Edouard VII,   **Ⓜ** Opéra
39 av. Opéra ✉ 75002   Closed 11-24 August,
   01 42 61 86 25   Saturday and Sunday
Fax 01 42 61 47 73
e-mail resto@anglopera.com **www**.anglopera.com

Menu € 29 (lunch) – Carte € 48/58

VISA
M/C
AE
DC

On the ground floor of the very chic Edouard VII, a fashionable restaurant managed by Gilles Choukroun, a young, talented chef with a taste for the avant-garde has a passion for inventing and blending flavours both sweet and savoury, spices and getting his inspiration from four corners of the globe. The result is a succinct menu that associates playful, sometimes bold associations, all of which are delicious. "Crème brûlée, radish, soya sauce, coffee and foie gras", "grapefruit, green tea, spinach leaves and rump steak" and for dessert "petits farcis, salted caramel, ginger, maple and chocolate". Give your taste buds a surprise! Snacks, quick lunches and pastries are sold at the bar.

Aux Lyonnais ☻

Lyonnais cuisine ✗

B1

32 r. St-Marc ✉ 75002
℘ 01 42 96 65 04
Fax 01 42 97 42 95
e-mail auxlyonnais@online.fr

Ⓜ Richelieu Drouot
Closed 20 July-18 August, Saturday lunch,
Sunday and Monday – Pre-book

Menu € 30 – Carte € 38/55

A/C
VISA
Ⓜ©
AE

This deliciously retro bistrot, open since 1890 and a member of the Alain Ducasse group, is very stylish with its mirrors, mouldings, earthenware, paintings and old zinc bar. Sitting comfortably on one of the banquettes, you are all set to read the menu (despite the tables being a bit too close). Explore the tasty Lyon recipes made with the best regional products: *cervelle de Canut, quenelles* and crayfish, *cochonnailles* (pork delicacies), *cervelas pistaché* (cured pork sausage and pistachios), *tarte aux pralines roses* etc. The cellar features wines from the Rhône and Burgundy regions. The attentive service, ambiance and good value for money (the wines, however, are a bit expensive) make this a true *bouchon lyonnais* in Paris.

Chez Georges

Traditional ✗

C2

1 r. Mail ✉ 75002
℘ 01 42 60 07 11

Ⓜ Bourse
Closed August, 24 December-2 January,
Saturday, Sunday and public holidays

Carte € 42/66

A/C
VISA
Ⓜ©
AE

A real institution in the Sentier district, near the Place des Victoires, this authentic Parisian bistrot has preserved its 1900s decor, with zinc bar, banquettes, stucco and mirrors, and its warm, friendly atmosphere. The owner loves to pamper diners; the purely traditional dishes are generous and designed to please food-lovers: *terrines de foie de volaille* (chicken liver terrine), *harengs-pommes à l'huile* (herring cured in oil with potatoes), *entrecôte grille* (grilled steak), *profiteroles au chocolat*, etc. Regulars have been coming to this place for a century (despite slightly high prices) with its top-quality produce – special praise going to meat dishes such as the famous *pavé de bœuf* –, perfect cooking and well-chosen French wines.

L'Écaille de la Fontaine

Fish and shellfish ✗

A2

15 r. Gaillon ✉ 75002
☎ 01 47 42 02 99
Fax 01 47 42 82 84

Ⓜ Quatre Septembre
Closed 9 August-1st September,
Saturday and Sunday
Number of covers limited, pre-book

Carte approx. €35

VISA
ⓂⒸ
AE

This is another restaurant run by Gérard Depardieu and Laurent Audiot, located almost across the street from Fontaine Gaillon, specialising in shellfish obtained from small oyster-farmers and fish merchants from Quiberon, Marennes, Oléron, etc. A small slate menu also features appetizing seafood recipes to go or to enjoy at the bar. Or, if you feel like taking your time, try the little upstairs dining room which is cosy and intimate. Have a look in any case. Depardieu has created an impressive "study" with photographs evoking his life as an artist. Note that this national star also supervises the wine list.

Le Mesturet

Traditional ✗

B2

77 r. de Richelieu ✉ 75002
☎ 01 42 97 40 68 **Fax** 01 42 97 40 68
e-mail lemesturet@wanadoo.fr **www**.lemesturet.com

Ⓜ Bourse

Menu (€20), €26 – Carte €27/38

A/C
VISA
ⓂⒸ
AE
Ⓞ

People crowd in to sit shoulder-to-shoulder in the keyed-up atmosphere at Le Mesturet! The passionate chef at this old-style bistro champions "homemade" food and real regional produce. The meat, cold meats, fruits, vegetables and cheese all come from small-scale producers whose names appear on the menu. You can enjoy the food here at any hour of the day, from old-fashioned dishes to more creative recipes, express menus for those in a hurry ("at the bar"), breakfasts, brunches and aperitifs. It also boasts a judicious selection of wines, a warm welcome and an authentic setting (stone and wood work, bottle drainers, bric-a-brac and banquettes). The price of success: the restaurant is full until closing time!

Pierrot

Traditional ✗

D3

18 r. Étienne Marcel ✉ 75002   Ⓜ Étienne Marcel
📞 01 45 08 00 10   Closed 30 July-22 August and Sunday
Fax 01 42 77 35 92

Menu (€ 28), € 50 bi – Carte € 34/50

A typical bistrot (banquettes, zinc bar, mirrors) with a warm and friendly atmosphere in the heart of Les Halles. Sound appealing? The flavours and fine products from the Aveyron region are another (really good) reason to try it. Farm-raised meat from Aubrac, confit de canard (preserved duck), homemade foie gras, etc. All these well-made, plain and simple, generous dishes are written up on the slate menu, complemented by the latest additions. The service is attentive, friendly and fast. In good weather you can eat on the sidewalk terrace and enjoy people-watching on busy rue Étienne-Marcel.

Le Saint Amour

Seafood ✗

A2

8 r. Port Mahon ✉ 75002   Ⓜ Quatre Septembre
📞 01 47 42 63 82   Closed 1st-15 August,
Fax 01 47 42 63 82   Saturday and Sunday
e-mail hervbrun@hotmail.fr

Menu (€ 25), € 34/46

The Saint Amour is a haven of peace and quiet amidst the hustle and bustle of this central district of Paris, home to the Opéra and the big department stores. On a small side street, it has two levels decorated in different styles – banquettes and exotic wood tables on the ground floor, country atmosphere with an antique dresser on the first floor. The overall effect remains simple, as the generous traditional cuisine is the main focus of attention here, featuring fresh fish and shellfish shipped directly from Brittany. They have quite a knack for hospitality at this friendly and convivial "pocket" restaurant, where the chef's mother greets you with a warm welcome.

Le Marais · Beaubourg

Adjoining the working-class Halles district, the 3rd arrondissement displays an equal vitality with its countless shops and boutiques and the highly popular Beaubourg museum. However it differs in one not-able respect, the soul of historic Paris can still be felt in the Marais, proud of its hectic, multicultural past and still a haven for differences of every nature…

GAY PARIS

The Marais owes its name to the marshes that used to border the Seine, turned into cottage gardens in the Middle Ages. Since then, the district has never ceased to prosper, changing personality with every era: aristocratic in the 17C, laboriously toiling in the 19C, it then floundered for a while, abandoned in indifference before being brought back to life again in the early 1980s with the arrival of the gay community.

The neighbourhood is frequently accused of being a museum-district because of its many cultural and historic sites (**Picasso, Carnavalet museums,** etc.). However for its inhabitants, the Marais is first and foremost a "village" such is its resemblance with a microcosm where everyone knows everyone. It has above all remained human in size because of its narrow streets that were typical of Paris prior to the Hausmannian revolution. A walk in the Marais is like embarking on a journey through time, past the half-timbered medieval houses and elegant town mansions in **rue des Archives** and **rue François-Miron.** Don't miss **place des Vosges,** lined in identical arcaded buildings, home to antique dealers and good restaurants, in the centre of which stands the majestic and very chic Louis XIII square.

Just behind lies the **rue des Francs-Bourgeois** dotted with fashion boutiques located in old bakers and butchers shops that have retained their original façades. The street is always packed with fashionistas, even on Sundays when the whole neighbourhood stays open for shopping addicts! Two steps away the picturesque **rue des Rosiers** abounds in tempting kosher shops, a throwback to its Jewish traditions. It is here that you can sample the best falafels and eastern European Jewish pastries of the capital.

Rue Vieille-du-Temple and the aptly named **rue du Trésor** swarm for their part with cafés and are ideal to start the evening. On **rue Ste-Croix-de-la-Bretonnerie** the rhythm increases a notch in the gay bars that have taken up residence here.

ART AND TECHNOLOGY

To the west, modern-day Paris once again rears its head in one of its best-known icons, the **Centre Georges Pompidou**, referred to as Beaubourg and

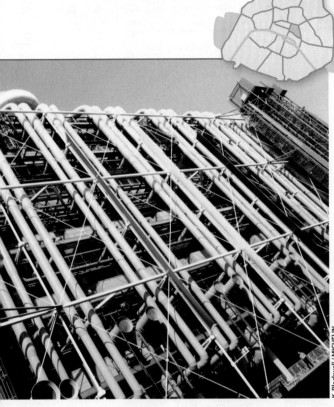

K. Blackwell / MICHELIN

known as much for its modern art museum as for its amazing (at the time) architecture. The "piazza" in front of the museum is undoubtedly the most popular location in the whole arrondissement and is frequented by an improbable mixture from students and tourists to street performers and portrait painters. If you're in the area, particularly at sunset, go up to the rooftop terrace of the restaurant and admire the stunning view of the roofs of Paris.

To the north, between the **Arts et Métiers Museum** (don't miss its surprising metro station) and République, you are in a "designer" land of confidential and more than trendy fashion addresses, art galleries and café-restaurants belonging to an amazing hotchpotch of registers from organic and world fusion. However let's not forget two institutions, the venerable **marché des Enfants Rouges** (1615), ideal for a quick bite between shops and the **carreau du Temple,** devoted to second-hand clothes and built out of glass and iron in tribute to the old Baltard pavilions of Les Halles.

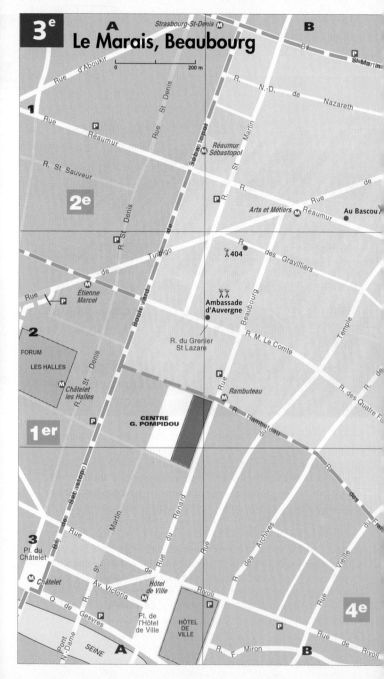

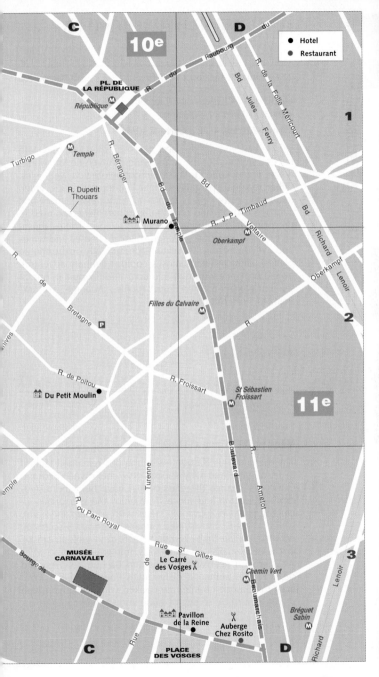

Ambassade d'Auvergne ☺

B2

22 r. Grenier St-Lazare ✉ 75003   Ⓜ Rambuteau
☎ 01 42 72 31 22 **Fax** 01 42 78 85 47
e-mail info@ambassade-auvergne.com
www.ambassade-auvergne.com

Menu (€ 20 bi), € 28 – Carte € 30/46

A/C
📶
VISA
Ⓜ©
AE

Where can you get the best *aligot* (mashed potatoes with cheese) in Paris? At the Ambassade d'Auvergne, of course, where it is whipped in a copper pot before your very eyes. Other regional specialities include pork delicacies, green lentils and *potée de porc fermier aux choux braisés* (pork and cabbage hotpot), and only the best ingredients are used in preparing these authentic, generous recipes. The establishment has a bountiful selection of local cheeses and wines (the Aveyron region also features prominently on the cheese platter). Here you can enjoy a copious culinary adventure from a province with rich traditions and flavours in one of the four elegant themed dining rooms – Auberge, Artisans, Peintres, and Rotonde.

Au Bascou

B1

38 r. Réaumur ✉ 75003   Ⓜ Arts et Métiers
☎ 01 42 72 69 25   Closed August, 24 December to 2 January,
Fax 01 55 90 99 77   Saturday and Sunday

Menu (€ 18) – Carte € 33/42

VISA
Ⓜ©
AE

The menu at this Basque institution has remained faithful to its origins. And why should new chef-owner Bertrand Guéneron change the classics that have built the restaurant's reputation and success? So enjoy the specialities including *piperades* (scrambled eggs with peppers and ham), *pimientos del piquillo* (stuffed pimentos), *chipirons sautés au piment d'Espelette* (baby squid), *fricassée d'escargots au jambon* (fricassee of snails), chestnut soup, foie gras ravioli, *axoa de veau* (ground veal with onions and Basque peppers) and *clafoutis*. The authentic dishes with fine ingredients fresh from the Basque country are cooked with loving care and served in a rustic setting of stone and vaulted ceilings.

Auberge Chez Rosito

D3

Corsican cuisine 🍴

4 r. Pas de la Mule ✉ 75003
📞 01 42 76 04 44
Fax 01 42 76 98 52

Ⓜ Bastille
Closed 8-23 August,
Saturday lunch and Sunday

Menu (€ 15) – Carte € 32/54

VISA
MC

The Corsican flag floats above this genuine ambassador of the Isle of Beauty. The proprietors extend a warm welcome, in a spirit of simple generosity. The retro dining room has been carefully decorated with frying pans, herbs, peppers, old posters and other objects from the island. Regulars – whether from Corsica or not – enjoy the homely feeling of this establishment serving the island's treasured gastronomy (game, fish and pork) and wine. You'll feel like you've taken a one-way trip to Ajaccio in the heart of this neighbourhood full of antique and design shops.

Le Carré des Vosges

C3

South-west of France 🍴

15 r. St Gilles ✉ 75003
📞 01 42 71 22 21
Fax 01 41 17 09 33
e-mail lecarredesvosges@yahoo.fr
www.lecarredesvosges.fr

Ⓜ Chemin Vert
Closed 5-25 August, 23-30 December,
Monday lunch and Sunday

Menu (€ 21), € 27 (lunch) – Carte € 34/60

A/C
VISA
MC

Those who were familiar with the Petit Pamphlet will remember its atmosphere characterised by lampoonist posters and engravings. Now they can explore its successor, Le Carré des Vosges, and its chic, new, contemporary bistro look (black lacquer bar, beige and taupe tones, orange banquettes, flowers and wall of mirrors). Other plus points at this new establishment include its convivial ambiance, friendly and informal service, and seasonal cuisine. The menu features pan-fried foie gras with red berries and apple chutney, lamb cooked for seven hours, and a *Tatin glacé à la crème d'Isigny*.

404

B2

69, r. des Gravilliers ✉ 75003   Ⓜ Arts et Métiers
✆ 01 42 74 57 81 **Fax** 01 42 74 03 41
e-mail 404resto@wanadoo.fr

Menu (€ 17), € 30 (lunch), € 50/80 – Carte € 30/50

Two of the specialities on the menu at this North African restaurant have gained it a solid reputation – its famous couscous and tajine dishes. Carefully prepared with high-quality ingredients, they attract a clientele that enjoys the exotic decor in this small establishment where the low wooden tables, superb *moucharabiehs*, finely worked lanterns and painted tableware from Morocco, Syria and Egypt create a true Arabian Nights decor. The quiet lunchtime atmosphere (with neighbourhood regulars) gets trendier in the evening, so be sure to book. Weather-permitting, try the delightful patio-terrace.

PANTAGRUEL OUT FOR THE COUNT!

The Club des Grands Estomacs was all the rage during the Second Empire. The name was quite unusual – and very explicit! The favourite activity of its 12 gourmet members was to meet from 6pm on Saturday to noon the next day, at a restaurant called "Chez Philippe" (on rue Montorgueil), where they ate three gigantic meals one after the other. They swallowed 30 dishes without respite – fatted chicken, veal tongue, turbot, sole, soup, beef filet, roast chicken, pudding, onion soup, patisseries, etc. – washed down with large quantities of wine and champagne. Naturally they needed a digestive after all that food, so they drank a whole bottle of cognac, kirsch or rum – per person! Bottom's up!

Île de la Cité
Île St-Louis · St-Paul

The seat of religious and political power since Antiquity, the islands of St-Louis and the Cité mark the heart of Paris. The home of some of the most emblematic (and tourist) monuments of the capital, they stand like timeless jewels cut off from the rest of Paris by the Seine. The unassuming village of St-Paul, just nearby, for its part is endowed with an almost provincial art de vivre…

From island
to island

Is it their isolation by the Seine that gives these islands such a special character in the Parisian landscape? Despite the affluence of tourists, nothing seems to trouble the serenity of their ancient facades, so sensibly aligned behind the trees.

Ile de la Cité remains singularly impressive, as it is home all on its own to the law courts, police headquarters (the "Quai des Orfèvres" of Clouzot and Jouvet), the medieval turrets of the Conciergerie (first prison of Paris), the court of trade and Hôtel-Dieu Hospital, a fact that explains the surplus of robed lawyers and policemen… You may also see many passers-by, nose up in the air desperately seeking the entrance to the Sainte-Chapelle, tucked away behind the law courts.

The island is also home to another gothic masterpiece, **Notre-Dame Cathedral,** as popular today as it was in past times. Once you've made your way across the esplanade, sidestepping the snap-shotters, souvenir vendors and roller bladers, venture indoors and enjoy the classical concerts that take place beneath its ribbed vaults – don't miss the evening organ concerts.

In contrast to these grandiose sites, you may want to take a breather at **place Dauphine**, the **flower market** or **square du Vert-galant,** as you head down towards **Pont Neuf** – in fact the oldest bridge of Paris. Beneath you boats of tourists and barges make their way up and down the Seine.

Walk over to **Île Saint-Louis** across the bridge of the same name – the only link between the two islands. The atmosphere here is much quieter and more peaceful. A throwback perhaps to when the island was little more than a field given over to cows, duels and washerwomen! A residential district since the 17C, its noble edifices are also reminders of the artists and poets who found refuge here in the 19C. In short it is a haven for romantic strolls. In the evening, walk up **rue Saint-Louis-en-l'Île,** the backbone of the island and the location of shops, galleries and restaurants, and also of the famous ice-cream maker, **Berthillon**.

R. Visage / SUNSET

ÎLE DE LA CITÉ • ÎLE ST-LOUIS • ST-PAUL

TOWN AND VILLAGE

A parenthesis in time, **village Saint-Paul** is an unexpected enclave with its tiny maze of lanes and ancient houses, now home to high-class antique dealers and also popular with strollers. Almost a medieval miniature, it is only a few steps from the modern traffic and bustle of **rue Saint-Antoine** and **rue de Rivoli.** The basement of the hundred-year-old Bazar de l'Hôtel de Ville (BHV) is heaven for do-it-yourself fans who, once their bolt found, can take a break at the café Boulon. Finally **place de l'Hôtel de Ville** resonates to the capital's major cultural, sporting and political events, while place Baudoyer, just behind, is where the only market in the 4th is held.

Bastille on one side and **Châtelet** on the other, the symbolic frontiers of this arrondissement, are high places of opera and theatre in the capital. Surrounded by brasseries and cafés that are open until early in the morning, they embody the personality of the city of light and revolution.

83

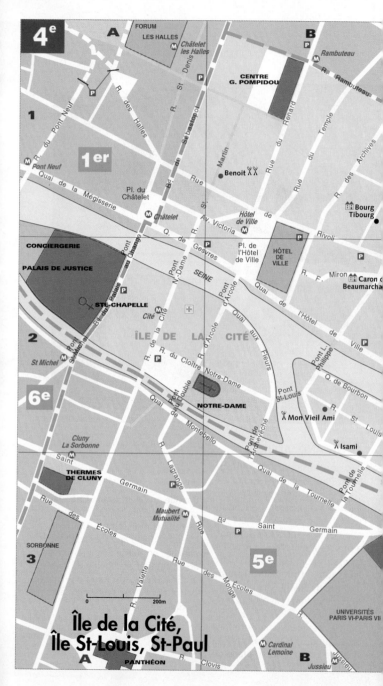

Île de la Cité,
Île St-Louis, St-Paul

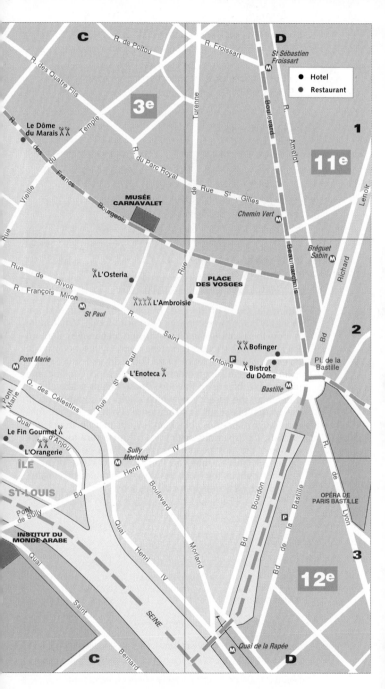

L'Ambroisie ✿✿✿

D2

9 pl. des Vosges ✉ 75004
✆ 01 42 78 51 45

Ⓜ St-Paul
Closed August, 23 February-11 March,
Sunday and Monday

Carte € 196/252

A/C

VISA
MC
AE

Owen Franken

Ambrosia: "food of the gods of Olympus, a source of immortality", and by extension, "exquisite food". What more is there to say about the divine cuisine prepared by Bernard Pacaud, whose success is matched only by his modesty? In an elegant reinterpretation of tradition, dishes feature painstakingly selected ingredients, with precision cooking and impeccable blends of flavours. These details make all the difference, the essence of which could be summed up in the words "classical" and "masterful".With its antique mirrors, huge tapestries, black-and-white marble floors and orchids, the luxurious setting – a 17th century townhouse on one of the most beautiful squares in Paris – is of the same calibre. It calls to mind an Italian palace – like being in Florence right on the Place des Vosges. Refined and elegant, a meal here is a delight for all the senses.

First Course

- Feuillantine de langoustines aux graines de sésame, sauce curry.
- Foie gras de canard au poivre gris, chutney de cerises noires.

Main Course

- Navarin de homard et pommes de terre fondantes au romarin.
- Poularde de Bresse rôtie au beurre d'estragon.

Dessert

- Tarte fine sablée au chocolat, glace vanille.
- Arlettes caramélisées au fromage blanc et framboises, cristallines de rhubarbe.

Benoit ✿

Traditional ✗✗

B1

20 r. St-Martin ✉ 75004
✆ 01 42 72 25 76
Fax 01 42 72 45 68
e-mail restaurant.benoit@wanadoo.fr
www.alain-ducasse.com

Ⓜ Châtelet-Les Halles
Closed 26 July-25 August and
25 February-2 March

Menu €38 (lunch) – Carte €55/88

A/C
⟷
VISA
Ⓜⓒ
ⒶⒺ

Marie Hennechart

For true Parisian bistro atmosphere – an endangered species – try this establishment at 20, Rue Saint Martin in the heart of Paris. Benoît opened its doors in 1912, when Les Halles still had its famous marketplace. Originally a *bouchon lyonnais*, this bistro remained for three generations in the Petit family, who shaped and preserved its old-fashioned charm. Every detail in the Belle Époque décor contributes to the authentic style – from the wood panelling, copper pots, mirrors, velvet banquettes, and closely-packed tables down to the plates with a "B" monogram. This is not one of those trendy ersatz bistros! And although it was bought by the Ducasse group in 2005, it hasn't lost any of its soul. The same holds true for the cuisine. The traditional fare blends ingredients from the terroir, perfect cooking and generous portions. Regulars know that "Benoît's is the place to eat, drink and be merry." Especially with its "plats canaille", which everyone knows but hardly ever eats – except here.

First Course

- Escargots en coquille, beurre d'ail, fines herbes.
- Têtes de cêpes farcies (autumn).

Main Course

- Filet de sole nantua, épinards à peine crémés.
- Tête de veau traditionnelle sauce ravigote.

Dessert

- Vacherin aux marrons glacés.
- Tarte tatin.

Bofinger

D2

Brasserie ✗✗

5 r. Bastille ✉ 75004   **Ⓜ** Bastille
✆ 01 42 72 87 82 **Fax** 01 42 72 97 68
e-mail ebern@groupeflo.fr **www.**bofingerparis.com

Menu (€24), €32 – Carte €32/79

Ⓐ/Ⓒ
▭
☞
VISA
Ⓜ/Ⓒ
AE
Ⓓ

When Frédéric Bofinger opened this brasserie in 1864, it was almost an immediate success. Parisians came to sample the draught beer on sale. The greatest craftsmen of art (Royer, Panzani, Spindler...) then shaped the capital's gourmet memorial. Of special note is the superb upstairs room (6-8 places) where the woodwork painted by Hansi represents kougelhopf, bretzel, storks, ladybirds and Alsatian ladies in local dress. The splendid decor is still just as fascinating today, with its magnificent glass dome with floral patterns, its stained glass windows, marquetry, vases and paintings. And the vistor's book is practically a 20th century Whos' Who!

Le Dôme du Marais

C1

Contemporary ✗✗

53 bis r. Francs-Bourgeois ✉ 75004   **Ⓜ** Rambuteau
✆ 01 42 74 54 17   Closed 10 August-4 September,
Fax 01 42 77 78 17   Sunday and Monday
e-mail ledomedumarais@hotmail.com

Menu €36/48 – Carte €50/70

VISA
Ⓜ/Ⓒ
AE

The two major attractions of this charming restaurant are in the name itself. First of all, the light emanating from the majestic dome, a legacy from the "Mont-de-Piété" once housed here, bathes the former auction room, where one may sample the chef's modern-day specialities. The pleasant glass-roofed dining room has been decorated in a winter garden style. Secondly, the location in the Marais, in the rue de Franc-Bourgeois, is another advantage of this venue much appreciated by tourists and Parisians alike.

L'Orangerie

C2

28 r. St-Louis-en-l'Île ✉ 75004
✆ 01 46 33 93 98
Fax 01 43 29 25 52
e-mail lorangerie75@orange.fr

Ⓜ Pont Marie
Closed 3-24 August,
Wednesday lunch and Tuesday

Menu €35 (weekday lunch), €75/130 – Carte €80/102

A/C
VISA
MC
AE
①

Remember actor Jean-Claude Brialy's restaurant, so popular with the artistic glitterati in its day? This Ile St-Louis establishment is now home to an experienced team whose dishes blend classical influences and inventiveness. The proof is in the pudding: fresh goat's cheese blancmange with young vegetables, passion fruit and olive oil, cep risotto, *ventrèche paysanne grillée* (grilled pork belly), as well as chocolate hazelnut sponge with light vanilla mousse, fresh and cooked raspberries, and ewe's milk frozen yoghurt. All this to be enjoyed between the 17th century walls decorated with modern paintings in a long, chic dining room. A place worth watching.

Bistrot du Dôme

D2

2 r. Bastille ✉ 75004
✆ 01 48 04 88 44
Fax 01 48 04 00 59

Ⓜ Bastille
Closed 1st-21 August

Carte €30/45

A/C
VISA
MC
AE

Painted earthenware decorating the façade tells it all. You are about to enter a bistrot truly dedicated to seafood. The décor inside confirms the restaurant's vocation, with marine-inspired paintings that enliven the two rather sober dining rooms. A bistrot-like atmosphere reigns on the ground floor, with lighting provided by artificial bunches of grapes on a vine arbour. Upstairs there's a brighter and more comfortable area. The menu offers fish, shellfish, crabs, all carefully chosen and prepared by the chef. All in all, it's a much appreciated venue a stone's throw from the Bastille.

L'Enoteca

C2

Italian ✗

25 r. Charles V ✉ 75004
✆ 01 42 78 91 44
Fax 01 44 59 31 72
e-mail enoteca@enoteca.fr
www.enoteca.fr

Ⓜ St-Paul
Closed 9-18 August and
lunch in August – Pre-book

Menu (€ 14 bi), € 30/45 bi – Carte € 30/45

VISA
ⓂⒸ
ⒶⒺ
🐾

What's the secret of this trattoria? Of course, the 500 or so
Italian wines, from a wine cellar of over 30,000 bottles!
This would be enough to attract Italian gourmets and lovers
of antipasti (buffet available on the ground floor) and other
"pasta del giorno". But the Enoteca's charm doesn't stop
there. Behind its 16th century walls, in the heart of the
Marais, original exposed beams and Murano chandeliers
provide a more than welcoming atmosphere, which is also
lively to say the least, especially in the evenings. This is for
a quick trip to Rome with friends rather than a romantic
escapade to Venice!

Le Fin Gourmet

C2

Contemporary ✗

42 r. St-Louis-en-l'Île ✉ 75004
✆ 01 43 26 79 27
Fax 01 43 26 96 08
e-mail contact@lefingourmet.fr
www.lefingourmet.fr

Ⓜ Pont Marie
Closed 1st-15 August, 5-20 January,
Tuesday lunch and Monday

Menu € 20 (weekday lunch), € 27/35 – Carte € 45/49

VISA
ⓂⒸ
ⒶⒺ
Ⓓ

There's no doubt about it – the name lives up to its
promise! Running the show are two passionate and congenial young associates who have made their childhood dreams come true with this restaurant. Chef Yo-
hann Gerbout likes to reinterpret classic recipes in his
flavourful up-to-date dishes, such as roasted rack of lamb
with black truffle puree, and John Dory in a herb crust
with leeks. David Magniez is in charge of welcoming
guests to the charming dining rooms, part-rustic (exposed
beams, period furniture, 17th century vaulted cellar),
part-contemporary (designer lighting, paintings by young
artists).

Isami

4 quai d'Orléans ✉ 75004   **Ⓜ Pont Marie**
☎ 01 40 46 06 97   Closed 5-25 August, 22 December-6 January, Sunday
      and Monday – Number of covers limited, pre-book

Menu (€ 30) – Carte € 42/75

A/C
VISA

Possibly the best raw fish in Paris is served here. That explains why this establishment is so popular with the Japanese, who know where to go for food "just like back home". The Parisian and international clientele know a good thing when they see it too – namely Katsuo Nakamura, who creates fabulous sushi and chirashi behind his counter. The exceptionally fresh, high-quality ingredients and fascinating knife-wielding have propelled this intimate restaurant into the top rung of Japanese addresses in the capital. There's no outdated folklore in the decor of the small dining room, just some calligraphy and the word "Isami" (meaning ardour or exaltation) etched on a wooden panel and displayed in a prominent place. Reservations are a must.

Mon Vieil Ami

69 r. St-Louis-en-l'Ile ✉ 75004   **Ⓜ Pont Marie**
☎ 01 40 46 01 35   Closed 1st-20 August, 1st-20 January,
Fax 01 40 46 01 35   Monday and Tuesday
e-mail mon.vieil.ami@wanadoo.fr
www.mon-vieil-ami.com

Menu € 41

VISA

AE

This old friend will do you no harm, according to Antoine Westermann! Foreign customers and Parisian gourmets flock to his rather chic bistrot, proof that the talented Alsatian chef knows how to add the "French touch" that may, or may not, bring universal success to these "new generation" establishments. Below the lofty ceilings of the former stables (5 metres high!) the decor is resolutely modern. Black and brown tones harmonise with the frosted glass walls. A long table to the left, and small, nicely set tables to the right give the restaurant the appearance of a trendy inn where the chef will delight you with savoury, traditional recipes with more modern touches and hints of Alsace.

L'Osteria

C2

10 r. Sévigné ✉ 75004
✆ 01 42 71 37 08
e-mail osteria@noos.fr

Ⓜ St-Paul
Closed August, Monday lunch,
Saturday lunch and Sunday – Pre-book

Carte € 33/102

There is no sign or menu on the façade of L'Osteria, which cultivates an exclusive private club feeling that suits the clientele of regulars and celebrities. In recognition of their favourite trattoria, a stone's throw from Saint-Paul, the latter have filled its walls with drawings, paintings and autographs of all kinds. But mere mortals need not fear – with a reasonable (Parisian) budget, they too can taste the chef's impeccable cuisine. All the irresistible stars of Italian cooking are featured here: gnocchi, risotto, octopus salad, tuna carpaccio, seasonal vegetables, panna cotta and tiramisu etc.

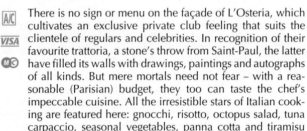

LADURÉE, MASTER OF THE PARISIAN MACAROON

Parisian macaroons are round, with a creamy filling, and come in two sizes – mini "Gerbets" (named after their inventor) and individuals – but are always gobbled up in one bite. They were created in the early 20C by a grandson of the Ladurée establishment (1862), freely inspired by the original recipe imported from Italy by Catherine de Medici. They soon stole the limelight from the crunchy almond biscuits that have remained a favourite in the Basque Country (St-Jean-de-Luz) and Lorraine (Boulay, Nancy) to this day. An infinite variety of sweet and savoury flavours were invented and reinvented from season to season. The height of fashion!

Panthéon · Jardin des Plantes · Mouffetard

An amphitheatre 2000 years old, a "mountain" of resistance, a garden of rare and exotic plants, a hi-tech museum and picturesque markets – the appeals of this surprising and rebellious district are countless.

KNOWLEDGE IN CAPITAL LETTERS

The district is home to the **Sorbonne**, Jussieu, Censier, **Collège de France** and to top secondary and prestigious business schools. Marked by a long history of idealistic combats, the neighbourhood between **St-Michel** and **Port-Royal** has been marked by legendary personalities such as Saint Geneviève – patron saint of Paris who defended the city on her hill when the town was still Lutèce, the "great freedom fighters" honoured for eternity under the cupola of the Pantheon, dissident theologians (Abélard, Sorbon), thinkers and the heroes of May 1968.

The **fountain** where Saint Michael slays the dragon remains a popular meeting-point to this day. From morning to night, the square never empties and is literally packed during Parisian rituals such as the Music Festival. It leads to a string of high-street chain stores along the wide **Boul'Mich** or to the delightful lanes of the old **St-Séverin** district. Students and tourists mingle on **quai de Montbello** and **quai de la Tournelle,** overflowing from the friendly bars

and tightly-packed café terraces.

In terms of cuisine, the 5th displays a marked taste for exotic flavours, particularly those of the Mediterranean and Asia. The nights are equally lively from the laid-back Irish pubs and cosy cellars playing acoustic jazz to the cafés that stay open until dawn of **rue du Petit-Pont.**

PHILOSOPHY AND CARTOONS

In terms of culture, the area is proud of its traditions! Ionesco's plays have been playing at the Théâtre de la Huchette since 1957, arthouse retrospectives abound, Shakespeare & Co, a mythical English bookshop, stays open until midnight with beds available upstairs for bohemian globe-trotters and the debates are always heated in the "cafés philo". However more up-to-date leisure activities are also available for today's online youth as the cyber cafés and cartoon-strip bookstores prove. The fifth arrondissement, despite its solemn, bourgeois air, has nonetheless retained its teenage spirit.

TRAVEL THROUGH TIME

Architecture in the 5th crosses the centuries and styles from gothic and neo-classical to contemporary, all of which creates a stunning cultural shock: the Gallo-Roman ruins of the **Arènes de Lutèce** and the **Thermes de Cluny** beneath

X. Richer / MICHELIN

the **Museum of the Middle Ages,** the classical **Val de Grâce** Hospital and modern **Institute of the Arab World.** From the rooftop of this glass and steel structure, the café commands a view of the Seine and **quai St-Bernard,** where improvised riverside performances of tango, salsa and capoeira take place in the summer evenings. For a taste of the orient, head for the **Paris Mosque!** You have a choice between a Turkish bath, mint tea and pastries in a unique setting.

Opposite, the **Jardin des Plantes** takes us back to our childhood. It is a traditional hit with families with a rose garden, zoo and the immense gallery of evolution of the **Natural History Museum.**

Finally take the time to savour the atmosphere of the district's many outdoor markets **(Maubert, Monge)** and busy shopping streets. If we were to recommend only one, it would be that of **rue Mouffetard** – a string of old-fashioned boutiques and handsome attic facades that stretch out between place de la Contrescarpe (lively cafés and hip intellectual atmosphere) and square St-Médard.

95

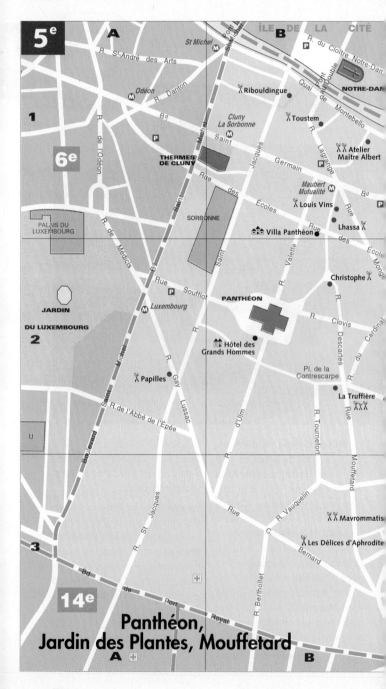

Panthéon,
Jardin des Plantes, Mouffetard

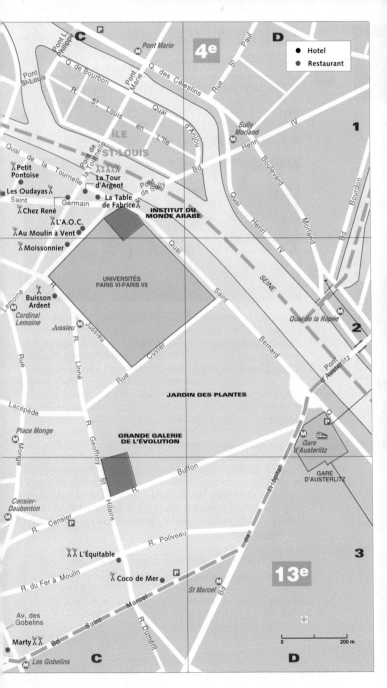

Hotel
Restaurant

4e

C · D

1

Pont L.
Philippe
P
Pont Marie
Pont Marie
Q. de Bourbon
Q. des Celestins
St. Paul
Rue
Pont
St-Louis
R. St. Louis
Quai d'Anjou
Quai de la Tournelle
ÎLE
ST-LOUIS
St. Louis en
L'Île
Sully
Morland
Henri
IV
Bd
Bourdon

Petit
Pontoise
Les Oudayas
Saint
Germain
Chez René
L'A.O.C.
Au Moulin à Vent
Moissonnier
La Tour
d'Argent
La Table
de Fabrice
INSTITUT DU
MONDE ARABE
Pont de Sully
Quai
Henri
IV
Morland
Boulevard
Morland

2

SEINE
Quai de la Rapée

Lemoine
Buisson
Ardent
Cardinal
Lemoine
Jussieu
R. Jussieu
R. Linné
Rue Cuvier
UNIVERSITÉS
PARIS VI-PARIS VII
Quai
Saint
Bernard
Pont
d'Austerlitz

Rue
Lacépède
Place Monge
Monge
R. Geoffroy St. Hilaire
JARDIN DES PLANTES
GRANDE GALERIE
DE L'ÉVOLUTION
Buffon
Gare
d'Austerlitz
GARE
D'AUSTERLITZ
P
Bd de l'Hôpital

3

13e

Censier-
Daubenton
R. Censier
P
L'Équitable
Coco de Mer
R. du Fer à Moulin
Saint
Marcel
Bd
R. Dumeril
St Marcel
Bd

Av. des
Gobelins
Marty
Bd
Les Gobelins

0   200 m

C · D

La Tour d'Argent ✿

C1

Traditional XXXXX

15 quai Tournelle ✉ 75005
✆ 01 43 54 23 31
Fax 01 44 07 12 04
e-mail resa@latourdargent.com **www.**latourdargent.com

🚇 **Maubert Mutualité**
Closed August and Monday

Menu € 70 (lunch) – Carte € 140/487

A/C
VISA
MC
AE
D

Tour d'Argent

This historic restaurant has been linked to the Terrail name
since 1912. First there was André, the founder, then his son
Claude, and now his grandson André. But the saga of the
Tour d'Argent began long before the Terrail family. In 1582
it was already an elegant inn, transformed into a restaurant
in 1780. The real legend started in the 20th century when
André Terrail bought it. His brilliant idea was to add another
floor onto the building for the dining room, providing a
unique panorama of the Seine and Notre-Dame. The plush
setting has retained all its splendour. The perfectly executed
service specialises in wonderful presentation, including the
famous ritual of the numbered Challans duck (invented by
Frédéric Delaire). The millionth duck was served to a diner
in 2003, the inimitable symbol of a type of cuisine that may
not be revolutionary but respects tradition. David Ridgway's
exceptional cellar (with a direct lift) is estimated at 500,000
bottles – a real museum that is opened on occasion for very
privileged clients.

First Course	*Main Course*	*Dessert*
• Quenelles de brochet "André Terrail".	• Noisette d'agneau des Tournelles.	• Poire caramélisée "Vie Parisienne".
• Foie gras des Trois Empereurs.	• Caneton "Tour d'Argent".	• Crêpes "Belle Époque".

La Truffière

Innovative ✗✗✗

B2

4 r. Blainville ✉ 75005
✆ 01 46 33 29 82
Fax 01 46 33 64 74
e-mail restaurant.latruffiere@wanadoo.fr
www.latruffiere.com

Ⓜ **Place Monge**
Closed 20-26 December,
Sunday and Monday

Menu € 24 (weekday lunch), € 105/180 – Carte € 71/164

A/C
VISA
MC
AE
DC
⋒

Where can you find an authentic establishment that smacks of tradition? Answer: at La Truffière. Christian Sainsard's restaurant enjoys the discreetly luxurious environment of a well-preserved 17C house. With its stonework, beams and vaulted rooms, the setting exudes a pleasant rustic refinement. The menu features truffle dishes and southwestern specialities, including *magret au miel* (magret with honey), *confit, foie gras, cassoulet* and seasonal game. The impressive cellar has over 2 500 bottles (châteaux petrus, lafitte, mouton, yquem, etc.). There's nothing like an after-dinner liqueur to round off such a fine meal. And why not enjoy a cigar in the lounge?

Atelier Maître Albert

Traditional ✗✗

B1

1 r. Maître Albert ✉ 75005
✆ 01 56 81 30 01
Fax 01 53 10 83 23
e-mail ateliermaitrealbert@guysavoy.com
www.ateliermaitrealbert.com

Ⓜ **Maubert Mutualité**
Closed 5-25 August, Christmas holidays,
Saturday lunch and Sunday lunch

Menu € 24 (weekday lunch), € 40/50 – Carte approx. € 44

A/C
🖗
VISA
MC
AE
DC

When chef Guy Savoy and architect Jean-Michel Wilmotte unite their talents to revive an old establishment across from Notre-Dame, the result is a chic contemporary restaurant-rotisserie which is full of tourists and regulars. Charcoal-grey tones, beams and stonework are featured in three different rooms: the lounge which looks like a New York bar, the dining room with its great medieval fireplace matching the rotisserie and open kitchen, and finally the more intimate wine-tasting area. The menu includes chilled oysters, roasted free-range chicken, spit-roasted veal shanks, and grapefruit terrine with tea sauce. This place has it all – from the ingredients and precision cooking to the presentation of the dishes and professional service.

L'Équitable

C3

Traditional XX

47bis r. Poliveau ⊠ 75005
✆ 01 43 31 69 20
Fax 01 43 37 85 52
e-mail equitable.restaurant@wanadoo.fr

Ⓜ St-Marcel
Closed Easter holidays, 5-25 August,
Tuesday lunch and Monday

Menu € 21 (weekday lunch)/32

VISA
ⓂⒸ
ⒶⒺ

And equitable it is indeed – both in price and in the generous menus which fulfill all their promises with dishes such as *œuf-cocotte* with cream of mushrooms, fillet of sea bass with olive paste, caramel duck and semolina scented with orange, *douceur au chocolat* and crème brûlée with saffron. You can sense the hand of Yves Mutin – formerly at Le Jules Verne, Le Vert Galant and l'Ambassade d'Auvergne – whose taste for spices gives unusual flavours to traditional recipes and makes something special out of seasonal dishes. The setting is attractive, like a perfect country inn with its stonework, beams, checked tablecloths, rustic counter and collection of scales. Not to mention the charming service.

Marty

C3

Brasserie XX

20 av. Gobelins ⊠ 75005
✆ 01 43 31 39 51 **Fax** 01 43 37 63 70
e-mail restaurant.marty@wanadoo.fr
www.marty-restaurant.com

Ⓜ Les Gobelins

Menu € 34 – Carte € 36/54

A/C
⟨⟩
VISA
ⓂⒸ
Ⓞ

This venerable Parisian brasserie, run by the same family since 1913, has entered the 21C with a new decor that has preserved its essence and soul, as evidenced by the mahogany wood panelling, chandeliers, stained glass, old furniture and paintings. Everything here evokes the retro atmosphere of the 1930s, from the bar and mezzanines to the veranda and terrace. Traditional dishes – huge seafood platters, AAAAA *andouillette* sausages, *choucroute*, grilled chateaubriand with béarnaise sauce, etc. – share the billing with more up-to-date selections. Save room for the *profiteroles au chocolat* – a classic, like this establishment!

Mavrommatis

B3

Greek XX

42 r. Daubenton ✉ 75005
☎ 01 43 31 17 17
Fax 01 43 36 13 08
e-mail info@mavrommatis.fr
www.mavrommatis.fr

Ⓜ Censier Daubenton
Closed 15 August-15 September,
Sunday and Monday

Menu (€ 28), € 37/60 – Carte € 49/70

A/C
⊡
VISA
ⓂⒸ
ÆE

If souvlaki, tzatziki and moussaka are all you know of Greek cuisine, then it's time you headed to Andreas and Evagoras Mavrommatis' restaurant for some delicious special education classes. Their establishment is, quite simply, the height of Hellenic cuisine in Paris. Instead of folklore, it features tradition (the dining room is very understated, evoking a 19C Athenian villa) and impeccably fresh ingredients. As a result, the dishes are refined and, as tradition dictates in Greece, tables are laden with the wonderful flavours of *tarama*, grilled octopus, swordfish with pickled peppers, quail roasted in honeyed vine leaves and thyme. To top it off, enjoy a glass of ouzo on the terrace lined with olive trees.

L'A.O.C.

C1

Grilled meat X

14 r. des Fossés St-Bernard
✉ 75005
☎ 01 43 54 22 52
e-mail aocrestaurant@wanadoo.fr
www.restoaoc.com

Ⓜ Maubert Mutualité
Closed August, Sunday and Monday

Carte € 28/57

VISA
ⓂⒸ

A self-proclaimed "bistro for initiates" or "carnivore's bistro", A.O.C. has what it takes to please fans of quality meat. Owner Jean-Philippe Lattron knows his business – or rather his passion. A former butcher, like his father and grandfather, he takes the meat through the maturation process himself. This proof of reliability is matched by another leitmotiv – the quality of the seasonal ingredients that are served with the beef from Normandy, Galicia, Bavaria (Simmental), etc. With its convivial ambiance, simple setting, blackboards and rotisserie behind the counter near the entrance, A.O.C. exhibits a cheerful countenance and a commendable eagerness to do things the right way.

Au Moulin à Vent

C1

20 r. Fossés-St-Bernard ✉ 75005   Ⓜ Jussieu
✆ 01 43 54 99 37   Closed 2-26 August, 31 December-8 January,
Fax 01 40 46 92 23   Saturday lunch, Sunday and Monday
e-mail alexandra.damas@au-moulinavent.fr
www.au-moulinavent.com

Carte € 46/61

VISA
MC

Don't judge this place by its modest façade. This very atmospheric bistro has a very pretty little eggshell-coloured dining room which hasn't changed since it opened in 1948. This is the Moulin à Vent, prized by both Parisians and tourists in search of a typically French spot. The long row of tables is simply set. On the left, a group of regulars savours a *bœuf ficelle*, calf's liver or *magret de canard* (breast of duck); on the right, an American couple enjoys delicious Burgundy snails and frog's legs *à la provençale*. Why not try one of these timelesss, down-to-earth dishes yourself? And don't forget the *viandes de Salers*, a house speciality. Desserts and wines are in keeping with the rest. Classically good!

Buisson Ardent 😊

C2

25 r. Jussieu ✉ 75005   Ⓜ Jussieu
✆ 01 43 54 93 02   Closed August,
e-mail jtlopez@noos.fr   Saturday lunch and Sunday
www.lebuissonardent.fr

Menu € 31/45

A/C
VISA
MC

This bistro close to the Jussieu towers is a favourite spot for students at the university. The atmosphere in this former (18C) post house evokes the sparkling days of the Roaring Twenties, particularly in the first dining room with its bar, mirrors, tiles and magnificent original frescoes. The second room, also quite charming, has a more contemporary look. The terrace is another option, weather permitting. The dishes are titillating: asparagus and mozzarella *croustillant* with citrus, calamari risotto with parmesan, peaches with basil and frozen yoghurt. Stéphane Mauduit has worked with some of the great chefs (including Rostang) and it shows in his fine cooking!

Chez René

Traditional ✗

C1

14 bd St-Germain ✉ 75005
✆ 01 43 54 30 23
Fax 01 43 54 33 57

Ⓜ Maubert Mutualité
Closed August, 24 December-2 January,
Sunday and Monday

Carte €24/65

Chez Réné, or the triumphant comeback of a real Parisian/ Lyonnais bistro. Remember this institution on the Boulevard St-Germain, where celebrities and regular folks have flocked since 1957? Although it hasn't made any radical changes, this emblematic restaurant from another era has gained a new lease of life under its new management. The decor has been rejuvenated and the walls repainted, restoring the sparkle to this place, which has lost none of its former conviviality. The food hasn't changed one bit, still featuring the same classic dishes: *cochonnailles*, *blettes en gratin* (Swiss chard), frogs' legs, *coq au vin*, *bœuf bourguignon*, veal kidneys, *crème caramel*, and *millefeuille*. Ideal for anyone who feels nostalgic for the good old days.

Christophe

Contemporary ✗

B2

8 r. Descartes ✉ 75005
✆ 01 43 26 72 49

Ⓜ Maubert Mutualité
Closed 5 August-5 September,
Sunday and Monday

Menu (€12), €19 (weekday lunch) – Carte €37/56

Although the Pantheon is a major sightseeing spot, this little gourmet bistro is anything but a tourist-trap. The tasteful decor, part minimalist, part Japanese-inspired, features spotless – and discreet – orange walls, and old black-and-white photographs of Paris. People come here for the "brainstorming" cuisine by Christophe Philippe, who trained with Eric Briffard. Alone in the kitchen, he invents new versions of bistro classics. In addition to *langoustines* with basil, try one of his unbeatable dishes such as the pork trilogy (pig's foot and ear ragout, and roasted loin and boudin sausage) or the crunchy Guanaja chocolate mousse with pralines. Attractive prices.

Coco de Mer

C3

Creole cuisine ✗

34 bd St-Marcel ✉ 75005   ⓜ St-Marcel
☎ 01 47 07 06 64   Closed Saturday lunch and Sunday lunch
Fax 01 43 31 45 75
e-mail contact@cocodemer.fr **www**.cocodemer.fr

Menu (€23), €28

VISA
MC
AE
OD

The holidays are over? As a consolation, book a table at Coco de Mer, where you will be whisked off to the Seychelles. Sitting comfortably with your bare feet in the sand (the terrace has been done up like a beach!) between marine frescoes and coconut trees, it's easy to dive into this exotic paradise. The authentic island food is half-Indian, half-African. The fish is imported directly from the Indian Ocean and delicately smoked, marinated, grilled or poached. After tasting the fresh tuna tartare with ginger, *bourgeois* (fish) with green mango chutney, octopus curried in cream with bananas, you'll be ready to hop on the first plane to Mahé!

Les Délices d'Aphrodite

B3

Greek ✗

4 r. Candolle ✉ 75005   ⓜ Censier Daubenton
☎ 01 43 31 40 39 **Fax** 01 43 36 13 08
e-mail info@mavrommatis.fr **www**.mavrommatis.fr

Menu (€20) – Carte €31/44

A/C
VISA
MC
AE

Although many people think this is an annexe of the Mavrommatis brothers' other restaurant, it is actually their first establishment, opened in 1981. At this convivial tavern, more laid-back than the gourmet restaurant on the rue Daubenton, you can enjoy fresh Greek Cypriot specialities full of sunny flavours. The puff pastry with sheep's-milk cheese, vine leaves stuffed with rice and pine nuts, cold meats marinated in red wine, aubergine purée and *mahalepi* (creamy pudding with orange-blossom water) are served with typical Hellenic generosity and friendliness. The blue-and-white setting straight from the Cyclades, ivy on the ceiling and vibrant rebetiko music in the background will make you feel like you're really there.

Lhassa

B1

Tibetan ✕

13 r. Montagne Ste-Geneviève ✉ 75005
📞 01 43 26 22 19 **Fax** 01 42 17 00 08

🚇 Maubert Mutualité
Closed Monday

Menu €11 (weekday lunch), €15/21 – Carte €17/25

VISA
MC

If you want to breathe in the air of the Himalayas without getting dizzy, just climb up the rue de la Montagne-Sainte-Geneviève. There lies Lhassa, one of the rare good Tibetan restaurants in Paris. Intimate lighting, antique rugs, embroidery, dolls, religious objects, a photograph of the Dalai Lama, and tourist brochures about the country and its culture. The peaceful atmosphere and soft background music have a calming effect, like entering a sacred temple. The kind welcome prolongs the immediate feeling of well-being. The food is full of foreign flavours, featuring steamed dishes, soup made with barley flour, spinach and meat, beef ravioli, balls of hot rice and raisins in yoghurt, and salted butter tea! Are you ready for the journey?

Louis Vins

B1

Bistro ✕

9 r. Montagne-Ste-Geneviève ✉ 75005
📞 01 43 29 12 12
www.fifi.fr

🚇 Maubert Mutualité

Menu (€24), €27

The recently opened Louis Vins – done up like an old bistro – is a happy addition to the capital's little family of wine bars. It has a crimson façade and 1900s brasserie-style interior decor with a walnut bar, mirrors, chandeliers and frescoes, as well as a glass cellar to delight the eye. That sets the tone for this establishment, run by a restaurateur who has been collecting fine bottles for thirty years. 280 wines, to be exact, which you can taste by the glass or *à la ficelle* (you pay for however much you drink). The menu features ingredients from the *terroir*, with generous blackboard recipes such as poached eggs with foie gras, monkfish cheeks in white sauce, and house desserts. Success is well-deserved given the reasonable prices.

Moissonnier

C2

Lyonnais cuisine ✗

28 r. Fossés-St-Bernard ⊠ 75005   **M** Jussieu
✆ 01 43 29 87 65   Closed August, Sunday and Monday
Fax 01 43 29 87 65

Menu €24 (weekday lunch) – Carte €29/51

VISA

MC

This establishment, a typical *bouchon lyonnais* across from the Institut du Monde Arabe, is not new, nor is the decor. This is a true bistro, where you feel at home surrounded by the shiny zinc bar, large moleskin banquettes, wooden tables and –an original touch – the mushroom-shaped lights and wine-harvester's basket and casks. Conviviality and good humour reign here. *Queue de bœuf en terrine* (ox tail terrine), *tablier de sapeur sauce gribiche, rognon de veau* (veal kidneys), *gras double* (tripe), *museau* (headcheese): rather than reinvent these traditional Lyon dishes, Philippe Mayet simply prepares them with delightful generosity, and serves them up with jugs of Beaujolais and Franche-Comté wines. Save a little room for dessert!.

Les Oudayas

C1

Moroccan ✗

34 bd St-Germain ⊠ 75005   **M** Maubert Mutualité
✆ 01 43 29 97 38
e-mail oudayas@oudayas.com

Menu (€15), €23/29 – Carte €31/44

A/C

🕁

VISA

MC

They couldn't have found a better spot! If you're in the mood for the colourful flavours of the Middle East, don't look any further. A stone's throw from the Institut du Monde Arabe, Les Oudayas, named after the Kasbah in Rabat, is sure to fulfil your expectations of an exotic culinary experience. Try one of the subtly reinterpreted Moroccan delicacies: *assiette de briouates* (goat's cheese, chopped meat and herb fritters); *harira* (soup); chicken *tajine* with preserved lemons, olives, violets and coriander; Berber *crêpe* with butter and honey; orange salad with cinnamon and orange blossom water. The same exotic ambiance is celebrated in the decor of this typically Moorish restaurant cum lounge, which doubles as a tea salon.

Papilles 😊

South-west of France 🍴

A2

30 r. Gay Lussac ✉ 75005
☎ 01 43 25 20 79
Fax 01 43 25 24 35
e-mail lespapilles@hotmail.fr

Ⓜ Luxembourg
Closed Easter holidays, 1st-21 August,
1st-8 January, Sunday and Monday

Menu € 31 – Carte € 36/43

VISA

ⓂⒸ

Is it to eat here, or to go? Not to worry – Papilles, Bertrand Bluy's restaurant-cellar-deli, is no fast food joint. Far from it! On one side are the wine racks where you help yourself (with just a corkage fee, known as a *droit de bouchon*); on the other side, the shelves of terrines, foie gras and jam for sale in addition to the fine bottles; and, in the middle, the tables (there's another room in the cellar with a television screen for watching the match). Monotony has been banned from the kitchen. Every day at lunchtime, the blackboard features different market-based dishes with a southwest flavour; for dinner, there is a fixed surprise menu. If you book the night before, you can find out what it is; but that takes all the fun out of it!

Petit Pontoise

Bistro 🍴

C1

9 r. Pontoise ✉ 75005
☎ 01 43 29 25 20

Ⓜ Maubert Mutualité

Carte € 31/52

A/C

VISA

ⓂⒸ

AE

There are very few restaurants where you really feel at home, but the Petit Pontoise is one of them. Yes it's small, yet so charming with its pure 50s decor, appetizing blackboard suggestions and cheerful ambiance. The regulars here like to take their time and know the establishment's golden rule – patience! – which can be slightly disconcerting for newcomers. The service is in keeping with the dishes, "made to order" as the sign in the restaurant says. Philippe Tondetta's bistro is still full for lunch and dinner. And when the dishes arrive, they are well worth it, including foie gras with figs, roasted sea bass with vanilla, and pan fried *girolle* mushrooms with chopped parsley and garlic. Subtle and genuine traditional cuisine.

PANTHÉON • JARDIN DES PLANTES • MOUFFETARD

Ribouldingue

B1

10 r. St-Julien le Pauvre
✉ 75005
✆ 01 46 33 98 80
Fax 01 43 54 09 34

Ⓜ Maubert Mutualité
Closed 1st-24 August,
Sunday and Monday

Menu € 27

VISA
ⓂⒸ

Tripe is in fashion! Go and see for yourself at Ribouldingue, a friendly neo-bistro that has replaced the former Fogon. The chef, Claver Dosseh, ex-second for Camdeborde, has taken up the bold challenge of reconciling diners with offal. And he has more than succeeded. To start off, try the fine Brittany artichokes, served with a smile by Nadège. Then come the melt-in-your-mouth dishes – classic or reinvented – including snouts, teats, brains, tongue and cheeks. The menu also has items for more delicate diners, such as asparagus, *foie gras* or *endives au gratin*. And everyone enjoys the desserts: *caillé de brebis* with chestnut honey and rice pudding with orange marmalade. A real favourite, at an affordable price.

La Table de Fabrice

C1

13 quai de la Tournelle ✉ 75005
✆ 01 44 07 17 57
Fax 01 43 25 37 55
e-mail latabledefabrice@orange.fr
www.restaurantlatabledefabrice.com

Ⓜ Pont Marie
Closed 5-25 August,
Saturday lunch and Sunday

Menu € 40 – Carte € 51/79

A/C
VISA
ⓂⒸ

After his solid training at Lasserre, Senderens and Robuchon, Fabrice Deverly decided to strike out on his own. The 17C house he found on the Quai de la Tournelle, across from the Île Saint-Louis, was the ideal spot for his restaurant, which opened in late 2005. Book a table upstairs for a wonderful view of the Seine and its barges. With its country look and original stonework, the long vaulted room is full of charm. As for the food, you have a choice between a set menu and the blackboard offerings, which change daily according to the chef's inspiration. His signature dishes include sweetbreads, *foie gras mi-cuit*, truffle risotto, crab *millefeuille* and raspberry tiramisu.

Toustem

South-west of France ✕

B1

12 r. de l'Hôtel Colbert
✉ 75005
✆ 01 40 51 99 87
e-mail toustem@helenedarroze.com

Ⓜ Maubert Mutualité
Closed Monday lunch,
Saturday lunch and Sunday

Menu (€ 24), € 32 (lunch) – Carte € 45/49

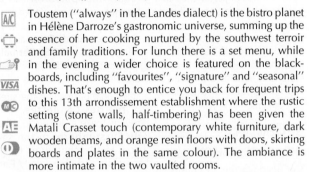

Toustem ("always" in the Landes dialect) is the bistro planet in Hélène Darroze's gastronomic universe, summing up the essence of her cooking nurtured by the southwest terroir and family traditions. For lunch there is a set menu, while in the evening a wider choice is featured on the blackboards, including "favourites", "signature" and "seasonal" dishes. That's enough to entice you back for frequent trips to this 13th arrondissement establishment where the rustic setting (stone walls, half-timbering) has been given the Matali Crasset touch (contemporary white furniture, dark wooden beams, and orange resin floors with doors, skirting boards and plates in the same colour). The ambiance is more intimate in the two vaulted rooms.

VISA

MC

AE

Ⓓ

5

PANTHÉON • JARDIN DES PLANTES • MOUFFETARD

St-Germain-des-Prés
Quartier Latin · Luxembourg

Has the sixth arrondissement become a model of chic urbane life? Such is the idea put forward by those nostalgic for their lost intellectual district, now a luxury shop window. From one legend to another, it is only a short step. True the left bank has changed but only to keep pace with its era and it remains a pleasure to walk the streets of this glossy part of Paris.

St-Germain:

THE ART OF FASHION

The headquarters of culture in Paris where one just has to be seen, St-Germain is dotted with mythical cafés, the famous meeting places of the French intelligentsia: **Deux Magots,** the (flawlessly classical) **Flore** and the **Brasserie Lipp,** said to be the canteen of politicians. They continue to attract a mixture of writers, dandies and tourists by surfing on their existentialist post-War hour of glory (Sartre, cellars, jazz, etc.). Some even award their own literary prizes.

Never one to be caught wrong-footed in terms of trend, St-Germain is a must for art, design and fashion. The arrival of top fashion houses may have upset the muted world of letters, ousting the publishing houses, but the neighbouring Académie française has yet to be disturbed. While it may still be distinguished to leaf the pages of the latest publications at **La Hune** bookshop (open until midnight), the world of fashion reigns undisputed on **rue de Rennes,** creating a closed circle with the antique shops and art galleries on **rue de Seine** and the design shops of **Bd St-Germain.** Heaven on earth for fashion addicts from the world over.

Traditional bistros line the street of **rue des Cannettes.** Afterwards make a detour to **place de Furstenberg,** in the shadow of the church, or to the romantic and very trendy **Pont des Arts.** In the evening, the cafés on **rue Mazarine** vibrate to "electro-funk". To complete your hedonist experience, stop at one of the master chocolate makers, **Hermé, Mulot** or **Hévin,** and sample their delicious wares.

Odéon:

THEATRE AND CINEMA

Recognisable by its lovely rotunda theatre, Odéon attracts students and tourists night and day. Lined in crêperies (pancake bars), pubs, sushi bars and independent cinemas, **rue St-André-des-Arts** and **rue Monsieur-le-Prince** are constantly lively and busy. The same is true of the handsome brasseries on **Carrefour de l'Odéon** and of the lively market stalls of **Carrefour Buci. Passage du Commerce St-André** is both peaceful and picturesque and fiercely atta-

R. Visage / SUNSET

ched to its past. It leads to **cour de Rohan** and the rear of the **Procope**, the oldest café in Paris, frequented by Voltaire and revolutionaries in their time. This is also the location of modern-day gastronomic restaurants, French and further afield, that make the headlines.

Bucolic pleasures

The vast Italian-style Luxembourg gardens are ideal to rest and relax. At all hours of the day, its flowerbeds, balustrades, ornamental pools and statues are popular with Parisians who move the green chairs about to catch the sun's rays. Lovers hand in hand wander past, joggers sprint along and whole families flock to the little boats on the pools, the swings, the tennis courts and the temporary photo exhibitions put up around the garden's railings.

To the southwest, **Notre Dame-des-Champs** changes register: it is a bourgeois "refuge" of stars and jet-setters, who you will run into at **Café de la Mairie** on **place St-Sulpice,** or as you go shopping around **Sèvres…**

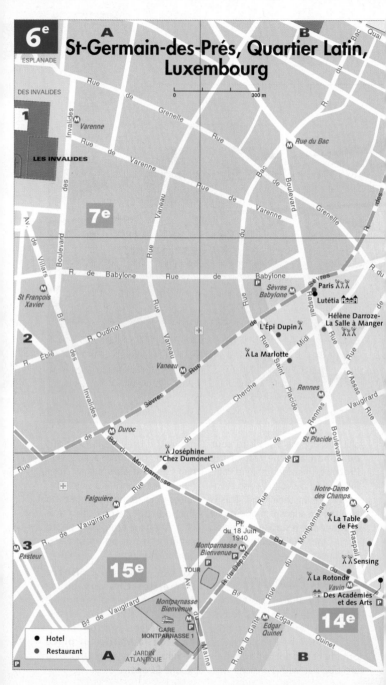

St-Germain-des-Prés, Quartier Latin, Luxembourg

ESPLANADE

DES INVALIDES

A **B**

1

LES INVALIDES

Rue de Grenelle

Varenne

Rue de Varenne

Rue du Bac

Rue de Varenne

Quai

R. du Bac

7^e

0   300 m

Av. de Villars

Boulevard des Invalides

St François Xavier

R. Oudinot

R. Éblé

R. de Babylone   Rue   de   Babylone

Rue Vaneau

Sèvres Babylone

Paris ✕✕✕

Lutétia ⌂⌂⌂

Hélène Darroze-
La Salle à Manger ✕✕✕

L'Épi Dupin ✕

✕ La Marlotte

2

Vaneau

Sèvres

Rue du Cherche

Rue Saint Placide

Rennes

Vaugirard

Rue d'Assas

Duroc

St Placide

Boulevard

Rue du Montparnasse

✕ Joséphine
"Chez Dumonet"

Rue de

3

Falguière

Rue de Vaugirard

R. de Vaugirard

Pasteur

15^e

Pl. du 18 Juin 1940

Montparnasse Bienvenue

TOUR

Av. du Maine

R. de Départ

Notre-Dame des Champs

Montparnasse

✕ La Table de Fès

Sensing ✕✕

✕ La Rotonde

Vavin

⌂⌂ Des Académies et des Arts

Bd du Montparnasse

Raspail

Montparnasse Bienvenue

GARE MONTPARNASSE 1

Bd de Vaugirard

Bd

Rue de la Gaîté

Edgar Quinet

14^e

A JARDIN ATLANTIQUE **B**

● Hotel
● Restaurant

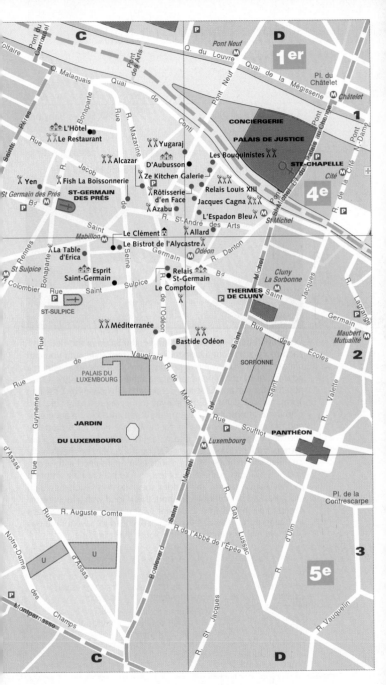

Hélène Darroze-La Salle à Manger ✿✿

B2

4 r. d'Assas ✉ 75006
✆ 01 42 22 00 11
Fax 01 42 22 25 40
e-mail reservation@helenedarroze.com

Ⓜ Sèvres Babylone
Closed lunch 19 July-30 August,
Monday except dinner 19 July-
30 August and Sunday

Menu €72 (lunch), €175/280 – Carte €111/189

Hélène Darroze

Which will it be – the Salle à Manger, the Salon or the Boudoir? Each room at Hélène Darroze has a different style, and you can choose what you want depending on your mood – either a gourmet meal or high-end tapas and other bite-size dishes. Once past the discreet black façade, decorated with flowers by Christian Tortu, all your cares will melt away in this impressively chic and glamorous atmosphere. The upstairs is soft and cosy, in aubergine and orange tones; downstairs the ambiance is airy, comfortable and contemporary. Born into a family of chefs and restaurant owners, Hélène Darroze gained recognition from her peers early on. Here she exhibits her enormous talent combined with strong intuition. Darroze packs a lot of feeling into her cooking, inspired by her native *terroir*, the Landes, her mentors (such as Alain Ducasse) and her curiosity. In short, this is food with a lot of heart. Exceptional ingredients, excellent wines, unrivalled Armagnacs and generosity – there's everything you need to have a fabulous experience at this enclave of the South West in Paris.

First Course

- Riz carnaroli acquarello noir et crémeux, chipirons au chorizo et tomates confites, jus au persil, émulsion de parmesan.

- Escaoutoun landais au brebis basque, cèpes, jus de volaille.

Main Course

- Grosses langoustines bretonnes rôties aux épices tandoori.

- Pigeonneau flambé au capucin et foie gras de canard des Landes grillé au feu de bois.

Dessert

- Chocolat, coriandre, chicorée et vanille bourbon.

- Véritable baba imbibé du bas armagnac " Francis Darroze".

Jacques Cagna ✿

D1

14 r. Grands Augustins ✉ 75006
✆ 01 43 26 49 39
Fax 01 43 54 54 48
e-mail jacquescagna@hotmail.com
www.jacques-cagna.com

Ⓜ St-Michel
Closed 27 July-24 August,
Monday lunch,
Saturday lunch and Sunday

Menu €48 (lunch)/100 – Carte €87/153

Jacques Cagna

Jacques Cagna's restaurant, unaffected by the diktats of current fashions, has remained a warm and intimate place, preserving its identity and discreet decor featuring wood (exposed beams, light oak walls) and Flemish paintings. You could almost forget the nearby banks of the Seine and the hustle and bustle of crowded, trend-conscious Saint-Germain-des-Prés. The 17th century mansion is a perfect fit for the delicious traditional cuisine. The food is generous and full of flavour (like the amazing Paris-Brest pastries), and matched by a well-stocked wine list with some rare bottles (priced accordingly). Its charms are slightly old-fashioned, yet eminently reassuring – to the delight of its refined clientele.

St-Germain-des-Prés • Quartier Latin • Luxembourg

First Course

- Langoustines de l'Atlantique en crousillant.
- Foie gras de canard poêlé aux fruits de saison caramélisés.

Main Course

- Noix de ris de veau en croûte de sel.
- Gibier (season).

Dessert

- Croustillant de pain d'épice, mousseline à la vanille bourbon, sauce au chocolat épicé.
- Baba au rhum, crème parfumée au thé.

Paris ❀

Contemporary XXX

B2

Hôtel Lutetia,
45 bd Raspail ✉ 75006
☎ 01 49 54 46 90
Fax 01 49 54 46 00
e-mail lutetia-paris@lutetia-paris.com **www**.lutetia-paris.com

Ⓜ **Sèvres Babylone**
Closed August, Saturday,
Sunday and public holidays

Menu €60 bi (lunch), €80/130 – Carte €98/130

 ♿ A/C 💺 🧼 VISA Ⓜ©️ ＡＥ ①

G.Corbic/MICHELIN

Don't be daunted by the huge sculpted façade of this grand hotel on the Left Bank; while the restaurant is very refined, the warm welcome will make you feel right at home. The Art Deco dining room is an exact replica of that on the cruise ship Normandie. The archetypal 1930s design, thankfully preserved in Sonia Rykiel's renovations, exudes intimate, discreet luxury and style, with period furniture, wood panelling, large mirrors covering an entire wall, and plants. Everything has been thought of to preserve the serene and pleasant atmosphere of former days. The chef deliberately limits the number of place settings, the elegant tables are well-spaced, and the service is efficient and discreet. The well-heeled local clientele clearly appreciates the consistent and dependable cuisine featuring excellent ingredients, prepared without fuss.

First Course

- Saint-Jacques marinées au caviar d'esturgeon blanc (oct. à avril).
- Araignée de mer au pamplemousse rose et avocat, jus parfumé de colombo.

Main Course

- Homard à la vanille, avocat à la tomate au citron vert.
- Agneau de lait des Pyrénées (January-May).

Dessert

- Clafoutis du Limousin aux cerises entières, crème épaisse.
- Tout chocolat d'un gourmand de cacao.

Relais Louis XIII ⁂ ⁂

Classic 𝗫𝗫𝗫

D1

8 r. Grands Augustins ⊠ 75006
𝒫 01 43 26 75 96
Fax 01 44 07 07 80
e-mail contact@relaislouis13.com
www.relaislouis13.com

🄼 **Odéon**
Closed August, 22 December-3 January,
Sunday and Monday

Menu € 50 (lunch), € 80/110 – Carte € 115/133

A/C

VISA
MC
AE
O
⁂

Relais Louis XIII

The Relais Louis XIII, built over the cellar of the former Saint-Augustin convent, is filled with history. When Henri IV was assassinated, on 14 May 1610, it was here that Louis XIII was informed of his father's death and of his subsequent accession to the throne. That information is important as you enter the dining room and are plunged into the past. The exposed beams and stonework, wood panelling, stained glass and wall hangings evoke a bygone era, with period collectors' items (paintings) dotting the room. This shrine to the glory of the Bourbon dynasty is the perfect setting for Manuel Martinez' delicious traditional cuisine. After working at Ledoyen, the Crillon and the Tour d'Argent (and winning the Meilleur Ouvrier de France award), Martinez took over here in 1996, and has captivated regulars and newcomers ever since. Worth noting too are the private rooms and a smoking area in the cellar.

First Course	*Main Course*	*Dessert*
• Ravioli de homard, foie gras et crème de cèpes.	• Caneton challandais rôti entier aux épices, cuisse confite en parmentier.	• Millefeuille, crème légère à la vanille bourbon.
• Quenelle de bar de ligne, mousseline de champignons au champagne.	• Sole de ligne, chou pointu, marinière de moules et crevettes grises.	• Assiette dégustation chocolat, sauce au vin de Maury.

ST-GERMAIN-DES-PRÉS • QUARTIER LATIN • LUXEMBOURG

Le Restaurant ❀

C1

Hôtel L'Hôtel,
13 r. Beaux Arts ✉ 75006
☎ 01 44 41 99 01

Ⓜ St-Germain-des-Prés
Closed August, 21-29 December,
Sunday and Monday

Menu (€ 38), € 75/125 bi – Carte € 74/83

A/C

VISA

MC

AE

DC

Le Restaurant

Despite its catch-all name, there is nothing conventional about Le Restaurant at L'Hôtel. On the contrary, its baroque, anachronistic and eclectic ambiance boasts an original personality created by designer Jacques Garcia, a fan of the Empire style. The décor, recently given a facelift, has been done up like a private room, with a wealth of drapes, velvet, banquettes, low armchairs, alcoves, gilded mouldings and fauve tones, evoking an Ingres painting from his Orientalist period. A bit over-the-top to some, pleasantly exotic for others – but spectacular in any case. In the delightful inner courtyard with a terrace and fountain you could even forget that you're in the heart of Paris. Chef Philippe Bélissent, formerly at Laurent and Ledoyen, has all the savoir-faire to satisfy the demands of the "happy few" clientele, including stars and other celebrities, who are fond of the intimacy and the many illustrious guests who have stayed here (Oscar Wilde, Borgès, etc.). His dishes are perfectly balanced in texture and flavour, reflecting the kind of refined cooking currently in vogue. Like everything else here, they too are anything but ordinary.

First Course	*Main Course*	*Dessert*
• Tourteau relevé à l'huile d'argan.	• Cabillaud rôti au beurre salé.	• Figue de Solliès rôtie au banyuls.
• Foie gras de canard cuit et pressé à la sangria.	• Volaille de Bresse cuite en cocotte.	• Chocolat en tartelette tiède.

Alcazar

C1

Fusion ✗✗

62 r. Mazarine ✉ 75006   Ⓜ Odéon
✆ 01 53 10 19 99 **Fax** 01 53 10 23 23
e-mail contact@alcazar.fr **www**.alcazar.fr

Menu € 20 (weekday lunch) bi/40 – Carte € 37/60

This is as trendy as it gets. A former cabaret, it was brought back to life in 1998 by design guru Terence Conran. The result has lived up to people's expectations, combining a contemporary decor with dance music, up-to-date food and a "fashionable" crowd charmed by the lounge ambiance. You can have a drink at the polished zinc bar up on the mezzanine, or downstairs in the light-filled and glass-roofed restaurant, with its wooden tables and red banquettes. Watching the kitchen staff at work, headed by Guillaume Lutard (formerly at Taillevent), is guaranteed to whet your appetite. The menu boasts traditional recipes with a modern twist, and an international selection of wines.

Bastide Odéon

C2

Contemporary ✗✗

7 r. Corneille ✉ 75006   Ⓜ Odéon
✆ 01 43 26 03 65   Closed 3-25 August,
Fax 01 44 07 28 93   Sunday and Monday
e-mail reservation@bastide-odeon.com
www.bastide.odeon.com

Menu € 26 (lunch)/40

Southern scents and flavours reign at the Bastide Odéon, located near the Luxembourg Gardens and the Théâtre de l'Europe. The change of scenery is guaranteed at this friendly establishment where the traditional floor tiles and ochre tones evoke a Provençal bastide. Snug wooden tables set with white porcelain and diffused lighting from wall sconces complete the convivial atmosphere in the main dining room (a private room is available upstairs for a more intimate setting). The Mediterranean-inspired cuisine featuring fresh market ingredients is up-to-date and crafted with a personal touch. The kitchen, with its young and highly motivated staff, is visible from the restaurant entrance.

119

Les Bouquinistes

Contemporary XX

D1

53 quai Grands Augustins ⊠ 75006
℘ 01 43 25 45 94
Fax 01 43 25 23 07
e-mail bouquinistes@guysavoy.com
www.guysavoy.com

Ⓜ St-Michel
Closed 5-23 August,
23 December-5 January,
Saturday lunch and Sunday

Menu € 25 (weekday lunch)/75 – Carte € 50/62

A/C
☞
VISA
MC
AE
①

This trendy restaurant overlooking the Seine, a stone's throw from the famous book-sellers' stands, is one of the branches of the Guy Savoy empire. The decor by Daniel Humair boldly blends a hip modern look with Art Deco and baroque influences, featuring designer banquettes, abstract paintings, wide mirrors and colourful lighting, and a wide picture window giving onto the street. The food is simple and sometimes inventive. Favourites include the *marinière de moules* (mussels cooked in white wine) with curried herb gnocchi, and the pig's cheeks simmered in *verjus* with Noirmoutier potatoes. The service is quick and efficient.

Méditerranée

Seafood XX

C2

2 pl. Odéon ⊠ 75006
℘ 01 43 26 02 30
Fax 01 43 26 18 44
e-mail la.mediterranee@wanadoo.fr
www.la-mediterranee.com

Ⓜ Odéon
Closed 22-28 December

Menu (€ 27), € 32 – Carte € 38/64

A/C
⟐
☞
VISA
MC
AE

This restaurant on an elegant little square across from the Théâtre de l'Europe is proud to display its marine heritage. The midnight blue façade with its lovely Cocteau drawing subtly evokes the mysterious depths of the sea. The three dining rooms form a pleasant decor which is very Parisian and also has a nice veranda. Not surprisingly, the menu features seafood, prepared with talent by the experienced staff. The carefully cooked bisques, fish and shellfish are extremely fresh, prepared Mediterranean-style with olive oil marinades, fragrant herbs and saffron flavours. All that is missing is the deep blue sea and the lapping of the waves!

Sensing

I n n o v a t i v e ✗✗

B3

19 r. de Bréa ⊠ 75006
✆ 01 43 27 08 80
Fax 01 43 26 99 27
e-mail sensing@orange.fr
www.restaurantsensing.com

Ⓜ Vavin
Closed August,
Monday lunch and Sunday

Menu (€25), €55 (weekday lunch), €95/140 – Carte €60/73

A haven of chic design lies behind the opaque smoked glass façade of Guy Martin's most recent restaurant, located on a small street near the Boulevard du Montparnasse. The sensational interior by Malherbe and Faillant Dumas is restrained and refined, featuring noble materials with clean lines, white marble floors, bare wooden furniture and chairs in purple velvet. Everything is deliberately modern here, down to the video images projected on the walls. The food is on a par, with a highly contemporary short menu created by a chef fond of cutting-edge techniques such as *sous-vide*, low-temperature or induction cooking using carefully chosen ingredients.

Yugaraj

I n d i a n ✗✗

C1

14 r. Dauphine ⊠ 75006
✆ 01 43 26 44 91
Fax 01 46 33 50 77
e-mail contact@yugaraj.com

Ⓜ Odéon
Closed 1st-4 May, 5-27 August,
1st-4 January, Thursday lunch and Monday

Menu €31/46 – Carte €36/60

Yugaraj, in business in Paris for three decades, is a sure bet for Indian cooking, more specifically that of the North, where the flavours are more powerful than in southern Indian food. Good judgement and the subtle use of spices are the chef's main secrets as he takes you on a culinary journey with his delicious dishes. Not to mention the high-quality ingredients (Bresse chicken, milk-fed lamb) which give the tandooris and curries here a taste you'll find nowhere else. The decor is also worth the detour – an exceptional, recently renovated setting that is like a highly refined museum decorated with precious silks, wood panelling and ancient statues. Truly exotic.

Allard

Traditional ✗

D1

1 r. l'Eperon ✉ 75006   Ⓜ St-Michel
✆ 01 43 26 48 23 **Fax** 01 46 33 04 02   Closed 3-25 August

Menu (€ 25), € 34 – Carte € 35/66

A/C
VISA
Ⓜ©
Æ
⓪

Allard has had top bistro billing since 1931 and has attracted many notable figures (President Pompidou's wife and Alain Delon among others), developing a loyal clientele generation after generation with its straightforward and authentic cuisine. While the dishes are simpler nowadays, they remain generous and rooted in traditional recipes. Your taste buds will be titillated by this fine chapter in French culinary heritage featuring Burgundy snails, cured herring with warm potatoes in oil, hare stew, and veal sweetbreads with morel mushrooms. The turn-of-the-century decor celebrates the same spirit with its zinc bar, leather banquettes, tiles and engravings. Incomparable charm.

Azabu

Japanese ✗

C1

3 r. A. Mazet ✉ 75006   Ⓜ Odéon
✆ 01 46 33 72 05   Closed 20 April-5 May, 27-30 July,
                    26-29 October, Sunday dinner and Monday

Menu € 19 (weekday lunch), € 33/59 – Carte € 36/50

A/C
VISA
Ⓜ©
Æ

In Tokyo, Azabu is a neighbourhood famous for gastronomy. In Paris, it's the name of a restaurant near the Carrefour de l'Odéon with a very discreet look that is typical of this kind of establishment. The interior decor displays a similar minimalist aesthetic – a Zen ambiance in which to enjoy a quiet meal. The menu, with no raw fish, features Japanese classics reinvented as *teppanyaki* (cooking table) dishes, including sautéed tofu with chicken sauce and grilled duck breast. While remaining faithful to tradition, the chef is open to Western influences. You can sit at the counter (for dinner) and admire him at work.

Le Bistrot de L'Alycastre

C2

2 r. Clément ⊠ 75006
☎ 01 43 25 77 66
Fax 01 43 25 77 66
e-mail jmlemmery@hotmail.com

Ⓜ Mabillon
Closed 12-27 August and
Monday lunch

Menu € 50/65 – Carte € 41/62

Modernity and authenticity blend together perfectly in this chic bistro, where the zinc bar, wooden stools and red banquettes mingle with trendy wicker chairs and walls in lilac and aubergine tones. The winning decor was designed by the owner, Jean-Marc Lemmery, former chef at Le Cap Vernet (8th arrondissement). His up-to-date recipes feature ingredients prepared with passion and simplicity. The excellent roasted sea bass is cooked to perfection, served on a bed of green beans and mangetout with cardamom. While velvet-textured Valrhona chocolate soup is topped with lightly whipped cream... A lovely surprise just across from the Marché St-Germain.

Le Comptoir

C2

Hôtel Relais-St-Germain,
9 carrefour de l'Odéon ⊠ 75006
☎ 01 44 27 07 97 **Fax** 01 46 33 45 30
e-mail hotelrsg@wanadoo.fr **www**.hotelrsg.com

Ⓜ Odéon
Number of covers limited,
pre-book

Menu € 45 (dinner) – Carte € 35/55 (lunch)

This new bistro run by Yves Camdeborde and his wife – adjoining their famous hotel, the Relais Saint-Germain – is a huge success. The setting has an intimate Art Deco look with its 1930s decor, snug tables and large windows overlooking a huge sunny terrace. The cuisine alternates between two complementary concepts: brasserie-style food with simple and well-prepared dishes at lunchtime, and more elaborate gourmet meals for dinner. The set menu changes daily according to the market and the chef's inclination, but the quality of the dishes and the ingredients are always outstanding. Tasty specialities from southwestern France.

St-Germain-des-Prés • Quartier Latin • Luxembourg

L'Épi Dupin 😊

B2

11 r. Dupin ✉ 75006
📞 01 42 22 64 56
Fax 01 42 22 30 42
e-mail lepidupin@wanadoo.fr

Ⓜ Sèvres Babylone
Closed 1st-24 August, Monday lunch,
Saturday and Sunday
– Number of covers limited, pre-book

Menu (€25 bi), €34

VISA
Ⓜ©

Don't be fooled by the rustic bistro look at this pocket restaurant in the Bon Marché area. The cuisine is refined – well worth the detour – and the prices are right too. The charming decor is unusual for Paris, with quarried-stone walls and exposed beams. Conviviality is assured, with diners packed cheek-by-jowl. The simple and tasty dishes are prepared with impeccably fresh ingredients in the best country tradition: duck with honey, calf's head, oxtail and pig's cheeks are all spot-on.

L'Espadon Bleu

D1

25 r. Grands Augustins ✉ 75006
📞 01 46 33 00 85
Fax 01 43 54 54 48
e-mail jacquescagna@hotmail.com
www.jacques-cagna.com

Ⓜ St-Michel
Closed August, Monday lunch,
Saturday lunch and Sunday

Menu (€25), €33 – Carte €39/74

[A/C]
☞🍴
VISA
Ⓜ©
ⒶⒺ
Ⓓ

Is this another annexe of the Jacques Cagna culinary empire? Or, rather, a pleasant variation on the theme of seafood? This brightly coloured bistro plays the ocean card to the hilt, featuring life-size swordfish on the walls, beams painted in the style of a St.-Malo inn, mosaic tables and blue-and-white striped banquettes colourfully evoking a meeting of the Mediterranean and the Atlantic. The sea bream-shaped blackboard lists some of specialities – including brill fillet *à la plancha* (grilled on a hot, dry griddle) and line-caught whiting in Isigny butter – mainly created with the freshest of fish caught in the Finistère region. The service and cellar are of the same calibre.

Fish La Boissonnerie

Bistro 𝒳

C1

69 r. de Seine ✉ 75006   **Ⓜ Odéon**
☎ 01 43 54 34 69   Closed one week in August,
                 one week in December and Monday
Menu € 22/34 (dinner)

Aℂ
VISA
Ⓜ©
🐾

Could this be the best of two worlds – combining the pleasures of an authentic gastropub with that of a wine bar? This establishment, in a former fishmonger's, with a charming façade covered in colourful mosaics, proposes straightforward quality food at attractive prices. The relaxed setting evokes both the fish shop and a Parisian bar, with its old zinc counter polished by the years, and a dining room with exposed beams, decorated with sculptures and drawings of marine fauna. The menu naturally features seafood, but doesn't neglect meat-lovers. The wines are excellent, including those from small producers and prestigious grand crus.

Joséphine "Chez Dumonet"

Traditional 𝒳

A3

117 r. Cherche-Midi ✉ 75006   **Ⓜ Duroc**
☎ 01 45 48 52 40   Closed Saturday and Sunday
Fax 01 42 84 06 83

Carte € 40/80

VISA
Ⓜ©
AE

This neighbourhood institution founded in 1898 was named after the wife of the first owner. Today this establishment is run by Jean Dumonet, and has preserved all its original charm, with its lustrous zinc bar, venerable banquettes, molten glass chandeliers and period mirrors giving this very Parisian bistro a slightly old-fashioned "Roaring Twenties" air. But the kitchen is a serious affair and the traditional dishes – beef bourguignon, leg or noisette of lamb, and cassoulet – are copious and carefully prepared. In addition to the friendly owner and efficient service, it also has a spectacular wine list which, however, does not incline one toward moderation.

ST-GERMAIN-DES-PRÉS • QUARTIER LATIN • LUXEMBOURG

6

125

La Marlotte

B2

55 r. Cherche-Midi ✉ 75006
✆ 01 45 48 86 79
Fax 01 44 07 28 93
www.lamarlotte.com

Ⓜ St-Placide
Closed 3-24 August,
Sunday and public holidays

Menu (€ 23), € 40/50 – Carte € 32/64

Once you get past the rustic inn look, this congenial bistro a stone's throw from the Bon Marché boasts a long and very pleasant dining room. The ambiance is warm and convivial, with soft lighting, tightly-packed tables and an amusing collection of plates and old keys. Excellent seasonal ingredients are celebrated in the tasty traditional food, including *œufs pochés en meurette* (poached eggs in a red wine sauce), lentil salad with shallots, *pavé de cabillaud rôti au pistou* (baked cod with basil and garlic), pan-fried calf's liver with honey, etc. The classic dishes are served at a good pace. As unpretentious as ever, the place has remained a favourite with publishers, gallery owners and politicians in the area, as well as visitors.

Rôtisserie d'en Face

D1

2 r. Christine ✉ 75006
✆ 01 43 26 40 98
e-mail la-rotisserie@orange.fr
www.jacques-cagna.com

Ⓜ Odéon
Closed Saturday lunchtime and Sunday

Menu (€ 25), € 29 (weekday lunch) – Carte € 39/63

Opposite (*en face de*) what? Jacques Cagna's main restaurant. Cagna opened this establishment to revive the rotisserie tradition – in a bistro spirit. The recipes, created by "the master", are prepared by the talented chef and offered at affordable prices. Just the place for sampling tasty market-based cuisine that reinvents the great classics, including terrine of hare, rib of beef, spit-roasted chicken, and pan-fried foie gras with raspberry vinegar. The ochretoned dining room with soft lighting and simply laid tables provides an elegant and relaxed ambiance. For your added enjoyment: an excellent wine list and efficient service.

La Rotonde 😳

Brasserie ⑂

B3

105 bd Montparnasse ⊠ 75006   Ⓜ Vavin
℡ 01 43 26 68 84 **Fax** 01 46 34 52 40

Menu (€17 bi), €35 – Carte €36/69

A/C
VISA
MC
AE

This is a real institution! Right in the heart of Montparnasse, and a stone's throw from the theatres on the rue de la Gaîté, La Rotonde has been the quintessential Parisian brasserie for nearly a century. The classic decor has a 1930s look with brass everywhere and red velvet banquettes where Picasso, Matisse and Trotsky once sat. The menu is a happy blend of true classics and more traditional dishes, like the Salers beef and oyster platters, two of their classics. The service goes until 2am, making this establishment a favourite with theatre-goers.

La Table d'Erica

Creole cuisine ⑂

C2

6 r. Mabillon ⊠ 75006   Ⓜ Mabillon
℡ 01 43 54 87 61   Closed August,
e-mail table-erica@proximedia.fr   Sunday and Monday
www.tablederica.com

Menu €13 (lunch)/29 – Carte €25/49

VISA
MC
AE
①

This family restaurant next to the Marché St-Germain (set back a bit from the street) specialises in Creole food. The colourful atmosphere is refreshing and bright – a hint of the cuisine to come – evoking all the richness of the islands, with exotic plants, guitars, parrots, fruits and vegetables from "over there" hanging from the beams, and paintings of tropical landscapes to complete the decor. Not to mention the recipes that will take your taste buds on a voyage straight to the Caribbean. After sampling the obligatory punch, try one of the house specialities: *accras de morue* (cod fritters), stuffed crab, *colombo de cabri* (kid), *poulet boucané à l'ancienne*, and for dessert, coconut milk blancmange.

La Table de Fès

Moroccan ✗

B3

5 r. Ste-Beuve ⊠ 75006
📞 01 45 48 07 22
Fax 01 45 49 47 88
e-mail digitalmedia@orange.fr

Ⓜ Notre Dame des Champs
Closed 24 July-30 August and
Sunday – Dinner only

Carte € 44/61

A/C
VISA
MC

This little gem of North African cuisine (from Morocco to be exact) is hidden behind a modest stucco façade between Raspail and Notre-Dame-des-Champs. The atmosphere is convivial, the decor warm, in a dining room which evokes both the desert and a verdant oasis. The very short menu focus on couscous, masterfully prepared here. The cook, clearly an expert in Moroccan cuisine, knows her subject by heart. The dishes are full of flavour, the food abundant and the service pleasantly simple. Note, the restaurant doesn't open in the evening until 8:30pm.

Yen

Japanese ✗

C1

22 r. St-Benoît ⊠ 75006
📞 01 45 44 11 18
Fax 01 45 44 19 48
e-mail restau.yen@wanadoo.fr

Ⓜ St-Germain-des-Prés
Closed Sunday

Menu (€ 31), € 55 (dinner) – Carte € 31/64

A/C
VISA
MC
AE
①

The outside of this typically Japanese restaurant is extremely discreet, with a modest side door and pale wood façade exemplifying Asian restraint. The same ambiance reigns inside, in the two dining rooms with carefully aligned teak tables and minimalist "zen" atmosphere. Thinly sliced buckwheat *soba* noodles cut in thin strips and seasoned in different ways are the chef's speciality here. Sushi fans will also find their share of raw fish on the menu. This place attracts a large Japanese clientele who enjoy the authenticity and fine service.

Ze Kitchen Galerie ⁂

Fusion 🍴

4 r. Grands Augustins ✉ 75006   Ⓜ St-Michel
☎ 01 44 32 00 32   Closed Saturday lunchtime and Sunday
Fax 01 44 32 00 33
e-mail zekitchen.galerie@wanadoo.fr **www**.zekitchengalerie.fr

Menu €36 – Carte €55/59

A/C

VISA

MC

AE

⓪

%

Bruno Delessard

Is it an art gallery, a cooking studio, or an artsy New York-style cafeteria? Ze Kitchen Galerie strives to bring art and cooking together by blurring the distinction between the two in its dishes and décor. The space, conceived by Daniel Humair, is streamlined without seeming cold, blending designer furniture and cutlery, raw materials and colourful paintings around a kitchen window showcasing the brigade's live performance. Chef William Ledeuil celebrates his passion for Asia (Thailand, Vietnam, and Japan) with flavours such as galanga, kachai, curcuma, wasabi and ginger. The herbs, roots and spices from far across the world add an exciting touch to his classic French recipes. The fusion menu – fish, broths, pasta and grilled food – features a range of polished, inventive and up-to-date dishes that are rich in flavour and colour. In short, this is "the" trendy establishment on the Left Bank.

First Course

- Légumes marinés et grillés, tomates, girolles, émulsion parmesan.
- Salade de poulpe, tomates et citron confit.

Main Course

- Joue de veau, jus thaï, marmelade de tomate, gingembre.
- Thon grillé,"aubergines de Chine" confites.

Dessert

- Chocolat gianduja, sésame, cacahuète, glace coco.
- "Mœlleux" mirabelle, gingembre, jus abricot.

Tour Eiffel
École Militaire · Invalides

The quiet and very green 7th arrondissement is no doubt the one that best personifies the Parisian upper class and bourgeois discretion. Wide avenues lined by century-old trees, listed buildings with flawless stone façades and luxurious private mansions hidden by cascades of greenery adorn this district, renowned for its genteel lifestyle, charming lanes and spectacular vistas. Avenue de Breteuil, whose manicured lawns lead to the Hôtel des Invalides where Napoleon is buried, is the main thoroughfare of this immense fan-shaped district that stretches as far as the Seine.

To the west, the district revolves around the Champ de Mars, an elongated stretch of greenery that runs from the Ecole Militaire to the Tour Eiffel. This emblematic neighbourhood is packed with tourists from all over the world, but as soon as you leave the immediate vicinity of the "Iron Lady", one is surprised by the almost timeless quality of the luxury flats, among the most sought-after of the capital. Two minutes away from the crowded grassy banks of the Champ de Mars, take the time to walk along the pedestrian rue Cler and the rue de l'Université, where you will find some of the finest grocery shops in Paris: bread (Poujaran), wine and cheese (Barthélémy) and even caviar (Pétrossian).

CUISINE AND POLITICS

Further east, the vast esplanades are replaced by the narrow crisscrossing of the opulent streets of rue de **Bourgogne,** rue de **Varenne** and rue de **Grenelle.** An uninterrupted succession of mansions hidden by high walls, this district concentrates practically all the headquarters of the country's political and administrative activity. The **Assemblée Nationale,** rising on the banks of the Seine, **Hôtel Matignon,** the **Quai d'Orsay** and the national headquarters of countless political parties keep company in edifices, whose well-worn façades have witnessed the legislative history of France.

However the country's political life also takes place in the many bistros tucked away behind the **Palais Bourbon,** to such an extent that the area is sometimes referred to as a second parliament. As a result, you won't be surprised to learn that these establishments serve dishes capable of satisfying the demanding palates of France's elected representatives.

ART AND CULTURE

Finally, it would be unthinkable to speak of the 7th arrondissement without referring to its outstanding cultural and artistic wealth. In addition to the **Invalides,** already mentioned, which are home to the **Musée de l'Armée** and Napoleon 1's tomb, the arrondissement is rich in other museums. First and foremost, the

S. Sauvignier / MICHELIN

Musée d'Orsay, located in the former railway station of the same name. Under its spectacular metal and glass roof, its collections of sculpture and paintings offer a magnificent insight into the artistic effervescence of the 19C and early 20C. On rue de Varenne, the Musée Rodin exhibits some of the best-known works of the sculptor, while those with a weakness for further-flung destinations will adore the recently inaugurated **Musée des Arts Premiers** on Quai Branly that features sumptuous collections of African, pre-Columbian and Oceanic art.

But if you're more of a shopping-type person, make sure you pay a visit to the **Bon Marché** department store, the temple of "left bank" good taste.

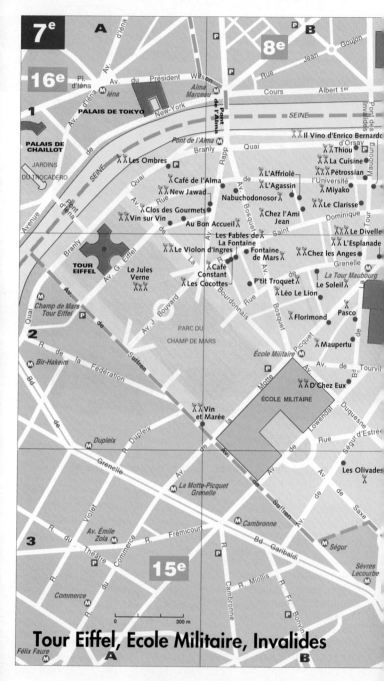

Tour Eiffel, École Militaire, Invalides

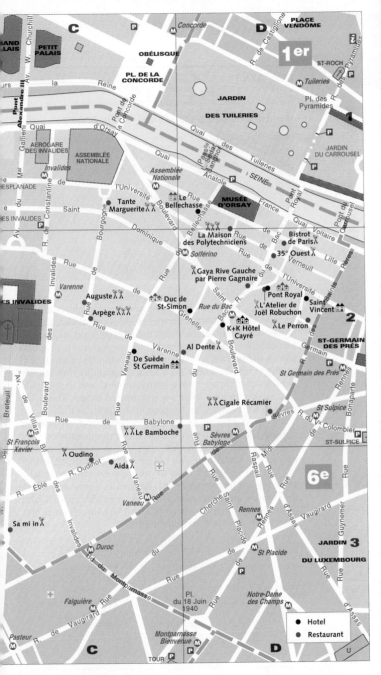

Arpège ✿✿✿

Innovative 𝕏𝕏𝕏

84 r. de Varenne ✉ 75007   Ⓜ **Varenne**
✆ 01 45 51 47 33 **Fax** 01 44 18 98 39   Closed Saturday and Sunday
e-mail arpege.passard@wanadoo.fr **www**.alain-passard.com

Menu €130 (lunch)/340 (dinner) – Carte €188/247

A/C
📺
VISA
MC
AE
⓪

Aurore Deligny

Alain Passard has had his restaurant near the Musée Rodin
for twenty years, in the same spot as L'Archestrate, his
mentor Alain Senderens' former establishment. This discreet
place, barely noticeable from the Rue de Varenne, resembles its chef. The serene modern decor features pear wood
panels highlighted by Lalique glass sculptures, wave motifs
on the windows, and a portrait of his grandmother Louise,
herself a chef. Space is at a premium here, and in the cellar
too, where there is room for just twelve diners. That's big
enough for Passard, an "Impressionist" artist and an expert
cook. The simplicity of his accomplished and streamlined
cuisine masks all the research and experimentation that
goes into it beforehand. For years he has explored vegetables in his outstanding and unconventional cooking, bringing out the noble qualities of ordinary ingredients usually
served as an accompaniment. Passard is highly attuned to
the seasons and even grows his own vegetables on his farm
in the Sarthe region – more proof of how much stock this
passionate man puts in authenticity.

First Course

- Épinard "géant d'hiver" fané au beurre salé, carotte à l'orange.
- Betterave au gros sel gris de Guérande.

Main Course

- Saint-Jacques de la Côte d'Émeraude, inflorescence de chou-fleur.
- Dragée de pigeonneau de Sologne à l'hydromel.

Dessert

- Avocat soufflé au chocolat noir, pointe de pistache.
- Millefeuille "caprice d'enfant" goûter croustillant.

Le Divellec ✿

Seafood 𝕏𝕏𝕏

B1

107 r. Université ✉ 75007   **Ⓜ Invalides**
✆ 01 45 51 91 96   Closed 25 July-25 August, 25 December-
Fax 01 45 51 31 75   2 January, Saturday and Sunday
e-mail ledivellec@noos.fr

Menu € 55 (lunch)/70 (lunch) – Carte € 105/205

A/C
VISA
MC
AE
D

Nicolas Lever

Jacques Le Divellec, a true maestro and incorrigible Breton, keeps on whistling the same tune. You can trust this "ambassador of the sea", as he likes to call himself, to offer the kind of cuisine that evokes his native town of La Rochelle at his (blue-and-white, yacht-like) Parisian pied-à-terre near the Invalides. He celebrates flavours from the ocean and the Mediterranean with the freshest, luxury ingredients. Quality and simplicity remain the top priorities. Witness the sea bass tartare, *cassolette de langoustines aux truffes* (Dublin Bay prawns with truffles) and turbot carpaccio in lemon aspic. A chic "conservatory" (perhaps a tad dated?) of seafood gastronomy, with impeccable service and a high-rolling clientele from the worlds of politics, showbiz and business, thrilled by the call of the sea.

First Course

- Carpaccio de turbot et truffe, citronnelle et huile d'olive.
- Harmonie d'huîtres chaudes et froides.

Main Course

- Homard bleu à la presse avec son corail.
- Saint-Pierre en "tajine" aux citrons confits et cumin.

Dessert

- Fondant chocolat noir au caramel à la fleur de sel.
- Soufflé glacé au café cognac.

Le Jules Verne

Contemporary XXX

A2

2nd floor Eiffel Tower, private lift,   Ⓜ Bir-Hakeim
South pillar ✉ 75007
✆ 01 45 55 61 44 **Fax** 01 47 05 29 41
www.lejulesverne-paris.com

Menu €75 (lunch), €155/450 – Carte €132/195

A/C

VISA

MC

AE

O

You don't have to climb the Eiffel Tower's 1,652 steps to reach the 2nd floor. Just head for the South pillar and take the lift straight up to the Jules Verne. Why revisit this restaurant perched atop the most famous monument in Paris? Because several changes occurred here in 2007. Since January the new team led by Alain Ducasse has offered contemporary French cuisine, and after the recent renovations diners can once again enjoy the exceptional panorama through the large picture windows and the brand new decor by French architect and designer Patrick Jouin

La Maison des Polytechniciens

Traditional XXX

D1

12 r. Poitiers ✉ 75007   Ⓜ Solférino
✆ 01 49 54 74 54   Closed 27 July-27 August, 23 December-3 January,
Fax 01 49 54 74 84   Saturday, Sunday and public holidays
e-mail le.club@maisondesx.com   – Number of covers limited, pre-book
www.maisondesx.com

Menu €36 – Carte €39/59

VISA

MC

AE

O

Despite its name, the Maison des Polytechniciens is not the exclusive preserve of Polytechnique students, and you'll run into more businessmen here than mortar boards. That is quite fortunate, given its prestigious historic setting in the delightful Hôtel de Poulpry, an early 18C townhouse with an ancient chandelier which creates a wonderful effect. It is impossible not to succumb to its charms, between the Napoleonic room, the hushed lounges (including one decorated by Watteau), the vaulted cellars, inner garden and idyllic terrace. Particularly with Pascal Chanteloup subtly playing with tradition in the kitchen. His contemporary cuisine is combined with a more classic wine list designed with Les Caves Taillevent.

Pétrossian

Seafood XXX

144 r. Université ✉ 75007   Ⓜ Invalides
✆ 01 44 11 32 32 **Fax** 01 44 11 32 35   Closed August,
Sunday and Monday

Menu €35 (weekday lunch), €45/100 – Carte €56/98

With her graceful bearing and iron will, chef Rougui Dia
has rewritten the rule book at this legendary restaurant, a
symbol of Russian and Armenian haute gastronomy since
1920, and the Parisian temple of caviar. The classic repertoire at "Le 144" (Alexandre III tartare with caviar, Kyscielli,
etc.) has opened up to more modern, more exotic influences, thanks to Dia's personal approach and taste for spices.
The shades of grey in the refined contemporary dining room
mirror the distinctive Pétrossian product: caviar.

Le Bamboche

Contemporary XX

15 r. Babylone ✉ 75007   Ⓜ Sèvres Babylone
✆ 01 45 49 14 40   Closed 27 July-10 August and Sunday lunch
Fax 01 45 49 14 44
e-mail lebamboche@aol.com **www.**labamboche.com

Menu (€28), €35 – Carte €60/71

You're likely to enjoy yourself at this discreet little restaurant
hidden behind the Bon Marché. The contemporary decor
with glamorous red armchairs is the ideal setting for smart
diners to cool their heels while waiting to sample the delicious dishes. The place might appear to be somewhat well-
behaved, but the boldness is all in the food, created by the
high-powered duo of Serge Arce and Philippe Fabert, who
have made their mark with tasty ingredients prepared in an
original way. Their inventions – caviar sorbet, smoked trout
and baby spinach, tomatoes and sorbets from the garden
(basil, olive oil, tomatoes), grilled sea bass with a delicate
compote of fennel and bacon – have plenty of appeal.

TOUR EIFFEL • ÉCOLE MILITAIRE • INVALIDES

Auguste

C2

Contemporary XX

54 r. Bourgogne ⊠ 75007
𝒞 01 45 51 61 09
Fax 01 45 51 27 34
www.restaurantauguste.fr

ⓜ Varenne
Closed 3-24 August,
Saturday and Sunday

Menu €35 (lunch) – Carte €58/76

A/C
MC
AE
①

A minimalist atmosphere at this restaurant on "ministry row". Gaël Orieux's small establishment – only thirty place settings – offers peace and quiet in an elegant contemporary setting with deceptively simple lines. White is the dominant tone, but the "purist" architecture is warmed up with a number of original touches, such as the bright red banquettes, charcoal grey parquet floor, flowers and amazing Buddha paintings on the walls. You'd expect to be served trendy food in a chic and "cool" space like this. But appearances can be deceiving, and the chef's dishes are on the contrary clearly more classical in style. Does the name refer to Auguste Escoffier, or to Auguste Rodin (the Rodin Museum being nearby)? A double allusion apparently – but first of all to Escoffier, who was the "king of chefs and chef of kings". The short menu changes frequently and is delightfully varied. The wine list is full of interesting finds at competitive prices.

First Course

- Fine gelée iodée aux huîtres creuses et bulots.
- Foie gras de canard poêlé, supions et enokis.

Main Course

- Saint-Pierre de pleine mer au poêlon.
- Noix de ris de veau croustillante aux cacahuètes caramelisées.

Dessert

- Soufflé au chocolat pur Caraïbes.
- Panna cotta, glace au miel d'acacia.

Chez les Anges

Traditional ✗✗

B2

54 bd de la Tour Maubourg   🅜 La Tour Maubourg
✉ 75007   Closed Saturday and Sunday
☎ 01 47 05 89 86 **Fax** 01 47 05 45 56
e-mail mail@chezlesanges.com **www**.chezlesanges.com

Menu (€ 25), € 34 – Carte € 44/73

A/C
⟨⟩
VISA
🅜🅒
AE
⧇

Tempted by the idea of dining in paradise? Designed by Alberto Bali in a sparse contemporary style, Les Anges has wide picture windows providing full daylight, a large central counter and lithographs of angels on the walls (a must, given the establishment's name). The tone is set. After a forty year hiatus, this brasserie won back its name (and spirit) in 2005. The market-based menu blends traditional and modern dishes, all well-prepared and authentic. The cellar is stocked with Burgundies (and the occasional Bordeaux). A warm welcome, good value for money and service that is positively angelic.

Cigale Récamier

Traditional ✗✗

D2

4 r. Récamier ✉ 75007   🅜 Sèvres Babylone
☎ 01 45 48 86 58   Closed Sunday

Carte approx. € 55

⌂
A/C
VISA
🅜🅒

A haven of peace and quiet, the Cigale Récamier is nestled in a cul-de-sac giving onto a garden, with a charming flowery terrace. Sweet and savoury soufflés are the speciality here, with an original menu renewed every month, along with foie gras terrines, grilled lamb chops with thyme, fillet of sea bream, etc. The classic bistro-style cuisine is cooked up by the owner, Gérard Idoux. The dining room has been revamped in a contemporary style with clean lines, lending it a more modern, convivial look. The calm, contemplative atmosphere draws a smart Parisian crowd, including members of the literary set.

Le Clarisse

Contemporary ✕✕

B1

29 r. Surcouf ✉ 75007
✆ 01 45 50 11 10
Fax 01 45 50 11 14
e-mail olivier.maria@leclarisse.fr

Ⓜ La Tour Maubourg
Closed August,
Saturday lunch and Sunday

Menu (€32), €39 (lunch)/56

A/C
VISA
M/C

Le Clarisse, a new establishment on a quiet little street in the 7th arrondissement, reflects the current trend in restaurants. The spare contemporary decor·is in black and white (walls, banquettes and chairs), with dark wood tables, a large chandelier and a more intimate dining room upstairs. It is elegant and refined, with jazz playing in the background, and not a false note. Your appetite is whetted by a glance at the menu featuring duck foie gras with beetroot caramel, seasonal fruits and vegetables, sea bream in a gingerbread crust, and a classic 1891 Paris-Brest (choux-based pastry). The dishes, prepared by the former chef at the Ferme Saint-Simon, are precise, with pronounced flavours. A promising start.

La Cuisine

Traditional ✕✕

B1

14 bd La Tour-Maubourg ✉ 75007
✆ 01 44 18 36 32 **Fax** 01 44 18 30 42
e-mail lacuisine@lesrestos.com
www.lacuisine.lesrestos.com

Ⓜ Invalides
Closed Saturday lunch

Menu (€28), €35 (weekday lunch)/42 – Carte €53/75

A/C
VISA
M/C
AE
Ⓞ

Cuisine, near the Quai d'Orsay, is well worth the detour. Created in 2000 by the Selles-Duboscq duo (seasoned restaurateurs formerly at the Georges V), it has been quietly gaining ground, confident of the excellent reputation it has earned with its clientele of gourmets who care about quality above all. They are rewarded with a selection of top ingredients brilliantly prepared in the finest tradition by the chef: langoustines served in bisque in a *chaud-froid*, John Dory on a bed of spinach, and cannelloni with a white chocolate garnish. Delicious! The contemporary dining room features modern paintings, mirrors and comfortable banquettes. Enjoy the veranda in the daytime and the soft lighting in the evening.

D'Chez Eux

Terroir ✕✕

B2

2 av. Lowendal ✉ 75007
☎ 01 47 05 52 55
Fax 01 45 55 60 74
e-mail contact@chezeux.com **www**.chezeux.com

Ⓜ École Militaire
Closed 1st-18 August and Sunday

Menu (€35), €40 (lunch) – Carte €46/77

A/C
VISA
Ⓜ©
Ⓘ

The name (roughly translated as "from their homeland") refers to the Southwest and Auvergne regions represented at this charming inn-like restaurant, run by Jean-Pierre Court (the owner) and François Casteleyn (the chef). The dining room looks right out of a postcard with its rustic furniture and checked tablecloths. Tradition is everywhere, in the regional ingredients, generous portions, extensive cellar – focusing particularly on Bordeaux and Burgundies – and smocked waiters. No wonder their formula has been a hit for over 40 years! Try the *panier de cochonnailles* (assortment of sausages and pâtés), frogs' legs, scallops with preserved shallots, duck breast, and of course the hearty *cassoulet* – all irresistible.

L'Esplanade

Contemporary ✕✕

B2

52 r. Fabert ✉ 75007
☎ 01 47 05 38 80 **Fax** 01 47 05 23 75

Ⓜ La Tour Maubourg

Carte €39/83

A/C
☞
VISA
Ⓜ©
AE

The Costes Brothers can boast that everything they touch turns to gold. Including hip places like the Esplanade, a successful blend of venue, ambiance and decidedly trendy cuisine. Here's the proof, four times over. First, the superb view of the Invalides, especially from the terrace. Secondly, the Jacques Garcia decor – a "lounge and military" atmosphere evoking Napoleon III, with comfortable armchairs and…cannons. The menu features updated brasserie classics in an "urban terroir" genre (tartare, organic boiled egg, etc.) or fusion-style with prawn risotto and coconut caramel duck. The stylish waiters and valet parking serve a clientele of celebrities and politicians. Verdict: rush over to see and be seen – after booking.

Il Vino d'Enrico Bernardo ✿

B1

13 bd La Tour-Maubourg ✉ **75007**   **Ⓜ Invalides**
☎ 01 44 11 72 00 **Fax** 01 44 11 72 02
e-mail info@ilvinobyenricobernardo.com
www.ilvinobyenricobernardo.com

Menu €50 bi (lunch), €100 bi/1000 bi – Carte €70/120

Bruno Delessard

You usually start by ordering your food, then the wine as an accompaniment. But they do things in a radically different way at Il Vino. Instead of mouth-watering dishes, the menu features only top vintage wines (the prestige menu composed of exceptional wines starts at 1,000 euros). Is this just the latest fad, thought up by owner Enrico Bernardo, voted the world's best sommelier in 2004? More like a new approach to matching food and wine in which the latter has landed the main role. Listen carefully to find out more about the cuisine offered. After selecting your fabulous wines, they will suggest the most appropriate dishes to go with them. Quite original, perhaps a bit disconcerting, and definitely exhilarating. One thing is sure – people who like surprises are in for a treat here. As for the decor, the warm colours from the days of Le Chamarré are gone, traded in for an ultra chic atmosphere blending discretion with contemporary designs, offset by a glassed-in cellar illustrating the house theme.

First Course
- Risotto aux cèpes.
- Saint-Jacques, topinambour et truffes.

Main Course
- Agneau de sept heures.
- Côte de veau, purée de pommes de terre.

Dessert
- Dacquoise à la poire.
- Tarte aux figues.

New Jawad

B1

Indian-Pakistani ✗✗

12 av. Rapp ⊠ 75007   **Ⓜ** École Militaire
✆ 01 47 05 91 37 **Fax** 01 45 50 31 27

Menu € 16/40 – Carte € 21/42

A/C
VISA
MC
AE
①

Enjoy the flavours of northern India in a peaceful atmosphere near the Eiffel Tower. Far from the effervescent local places in Paris' Indiatown, the New Jawad offers a cosy, hushed setting worthy of a private townhouse. The extremely chic 7th arrondissement has clearly left its mark on this Indo-Pakistani establishment, which has done away with all outer signs of exoticism apart from a few precious engravings. The voyage is all in the food. Try a classic menu of assorted starters (*samosas, pakoras, bahjis*), curries and *biryanis*, light-tasting *nans*, and *lassi* or wine – more conventional, and pricier – to experience a delightful gourmet pause in the land of Maharajas.

Les Ombres

A1

Contemporary ✗✗

27 quai Branly ⊠ 75007   **Ⓜ** Alma Marceau
✆ 01 47 53 68 00 **Fax** 01 47 53 68 18
e-mail ombres.restaurant@elior.com **www**.lesombres.fr

Menu € 37 (lunch)/95 – Carte € 61/98

A/C
P
VISA
MC
AE
①

Futuristic architecture, colourful cubes and vertical gardens are part of the strikingly original look of the Musée du Quai Branly designed by Jean Nouvel. The popular restaurant perched on its rooftop terrace – all in wood, rattan and steel – is a unique spot up in the clouds with an airy and contemporary glass design. At lunch, enjoy the breathtaking view of the Eiffel Tower and its majestic play of light and shadows (thus the restaurant's name), sure to dazzle tourists and celebrities alike. Dishes on the enticing up-to-date menu, composed by a chef with a pedigree featuring stints at Laurent and Robuchon, include the likes of aubergine puree, grilled chicken breast, chocolate-pistachio-cake with barley syrup ice cream and red berry tiramisu.

Tante Marguerite

C1

Traditional ✗✗

5 r. Bourgogne ✉ 75007
✆ 01 45 51 79 42
Fax 01 47 53 79 56
e-mail tante.marguerite@bernard-loiseau.com
www.bernard-loiseau.com

Ⓜ Assemblée Nationale
Closed August, Saturday and Sunday

Menu € 47

A/C
⟨⟩
VISA
ⓂⒸ
AE
Ⓓ

By a funny coincidence, Tante Marguerite, a well-known restaurant specialising in cuisine from Burgundy, is located on the rue de Bourgogne. The good news is that this institution in the Bernard Loiseau group has had a face lift, with a new bronze-grey contemporary decor – an ode to the Morvan forests – and a new chef, Jean-François Robert (who worked with Savoy, Dutournier and Darroze). The menu features Loiseau-style recipes from the *terroir* and more modern dishes like the *mosaïque de raie aux aromates* (mosaic of skate with seasoning) or the goat cheese *croustillant* with dates. Political figures love this place for its elegant cuisine, intimacy and soft lighting for hushed conversations. A place worth (re)discovering.

Thiou

B1

Thai ✗✗

49 quai d'Orsay ✉ 75007
✆ 01 40 62 96 50
Fax 01 40 62 97 30

Ⓜ Invalides
Closed August,
Saturday lunch and Sunday

Carte € 46/91

A/C
VISA
ⓂⒸ
AE

V.I.P. – three letters that sum up the "glitter and gloss" ambiance here, prized by the in-crowd on the lookout for chic venues. The owner, Thiou, is also quite media-savvy. The many talents of this self-taught woman from China, already spotted when she was the chef at the (famous nightclub) Les Bains Douches, are evident in her refined exotic touch. Witness the discreetly ethnic dining room (bamboo and warm tones ranging from copper to chocolate), and above all the beautifully-presented cuisine. Celebrities can get a change of scenery without fear of jet-lag while enjoying the Thai and vegetarian dishes. The Crying Tiger (grilled marinated beef) – the house speciality – is a real crowd-pleaser, and no one seems worried about the bill (lots of euros).

Vin et Marée

Seafood 🍴🍴

A2

71 av. Suffren ✉ 75007   Ⓜ La Motte Picquet Grenelle
☎ 01 47 83 27 12 **Fax** 01 53 86 98 26
e-mail vmsuffren@vin-et-maree.com **www**.vin-et-maree.com

Menu (€ 21) – Carte € 32/58

A/C

VISA

MC

AE

Failing a trip to the seaside, you can always take refuge in the comfortable dining room of this first of the Vin et Marée restaurants in Paris. A sure bet, it has held a steady course ever since it opened. Its formula for success is simple, offering only the freshest of ingredients – bought at the morning fish auction – in flawless and appetising dishes. The smoothly run operation is sure to please. Blackboard selections change with daily deliveries, spotlighting a wide range of fish and shellfish. There are even two dishes on the menu for strict carnivores. And the delicious food is not all. Vin et Marée is also a delight to the eye, with a tailor-made decor featuring an ultramarine façade and plush interior.

L'Affriolé 😊

Contemporary 🍴

B1

17 r. Malar ✉ 75007   Ⓜ Invalides
☎ 01 44 18 31 33   Closed 3 weeks in August, Sunday and Monday

Menu (€ 23), € 29 (lunch)/34

A/C

VISA

MC

With its bits-and-pieces bistro decor (knick-knacks, stucco, mosaic tables), Thierry Vérola's restaurant has some nice gastronomic surprises up its sleeve among the daily blackboard suggestions. And it doesn't take the easy way out, changing its menu by the month. Following the market and his own inclinations, the chef composes generous dishes with a modern touch, such as ham hock croquettes with lentils, swordfish hamburger with fennel, *nonnette* (tart) made with salted butter. People come here for the relaxed yet well-prepared meals, the warm and friendly reception, and attentive service (appetizers with radishes, pots of cream) – all at reasonable prices. Tempting, isn't it?

Vin sur Vin ✿

A1

Traditional 𝕏𝕏

20 r. de Monttessuy ✉ 75007   Ⓜ Pont de l'Alma
✆ 01 47 05 14 20

Closed 1st-11 May, 27 July-25 August,
22 December-6 January, Monday except dinner from
mid September to end-March, Saturday lunch and Sunday

Carte €68/118   Number of covers limited, pre-book

A/C

VISA

MC

G.Corbic/MICHELIN

"It's a private place that we open to the public," explains owner Patrice Vidal, summing up the atmosphere here. With its ten tables and fifteen place settings, this discreet and unique restaurant is almost like a family dining room. Busy in the kitchen are chef Pascal Toulza, a native of the South West, and his assistant Mustapha Rednaoui, who trained in Marrakech. Together they cook up expert and excellent traditional dishes paired with excellent wines, a key feature of this establishment. The owner is passionate about good wine, and the cellar boasts several hundred references that were patiently and lovingly unearthed. The Vin sur Vin may not be a "fashionable address", but its popularity has yet to fail in twenty years.

First Course	*Main Course*	*Dessert*
• Saint-Jacques d'Erquy (October-March).	• Gros turbot sauvage.	• Crème brulée.
• Galette de pieds de cochon.	• Ris de veau de lait français.	• Soufflé.

Le Violon d'Ingres ✿

Contemporary ✕✕

B2

135 r. St-Dominique ✉ 75007
✆ 01 45 55 15 05
Fax 01 45 55 48 42
e-mail violondingres@wanadoo.fr **www**.leviolondingres.com

Ⓜ École Militaire
Closed in August, Sunday and Monday

Menu €48/65 – Carte €50/67

A/C
VISA
Ⓜ©
AE
Ⓓ

Violon d'Ingres

Pun intended? Violon d'Ingres, the French term for hobby, could mean that chef Christian Constant's passion for cooking is his favourite pastime. Or it might refer to the fact that he comes from Montauban, like the painter Ingres. It's also the name of his first restaurant, launched after a brilliant career in a number of luxury hotels and famous establishments (Ledoyen, Ritz, Crillon). But Christian Constant has left behind the large kitchen brigades, exclusive and ultra-chic environments and recipes designed above all to turn heads. Since running his own show, Constant has taken a 180° turn. Now he prefers simplicity and a small staff in what could be described as a luxury neo-brasserie that is discreet and contemporary. The long dining room is bathed in white, cream and grey tones, giving it a feeling of space and serenity. The modern cuisine de terroir has a strong traditional base (and perfect technical mastery) with southwestern roots, enhanced by an excellent wine list. It's always packed here – the price of success – so don't forget to book.

First Course

- Millefeuille de langue et foie gras façon Lucullus.
- Foie gras en brioche.

Main Course

- Cassoulet montalbanais.
- Andouillette et pied porc pané.

Dessert

- Soufflé vanille, sauce caramel au beurre salé.
- Tarte chocolat.

L'Agassin

B1

8 r. Malar ✉ 75007
✆ 01 47 05 18 18
Fax 01 45 55 64 41

Ⓜ La Tour Maubourg
Closed August, Sunday and Monday

Menu € 23 (lunch)/34

VISA
Ⓜ©
Ⓐ🄴

In case you were wondering what the name means, it refers to the lowest bud on the vine, which doesn't bear fruit. In Côtes du Rhône vineyards they are known as "gourmands". That says a lot about chef-owner André Le Letty's passion for wine as an essential accompaniment to fine cooking. His up-to-date cuisine is featured on the menu or as suggestions of the day. And the iconic dishes from Anacréon (where he was the chef for over 10 years) are as mouth-watering as ever: *terrine de lapin au foie gras et légumes*, *clafoutis aux pruneaux*, etc. The same sense of simplicity comes through in the clean lines of the decor – the new template for stylish contemporary bistros.

Al Dente

D2

38 r. Varenne ✉ 75007
✆ 01 45 48 79 64

Ⓜ Rue du Bac
Closed 20 July-20 August, 25 December-
1st January, Sunday and Monday

Carte € 29/48

VISA
Ⓜ©
Ⓞ

As everyone knows, all roads lead to Rome. And perchance to Italian cuisine, judging from this recent neighbourhood trattoria run by Sylvain Lindon (actor Vincent's brother), who traded in his job as a television adman for that of restaurateur. Lacking all pretension – but not lacking in quality – his establishment welcomes you just like at home. The setting is simple, with red banquettes, dark wood furniture, and sienna and ochre tones – for that touch of sun. It's almost like being in Tuscany. As for the dishes, they speak for themselves: fettucine with courgettes and pecorino, three-cheese rigatoni, papardelle with aubergines, tomatoes and mozzarella, pizza with rocket and bresaola. Simple, modern, and *al dente*.

Aida ✿

C3

Japanese 𝗫

1 r. Pierre Leroux ✉ 75007
☎ 01 43 06 14 18
Fax 01 43 06 14 18
www.aidaparis.com

Ⓜ Vaneau
Closed 5-25 August, February holidays, Tuesday lunch,
Saturday lunch, Sunday lunch and Monday
Dinner only – Number of covers limited, pre-book

Menu €90/160 – Carte €87/200

Bruno Delessard

The white façade of this small Japanese restaurant blends in so well with the urban landscape that you could easily walk right by without even noticing it. But don't! Hidden inside is a secret which is jealously kept by informed gourmets – a delicious Japanese establishment. The ultra-zen, subdued interior is a chic, welcome change of scenery. You can choose between the red lacquer counter (to be in the first row, across from the huge hot plates) or in the private room. The menu features refined cutting-edge cuisine, a blend of Japanese and French. A lovely marriage of lobster, chateaubriand and calf sweetbreads with teppan-yaki – which gets the better of sushi here – and Burgundies passionately chosen by the chef, an expert œnologist.

First Course	*Main Course*	*Dessert*
• Pot au feu japonais. • Sashimi.	• Huîtres sautées au beurre d'algues sur lit de cresson. • Chateaubriant cuit au teppanyaki.	• Glace vanille et crème de marron à la truffe. • Sorbet maison.

L'Atelier de Joël Robuchon ❀❀

D2

Innovative ✗

5 r. Montalembert ✉ 75007   Ⓜ Rue du Bac
✆ 01 42 22 56 56   Open from 11.30 am to 3.30 pm and from 6.30 pm
Fax 01 42 22 97 91   to midnight. Reservations only for certain services:
e-mail latelierdejoelrobuchon@wanadoo.fr   please enquire

Menu € 110 – Carte € 53/100

A/C
VISA
MC

L'Atelier de Joël Robuchon

You can't book here – except for the 11:30am and 6:30pm sittings. You've been warned! The intriguing Atelier de Joël Robuchon is in a category of its own on the gastronomic landscape, brushing aside conventions but not overlooking a certain taste for luxury. The deliberately subdued lighting immediately creates a different kind of space for the senses. Diners sitting on high stools at the two bars can watch the chefs preparing their food right in front of them in the central kitchen.

The trendy decor boasts black lacquer furniture, dark granite floors, intimate lighting disseminated in glowing red beams, and jars of spices and preserved vegetables. Architect Pierre-Yves Rochon's design is a perfect match for this original Parisian version of Robuchon's concept, opened all over the world since then.

This "chic canteen", a Western version of Japanese teppanyakis and sushi bars, features tailor-made tasting menus and a fine selection of wines by the glass.

First Course

- Langoustine en papillote croustillante au basilic.
- L'œuf cocotte à la crème de girolles.

Main Course

- Merlan frit colbert, beurre aux herbes.
- Le ris de veau clouté de laurier frais à la feuille de romaine farcie.

Dessert

- Chartreuse en soufflé chaud et sa crème glacée à la pistache.
- La vanille et le chocolat en petits pots crèmeux.

Au Bon Accueil ☺

Bistro ✗

A1

14 r. Monttessuy ✉ 75007
✆ 01 47 05 46 11
Fax 01 45 56 15 80

🅜 Pont de l'Alma
Closed 7-20 August,
Saturday and Sunday

Menu €27/31 – Carte €50/75

A/C
VISA
M©
AE

This gourmet bistro has more than one trick up its sleeve to win the hearts of its diners. First, there is the lovely terrace ideally located a stone's throw from the Champ de Mars, with the Eiffel Tower in the background. When the weather is less inviting, you can happily take refuge in the dining room and lounge, offering a contemporary setting which is rather hip in its own 7th arrondissement way. The daily blackboard selections are created according to the market and quality ingredients. The up-to-date dishes and seasonal game have clear and simple flavours, enhanced by vintage Rhône and Burgundy wines. As for the welcome and service, all you have to do is read the sign to know it will be friendly, efficient and spirited.

Bistrot de Paris

Bistro ✗

D2

33 r. Lille ✉ 75007
✆ 01 42 61 16 83
Fax 01 49 27 06 09

🅜 Musée d'Orsay
Closed August, 24 December-1st January,
Sunday and Monday

Carte €22/68

VISA
M©
AE

This historic Parisian establishment, former "soup kitchen" famously frequented by writer André Gide, is the kind of timeless place that never loses its appeal. People love the genuinely charming 1900s decor (remodelled by Slavik) that embodies a certain Parisian style, with its chandeliers, copperware and mirrors, red and gold tones and closely-spaced tables. It is often packed, but the attentive service is up to the job. The bistro cuisine, paired with a hundred or so wines, is brilliantly simple and on the mark. A real godsend in this antique shop district.

Café Constant

B2

139 r. Saint-Dominique ✉ 75007
℘ 01 47 53 73 34
Fax 01 45 55 48 42

Ⓜ École Militaire
Closed 2 weeks in August,
Sunday and Monday

Menu (€16), €31/35

VISA
Ⓜ©
Ⓘ

Slowly but surely, Christian Constant, the former chef at the Crillon, is turning the rue Saint-Dominique into a real gourmet haven. This annexe a stone's throw from the Violon d'Ingres, his gastronomic restaurant, was opened in a little corner bistro with no pretentions – and no reservations! Simplicity is the watchword here - there is nothing flashy about the decor. The food shows a keen understanding of ingredients, retaining some of the spirit of the great Parisian tables (without the fussiness and high prices). The blackboard features tasty market-based dishes such as *œuf mimosa*, cream of pumpkin soup, fillet of beef with pepper sauce, and profiteroles. The service is friendly and the ambiance feisty. A Constant source of amazement!

Café de l'Alma

B1

5 av. Rapp ✉ 75007
℘ 01 45 51 56 74 **Fax** 01 45 51 10 08
e-mail cafedelalma@wanadoo.fr

Ⓜ Alma Marceau

Carte €35/70

⌂
A/C
☞
VISA
Ⓜ©
AE
Ⓘ

With its plum, anise green and beige colours and wenge wood, the Café de l'Alma stylishly contrasts with the clichéd image of a Parisian brasserie. There is no zinc counter worn by the years, no moleskin or bistro furniture here. The decor is by architect François Champsaur, designed in a highly contemporary spirit made for cocooning, with cosy nooks upstairs and banquettes for lounging comfortably from morning until night. The food is also up-to-date, with the likes of coconut shrimp tempura, fish and chips with *sauce tartare* and aged sherry, *hachis parmentier de pot-au-feu* (shepherd's pie), caramel tart, etc. The wines are of the same calibre, with a wide selection of bottles from around the world.

Chez l'Ami Jean

B1

Terroir ✗

27 r. Malar ✉ 75007
☎ 01 47 05 86 89
Fax 01 45 55 41 82

Ⓜ La Tour Maubourg
Closed August, 23 December-2 January,
Sunday and Monday

Menu € 32

Wood furniture, blackboard specialities of the day, *piments d'Espelette, chistera*, old rugby posters and photographs make up the "regionalist" decor of this authentic bistro, quite up-to-date despite its 70 years. Stéphane Jégo, the chef here since 2002, has been given high marks from the gourmets, who enjoy spending time with friends in the open and convivial atmosphere. The market-based cuisine is generous and tasty, alternately featuring seafood – the chef is from Brittany – and Basque-Béarnais dishes (he was the assistant to Camdeborde at La Régalade). A big success, it is always packed, lively and fun.

Clos des Gourmets

B1

Contemporary ✗

16 av. Rapp ✉ 75007
☎ 01 45 51 75 61
Fax 01 47 05 74 20
e-mail closdesgourmets@wanadoo.fr
www.closdesgourmets.com

Ⓜ Alma Marceau
Closed 10-25 August,
Sunday and Monday

Menu (€ 25), € 29 (weekday lunch)/35

The Clos des Gourmets has a very fitting name! This restaurant, which opens onto a veranda and a terrace, is on the lips of many a food-lover. The well-deserved success is due to the talented chef, Arnaud Pitrois, who hasn't forgotten the lessons learned from his teachers (Guy Savoy, Christian Constant, Éric Fréchon). He skilfully prepares food with a personal touch where old-time specialities (stuffed cabbage, duck breast with blueberries) are on a par with more inventive recipes - avocado in puff pastry and preserved lemons with aged rhum, reinette apples with salty caramel sauce and thyme ice cream. The wines come from France and all around the world. Do we need to add that the prices are low to convince you to rush over here?

Les Cocottes

B2

135 r. St-Dominique ⊠ 75007
Fax 01 45 55 00 91
e-mail violondingres@wanadoo.fr

Ⓜ École Militaire
Closed Sunday

Carte € 24/34

VISA
ⓂⒸ
ⒶⒺ

And the latest brainchild of Christian Constant here in his gourmet stronghold (i.e. the rue Saint-Dominique)? Food in cast iron casserole dishes, made by Staub, served up in a modern decor in this unclassifiable establishment, neither restaurant nor bistro. Picture a long, stylish looking counter top with tall stools, clean lines and gourmet delicatessen products. The concept is that of a friendly snack bar for gourmets in a hurry, with Kilner jars, earthenware and cast iron dishes containing the likes of fillet of sea bream with summer vegetables and roast pigeon with peas. Another clever idea here is the continuous service from breakfast to late-night dinner with no advance booking (but beware of the crowds!), and they also do takeaway.

Fontaine de Mars

B2

129 r. St-Dominique ⊠ 75007
✆ 01 47 05 46 44 **Fax** 01 47 05 11 13
e-mail lafontainedemars@orange.fr

Ⓜ École Militaire

Carte € 35/68

If you still haven't been to this bistro, take the litmus test by walking past it and seeing if you can resist its charming terrace across from the Fontaine de Mars (dedicated to the god of war). It's virtually impossible, right? Sheltered under an arcade, this precious haven of peace is a godsend in Paris. Inside are two delightful (and perfectly restored) little Art Deco rooms with red-and-white checked tablecloths. The relaxed atmosphere is no surprise either, given the friendly proprietors. The simple traditional dishes, including fricassee of rabbit with mustard, black pudding with apples, *cassoulet*, preserved duck, *cochonnailles*, and *tourtière landaise* are always a treat. Choice wines.

Les Fables de La Fontaine ✿

B2

131 r. Saint-Dominique ✉ 75007
✆ 01 44 18 37 55 **Fax** 01 44 18 37 57

Ⓜ École Militaire
Closed 23-28 December

Menu (€35) – Carte approx. €50

Les Fables de La Fontaine

One of the three adjoining restaurants that belong to Christian Constant on the Rue Saint-Dominique (which they might think about renaming in his honour!).There's nothing superfluous about the decor, done in a chic contemporary bistro style. The long dining room is streamlined without seeming austere, with a few well-aligned tables in dark wood (like the façade), a bar counter near the entrance, and a tiny kitchen where you can watch the chef at work. The colours are well-matched (browns and whites), complemented by orange banquettes, while blackboards on the walls announce daily suggestions based on the market. Simple and high-quality pretty much sums up the Constant style.

Here, the cuisine highlights fish, accompanied by a fine selection of white wines. The technical mastery displayed in the dishes never overshadows the excellent ingredients: authenticity is the top priority. The reasonable prices are an added bonus.

First Course

- Émietté de tourteau, chiffonnade de sucrine, mousse piquillos.
- Croustillant de gambas au basilic, vinaigrette d'agrumes.

Main Course

- Merlu rôti au lard, caviar d'aubergine fumé, velouté de cèpes.
- Saint-Jacques à la plancha, velouté de topinambour à la truffe noire.

Dessert

- Gateau Basque.
- Tiramisu.

Florimond

B2

Traditional ✗

19 av. La Motte-Picquet
✉ 75007
✆ 01 45 55 40 38
Fax 01 45 55 40 38

Ⓜ École Militaire
Closed 28 April-4 May, 28 July-17 August,
22 December-4 January,
Saturday lunch and Sunday

Menu € 21 (weekday lunch)/36 – Carte € 38/54

VISA
MC

Florimond's name comes from the gardener at Monet's estate in Giverny. Does that mean the cuisine here is impressionistic and fussy? Not on your life. This little place is famous for its generous traditional cuisine, featured on a regular menu and a daily blackboard. The chef is skilful at integrating genres, proposing dishes that range from market-inspired to terroir, "canaille" (hearty) and gourmet. He likes to reinvent classics, serving up traditional specialities (stuffed cabbage, duck breast with blueberries) and more up-to-date dishes. Simplicity is the name of the game – also reflected in the discreet bistro-style setting.

Léo Le Lion

B2

Seafood ✗

23 r. Duvivier ✉ 75007
✆ 01 45 51 41 77
Fax 01 45 51 41 77
e-mail restaurantleolelion@hotmail.com

Ⓜ École Militaire
Closed August, 25 December-1st January,
Sunday and Monday

Carte € 40/50

VISA
MC

This bistro has resisted the sirens of fashion and appeals to people precisely because of its delicious retro setting and atmosphere still plunged into the days of the 1930s. The fine counter, wood-fired grill and velvet banquettes compose the warm and rustic spirit of the establishment, with its friendly service. Fish are featured on the menu year round – chef Didier Méry is an expert after his long turn at the famous seafood restaurant Le Divellec – and game shows up in season. Good catches include the crayfish in raspberry vinegar, snail *cassolette* in champagne, and the fillet of sea bass. For dessert, the crème brûlée with honey is an offer you can't refuse.

Gaya Rive Gauche par Pierre Gagnaire ✿

D2

44 r. Bac ✉ 75007
✆ 01 45 44 73 73
Fax 01 45 44 73 73
e-mail p.gagnaire@wanadoo.fr
www.pierre-gagnaire.com

Ⓜ Rue du Bac
Closed 3-24 August, 23 December-
4 January, Sunday and public holidays

Menu (€35) – Carte €63/102

A/C
VISA
MC
AE

Gaya Rive Gauche par Pierre Gagnaire

TOUR EIFFEL • ÉCOLE MILITAIRE • INVALIDES

Pierre Gagnaire – who already owns Sketch in London and another branch in Tokyo – wanted his second restaurant in Paris to be "elegant, fun and original", a more accessible, everyday restaurant where the food would be "good and also rather amusing". And he did just that at the Gaya Rive Gauche, open since September 2005.

The décor by Christian Ghion is indeed entertaining, with its literal illustrations of the dishes awaiting you, i.e. fish! You'll soon be in the same boat, among the sardine grey and ocean blue tones, the luminous bar with optical effects (a grid seen through wavy water), the scale-shaped wall and tables with seaweed patterns!

The food here is cleverly prepared and the atmosphere relaxed. The delicate and creative dishes feature a variety of fresh seafood, ranging from more "high-end" fish like sole and red mullet to the more "modest" hake and whiting.

First Course
- Croque-monsieur noir.
- Terrine de maquereau au vin blanc.

Main Course
- Langoustines.
- Bonite confite aux aromates.

Dessert
- Gâteau au chocolat.
- Parfait glacé aux poivrons.

157

Maupertu

B2

Traditional ✗

94 bd La Tour-Maubourg
✉ 75007
✆ 01 45 51 37 96 **Fax** 01 53 59 94 83
e-mail info@restaurant-maupertu-paris.com
www.restaurant-maupertu-paris.com

Ⓜ École Militaire
Closed 5-25 August and Sunday

Menu (€23), €32

VISA
ⓂⒸ

Le Maupertu isn't new, but its bistro decor has had a facelift, with bordeaux-coloured walls, modern paintings, wooden chairs and soberly dressed tables, subdued lighting and a lovely streetside veranda. The atmosphere has remained unpretentious and convivial, with a faithful local clientele. The menu specialises in dishes with a traditional base, particularly from Provence: tuna tartare with young vegetables, pike-perch with aubergine caviar and anise sauce, and home-made desserts, all promptly served. The terrace is the best spot in the house, with a stunning view overlooking the Esplanade des Invalides.

Miyako

B1

Japanese ✗

121 r. Université ✉ 75007
✆ 01 47 05 41 83
Fax 01 45 55 13 18

Ⓜ Invalides
Closed 1st August-1st September,
Saturday lunch and Sunday

Menu €14 (weekday lunch), €18/30 – Carte €26/43

Ⓐ/Ⓒ
VISA
ⓂⒸ
ⒶⒺ

On one wall of the dining room is a fresco of the Eiffel Tower and the Esplanade des Invalides, while plants and porcelain dolls on the other wall evoke the Land of the Rising Sun. Welcome to Miyako ("heart" in Japanese), a restaurant which pleasantly cultivates French and Japanese culture in its decor. The food, however, is rooted in the traditions of the archipelago. The menu has a large variety of typical dishes, enjoyed to the sound of classical music. Sushi, sashimi, maki, vegetable ravioli, chicken meatballs and red bean paste are all carefully prepared by Julie Shen, busy at work behind the large bar. The welcome is warm, and as they say over there before a meal, *Itadakimasu!*

Nabuchodonosor

Traditional ✕

B1

6 av. Bosquet ✉ 75007
✆ 01 45 56 97 26
Fax 01 45 56 98 44
e-mail rousseau.e@wanadoo.fr
www.nabuchodonosor.net

Ⓜ Alma Marceau
Closed 2-25 August,
Saturday lunch and Sunday

Menu €28 (lunch), €32/50 bi (dinner) – Carte €37/66

[A/C]
[VISA]
[MC]

The name refers to the largest sized champagne bottle, an apt metaphor for the aspirations of this elegant restaurant near the Place de l'Alma. The dishes are first rate here, and everything possible is done to make sure you enjoy a great meal. The Nebuchadnezzars sit majestically on the bar, if not on your table. The plush and comfortable setting delights the refined clientele, with its sienna-coloured walls and oak panelling, its spacious and well-laid tables and soft lighting. The chef prepares subtle market-based dishes using various seasonal ingredients from the *terroir*.

Les Olivades

Provence cuisine ✕

B3

41 av. Ségur ✉ 75007
✆ 01 47 83 70 09
Fax 01 42 73 04 75

Ⓜ Ségur
Closed August, Saturday lunch,
Monday lunch, Sunday and public holidays

Menu (€20), €25 (lunch) – Carte €40/53

[A/C]
[VISA]
[MC]
[AE]

This restaurant with a contemporary decor is an ardent champion of the flavours and aromas of southern France. The *Midi* is everywhere, from the olive-oil-based recipes to the beautiful photographs on the walls. But the real proof is in the menu, featuring creamy courgette soup with ratatouille, tuna *pain bagnat*-style, gambas with papaya, peppers, lemon and coriander, and apple tart with *calissons d'Aix* ice cream. The man behind all these appetising creations is Bruno Deligne, a passionate chef who has passed through the kitchens of various top restaurants (Pic, Maximin, Fauchon, Copenhague, the Ritz). The friendly welcome from his charming wife, Chantal, will get your meal off to the perfect start.

Oudino

C3

Traditional ✗

17 r. Oudinot ✉ 75007   Ⓜ Vaneau
☎ 01 45 66 05 09   Closed 9-19 August, 25 December-2 January,
Fax 01 45 66 53 35   Saturday lunch and Sunday
www.oudino.com

Menu € 16 (weekday lunch) – Carte € 26/43

A/C
VISA
MC
OD

The Oudino, an elegant establishment in the government ministry district, has everything it takes to please its regular clientele. The ambiance is stylish yet relaxed and the dining room understated – a streamlined modern replica of an Art Deco bistro (with mirrors, chandeliers, dark wood furniture and ivory walls creating a deeply soothing "yin & yang" effect). The food is made with quality ingredients and keeps up with current trends: dishes like cream of pumpkin soup, swordfish steak and fresh fruit salad in coconut milk follow the seasons, the market and ideas from all over. As a bonus, there are fine wines listed on the blackboard and a friendly welcome that fits in with the restaurant's motto of "making diners feel right at home".

Pasco

B2

Traditional ✗

74 bd La Tour-Maubourg   Ⓜ La Tour Maubourg
✉ 75007   Closed Monday
☎ 01 44 18 33 26 **Fax** 01 44 18 34 06
e-mail restaurant.pasco@wanadoo.fr

Menu (€ 21), € 26 – Carte approx. € 38

Pasco is run by two Pascals! This decisively Mediterranean restaurant grew out of the solid friendship between Pascal Mousset and Pascal Vignes, two professionals who trained at some of the finest establishments. Pasco, which opened in 2003, is just like them – friendly and sincere. Success came instantly to this fun place with a lot going for it: a wood and brick Provençal decor (refined without being stiff), a terrace with a view of the Invalides dome, and an olive oil-based southern French menu featuring vegetables and fish. Not to mention the warm welcome, valet parking and – a rarity in this neighbourhood – very reasonable prices. Definitely a place with a bright future.

Le Perron

D2

Italian 𝒳

6 r. Perronet ✉ 75007
☎ 01 45 44 71 51
Fax 01 45 44 71 51

Ⓜ St-Germain-des-Prés
Closed in August and Sunday

Carte € 36/46

A/C
VISA
MC
AE

Cooking has at least one thing in common with film –
beyond its own borders, it should only be experienced in
the original version! Such is the case at Le Perron, a congenial Italian restaurant that makes no bones about its origins: 100% *tradizionalissima*! That could be the motto of the
chef here, who cooks up traditional recipes from Italy, in
particular from the south – Sardinia, Sicily and the Abruzzi.
In addition to the antipasti, fresh pasta and home-made
desserts, we have a soft spot for the truly "cooked-to-order"
risotti. The dining room is both rustic (stonework, exposed
beams) and intellectual (with its bookcase, a nod to the
publishers and writers who are regulars here).

P'tit Troquet

B2

Traditional 𝒳

28 r. L'Exposition ✉ 75007
☎ 01 47 05 80 39
Fax 01 47 05 80 39

Ⓜ École Militaire
Closed 1st-24 August, Saturday lunch, Monday lunch
and Sunday – Number of covers limited, pre-book

**Menu (€ 20), € 28 (weekday lunch)/32 – Carte approx.
€ 40**

VISA
MC

OK, it's a tiny place, but what atmosphere! The quirky
nostalgia-filled decor celebrates objects picked up over the
years – old advertisements, siphons, coffee pots – all rem-
nants from the 1920s. Not to mention the original zinc
counter, wood panelling and tightly-packed tables. This
charming little "museum" – sure to please the tourists – is
bubbling with life at mealtimes. Regulars enjoy the traditional recipes such as marinated sardine lasagna, fillet
mignon of pork in lemon and honey, stuffed rabbit, and
home-made pastries. And with fast and friendly service, the
staff take good care of them.

Sa Mi In

C3

74 av. Breteuil ✉ 75007
℘ 01 47 34 58 96
Fax 01 47 34 58 96
e-mail han@samiin.com

Ⓜ Sèvres-Lecourbe
Closed Saturday lunch and Sunday lunch

Menu € 15 (weekday lunch), € 30/50 – Carte € 32/91

VISA
MC

This authentic little Korean establishment with its atmosphere of Asian serenity is discreet and refined. The dining room is "zen" without being overly minimalist, with flowers and watercolours creating a delicate aesthetic, contemporary lighting in keeping with the clean lines of the furniture, and beige-moka tones for an intimate feeling, enhanced by the background music. Everything is made to calm the mind. But not the appetite! The menu proposes authentic, original and flavoursome dishes that are little known to Western palates, such as *bulgogi, gyoza, bibimbap*, as well as a vegetarian menu. This charming, friendly place is well worth a visit. You'll have every reason to dream of the sweet land of morning calm – and to believe in it.

Le Soleil

B2

153 r. Grenelle ✉ 75007
℘ 01 45 51 54 12

Ⓜ La Tour Maubourg
Closed August,
Monday lunch and Sunday

Menu € 28/66 bi

A/C
VISA
MC
AE

Le Soleil, owned by Jacques-Louis Vannucci (proprietor of the identically-named restaurant in St-Ouen), is doing rather well at its location in the heart of the distinguished 7th arrondissement. The food and decor celebrate the Mediterranean sea and sun, with terracotta walls, wrought-iron chairs, banquettes and mirrors creating a warm atmosphere. You may even run into some other talented chefs – friends of the owner – who enjoy coming here. But let's get to the point – the flavourful, traditional southern French food that's a treat from start to finish: Sicilian-style seafood fricassee with basil, porcini mushrooms pan-fried in garlic and parsley, *petits farcis niçois* (a speciality), and Corleone-style cannoli (with mascarpone, ricotta, orange blossom and candied fruit).

35° Ouest

Seafood ✗

D2

35 r. Verneuil ✉ 75007
✆ 01 42 86 98 88 **Fax** 01 42 86 00 65
e-mail 35degresouest@orange.fr

Ⓜ Rue du Bac
Closed 3-25 August,
Sunday and Monday

Menu (€30 bi) – Carte €31/94

A/C
🛋
VISA
ⓂⒸ
AE

They specialise in fine seafood at this elegant restaurant, located at 35, rue de Verneuil, opened by the former manager of the Gaya Rive Gauche. The decor is in the current style (tasteful and refined minimalist look in green-grey tones), with sleek tables and a few places at the wooden counter (handy for the 7th arrondissement suit-and-tie clientele, sometimes rather pressed for time). In the kitchen, the chef shows a certain originality. Examples from the short menu include foie gras and smoked eel sushi wrapped in thin sheets of green apple, and pan-fried langoustines and pumpkin with a ginger mousse. The dishes are well-executed and the service is polished; the only downside is the rather steep bill.

Tour Eiffel • École Militaire • Invalides

Champs-Élysées
Concorde · Madeleine

It is rare to come across a Parisian who actually lives in the 8th, as the arrondissement seems almost entirely the preserve of embassies, luxury boutiques and tourism. Bordered by the 9th, the Seine and place de l'Étoile, the district is home to no less than 40 embassies and general consulates, including those of the United States and the People's Republic of China, as well as the Palais de l'Elysée, permanent residence of the president of the French republic. Understandably, business and commerce play an important role in this district which is the location of a record number of corporate headquarters.

To such an extent, that the streets of the 8th, while they might not be the most congested of the city, can boast the highest concentration of luxury cars. No other part of the capital gives such an impression of being a "global metropolis" and the international diplomatic, political and economic vocation of Paris is expressed here visibly, sometimes to excess. The area also boasts a cultural vocation due to monuments that modelled its history: the obelisk of the Concorde, brought back by Napoleon from Egypt and erected on the former place Louis XV, the Grand Palais and its recently restored glass and steel dome roof, and the Arc de Triomphe, of course, built in honour of Napoleon's military victories.

FICTION AND REALITY

It is difficult to do otherwise than start with the Champs-Elysées, the central artery of this arrondissement and claimed by some to be the most beautiful avenue in the world. Real Parisians, not fooled, know that the avenue is also the scene of some of the capital's most unpleasant aspects. It is nonetheless known the world over for its vast quantity of shops and spectacular perspective and it would be ungracious not to admit that the "Triumphal Way" imagined by Le Nôtre under Louis XIV that links the Louvre to the Arche de la Défense today, continues to offer a vista of rare majesty.

Another myth, according to which the entire 8th is a soulless arrondissement devoted to mass tourism and traffic jams, reveals an ignorance of the many authentic Parisian bastions that continue to hold out, hidden between the showy avenues and legions of chain stores. Rue Marbeuf and rue La Boétie, like the tiny alleys around the church of La Madeleine, are home to a plethora of establishments of character that make good food in Paris a genuine way of life.

8TH GASTRONOMIC MARVEL

The gourmet, keen to imprint his or her taste buds with a Parisian experience could do no better

X. Richer / MICHELIN

than choose this district due to its quantity of legendary restaurants. The 8th is home to nearly 25 starred establishments, including a few of the capital's most prestigious three-star restaurants; however a culinary portrait of the 8th would not be complete without a reference to its innumerable luxury hotels and gourmet grocery stores.

To be brief, anyone interested in tasting the best of French cuisine will want to come here. However those who prefer simpler fare should head for the outskirts of the arrondissement and explore its markets: the one in avenue des Batignolles is specialised in organic produce in particular, and the delightful flower market around la Madeleine provides a colourful picture in all seasons.

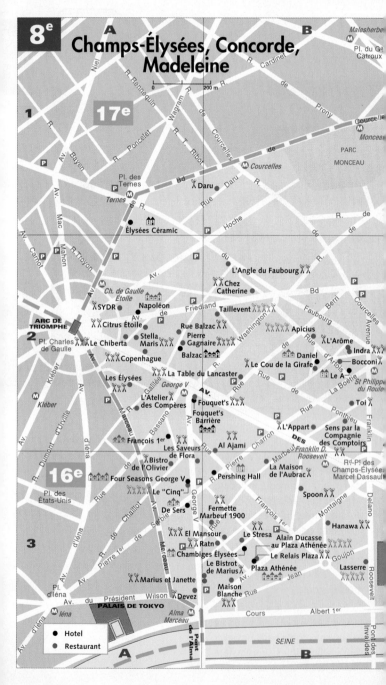

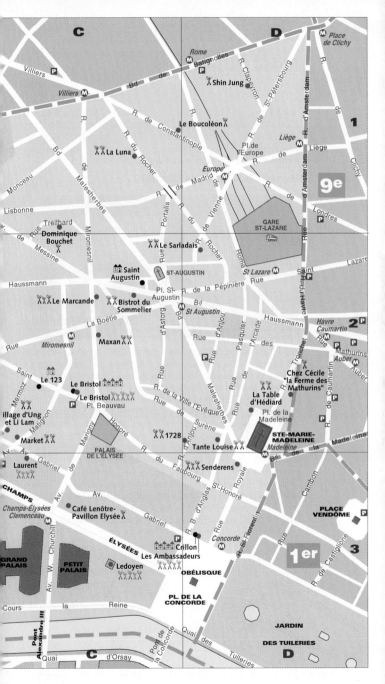

Alain Ducasse au Plaza Athénée ❀❀❀

B3

Innovative XXXXX

Hôtel Plaza Athénée,
25 av. Montaigne ✉ 75008
✆ 01 53 67 65 00
Fax 01 53 67 65 12
e-mail adpa@alain-ducasse.com **www**.alain-ducasse.com

Ⓜ Alma Marceau
Closed 18 July-25 August, 19-30 December,
Monday lunch, Tuesday lunch,
Saturday and Sunday

Menu € 240/340 – Carte € 180/330

A/C
VISA
MC
AE
O

Alain Ducasse au Plaza Athénée

Excellence, tradition, luxury, refinement – that's the Plaza Athénée, the legendary luxury hotel which has dominated the prestigious Avenue Montaigne since 1911. Alain Ducasse commissioned designer Patrick Jouin to give the dining room a new look. He created a "magical and poetic" interior design, "as though the decor had added its own extensions overnight". With its Regency-style furniture, chandelier with thousands of luminous pendants wrapped in metallic organza, ceiling painted in gold leaf and light tones, the result is a perfect match for the classical yet contemporary cuisine. Not to mention the totem at the entrance inscribed with pithy culinary expressions (here, "we struggle, we tie, we assemble, we dice, we chop, we slice, we coat in breadcrumbs, we gut"). The cuisine celebrates precision and hard work, both qualities clearly exhibited by chef Christophe Moret. His fine-tuned cooking is presented on a straightforward menu featuring seasonal and traditional specialities, enhanced by an amazing choice of fine wines from around the world.

First Course

- Légumes et fruits cuits/crus, marmelade tomato/truffe.
- Saint-Jacques snackées coco/curry.

Main Course

- Bar de ligne agrumes/poivres, vert et blanc de blette.
- Pigeonneau rôti, garniture d'une diable, pommes gaufrettes.

Dessert

- Fraises des bois en coupe glacée, sablé coco.
- Caillé de brebis, caramel-poivre, miel d'arbousier.

Les Ambassadeurs ✿✿

D3

Hôtel Crillon,
10 pl. Concorde ✉ 75008
☎ 01 44 71 16 16 **Fax** 01 44 71 15 02
e-mail restaurants@crillon.com **www**.crillon.com

Ⓜ Concorde
Closed August, 1st-8 January,
Sunday and Monday

Menu €75 (weekday lunch)/200 – Carte €156/275

Philippe Forestier

CHAMPS-ÉLYSÉES • CONCORDE • MADELEINE

Jean-François Piège, the chef at Les Ambassadeurs since 2004, likes to take liberties with high culinary tradition. Combining classicism and modernity, he has taken a new look at the fundamentals of top-flight cuisine. He has no desire to be deferential, but he does have technical mastery and a love of fine ingredients. This Ducasse disciple, who as a child dreamed of being a gardener, has breathed new life and inventiveness into the kitchens of the Crillon. "Preserving the flavour of the produce and giving it the taste of memory" sums up his philosophy, reflecting the refined and playful dishes he creates. Things seem to be in perpetual motion here, with a decidedly short menu and matching cellar. Highlighting the food, the decor in this 18th century former ballroom fits right in with the chef's style. A new contemporary look features light tones that match the Sienna marble, and clever lighting at dinnertime, while the impeccable service worthy of a luxury hotel and the hushed, somewhat affected atmosphere create a theatrical effect.

First Course	*Main Course*	*Dessert*
• Blanc à manger d'œuf, truffe noire (January-March).	• Bar de ligne, tapioca d'huître, fleur-feuille de bourrache.	• "Paquet gâteau" à manger, chocolat, banane.
• Saint-Jacques comme une tarte flambée, cuite, marinée.	• Ris de veau blanc/brun, spaghetti carbonara.	• Poire belle-Hélène version 2006.

Apicius ✿ ✿

Innovative XXXXX

B2

20 rue d'Artois ✉ 75008
✆ 01 43 80 19 66 **Fax** 01 44 40 09 57
e-mail restaurant-apicius@wanadoo.fr
www.restaurant-apicius.com

Ⓜ St-Philippe-du-Roule
Closed August, Saturday,
Sunday and public holidays

Menu € 150 (lunch), € 160/180 – Carte € 89/166

Apicius

Jean-Pierre Vigato, a chef for over forty years, has proven that training with great cooks is not the only way to make it to the top. Self-taught, he has conquered even the most blasé diners through his straightforward "cuisine vérité" (i.e. authentic) with a personal touch, spotlighting ingredients – he has a penchant for "plats canaille" (hearty dishes) – and bourgeois cooking, contrary to a certain modernist trend. In 2004, Apicius (named in honour of a Roman Epicurian said to have written the first cookbook) was opened on the ground floor of a listed town-house with the impressive look of a small palace – with a fine garden. Although the space is superlatively ample (with three successive dining rooms on the garden side and two more rooms on the other side), the atmosphere remains relaxed. The service contributes greatly to that feeling, as does the decor featuring theatre chandeliers, antique objects, niches adorned with huge bouquets, colourful tableware, a bar with antique columns, and cherubs on the ceiling. So is it old-style, Rococo, contemporary or trendy? It's all that, and the effect is stunning!

First Course	*Main Course*	*Dessert*
• Foie gras de canard poêlé "classique Apicius". • Déclinaison sur le thème de la langoustine.	• Tête de veau, langue et cervelle ravigotées. • Saint-Pierre grillé sur la peau, pâtes en risotto d'anchois.	• Soufflé au chocolat noir et chantilly sans sucre. • Grand dessert "tout caramel".

Le Bristol ❀ ❀

Innovative XXXXX

C2

Hôtel Bristol,   Ⓜ Miromesnil
112 r. Fg St-Honoré ✉ 75008
✆ 01 53 43 43 00 **Fax** 01 53 43 43 01
e-mail resa@lebristolparis.com **www.**lebristolparis.com

Menu €95 (lunch)/210 – Carte €118/222

Le Bristol

The distinctive feature of this ultra-classic luxury hotel? Its restaurant, where you can eat in one of two dining rooms, depending on the season. The oval winter dining room (built over the ruins of a private theatre) exudes old-fashioned luxury with its sculpted Regency panelling in Hungarian oak, gold leaf ceiling, paintings, tapestries and Baccarat crystal chandeliers. The airy summer restaurant is in a French-style garden inside the hotel with a terrace and tables set up by a lawn – a true haven of peace. The decor boasts chairs with light fabrics, canopies and striped draperies in a range of beige, green and red tones.In the kitchen, chef Éric Fréchon – winner of the Meilleur Ouvrier de France award and a brilliant sauce-maker – presides masterfully over his brigade. While he remains within the mainstream culinary tradition, highlighting superb ingredients from the terroir, he also likes to rework the classics in a more creative way – whatever the season.

First Course	Main Course	Dessert
• Macaroni farcis, truffe noire, artichaut et foie gras de canard, gratinés au parmesan.	• Merlan de ligne en croûte de pain aux amandes, tétragone mi-cuite, huile de péquillos.	• fraises des bois, crème brulée citronnelle, allumettes crousti-fondantes.
• Œuf de poule cuit en coque, goût de morilles et air d'amaretto.	• Poularde de Bresse cuite en vessie aux écrevisses, royale d'abats et morilles.	• Crèmeux noir, sablé croquant, noisette torréfiée, glace café, émulsion caramel.

171

Pierre Gagnaire ✿✿✿

Innovative XXXX

6 r. Balzac ✉ 75008
✆ 01 58 36 12 50
Fax 01 58 36 12 51
e-mail p.gagnaire@wanadoo.fr
www.pierre-gagnaire.com

Ⓜ George V
Closed 2-22 August, 22 December-4 January,
Sunday lunch and Saturday

Menu €95 (weekday lunch), €250/350 – Carte €230/449

A/C

VISA
MC
AE
①

Pierre Gagnaire

An "overbooked" chef who juggles establishments in Paris, London and Tokyo, Pierre Gagnaire is a trailblazer. His inventive, passionate and excessive cooking is like no one else's. This talented "tightrope walker" – and lover of jazz music and contemporary art – is always open to new things. For Gagnaire, excellence is all in the details. But he also knows when to stop. "I try to streamline and avoid false good ideas," he says. He never writes down his recipes, but composes a menu that resembles a poem, triggering your imagination and thrilling your appetite before the meal has even begun. Get ready for a dinner fit for a king – a festival of flavours for all the senses! The avalanche of dishes awaiting you demands only curiosity and an open mind on your part. The tastefully modern decor is refined and discreet, a perfect match with the thoughtful service.

First Course	*Main Course*	*Dessert*
• Langoustines de quatre façons.	• Pièce d'agneau de Lozère.	• Grand dessert Pierre Gagnaire.
• L'insolite.	• Tronçon de gros turbot rôti à l'arête.	• Soufflé caramel et angélique.

Le "Cinq" ✿✿

A3

Hôtel Four Seasons George V,   Ⓜ George V
31 av. George V ✉ 75008
✆ 01 49 52 71 54 **Fax** 01 49 52 71 81
e-mail par.lecinq@fourseasons.com **www**.fourseasons.com

Menu €75 (lunch), €135/210 – Carte €136/360

A/C
🛏
☞
VISA
MC
AE
①
🐾

Le "Cinq"

CHAMPS-ÉLYSÉES • CONCORDE • MADELEINE

Any self-respecting luxury hotel has got to have the best. Including this restaurant at the Hôtel Georges V, which has the art of making the everyday seem exceptional, and vice versa. Since reopening, Le Cinq has been a brilliant success thanks in part to its magnificent Louis XVI dining room that was given a complete facelift by architect Pierre-Yves Rochon. This is French elegance and splendour at its finest, with lofty columns, huge crystal chandelier, mouldings, paintings, high sprays of flowers and palm trees, and comfortably spaced tables – all in well-matched shades of ivory, gold and grey and bathed in soft lighting from the inner garden. The cuisine reflects the same sense of refinement. Drawing upon traditional French culinary techniques, it will satisfy the most discriminating palates with classic dishes offering sublime, harmoniously-paired flavours. The best ingredients, an outstanding cellar and a staff led by Éric Beaumard (one of the best restaurant directors in France) – the essence of luxury.

First Course	*Main Course*	*Dessert*
• Tarialini à la fonduta et à la truffe d'Alba (October-December).	• Turbot de ligne rôti aux oignons doux et au pralin.	• Millefeuille allégé à la vanille bourbon rafraîchi aux kumquats.
• Poireau cuit à la ficelle aux saveurs d'hiver et à la truffe noire (December-March).	• Poularde de Bresse et homard Georges V en cocotte lutée.	• Soufflé au chocolat Caraïbes, glace au poivre sauvage.

Lasserre ✿ ✿

Traditional XXXXX

17 av. F.-D.-Roosevelt
✉ 75008
✆ 01 43 59 53 43
Fax 01 45 63 72 23
e-mail lasserre@lasserre.fr **www**.restaurant-lasserre.com

Ⓜ Franklin D. Roosevelt
Closed August, Saturday lunchtime, Monday lunchtime,
Tuesday lunchtime, Wednesday lunchtime and Sunday

Menu € 75 (lunch)/185 – Carte € 125/233

A/C

VISA
MC
AE

Lasserre

René Lasserre, who died in 2006, came to Paris as an adolescent to learn the business and turned his restaurant into one of the most prestigious establishments in the capital. The delightfully retro decor in this small Directoire townhouse near the Champs-Élysées is unforgettable. The first floor dining room boasts a roof that opens up to the Paris sky, illuminating the tables throughout the seasons. Other features adding to the carefully preserved magic are the central space surrounded by pillars, window boxes full of orchids and greenery, silver tableware and baubles, and Chinese porcelain under a ceiling of dancers painted by Touchagues. As for the cuisine, the Lasserre legend continues under the guidance of chef Jean-Louis Nomicos, who was formerly with Ducasse and at starred restaurants on the Riviera. The house's emblematic dishes – superbly classical – are still a given, sharing the billing nowadays with more up-to-date creations with a Mediterranean touch, bringing a bit of the sunny south to the Champs Elysées!

First Course	Main Course	Dessert
• Macaroni aux truffes noires et foie gras.	• Pigeon André Malraux.	• Tarte soufflée au chocolat.
• Langouste à la parisienne.	• Turbot aux cèpes et échalotes, palourdes gratinées (September-October).	• Timbale Elysée Lasserre.

Ledoyen ✿✿✿

Innovative XXXXX

C3

carré Champs-Élysées
✉ 75008
✆ 01 53 05 10 01 **Fax** 01 47 42 55 01
e-mail pavillon.ledoyen@ledoyen.com
www.ledoyen.com

Ⓜ Champs Élysées Clemenceau
Closed 2-24 August, Monday lunch,
Saturday and Sunday

Menu €88 (lunch), €198/284 bi – Carte €149/227

A/C

P

VISA

MC

AE

Ledoyen

Ledoyen, the legendary Parisian restaurant, has been totally rejuvenated and has regained its prestige thanks to Christian Le Squer, the discreet but ever-so-inventive chef. This neo-Classical establishment dating back to 1848 is now one of the stars, offering an exceptional meal in an exceptional setting a stone's throw from the Champs-Élysées, yet far from the madding crowd. The 18th century tavern run by a caterer named Doyen is only a memory now, covered over by Hittorff's Second Empire architecture, with an entrance awning, columns, light wood panelling, old paintings, Napoleon III trimmings and furnishings in a luxurious decor opening onto the garden. Everything exudes refinement, including the well-orchestrated service and the superb and masterful cuisine presenting an original and varied menu (part-classical, part-modern). The subtle "from land and sea" dishes betray the chef's Breton origins, while the wines are always well-paired. In short, a sure bet. Extremely sure.

First Course

- Grosses langoustines bretonnes, émulsion d'agrumes.
- Araignée de mer rafraîchie d'une émulsion crémeuse liée de corail.

Main Course

- Blanc de turbot de ligne braisé, pommes rattes truffées.
- Ris de veau en brochette de bois de citronnelle, jus d'herbes.

Dessert

- Le "Grand Dessert Ledoyen" en cinq compositions.
- Croquant de pamplemousse cuit et cru au citron vert.

Taillevent ✿ ✿

Classic 🗶🗶🗶🗶🗶

B2

15 r. Lamennais
✉ **75008**
☎ 01 44 95 15 01
Fax 01 42 25 95 18
e-mail mail@taillevent.com **www**.taillevent.com

Ⓜ **Charles de Gaulle-Étoile**
Closed 26 July-25 August, Saturday, Sunday and holidays
Number of covers limited, pre-book

Menu €70 (lunch), €140/190 – Carte €116/204

A/C

VISA
Ⓜ©
AE
Ⓓ

Taillevent

This establishment, which needs no introduction, is proud of its traditions. To begin with, its owners, the Vrinat family, who for three generations have built its reputation as a leading restaurant. Then there's the name – from the author of the *Viandier*, the first recipe book published in France (in about 1379). And finally the decor, in this (19th century) former townhouse of the Duc de Morny, with its dining rooms on two floors, and hushed classical setting conducive to political meetings and business lunches. The soft lighting and shades of brown, red and beige create an intimate atmosphere, embellished in 2004 by the addition of contemporary artwork. A way of connecting with the times – like chef Alain Solivérès, who blends old and new, and up-to-date Mediterranean touches with haute cuisine recipes. The icing on the cake? The Taillevent cellar, among the finest in the city with its plethora of rare (and expensive) wines.

First Course	*Main Course*	*Dessert*
• Rémoulade de tourteau à l'aneth. • Épeautre du pays de Sault en risotto, homard et curry.	• Saint-Pierre aux coquillages, huile d'argan et citron confit. • Foie gras de canard au banyuls, fruits et légumes caramélisés.	• Tarte renversée au chocolat et au café grillé. • Trilogie gourmande.

Laurent ⣐

Contemporary 𝕏𝕏𝕏𝕏

C3

41 av. Gabriel
✉ 75008
☏ 01 42 25 00 39
Fax 01 45 62 45 21
e-mail info@le-laurent.com **www**.le-laurent.com

Ⓜ Champs Élysées Clemenceau
Closed 25 December-2 January,
Saturday lunch, Sunday and public holidays

Menu € 80/160 – Carte € 130/216

Laurent

No one really knows why the name of Mr. Laurent, who acquired the restaurant in1860, is the one that stuck. The former Café du Cirque was designed by Hittorff – who also built Ledoyen – in 1842. It's all part of the legend at this venerable establishment located in the gardens of the Rond-Point des Champs-Elysées. Whether a hunting lodge belonging to Louis XIV or an open-air café during the Revolution – the legend varies on this point too – Laurent has preserved the traditional neo-classical setting that was in vogue when it first opened. The pilasters, columns, pediments and antique capitals blend in with comfortable banquettes to create the (somewhat old-fashioned) charm and elegance of the dining rooms and private salons. Alain Pégouret's classic cuisine matches this setting to perfection, respecting and enhancing the codes of the French culinary tradition. No wonder Paris' top politicians and businessmen are so fond of dining here, especially in fine weather on the terrace overlooking the garden. A very special place indeed.

First Course

- Araignée de mer dans ses sucs en gelée, crème de fenouil.
- Foie gras de canard grillé, posé sur une "cracotte".

Main Course

- Flanchet de veau braisé, blettes à la mœlle et au jus.
- Suprêmes de pigeon caramélisés d'une mignonnette d'épices.

Dessert

- Canon de chocolat noir cacahuèté, crème glacée au baileys.
- Soufflé chaud au thym citron.

Le Chiberta ✿

Innovative XXX

A2

3 r. Arsène-Houssaye
✉ 75008
✆ 01 53 53 42 00
Fax 01 45 62 85 08
e-mail chiberta@guysavoy.com **www**.lechiberta.com

Ⓜ Charles de Gaulle-Étoile
Closed 2-24 August,
Saturday lunch and Sunday

Menu €60/100 – Carte €73/120

A/C

▢

VISA

Ⓜ©

AE

Ⓞ

Stevens Fremont

Guy Savoy's Le Chiberta has adopted black as its colour, wine as its symbol and inventiveness as its main culinary theme. The soft, quiet and discreet atmosphere envelops you the minute you walk in – perfect for business lunches and more private occasions. The strikingly minimalist – almost radically austere – dining rooms, lounge and bar designed by architect Jean-Michel Wilmotte are in reality discreet and stylish. The "vertical wine cellar" remains the most original feature here, with vintage bottles decorating the walls like works of art or books in a library. Abstract modern paintings between the lines of bottles add a sudden note of colour to a space dominated by wood and slate tones. Although you can have a snack at the bar, a table gives a better taste of the cuisine – supervised by the "boss" – featuring delightfully updated traditional dishes. Other important things to know: the market-based menu changes daily, the service is flawless, and the cellar is naturally first rate.

First Course

- Crème de carottes citronnelle-gingembre, langoustines éclatées.
- Terrine de foie gras et canette de challans.

Main Course

- Côte de Bœuf Hereford rôtie, sabayon ciboulette.
- Saint-Pierre rôti au bois de fenouil, tian de légumes.

Dessert

- Mœlleux guanaja au pralin feuilleté.
- Soufflé à la châtaigne, sorbet chartreuse verte.

Copenhague ✿

Scandinavian XXX

A2

142 av. Champs-Élysées ✉ 75008
☎ 01 44 13 86 26 **Fax** 01 58 05 44 98
e-mail reservation.copenhague@blanc.net
www.floradanica-paris.com

Ⓜ George V
Closed 2-24 August, Saturday,
Sunday and public holidays

Menu €50 (lunch), €69/109 – Carte €74/115

Copenhague

The Maison du Danemark has always been a favourite haunt of fans of the "exotic North". This culinary ambassador on the Champs-Élysées has provided incomparable Franco-Danish creations since 1955. Georges Landriot's menu spotlights fish, with salmon (a must!) in the forefront. Two kinds of ambiance are offered – for serious dinners or relaxed lunches, depending on how you feel. For the gourmet option, head for the Copenhague (upstairs), where a large portrait of Queen Margaret welcomes guests. The decor is streamlined without excess (tasteful furniture offset by red leather chairs and a large bay window overlooking a terrace), perfect for an intimate meal featuring Baltic flavours accompanied by a choice of Danish beers, vodkas and aquavit. More intimate and convivial, Flora Danica boasts a contemporary Scandinavian aesthetic with cosy banquettes, subdued lighting from original lamps, and hanging gardens – a design from a cool climate that won't leave you cold.

First Course

- Foie gras poché à la bière.
- Blinis servis selon la tradition scandinave au saumon fumé sauvage de la mer Baltique.

Main Course

- Cabillaud rôti et braisé au fumet de palourdes, émulsion aux coquillages.
- Renne légèrement fumé et rôti, champignons, légumes et fruits de saison.

Dessert

- Riz gonflé au lait cannelle-vanille, lait d'amande glacé.
- Le chocolat en soufflé, quelques arachides salées et givrées.

El Mansour

B3

7 r. Trémoille ✉ 75008
✆ 01 47 23 88 18
Fax 01 40 70 13 53

Ⓜ Alma Marceau
Closed Monday lunch and Sunday

Carte €43/69

Ⓐ/Ⓒ
VISA
Ⓜ/Ⓒ
ⒶⒺ
Ⓞ

An elegant establishment in the Golden Triangle which cultivates the art of North African hospitality, with a decor worthy of the finest restaurants in Casablanca – oak wood panelling, sofas, large tables, lovely tableware, velvet armchairs – and discreet and efficient service. Chef Mohamed Ezzyat knows Moroccan gastronomy like the back of his hand (he trained at La Mamounia in Marrakech). The dishes include traditional *pastillas, tajines* and couscous, all well-prepared and generously served. And the extra touch? They serve the couscous on a little side table, an original and much appreciated gesture. The short wine list has a few sunny North African vintages.

Fouquet's

A2

99 av. Champs Élysées ✉ 75008
✆ 01 40 69 60 50 **Fax** 01 40 69 60 35
e-mail fouquets@lucienbarriere.com **www.**lucienbarriere.com

Ⓜ George V

Menu €78 – Carte €60/142

🏠
🛗
VISA
Ⓜ/Ⓒ
ⒶⒺ
Ⓞ

From the beginning it has hosted the winners of the Molières and Césars awards; and every year the Jean Gabin, Romy Schneider, Louis Delluc and Marcel Pagnol Prizes are awarded here. As early as 1914, young aviators came here to celebrate their exploits at the Bar de l'Escadrille. The famous sidewalk terrace on the "most beautiful avenue in the world" has been a meeting point for the Parisian smart set since time immemorial. Fouquet's is a legendary place, a luxury brasserie which people visit as they would the Eiffel Tower when in Paris. Renovated by Jacques Garcia in 1999, its beautiful interior, on the list of Historic Monuments, attracts prestigious and unknown patrons from around the world. An emblematic venue in the capital.

Les Élysées ❀ ❀

Innovative 🗙🗙🗙

Hôtel Vernet,
25 r. Vernet ✉ 75008
☎ 01 44 31 98 98
Fax 01 44 31 85 69
e-mail elysees@hotelvernet.com **www.**hotelvernet.com

Ⓜ Charles de Gaulle-Étoile
Closed 26 July-25 August,
Monday lunch, Saturday and Sunday

Menu €64 (lunch), €105/140 – Carte €102/159

A/C

VISA
MC
AE
①

Les Élysées

To reach the sumptuous dining room at Les Élysées, first you walk through the lobby of the Hotel Vernet, then across a small lounge with antique furniture and orchid floral displays. The dazzling space is illuminated by the eye-catching glass roof with a metallic structure designed by Gustave Eiffel. The beauty alone of this hidden treasure in the 8th arrondissement is worth the detour. The decor – a happy blend of traditional and modern – highlights comfort and intimacy, with spacious round tables, raspberry-coloured velvet chairs and modern canvasses on the walls and light parquet floors. The same refinement is evident in the cuisine prepared by Éric Briffard, a Robuchon disciple. This highly skilful chef (Meilleur Ouvrier de France award) is not inclined to follow culinary fashions, preferring – like all the best chefs – to create his own signature dishes. And, while respecting the past, he also unleashes his creativity by reinterpreting tradition. Diners on a tight schedule will be delighted to know that, upon request, everything on the menu can be served in exactly one hour.

First Course

- Girolles de Sologne en fricassée aux abricots et pointes d'asperge, croustille d'œuf mollet.
- Tourteau breton, pétales de daïkon marinés au miel-épices.

Main Course

- Tronçon de turbot sauvage breton cuit au plat, ragoût de cocos paimpolais.
- Épaule d'agneau de Lozère fondante à l'orientale.

Dessert

- Chocolat noir grand cru Saint-Domingue, tarte fine au romarin, sorbet chocolat.
- Fruits rouges gelée d'hibiscus.

Indra

Indian 🍴🍴🍴

10 r. Cdt-Rivière ✉ 75008
☎ 01 43 59 46 40
Fax 01 42 25 70 32
e-mail toutounat@wanadoo.fr **www**.restaurant-indra.com

Ⓜ St-Philippe-du-Roule
Closed Saturday lunchtime and Sunday

Menu €40 (lunch), €44/65 – Carte €40/59

A/C
VISA
MC
AE
DC

In 1976, talented and visionary businessman Yogen Gupta opened one of the first Indian restaurants in the land of foie gras and baguettes. Today it is as magical as ever. The secret? A refined decor with just the right touch of the exotic – patchwork quilts on the walls, finely sculpted wood panelling, well-laid-out tables and large mirrors. The kitchen adapts to Western palates while respecting Hindu gastronomic traditions. Northern India is particularly well-represented, as flavours from the South are considered more powerful. For the full experience, try the *thali* – a meal in itself served on a silver platter – to satisfy your food-lover's curiosity!

Maison Blanche

Innovative 🍴🍴🍴

15 av. Montaigne ✉ 75008
☎ 01 47 23 55 99
Fax 01 47 20 09 56
e-mail info@maison-blanche.fr **www**.maison-blanche.fr

Ⓜ Alma Marceau
Closed Saturday lunch and Sunday lunch

Menu (€30), €55 bi (lunch)/65 bi (lunch) – Carte €77/139

A/C
VISA
MC
AE
DC

The Pourcel Brothers' Parisian establishment boasts an absolutely grandiose setting. Like a cube placed on the roof of the Théâtre des Champs-Élysées, the restaurant appears to be looking out at the dome of Les Invalides and off to the West of the city through its huge windows. The view of the Eiffel Tower from the terrace is stunning, and everywhere you look in this ultra-contemporary duplex loft is a feast for the eyes! Nestled in one of the alcove-banquettes or up on the mezzanine, one never tires of the show. The chic brasserie food reflects the twins' native Languedoc. Excellent choice of wines.

Le Marcande

Classic ✗✗✗

C2

52 r. Miromesnil ✉ 75008
℘ 01 42 65 19 14
Fax 01 42 65 76 85
e-mail info@marcande.com
www.marcande.com

Ⓜ Miromesnil
Closed 11-25 August, 24 December-5 January,
Friday dinner from October to April,
Saturday except dinner from
May to September and Sunday

Menu €35/41 – Carte €54/83

VISA
ⓂⒸ
ⒶⒺ

The delicious patio-terrace nestled in this restaurant is a rarity in Paris. A few seconds are all it takes to forget the hustle and bustle of the city in this oasis of calm where flowers, ivy and bamboo blend in with the sound of a murmuring fountain. If the sun is conspicuous by its absence, not to worry – it forms a well of light, bathing the two part-traditional, part-contemporary dining rooms in an amazing clarity. Stéphane Ruel, who has run the kitchen since 2003, masterfully prepares traditional recipes such as pikeperch *en meurette, entrecôte marchand de vin,* and five-pepper duck breast. Follow the excellent advice of sommelier and proprietor Emmanuel Cazaux in choosing your wine.

Al Ajami

Lebanese ✗✗

B2

58 r. François 1ᵉʳ ✉ 75008
℘ 01 42 25 38 44 **Fax** 01 42 25 38 39
e-mail ajami@free.fr **www**.ajami.com

Ⓜ George V

Menu (€19), €25 (weekdays)/46 – Carte €36/61

Ⓐ/Ⓒ
VISA
ⓂⒸ
Ⓘ

Tourists from the Middle East, Parisians of Lebanese origin and businessmen from the city make up the clientele of this restaurant on the corner of rue François 1ᵉʳ and rue Lincoln. This ambassador of traditional Lebanese cuisine is a Parisian offshoot of an establishment created in Beirut in the 1920s, with branches around the world. The decor is also inspired by the Land of Cedars, with its Middle Eastern objects, vases, watercolours, wood panelling, purple-and-gold striped wallpaper, comfortable sofas, soft cushions and background music. Professional service and family hospitality. Try the tasting menu with its assortment of fragrant and flavoursome dishes.

Senderens ✿✿

9 pl. Madeleine ✉ 75008
✆ 01 42 65 22 90 **Fax** 01 42 65 06 23
e-mail restaurant@senderens.fr
www.senderens.fr

Ⓜ Madeleine
Closed 3-25 August

Carte €72/91

A/C
VISA
Ⓜ©
AE
Ⓞ

Roberto Frankenberg

This institution on the Place de la Madeleine has indeed changed. For the record, the Lucas-Carton establishment, which opened in 1925, became Senderens in 2005.Neither bistro nor brasserie, it is a more relaxed kind of gourmet restaurant, with an unusual look that blends retro and futurist. Imagine the listed turn-of-the-century Majorelle wood panelling sharing the billing with curved ceiling fixtures bathing the ground floor dining room in soft lighting; the tables, while chairs and banquettes assert their contemporary style in shades of grey, white and beige. Without so much as a glance back at the past, Senderens is a chef who is in sync with the times, as illustrated by his young waitstaff, the less grave service, and his mindset in the kitchen. The chef has opted for simpler ingredients (thus a considerably reduced bill for diners), well-paired wines and various options for your meal, including creative preparations and an eclectic menu at the bar (tapas, sushis, etc.). For all tastes.

First Course

- Foie gras de canard rôti, salade de figues, éclats d'amande.
- Langoustines croustillantes, chou pak-choï, coriandre et livèche.

Main Course

- Suprême de pigeon rôtis, cuisses en pastilla, navets caramélisés
- Agneau de lait de Castille, péquillos et cocos.

Dessert

- Mille-feuille à la vanille de Tahiti.
- Tarte tatin aux coings, glace séchouan et orange (autumn-winter).

Stella Maris ✿

Contemporary 🗙🗙🗙

A2

4 r. Arsène Houssaye
✉ 75008
☎ 01 42 89 16 22
Fax 01 42 89 16 01
e-mail stella.maris.paris@wanadoo.fr **www.**stellamaris.com

Ⓜ Charles de Gaulle-Étoile
Closed 10-24 August, Saturday lunch,
Sunday and lunch on public holidays

Menu € 49 (lunch), € 99/130 – Carte € 112/156

A/C
VISA
MC
AE
DC

Stella Maris

CHAMPS-ÉLYSÉES • CONCORDE • MADELEINE

The man behind Stella Maris is Tateru Yoshino, a Japanese chef who fell in love with French gastronomy and has devoted himself to it ever since. He came to France in 1979 to learn the ins and outs of French cooking at all the right places, in particular with Robuchon and Troisgros. A devotee of the pure French tradition, he became its ambassador at two establishments in the Land of the Rising Sun, including his first Stella Maris in Odawara. His countrymen were soon won over by his remarkable approach. In 1997 he settled in Paris and took over the former Vancouver restaurant. It is an extremely refined place, at the crossroads of two cultures. The streamlined decor combines Art Deco style with a spacious modern-looking room done in a Zen spirit (long lamps hanging from the high ceiling, discreet flowers, tableware designed by Tateru and his wife, small mezzanine room). Needless to say, the cuisine exudes talent and subtlety. Both precise and original, it features the most natural of ingredients and strives to find the best-matched flavours – in the most delicate possible way.

First Course

- Duo de foie gras de canard, au torchon et mariné aux fruits secs.
- Huîtres en gelée au vin blanc et cresson.

Main Course

- Saumon mi-cuit à l'émulsion de pois gourmand.
- Tête de veau en cocotte, crête de coq, œuf frit, jus en tortue.

Dessert

- Mont-Blanc maison, quatre-quarts aux marrons glacés, glace à la vanille de Madagascar.
- Streuzel de mousse au chocolat des Caraïbes, sauce praliné.

La Table du Lancaster ✿

Contemporary XXX

Hôtel Lancaster,
7 r. Berri ✉ 75008
✆ 01 40 76 40 18 **Fax** 01 40 76 40 00
e-mail restaurant@hotel-lancaster.fr **www**.hotel-lancaster.fr

Ⓜ George V
Closed Saturday lunch

Menu €52 (weekday lunch)/120 – Carte €73/132

La Table du Lancaster

Ⓓ Could the owners of the Lancaster be visionaries? Well, they're certainly clever to have asked Michel Troisgros to run their restaurant, to which he has added a nice touch of vitality and a bit of the exotic. The "Master of Roanne" put together a free-wheeling menu influenced by his travels (to Asia, Russia, and the United States), then passed the baton on to Fabrice Salvador for the execution phase. The original menu spotlights themes and ingredients chosen according to the sensations they provide: "the sharpness of lemons and citrus fruit", "the greenery of veg-etables, herbs and fruits", the "spirit of the tomato" and "the lactic bite of dairy products". It's a whole new vocabulary for the senses. The new flavours go hand in hand with a new ambience for this hotel restaurant that is no longer restricted to guests staying here. The elegant room is a mixture of French-style luxury and the current cosmopolitan look (clean lines, Chinese engrav-ings). Don't forget to take at least a quick look at the Zen-style garden-courtyard with its amazing chic minimalism beautifully offsetting the red decor with green vegetation.

First Course

- Melba de Saint-Jacques à l'écorce de yuzu.
- Cuisses de grenouilles au tamarin, chou-fleur en copeaux.

Main Course

- Pièce de thon au ponzu, sur un riz "koshi hikari".
- Pigeon et pamplemousse frits comme un beignet.

Dessert

- Soufflé au citron vert et sirop au miel d'acacia.
- Tartelette au chocolat et noisettes, glace à l'huile de noisette.

L'Angle du Faubourg ✿

Contemporary ✗✗

B2

195 r. Fg St-Honoré ✉ 75008 — **Ⓜ Ternes**
✆ 01 40 74 20 20
Fax 01 40 74 20 21
e-mail angledufaubourg@cavestaillevent.com
www.angledufaubourg.com

Closed 26 July-25 August, Saturday,
Sunday and public holidays

Menu € 35/70 (dinner) – Carte € 45/71

A/C
VISA
MC
AE
①
✿

L'Angle du Faubourg

This Taillevent annex on the corner of Rue du Faubourg St-Honoré and Rue Balzac – next to its famous Caves – boasts a much more contemporary style than the "main branch", more a place for big occasions. You are sure to feel right at home in its neither too modern nor too classic decor with a discreet and comfortable dining room featuring red ochre walls embellished by contemporary paintings. The friendly service maintains the same high standards, working with remarkable thoughtfulness and precision. The dishes are classic, colourful and full of flavour – in tune with the times. And they are paired to perfection with the divine wine list, the most obvious asset of this Angle. The selection of wines comes from Languedoc, the rest of France and all over the world. The fine bottles – many of them available by the glass – are just waiting to be brought to you by the sommelière, who will share her knowledge and passion to help you find the best gourmet pairings.

First Course	Main Course	Dessert
• Tarte à la tomate au pistou.	• Turbot rôti, barigoule de légumes.	• Macaron au café et à la noisette.
• Sablé de thon aux épices.	• Râble de lapin rôti à la marjolaine.	• Cannelloni au citron, sorbet basilic.

Bistrot du Sommelier

C2

97 bd Haussmann ⊠ 75008
℘ 01 42 65 24 85
Fax 01 53 75 23 23
e-mail bistrot-du-sommelier@noos.fr
www.bistrotdusommelier.com

Ⓜ St-Augustin
Closed 25 July-24 August, 24 December-
5 January, Saturday and Sunday

Menu (€ 32), € 39 (lunch), € 60 bi/100 bi – Carte € 47/56

A/C
⟨⟩
VISA
MC
AE
&

It could also be called the Bistrot With the World's Best Sommelier, 1992 vintage, the title awarded at this prestigious contest's seventh ceremony to Philippe Faure-Brac, who has run this restaurant for the past 20 years. It is a true pleasure to taste the wine and food pairings invented by this sommelier and his chef partner, Jean-André Lallican, in the comfortable dining room and decor entirely devoted to Bacchus, with a convivial atmosphere and superb cellar with a host of labels. Winemakers' Fridays (*vendredis du vigneron*) are the latest concept, where proprietors present their estates and wines at thematic wine tasting-meals, an approach which is both gastronomic and educational.

Chez Catherine

B2

3 r. Berryer ⊠ 75008
℘ 01 40 76 01 40
Fax 01 40 76 03 96

Ⓜ George V
Closed Saturday,
Sunday and public holidays

Menu (€ 43), € 49

A/C
VISA
MC
AE
Ⓓ

Two olive trees and the pretty white façade tell you that you have arrived Chez Catherine. But don't bother looking for her when you walk in. She'll be in the kitchen, busy cooking up one of her specialities (*petits farcis niçois, pressé de foie gras* with crabmeat, duck breast with spices, baked tuna with dried fruits) or creating her "surprise menu". To try it out, have a seat in one of the two chic and modern dining rooms featuring pearl grey walls, contemporary paintings, velvet armchairs, a glass partition and a view into the kitchen. Follow the sommelier's advice in choosing a bottle from the excellent selection of French wines in the cellar.

Citrus Étoile

Contemporary 🍴🍴

A2

6 r. Arsène-Houssaye
✉ 75008
✆ 01 42 89 15 51
Fax 01 42 89 28 67
e-mail info@citrusetoile.fr **www**.citrusetoile.fr

Ⓜ Charles de Gaulle-Étoile
Closed 8-19 August, 21 December-3 January,
Saturday, Sunday and public holidays

Menu €39/90 – Carte €77/91

Chef Gilles Épié, who won his first Michelin star at the age of 22, is back in Paris after ten years in California. He has taken over the former Bouchon with his wife Élizabeth, who designed the décor (streamlined, with modern paintings and bright orange colours) and greets diners with a charming welcome. Épié invents new flavours influenced by his experience in America and Asia. Imagine cod marinated in soy sauce and sake, grilled and served with courgettes sautéed in olive oil, and for dessert, a coconut ice cream fritter. Other items of note are the glassed-fronted cellar, and the goldfish on every table – unique!

Fermette Marbeuf 1900

Traditional 🍴🍴

B3

5 r. Marbeuf ✉ 75008
✆ 01 53 23 08 00 **Fax** 01 53 23 08 09
e-mail fermettemarbeuf@blanc.net **www**.fermettemarbeuf.com

Ⓜ Alma Marceau

Menu (€24), €32 – Carte €35/63

And to think that this exceptional establishment – an extraordinary Art Nouveau dining room (1898) evoking a winter garden with its cast-iron armature, superb stained glass and ceramics – might have sunk into oblivion! Discovered by accident during renovations, this work by architect Emile Hurté and painter Wielhorski has been admired by people from all over the world. Don't forget to ask for a table in the main room, even if the other rooms are also lovely. The excellent dishes prove that the decor is not the only reason to come here, and the classic, seasonal cuisine gets it just right. The faithful staff – the chef has been here since 1979! – and the discreet and friendly service are two more serious assets.

Hanawa

Japanese ✗✗

26 r. Bayard ⊠ 75008
✆ 01 56 62 70 70
Fax 01 56 62 70 71
e-mail hanawa2007@free.fr **www**.kinugawa-hanawa.com

Ⓜ Franklin D. Roosevelt
Closed Sunday

Menu €34 (lunch)/125 – Carte €34/89

  ♿
  A/C
  VISA
  MC
  AE
  Ⓓ

With its 1100m² on three floors featuring eight different themed settings, this mega-size Japanese restaurant does things in a big way. Contrary to the two Kinugawas, the owner's earlier and more traditional Parisian establishments, Hanawa has reached beyond the gastronomic borders of Japan, with chefs skilled in cooking both Japanese and French specialities. The latter can be sampled in the basement (a semi-circular salon and several Teppanyaki counters). For Asian gastronomy, head up to the first floor, which also has a sushi bar. The refined and understated style (wood, flowers) is ideal for business lunches, and you may even get a glimpse of a famous face or two.

La Luna

Fish ✗✗

69 r. Rocher ⊠ 75008
✆ 01 42 93 77 61
Fax 01 40 08 02 44
e-mail laluna75008@yahoo.fr

Ⓜ Villiers
Closed 30 July-26 August and Sunday

Carte €68/105

  A/C
  VISA
  MC
  AE

The ultramarine façade is the giveaway – La Luna is a place where people come to enjoy fish and shellfish specialities. This establishment with an updated Art Deco interior (including a Lalique fresco) is chic and discreet (light grey and red tones), attracting a business clientele that likes to lunch here. The frequently renewed menu celebrates seafood, proposing recipes with a touch of the exotic, such as large roasted gambas with vanilla oil and sea bream with ginger cooked in a banana leaf. Dessert-lovers should save room for the restaurant's famous *Baba de Zanzibar*.

Marius et Janette

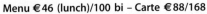

Seafood ✗✗

A3

4 av. George V ⊠ 75008
☎ 01 47 23 41 88 **Fax** 01 47 23 07 19

Ⓜ Alma Marceau
Closed 27 July-5 August

Menu €46 (lunch)/100 bi – Carte €88/168

Could the name refer to l'Estaque and Robert Guédiguian's films? It looks more like Saint-Tropez, to judge from the decor in the dining room evoking a yacht, and by the select clientele seated amongst the fishing poles, nets, plastic swordfish on the walls and brass portholes. As soon as the sun comes out, the decor changes altogether, and it's time to show off trendy sunglasses and suntans on the terrace on the Avenue Georges V. The cuisine also has a maritime bent, with a short menu featuring fish and shellfish dishes.

Market

Fusion ✗✗

C2

15 av. Matignon ⊠ 75008
☎ 01 56 43 40 90 **Fax** 01 43 59 10 87
e-mail prmarketsa@aol.com **www**.jean-georges.com

Ⓜ Franklin D. Roosevelt

Menu €34 (lunch) – Carte €49/87

In 2002 Jean-Georges Vongerichten, the "most Alsatian of New Yorkers", came back to France and opened his own restaurant in Paris. With associates Luc Besson and François Pinault he adapted his winning formula to French tastes. The result is this chic bistro with a discreetly contemporary decor designed by Christian Liaigre (raw finishes, grey, beige and white tones, African masks), and a friendly young staff presiding over the two dining rooms, including one that gives onto a courtyard. The fusion cuisine on the menu, created by Wim Van Gorp, blends French, Italian and Asian influences to produce dishes such as pizza with black truffles, crab salad with mango, and crisp tuna rolls with a green soy coulis.

CHAMPS-ÉLYSÉES • CONCORDE • MADELEINE

Maxan

Contemporary XX

37 r. Miromesnil ✉ 75008
✆ 01 42 65 78 60
Fax 01 49 24 96 17
e-mail rest.maxan@wanadoo.fr
www.rest-maxan.com

Ⓜ Miromesnil
Closed 5-28 August, 24 December-2 January,
Monday dinner, Saturday lunch and Sunday

Menu (€30), €38 (lunch)/45 (dinner) – Carte €48/75

[A/C]
[⟐]
[VISA]
[MC]
[AE]

The first surprise when you walk into Maxan – a contraction of Maxime and Andrea, the children of chef-owner Laurent Zajac – is the look created by Pierre Pozzi, an artist known for his use of paper and cardboard. Paper is king here – on the walls (cream-coloured or in multicoloured stripes), on the ceiling, in strips or in balls. Wood panelling and discreet bistro furniture are another element of the designer decor. The second surprise comes from the simple and creative food (Zajac studied with Gérard Vié and Alain Dutournier). The seasonal, up-to-date dishes (almond milk gaspacho with crabmeat, curried mackerel *tartare* in toast *millefeuille*) are absolutely delicious.

1728

Contemporary XX

8 r. d'Anjou ✉ 75008
✆ 01 40 17 04 77
Fax 01 42 65 53 87
e-mail restaurant1728@wanadoo.fr
www.restaurant-1728.com

Ⓜ Madeleine
Closed 5-25 August,
Sunday and public holidays

Menu (€35) – Carte €55/110

[A/C]
[VISA]
[MC]
[AE]

This townhouse is well worth a visit for the decor full of history. Built in 1728 by Antoine Mazin, it was the home of La Fayette from 1827 until his death. The sumptuous salons still have their period wood panelling and furniture, as well as the original wall hangings and paintings. Nothing seems to have changed, and the scrupulous restoration work has put all the charm and sparkle back into this unique and superb place. The food has zoomed into the 21C with creative chef updating recipes from five continents, using aromatic plants and spices. You'll find some very fine bottles in the carefully composed wine list.

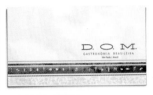

To enhance great foods
they choose great waters.

The delicate complex flavours of the finest cuisine are
best appreciated by an educated palate. And in the
same way that the right wine can release the nuances
of a dish, the right water can subtly cleanse the
palate, enhancing the pleasure and experience of both.
To discover why S.Pellegrino and Acqua Panna are seen
on all the best tables, go to WWW.FINEDININGWATERS.COM

ACQUA PANNA AND S.PELLEGRINO. FINE DINING WATERS.

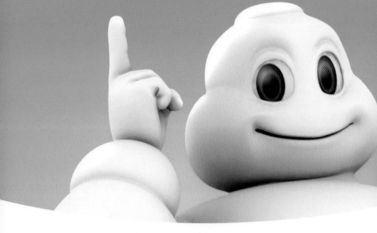

Ratn

Indian ✗✗

B3

9 r. de la Trémoille ✉ 75008   Ⓜ Alma Marceau
☎ 01 40 70 01 09 **Fax** 01 40 70 01 22
e-mail contact@restaurantratn.com **www**.restaurantratn.com

Menu (€ 21), € 39 – Carte € 39/50

VISA
MC
AE

Ratn has all the ingredients of a good Indian restaurant, starting with a "real" name – it means "jewel" – from the land of the Maharajas. The finely worked wood façade is like an invitation to embark on a journey. The interior is pleasantly understated and chic with its golden fabrics on the walls, velvet banquettes, sculpted wood panelling, statue of Shiva and hanging lamps. Another sign of authenticity is the Indian chef-proprietor's inexhaustible knowledge of the country and its gastronomy. His tasty dishes have just the right dose of spices. The service is very friendly.

Le Relais Plaza

Classic ✗✗

B3

Hôtel Plaza Athénée,   Ⓜ Alma Marceau
25 av. Montaigne ✉ 75008   Closed August
☎ 01 53 67 64 00 **Fax** 01 53 67 66 66
e-mail reservation@plaza-athenee-paris.com
www.plaza-athenee-paris.com

Menu € 50 – Carte € 76/148

A/C
VISA
MC
AE
Ⓞ

This brasserie frequented by the Parisian smart set is the chic and intimate "local" for the nearby couture houses. The Relais Plaza has certainly seen its share of celebrities, including Grace Kelly, Charles Aznavour, Liza Minelli, Yves Saint Laurent, John Travolta, Albert of Monaco and Junko Koshino. The carefully preserved setting has an elegant, subtly renovated Art Deco interior inspired by the ocean liner, Le Normandie. Alain Ducasse has put Philippe Marc in charge of the kitchen, and the result is classic dishes with a certain twist and an original menu where club sandwiches rub shoulders with tournedos Rossini.

CHAMPS-ÉLYSÉES • CONCORDE • MADELEINE

Rue Balzac

Contemporary ✗✗

A2

8 r. Lord Byron ✉ 75008
✆ 01 53 89 90 91
Fax 01 53 89 90 94
e-mail ruebalzac@wanadoo.fr

Ⓜ George V
Closed 1st-20 August,
Saturday lunch and Sunday lunch

Carte €32/80

A/C

VISA

MC

AE

Rue Balzac was created by a line-up of stars including Johnny and Laëticia Hallyday, Claude Bouillon and Michel Rostang. The six-bistro chef hired one of his students, Yann Roncier, to run the kitchen, and he does it with originality. Presented by theme and size of ingredients (small or large), the menu features their favourite recipes – thin pasta with green olives and parmesan for Johnny, langoustines for Laëticia – and their associate's creations such as beef tartare. These "star acts" are often embellished with new, carefully prepared and up-to-date inventions. The huge dining room looks like a stylish contemporary apartment with a touch of the Baroque.

Le Sarladais

South-west of France ✗✗

D2

2 r. Vienne ✉ 75008
✆ 01 45 22 23 62
Fax 01 45 22 23 62
www.lesalardais.com

Ⓜ St-Augustin
Closed 30 April-12 May, August, 24-31 December,
Saturday except dinner from 20 September to
30 April, Sunday and public holidays

Menu €38/64 – Carte €48/124

A/C

VISA

MC

AE

The robust and nourishing food here will satisfy any appetite and all cravings for foie gras and preserved *gésiers* (gizzards). Fans of Périgord specialities are fully aware that southwestern cooking is featured at this restaurant located between Saint-Augustin Church and Saint-Lazare Station. Seafood dishes are also on the menu, including sole (grilled or *meunière*), pikeperch steak grilled with thyme flowers, and market favourites depending on the catch of the day. The fine ingredients arrive straight from Carantec (Brittany). The decor is simple, with warm tones, wood panelling, floral compositions and paintings (for sale).

Les Saveurs de Flora

Contemporary XX

A3

36 av. George V ⊠ 75008
✆ 01 40 70 10 49
Fax 01 47 20 52 87
www.lessaveursdeflora.com

Ⓜ George V
Closed August, February half-term holidays,
Saturday lunch and Sunday

Menu (€ 28), € 38/68

Flora's flavours? They are brimming with originality and come from all over the world. Inspired by her travels, the proprietress reinvents traditional French and foreign recipes, making them more modern and "exotic". A dash of spice here and some herbs there, a sweet-and-savoury mixture or a blend of unexpected textures – and there's your new dish! This artist-chef's creative style is also evident in the decor of the three chic dining rooms (and a small lounge) designed with Dorothée Boissier, a follower of Starck. With its naive wallpaper, Venetian mirror wall lamps, *fauteuils à médaillon* reupholstered in leather, climbing flowers, and paste butterflies, this is a charming place with a very personal touch.

A/C
VISA
MC
AE

Sens par la Compagnie des Comptoirs

Contemporary XX

B2

23 r. de Ponthieu
⊠ 75008
✆ 01 42 25 95 00 **Fax** 01 42 25 95 02
e-mail resacdcparis@wanadoo.fr
www.lacompagniedescomptoirs.com

Ⓜ Franklin D. Roosevelt
Closed 1st-21 August, Saturday lunch,
Sunday and Monday

Menu € 45 (weekday lunch), € 75 bi/90 bi – Carte € 36/72

Shades of grey set the tone in this second Parisian restaurant belonging to the Pourcel Brothers, with its "lounge" atmosphere clearly designed by their favourite architect, Imaad Rahmouni. It is contemporary, discreet and refined, with comfortable banquettes, Louis XVI chairs, little red lamps and a giant screen where films are projected. It is truly a delight to feel the spring sun flooding into the dining room through the huge glass window, and to enjoy the sunny southern flavours permeating all the recipes prepared by the famous twins year round. The cheerful and professional waiters are an additional bonus!

A/C
VISA
MC
AE
Ⓞ

Spoon

Innovative XX

B3

12 r. Marignan ⊠ 75008
✆ 01 40 76 34 44
Fax 01 40 76 34 37
e-mail spoonfood@hotelmarignan.fr
www.spoon.tm.fr

Ⓜ Franklin D. Roosevelt
Closed 2 August-1st September,
25 December-5 January, Saturday and Sunday

Menu €47 (lunch)/89 – Carte €57/84

A/C
☞♿
VISA
Ⓜ©
AE
⓪
⅋

Until now Spoon, Alain Ducasse's playful restaurant, belonged to the fusion genre. The concept was simple. Diners composed their own meals – inspired by the five continents – according to their desires and needs, choosing a dish, a condiment or sauce, and a side dish. Perfect for "zapping" gourmets. Now Spoon has diversified, offering two menus: "Spoon Origins", like the original version, and "Spoon Now" highlighting the French tradition. The delicious dishes are presented and combined in striking ways, and paired with a superb selection of wines from around the world. The journey continues with the decor – redone in a "nouveau chic" look featuring a view of the kitchen. Don't forget to book your seat!

Le Stresa

Italian XX

B3

7 r. Chambiges ⊠ 75008
✆ 01 47 23 51 62

Ⓜ Alma Marceau
Closed 1st-8 May, August, 21 December-
3 January, Saturday and Sunday – Pre-book

Carte €57/105

A/C
VISA
Ⓜ©
AE
⓪

This tiny, chic trattoria is a favourite hangout of French and international "beautiful people", and both Alain Delon and Jean-Paul Belmondo are said to be regulars at Le Stresa; so the average mortal will have to book way in advance to get a table at this place run by the Faiola Brothers. Antonio is the one who welcomes diners into this timeless decor with paintings by Buffet and sculptures by César. The kitchen is Marco's domain, where he pampers demanding gourmet diners with his no-fuss Italian dishes prepared "just like at home" with generous portions and only the best ingredients. The prices are typically Parisian.

La Table d'Hédiard

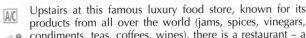

Traditional XX

D2

21 pl. Madeleine ⊠ 75008 · **Ⓜ Madeleine**
℘ 01 43 12 88 99 **Fax** 01 43 12 88 98 · Closed August and Sunday
e-mail latablehediard@hediard.fr **www**.hediard.fr

Carte € 47/71

[A/C]
☞
VISA
Ⓜ Ⓒ
AE
Ⓓ

Upstairs at this famous luxury food store, known for its products from all over the world (jams, spices, vinegars, condiments, teas, coffees, wines), there is a restaurant – a chic and refined place with a colonial-style decor. The exotic setting suits the cosmopolitan business clientele and lends itself perfectly to the house recipes. Among the appetising dishes are lightly-cooked swordfish with pepper and a saffron emulsion, *jus vert*, and seasonal vegetables, filet de *cannette rôti à la lavande* (duck with lavender), citrus tart, and *millefeuille à la vanille*. The menu is a blend of classic flavours and faraway fragrances, remaining faithful to the Hédiard image characterised by refinement and quality. Attentive welcome and meticulous service.

Tante Louise

Traditional XX

D2

41 r. Boissy-d'Anglas ⊠ 75008 · **Ⓜ Madeleine**
℘ 01 42 65 06 85 · Closed August, Saturday,
Fax 01 42 65 28 19 · Sunday and public holidays
e-mail tantelouise@bernard-loiseau.com
www.bernard-loiseau.com

Menu € 36 (lunch)/40 – Carte € 47/67

[A/C]
☐
VISA
Ⓜ Ⓒ
AE
Ⓓ

Tante Louise – part of the Bernard Loiseau group – owes its name to Louise Blanche Lefeuvre, the Parisian "Mama" who founded this restaurant in 1929. The pretty Art Deco façade is a fitting invitation to take a seat in the 1930s dining room with its carefully preserved, rather plush decor. Or you might prefer to sit in the comfortable mezzanine with its warm pale wood panelling and large clock. In either case, the food is traditional and faithful to the principles of the master of Saulieu – simple, good and of course influenced by his native Burgundy, like the wine list elaborated by a sommelier who works at the famous Relais.

Village d'Ung et Li Lam

Thai ✗✗

C2

10 r. J. Mermoz ⊠ 75008
✆ 01 42 25 99 79
Fax 01 42 25 12 06

Ⓜ Franklin D. Roosevelt
Closed Saturday lunchtime and
Sunday lunchtime

Menu €19/35 – Carte €25/40

A/C
VISA
MC
AE
D

Ung and Li Lam extend a warm welcome at their Asian "Village" a stone's throw from the Champs-Élysées. The restaurant's unusual decor is truly worth seeing, with its molten glass floor inlaid with grains of sand and pottery shards, aquariums hanging from the ceiling and live kitchen action seen through a picture window. The exciting menu features the great classics of Chinese and Thai cuisine prepared with the utmost professionalism, including an assortment of ravioli, caramel spare ribs, beef sautéed with basil, and a host of other indispensable and flavourful recipes! Simple, good and entertaining – no wonder the place is so often booked up.

L'Appart'

Traditional ✗

B2

9 r. Colisée ⊠ 75008
✆ 01 53 75 42 00 **Fax** 01 53 75 42 09
e-mail boris.terdjman@blanc.net **www**.lappart.com

Ⓜ Franklin D. Roosevelt

Menu €23 (lunch), €30/55 (dinner) – Carte €29/58

A/C
VISA
MC
AE

With its dining room, lounge, bookshelves and open kitchen, this restaurant has reproduced the atmosphere of a large and comfortable apartment on several floors. The look they're going for is intimate and chic (counter top, wood panelling, lamps with red shades to soften the lighting, and paintings). The "genteel family home" ambiance, both cosy and trendy, has developed a following – businessmen at lunch, and hip young jet setters for dinner. Whatever the time of day there is always a good reason to "squat" this "apartment" and sample the smoked salmon with mild horseradish sauce, the pan-fried sea bass with curry, the brioche French toast, *caramel laitier*, and vanilla ice cream.

L'Arôme

B2

Contemporary ✗

3 r. St-Philippe-du-Roule
✉ 75008
✆ 01 42 25 55 98
Fax 01 42 25 55 97
e-mail contact@larome.fr **www**.larome.fr

Ⓜ St-Philippe-du-Roule
Closed August, 22-29 December,
Saturday and Sunday

Menu (€ 27), € 34 (lunch), € 45/60 – Carte € 45/59

A/C
VISA
ⓂⒸ
ÆE

Aroma, fragrance and bouquet are the watchwords at this restaurant created by Éric Martins, a top-level restaurateur. The chic and discreet decor envelops you in its coral and taupe tones the minute you walk in. The Murano glass chandeliers create a softer atmosphere in the evening. Young chef Thomas Boullault (formerly at the George V) cooks according to his moods and boundless imagination. The result is a superb range of flavours in dishes such as pan-fried scallops with white beans, and pan-fried duck foie gras with bitter cocoa. The well-balanced cellar has a blend of great vintages and more modest wines to enhance your meal. A true gem, not to be missed.

L'Atelier des Compères

A2

Terroir ✗

56 r. Galilée ✉ 75008
✆ 01 47 20 75 56
e-mail contact@atelierdescomperes.com
www.atelierdescomperes.com

Ⓜ George V
Closed August,
Christmas holidays, Saturday,
Sunday and public holidays
– Number of covers limited, pre-book

Menu (€ 40), € 50/65

VISA
ⓂⒸ
ÆE

These talented fellows set up their establishment in a cobblestone courtyard! A strange but charming idea – like walking into a chic *guinguette* with contemporary furniture and attractively set tables, covered by a large tarpaulin (adjustable depending on the season). Unaffected by fickle weather, it is open in winter and summer, when they let the sunshine in. Jacques Boudin and Eric Sertour were intent on making this little corner of paradise a convivial and inviting place. To whet your appetite, the market-based dishes on the blackboard – changed daily – include roasted Guinea fowl with cabbage, medallion of veal with morel mushrooms, and pineapple and pear crumble. Naturally this haven of peace is always packed.

Le Bistrot de Marius

Seafood ✗

6 av. George V ✉ 75008 **Ⓜ** Alma Marceau
✆ 01 40 70 11 76 **Fax** 01 40 70 17 08

Menu (€ 28), € 32 (weekday lunch) – Carte € 32/63

VISA

ⓜⓒ

ⒶⒺ

Ⓓ

If, when in Paris, you can't have a game of *pétanque* (bowls), a glass of *pastis* under the southern sun or a bouillabaisse on a lively quayside, then head for this bistro – just like the ones on the old port of Marseille! Sitting at your snug table in the dining room decorated in Provençal colours, the "Bonne Mère" won't seem so far away as you sample the excellent market cuisine featuring seafood dishes. Particularly since the prices seem to have remained closer to Marseille than to Paris. This is an authentic and convivial place with no frills. Booking advised!

Bistro de l'Olivier

Provence cuisine ✗

13 r. Quentin Bauchart ✉ 75008 **Ⓜ** George V
✆ 01 47 20 78 63 Closed August, Saturday lunch and Sunday
Fax 01 47 20 74 58 – Number of covers limited, pre-book

Menu (€ 28), € 35 – Carte € 68/82

A/C

VISA

ⓜⓒ

ⒶⒺ

Ⓓ

Time flies at this warm bistro near the Champs-Élysées; and the bill is remarkably merciful given its location and quality. Naturally, the clientele from the neighbourhood know a good thing when they see it, so they have become regulars. What is the secret of this "eldorado" ? Sun, sun, and more sun : in the colourful decor (walls in yellow tones, red banquettes, and regionalist paintings) and in the cuisine carefully prepared by chef Aurélien Marion. The menu changes frequently, featuring meticulously selected fresh ingredients in precise and tasty dishes with a Provençal flavour. This is the place to go when you need an antidote to grey Parisian skies!

Bocconi

Italian ✗

B2

10bis r. Artois ✉ 75008   Ⓜ St-Philippe-du-Roule
☎ 01 53 76 44 44   Closed Saturday lunchtime and Sunday
Fax 01 45 61 10 08
e-mail bocconi@wanadoo.fr **www**.trattoria-bocconi.fr

Carte €41/55

This is one of a group of chic and trendy trattorias in Paris. Bonuses include its unique location just behind the shopping galleries on the "most beautiful avenue in the world" and its really pleasant sidewalk terrace in summer. The decor is discreetly contemporary (yellow and reds tones, banquettes and cushions) and the typically Italian cuisine, featuring fresh homemade pasta and other classics from across the Alps. Shared starters, which you can sample if there are several people in your party, are an original touch. A fun Italian jaunt!

Le Boucoléon

Traditional ✗

C1

10 r. Constantinople ✉ 75008   Ⓜ Europe
☎ 01 42 93 73 33   Closed 10-25 August, Saturday lunch,
Fax 01 42 93 95 44   Sunday and public holidays
     Number of covers limited, pre-book

Menu (€24) – Carte €34/44

All the charm of the Southwest seems to have been "contained" within this friendly neighbourhood establishment. Bright colours such as ocean blue - on the façade and in the paintings - light up the dark up-to-date setting (exposed stonework, immaculate walls, bistro floors and furniture) into which Richard Castellan welcomes you. A few souvenirs and posters are devoted to the sacrosanct rugby ball, of which the owner is a fan – did you ever doubt it for a moment? The warm ambiance is perfectly paired with the generous and delicious food made with ingredients from the Basque country; the menu changes every two months. *Dagizula* (bon appétit)!

Café Lenôtre - Pavillon Élysée

Brasserie 🍴

C3

10 av. Champs-
Élysées ✉ 75008
☎ 01 42 65 85 10
Fax 01 42 65 76 23
www.lenotre.fr

Ⓜ Champs Élysées Clemenceau
Closed 3 weeks in August, 1 week in February,
Monday dinner from November to
February and Sunday dinner

Carte € 44/64

The Pavillon Élysées is a kind of showcase for the famous
Parisian caterer, with a shop, cooking school and restaurant. This mecca for food-lovers found the perfect setting
– a magnificent and superbly restored Napoleon III pavilion, originally built for the 1900 World's Fair. The decidedly contemporary Café Lenôtre looks onto a very popular
terrace, from which you can see the busiest avenue in the
city. The appetizing menu features dishes with an international theme (Paris Oslo, Paris Cannes, Paris Bangkok),
"Pasta Inventions", and updated traditional dishes. A most
enjoyable place!

Chez Cécile
La Ferme des Mathurins

Traditional 🍴

D2

17 r. Vignon ✉ 75008
☎ 01 42 66 46 39
e-mail cecile@chezcecile.com
www.chezcecile.com

Ⓜ Madeleine
Closed Saturday lunch and Sunday

Menu € 34 (lunch)/37

It's always a pleasure to dine at this Madeleine area institution. But why? Is it the friendly ambiance that reigns
within these venerable walls? Or the faithful good-hum-
oured clientele? Probably a bit of both. This old-fashioned
bistro – where Georges Simenon was a regular – hasn't lost
any of its charm, with its traditional banquettes, tightly-
packed tables and counter top. The new management has
gone all out in the kitchen, offering copious and well-
prepared dishes (traditional, seasonal and market-based)
served by friendly and enthusiastic waiters. Jazz evenings
on Thursdays. Don't forget to book!

Le Cou de la Girafe

Contemporary ✗

B2

7 r. Paul Baudry ✉ 75008
☎ 01 56 88 29 55
Fax 01 42 25 28 82
e-mail nicolas-richard@wanadoo.fr
www.restaurantlecoudelagirafe.com

Ⓜ St-Philippe du Roule
Closed 1st-20 August,
Saturday lunch and Sunday

Menu (€ 24), € 30/50 – Carte € 34/55

A/C

VISA

MC

AE

DC

A trendy bistro? It does have all the necessary ingredients :
a privileged location near the Champs-Élysées, contemporary decor designed by the highly sought-after Pierre-Yves
Rochon (wood and shades of yellow and chocolate), hushed atmosphere and a clientele of regulars and businessmen
at lunchtime. The cuisine is riding on the wave of current
tastes, of course. But it pulls it off well - due to the talented
chef who is a master of his art. The menu also features some
fine fish recipes and *canaille* dishes. As a result, this establishment stands out from a good many other fashionable
places. The little sidewalk terrace is enjoyable in summer.

Daru

Russian ✗

B1

19 r. Daru ✉ 75008
☎ 01 42 27 23 60
Fax 01 47 54 08 14
e-mail restaurant.daru@orange.fr **www**.daru.fr

Ⓜ Courcelles
Closed August and Sunday

Menu (€ 29) – Carte € 40/70

A/C

VISA

MC

AE

This is the first Russian grocer's – created by one of Nicolas
II's officers in 1918 – and oldest Russian restaurant in the
city. The red-and-black decor bursting with warmth and
conviviality will take you right back you to old Russia,
with its casks, bottles of rare vodka, portraits of the Czars,
precious paintings and materials, dark wood panelling,
and dolls. Traditions are still strong here, where they treat
guests to *zakouskis* (*tarama* for two, sea urchins, smoked
salmon, marinated herring, etc.), caviar and the quintessential beef Stroganoff with paprika and potato blinis.
Enjoy the balalaika music in the background while sipping
your vodka.

Devez

A3

5 pl. de l'Alma ✉ 75008   Ⓜ Alma Marceau
☎ 01 53 67 97 53 **Fax** 01 47 23 09 48
e-mail contact@devezparis.com **www**.devezparis.com

Carte €33/67

Devèses are large pastures found over the basaltic terrain of the Aubrac region – the pride and joy of stockbreeders in the Aveyron, like Christian Valette, who loves his native region and came to Paris to "sing its praises". This is his second establishment celebrating the famous breed of Aubrac beef. To give it the greatest chance of pleasing his diners, the chef cooks it different ways – simmered, roasted, *à la plancha* – and even serves it as an appetizer ("gourmet tapas"). The decor is warm and up-to-date (wood everywhere and clean lines), and there is a heated terrace.

La Maison de L'Aubrac

B3

37 r. Marbeuf ✉ 75008   Ⓜ Franklin D. Roosevelt
☎ 01 43 59 05 14 **Fax** 01 42 25 29 87
e-mail ldurot.aubrac@wanadoo.fr

Menu (€30), €55 – Carte €34/54

The name, La Maison de l'Aubrac, is very fitting. Christian Valette – a restaurateur who breeds cattle in Laguiole and loves his *terroir* – has made it a showcase for the Aubrac region. The rustic interior emulates that of a farm in the Aveyron, while the highly convivial atmosphere is sometimes a bit over-excited (only natural given the proximity of the Champs-Élysées). Beef – from Aubrac, naturally! – is featured in recipes from Aveyron, Lozère and Cantal. The straightforward and well-prepared dishes are accompanied by a very fine choice of wines (in particular the old vintages). And it is open 24 hours a day, 7 days a week. Fancy a rib of beef after an evening of clubbing?

Dominique Bouchet ✿

Contemporary ✕

C1

11 r. Treilhard ✉ 75008
✆ 01 45 61 09 46
Fax 01 42 89 11 14
e-mail dominiquebouchet@yahoo.fr
www.dominique-bouchet.com

Ⓜ Miromesnil
Closed in August,
Saturday and Sunday – Pre-book

Menu (€ 46), € 55/87 – Carte € 55/75

Dominique Bouchet

Dominique Bouchet chose to go from luxury restaurants to a bistro. After running the brigades at the Crillon and the Tour d'Argent (and even participating in the latter's Japanese adventure), he aspired to something lighter and perhaps with a bit more freedom. With nothing left to prove as a gourmet cook, he wanted to make way for the up-and-coming generation and finally open a restaurant in his own name (he had also decided to stop chasing after perfection and awards). Now installed at "his own place" he can get back to basics: fine classical cuisine that may be too tame for some but is indisputably the work of a master. The selection of quality wines by the glass is an added bonus. Restraint, intimacy and calm sum up the atmosphere in the long dining room, with its exposed stone walls, wenge wood tables, paintings and open kitchen. Meals progress without a false note – like a long and peaceful river.

First Course	*Main Course*	*Dessert*
• Tête de veau croustillante sauce gribiche.	• Gros macaroni de homard sur purée de champignons, noyé de sa bisque.	• Tarte chaude aux pommes et miel de montagne, glace vanille bourbon.
• Charlotte de crabe et tomate, chiffonnade de laitue, mangue fraîche et basilic (April-September).	• Gigot d'agneau de sept heures, sauce parfumée au cacao torréfié, pomme purée.	• Mœlleux au chocolat mi-cuit, glace au cacao amer.

CHAMPS-ÉLYSÉES • CONCORDE • MADELEINE

Shin Jung

D1

7 r. Clapeyron ✉ 75008   **Ⓜ Rome**
𝒫 01 45 22 21 06   Closed Sunday lunchtime and
Fax 01 42 94 10 96   lunch on public holidays
e-mail printemp0706@aol.fr

Menu €9 (lunch), €15/36 (dinner) – Carte €19/37

A/C

VISA

MC

Regulars at this friendly family establishment come here for the really fine, authentic Korean cooking – less well-known than cuisine from neighbouring Asian countries but equally appetising. The typical Korean specialities – in-between traditional Chinese and Japanese recipes – include raw fish and barbecue dishes. The *bibimbap*, another Korean speciality, is delicious here, and absolutely authentic. The Zen-like space is as pure as a blank page, with just a few calligraphy drawings on the walls adding a personal touch to the ultra-spare decor. The service is fast and unfussy.

SYDR

A2

6 r. de Tilsitt ✉ 75008   **Ⓜ Charles de Gaulle-Étoile**
𝒫 01 45 72 41 32   Closed August, Sunday and Monday
Fax 01 45 72 41 79
e-mail sydrerie@orange.fr

Menu €27 (lunch)/39 bi – Carte €33/53

♿

A/C

VISA

MC

AE

Three, two, one, zero – countdown for the1st match of the 2007 Rugby World Cup and the opening of this new "playing field" for fans! The concept was designed by two pros: starred chef Alain Dutournier, and Philippe Sella, a legendary figure on the French rugby team. In the lobby entrance are two black lateral bars and a lounge area for sampling tapas and cider (thus the name SYDR). The dining room under a glass dome offers an ultra-streamlined minimalist setting. The southwestern-style cuisine features spit-roasted chicken, rib steak *à la plancha*, etc. A large picture window provides a view of the brigade at work at the grill. Giant plasma screens and collectors' jerseys complete the decor.

Toi

Contemporary 🍴

B2

27 r. Colisée ✉ 75008   Ⓜ Franklin D. Roosevelt
✆ 01 42 56 56 58
Fax 01 42 56 09 60
e-mail restaurant.toi@wanadoo.fr **www**.restaurant-toi.com

Menu (€17), €24/69 bi – Carte €35/79

A/C
VISA
MC
AE
①

The 70s decor, contemporary design and red and orange "Pop" colours blend together nicely in this trendy restaurant conceived by designer Cherif. The hip, chic and original setting on three levels – ground floor, lounge bar, and mezzanine – mirrors the inventive spirit celebrated in the cuisine. The daring and talented chef, who trained at top establishments (Ritz, Crillon), cooks up some fantastic combinations, including *Cupid* tomatoes and mozzarella brochettes, pan-fried gambas flambéed in pastis with quinoa, and pistachio macaroons with fresh raspberries and apricot sorbet. Diners in search of trendy spots will enjoy it here, and the fixed-price dinner menu is very reasonable. Buffet brunch on Sundays.

Opéra
Grands Boulevards

Opéra, the Grands Boulevards, Saint-Lazare form a triangle. The 9th is central, busy, commercial and larger than the tiny riverside arrondissements, but it is also denser, more dynamic and smaller than the arrondissements closer to the ring road. It is a concentrate of Paris and symbolises the movement and variety that endow the capital with its distinctive character. Wedged between place Pigalle, boulevard des Italiens and the rue d'Amsterdam and rue du Faubourg Poissonnière, it has a little of everything and lacks nothing: one of the largest railway stations in France (Saint-Lazare), an international calibre opera house, several outstanding churches and more department stores than one could ever hope to raid in an entire lifetime… .

A BIT OF HISTORY…

The Opéra district was born out of Napoleon III's desire to leave his imprint on Paris: the new avenues that were to be built and would soon be qualified as "Haussmannian" needed a focal point, an architectural and aesthetic construction that would draw the eye. Designed by Garnier, the Opéra de Paris is now the "Palace of Dance" but has retained all its original splendour and decor including an abundance of marble and stucco work and a profusion of grandiose frescoes and gilt-trimmed facades that create a somewhat extravagant picture. Yet despite its luxury and

massive outline, the edifice continues to inspire a certain lightness. The immediate vicinity was built in the same style despite an impressive number of banks, whose headquarters are fully capable of holding their own next to the imperial constructions. At lunchtimes, the district is awash with employees and businessmen in a hurry, mingling with the crowds of tourists in a joyful pandemonium, which is also probably the reason for the high density of restaurants and pubs, particularly around Havre-Caumartin, serving lunchtime specials and offering happy hours to appeal to this wide ranging clientele.

FROM
THE GOLDEN ERA TO THE GOUTTE D'OR

The Grands Boulevards – Italiens, Haussmann and Poissonnière – were initially designed to decongest Paris but soon became well-known districts devoted to entertainment and pleasure. Popular with walkers right from the start, they were quickly engulfed with cafés, theatres, shops and restaurants. Today the area is home to all the leading high-street chain stores, temples of fashion and consumerism, in addition to a number of cinemas beloved by Parisians such as the Grand Rex and the Max Linder which continue to uphold French cinema loving traditions.

A. Chicurel / HEMIS.FR

All around the brasseries and cafés overflow with customers to such a point that the area sometimes resembles an anthill. It is however not difficult to find a little peace and quiet by heading north along one of the streets that lead to Pigalle. The steeple of the church of La Trinité, characteristic of the second Empire, dominates the surrounding, quieter and more residential streets.

Further east, rue des Martyrs will thrust you into the joyful and effusive atmosphere near Montmartre whose sun-drenched markets, food shops of every possible type and unlikely bars are already a foretaste of the north of Paris and the nearby Goutte d'Or district – so very different from the sumptuous luxury of the Emperor's court.

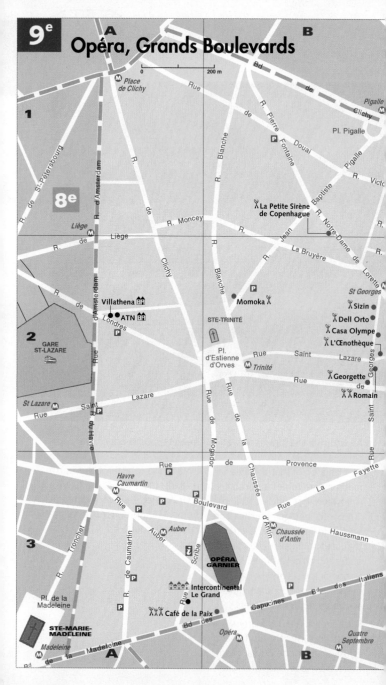

9e

Opéra, Grands Boulevards

0 — 200 m

8e

GARE ST-LAZARE

Place de Clichy

Pl. Pigalle

La Petite Sirène de Copenhague

Villathena

ATN

Momoka

STE-TRINITÉ

Sizin

Dell Orto

Casa Olympe

L'Œnothèque

St Georges

Pl. d'Estienne d'Orves

Trinité

Georgette

Romain

St Lazare

Rue de Provence

Havre Caumartin

Auber

OPÉRA GARNIER

Intercontinental Le Grand

Pl. de la Madeleine

STE-MARIE-MADELEINE

Café de la Paix

Madeleine

Opéra

Quatre Septembre

Chaussée d'Antin

Haussmann

Café de la Paix

Contemporary 🍴🍴🍴

Intercontinental Le Grand,   🇲 Opéra
12 bd Capucines ✉ 75009
✆ 01 40 07 36 36 **Fax** 01 40 07 36 13
e-mail reservation@cafedelapaix.fr **www**.cafedelapaix.fr

&♿ **Menu (€35), €45 (lunch)/85 – Carte €51/118**

Surely it needs no introduction. The legendary brasserie of
the Grand Hôtel Intercontinental (1862) is without a doubt
where the Parisian smart set, and well-to-do tourists, love
to meet. And well they should, for the setting is sublime,
with a magnificent painted ceiling, beautiful frescoes (by
Garnier), gilded wood panelling, and Second Empire-style
furniture. It is luxurious and unique. So, you may have to
wait a bit between courses, and the bill is not what you'd
call skimpy; but this is the Café de la Paix, where Maupassant, Oscar Wilde, Gide and Zola were once regulars. The
service plays out in three acts (from 7am to midnight),
featuring a smooth, updated classical repertoire.

Au Petit Riche

Traditional 🍴🍴

25 r. Le Peletier ✉ 75009   🇲 Richelieu Drouot
✆ 01 47 70 68 68   Closed Saturday from 14 July to
Fax 01 48 24 10 79   20 August and Sunday
e-mail aupetitriche@wanadoo.fr
www.aupetitriche.com

Menu (€24), €27/36 – Carte €30/62

This is truly an institution, mentioned by Maupassant in *Bel
Ami*, and frequented by Mistinguett and Maurice Chevalier.
Its 19C dining rooms haven't changed a bit since it opened
in 1854, with its red velvet banquettes, finely chiselled mirrors, *chapelières*, elegant snug tables, etc. The only change
of note is the clientele. Bankers and stockbrokers have made
it their "local", while stars and theatre-goers flock here until
the midnight hours. Its charm remains intact. Enjoy the
recipes inspired by Touraine cuisine at this historic venue,
along with a bottle chosen from the superb list featuring
wines from the Loire Valley.

Bistrot Papillon

D2

Traditional ✗✗

6 r. Papillon ✉ 75009
✆ 01 47 70 90 03
Fax 01 48 24 05 59

Ⓜ Cadet
Closed 1st-12 May, 6-31 August, Saturday except
dinner from October to April and Sunday

Menu € 29 – Carte € 36/48

A/C
VISA
MC
AE
Ⓓ

The Papillon in a nutshell? Classic, without a doubt. And that's what people like here – its "definitive", "exemplary" and almost "endangered species" side. It feels like one of those country inns where everything seems to have been carefully preserved for decades. The authentic Belle Epoque decor features wood panelling and bouquets of flowers everywhere, fabrics creating more privacy between tables, and pretty bistro chairs. The ideal setting for enjoying the great culinary classics "reverently" recreated by Jean-Yves Guion. Since 1983 he has been regaling regulars, businessmen and tourists in the family atmosphere expertly maintained by his wife Evelyne.

Carte Blanche 😊

C2

Traditional ✗✗

6 r. Lamartine ✉ 75009
✆ 01 48 78 12 20
Fax 01 48 78 12 21
e-mail rest.carteblanche@free.fr
www.restaurantcarteblanche.com/cuisine-inventive/

Ⓜ Cadet
Closed 1st-20 August,
Saturday lunch and Sunday

Menu € 26/40 – Carte approx. € 43

A/C
VISA
MC
AE

Who says all new bistros have to be trendy? This one has its own particular charm behind the simple façade – neither overly fashion-conscious nor neutral, with stone walls, exposed beams, clean lines, exotic photographs and tableware adding a personal touch to the decor. The two globe-trotting owners have drawn their inspiration from all over the world, and it shows. That cosmopolitan taste is also reflected in their culinary style featuring well-chosen ingredients and original dishes blending French traditions and faraway flavours – an adventure that will delight your taste buds!

Jean ❀

C2

8 r. St-Lazare ✉ 75009
☏ 01 48 78 62 73
Fax 01 48 78 66 04
e-mail chezjean@wanadoo.fr
www.restaurantjean.fr

Ⓜ Notre-Dame-de-Lorette
Closed 28 July-25 August, 25 February-3 March,
Saturday and Sunday

Menu (€38), €46 (lunch), €60/75 – Carte €63/71

A/C

VISA
MC
AE
①

Jean

Twenty years of good and faithful service at Taillevent, where
Jean-Frédéric Guidoni was the head maître d'hôtel, forms a
person's character. Guidoni lacks neither courage nor flair,
and took the plunge in 2002, becoming the new owner of
"Chez Jean", which he rechristened "Jean". This former traditional bistro has preserved some of its patina (fine proportions,
counter, oak panelling, banquettes, floor mosaics) as well as
an oriental lounge upstairs that was once a kind of culinary
laboratory. Simplicity is the watchword at Jean – in the welcome you receive, the setting and the ingredients. The chef,
Benoît Bordier, has had a free hand in putting together his
highly flexible contemporary menu. He likes to shake up
habits – the only unchanged dish is the "Monsieur cochon",
poitrine slow-cooked for eight hours – to test new and improbable pairings, and to create unusual ways of presenting and
formulating dishes. Sure, his cooking is edgy, playful and
precise, but even more than that, it's exciting.

First Course

- Jus tremblotant de crevettes grises, herbes parfumées.
- Comme un œuf au plat, jus de piperade et légumes à la cardamome, brioche toastée, chorizo.

Main Course

- Noix de veau, yaourt à l'anchois et jus de prune à l'orchidée.
- Râble de lapin et boudin de cuisses, navets au sarrasin et parmesan.

Dessert

- Dacquoise à la fleur d'oranger, chasselas, sorbet bière blanche.
- Jeu de saveurs et textures au chocolat, parfum de fenouil.

Romain

Italian ✕✕

B2

40 r. St-Georges ✉ 75009
✆ 01 48 24 58 94 **Fax** 01 42 47 09 75
e-mail restaurant_romain@yahoo.fr

Ⓜ St-Georges
Closed August,
Sunday and Monday

Menu €33 – Carte €36/67

VISA
MC
AE
Ⓓ

Romain is among the better Italian restaurants in Paris. Its French owners, the Bürkli family, fell in love with Italy and are eager to share that passion. In the kitchen, Mr. Bürkli renews his short menu every month – offering the freshest and choicest ingredients, including home-made pasta, excellent cold meats and a range of other refined and flavourful dishes. Mrs. Bürkli extends a warm welcome and oversees the service in the dining room, a stylish and airy setting adorned with paintings and flowers. Their son Romain, after whom the restaurant was named, is a connoisseur of Italian wines who will help you find the perfect bottle for your meal.

Casa Olympe

Traditional ✕

B2

48 r. St Georges ✉ 75009
✆ 01 42 85 26 01
Fax 01 45 26 49 33

Ⓜ St-Georges
Closed 1st-12 May, 1st-25 August,
23 December-3 January, Saturday and Sunday
Number of covers limited, pre-book

Menu (€29), €38/60

A/C
VISA
MC

Dominique Versini, alias Olympe (also her mother's name), was the culinary mastermind of the 1980s. She was one of the first women chefs and creators of "nouvelle cuisine". Out of the limelight these days, she presides over two small ochre dining rooms on the Rue Saint-Georges. Nothing appears to have changed. She still has the same strong character and the same faculty for reinventing traditional cuisine inspired by "hearty" dishes with a Mediterranean touch. Financiers and insurance men fight over tables at their "local" for lunch, while artists fill it up in the evening. Who cares if the tables are a bit small? The food is well worth the close quarters!

Dell Orto

B2

45 r. St-Georges ✉ 75009
📞 01 48 78 40 30

Carte €32/64

Ⓜ St-Georges
Closed August, Christmas holidays,
Sunday and Monday – Dinner only

VISA
ⓂⒸ
ⒶⒺ

Honouring Italian cuisine while adding his own creative touch is the leitmotiv of the chef-proprietor of this friendly restaurant which is only open for dinner. Why not at lunchtime? Because Patrizio Dell'Orto needs time to put together the daily market-based dishes which complete his short menu, to make his fresh pasta and think up appetising names for his creations. It is well worth the wait; the recipes from his native land, subtly seasoned with spices from afar, have already earned him a wide following. The same Mediterranean influence is present in the decor of the two dining rooms, with a warm and charming interior blending Italian and North African designs.

Georgette

B2

29 r. St-Georges
✉ 75009
📞 01 42 80 39 13

Ⓜ Notre-Dame-de-Lorette
Closed Easter holidays, August,
autumn half-term holidays,
Saturday, Sunday and Monday

Carte €27/44

VISA
ⓂⒸ
ⒶⒺ

Eating at Georgette's is like going into a time warp back to the 60s. Behind the retro sign is a friendly bistro sure to delight anyone pining for multi-tone formica tables and olive green imitation-leather chairs. The unusual cachet also thrills tourists in search of authenticity who enjoy the atmosphere from a bygone era. The "back to your roots" leitmotif also infuses the tradition-inspired cooking, featuring vegetables and other fresh ingredients. Diners love the chef's potato salad with mild herring, poached egg with Auvergne ham, *croustillant de veau pommes sautées* (veal turnover with sauteed potatoes), and *pâté en croûte façon Ducloux*. Still feeling peckish? Try the *crème brûlée* or rice pudding.

I Golosi

Italian ✗

C3

6 r. Grange Batelière ✉ 75009
✆ 01 48 24 18 63
Fax 01 45 23 18 96
e-mail i.golosi@wanadoo.fr

Ⓜ Richelieu Drouot
` Closed 5-20 August,
Saturday dinner and Sunday

Carte €25/41

Murano glass lamps and "Venetian terrace" floors are just part of the magic at this trattoria on the Passage Verdeau. The contemporary decor upstairs, combined with the waiters' accents, has given this establishment an incomparably chic air – and a solid reputation to go with it. And it's no wonder, with its extensive list of Italian wines (over 500 vintages, many of them served by the glass), huge variety of antipasti, seasonal soups and pasta dishes which change by the week. Can't resist? You can find all these flavours from Italy at the adjoining shop to take home with you – your own secret weapon. Booking advised!

Momoka

Japanese ✗

B2

5 r. Jean-Baptiste Pigalle
✉ 75009
✆ 01 40 16 19 09
Fax 01 40 16 19 09
e-mail masayohashimoto@aol.com

Ⓜ Trinité d'Estienne d'Orves
Closed August, Saturday lunch,
Sunday, Monday and public holidays

Menu (€25), €35 (lunch), €48/68

The word "miniscule" is no exaggeration in describing this restaurant that can only serve 14 people at a time! But, however small, Momoka has earned a reputation among fans of Japanese food, who even got a bit alarmed when it was rumoured to be closing. Not to worry – Masayo, the peerless and discreet chef, is still there, assisted by her French husband who takes care of the service. She updates traditional dishes from her childhood with obvious delight and reinvents the menu according to the market and her own inspiration: salads, *tofu*, *tempura*, seaweed, *donburi* (rice with marinated chicken, beef or tuna), vanilla blancmange with red berries and black sesame seeds. The ambiance is "just like being at home". But don't forget to book.

OPÉRA • GRANDS BOULEVARDS

L'Œnothèque

Traditional 🍴

20 r. St-Lazare ✉ 75009
✆ 01 48 78 08 76
Fax 01 40 16 10 27

Ⓜ Notre-Dame-de-Lorette
Closed 1st-8 May, 2 weeks in August,
24 December-1st January, Saturday and Sunday

Carte € 25/53

A/C
VISA
MC
AE
①
🍇

The name of this pocket bistro pretty much sums up its underlying principle. Daniel Hallée, a former sommelier at the prestigious restaurant Jamin, is in charge of this elegant place (the warm contemporary dining room is decorated in red tones) that doubles as a boutique. The chef spotlights market ingredients and flavours from the *terroir* in his mouth-watering dishes, chalked up on the blackboard. From the wide selection of wines and spirits (over 450), it's clear that they worship Dionysus here. No wonder the place is so popular – and not just with wine buffs.

L'Office

Contemporary 🍴

3 r. Richer ✉ 75009
✆ 01 47 70 67 31
Fax 01 47 70 67 31

Ⓜ Poissonnière
Closed 3-25 August, Saturday lunch,
Sunday and Monday
Number of covers limited, pre-book

Menu (€ 13,50), € 16 (weekday lunch)/26

VISA
MC

One of the up-and-coming establishments in the area, run by a self-taught young chef, passionate about food. His background? A law degree and various cooking stints on the other side of the Channel, most notably at Jamie Oliver's restaurant Fifteen. The decor at this pocket-sized bistro is simple and unpretentious (wooden tables, counter-top bar) – so discreet you could walk right by without even seeing it. But the menu in the window draws you in: *minestrone*, *onglet de veau*, pear and chocolate terrine served with *crème fraîche*, and other, daily-changing, Italo-French dishes. A real surprise.

La Petite Sirène de Copenhague ☺

Danish ✗

B1

47 r. N.-D. de Lorette ✉ 75009   Ⓜ St-Georges
✆ 01 45 26 66 66   Closed 2-25 August, 23 December-5 January, Saturday lunch, Sunday and Monday – Pre-book

Menu €29 (lunch)/34 – Carte €43/71

VISA
MC
AE

You'll be under its spell the minute you walk into this genuine ambassador of Danish cuisine. But rather than charming you with her singing, this siren catches gourmets in her net with delicious sweet-and-sour herring and incomparable smoked salmon, two undisputed stars on this sweet and savoury menu from the land of Hans Christian Andersen. The rest is naturally in the same spirit. Peter and his friendly staff take your order with their delightful Nordic accents, while proposing an excellent *øl* (Danish beer) or obligatory aquavit – to be enjoyed in moderation of course. The warm decor completes the local colour with its polished floor tiles, whitewashed walls, soft lighting, candles and paintings by Scandinavian artists. A real treat!

Le Pré Cadet ☺

Traditional ✗

C2

10 r. Saulnier ✉ 75009   Ⓜ Cadet
✆ 01 48 24 99 64   Closed 1st-8 May, 3-21 August, 24 December-
Fax 01 47 70 55 96   1st January, Saturday lunch and Sunday
    Number of covers limited, pre-book

Menu €30/45 – Carte €39/52

A/C
VISA
MC
AE
Ⓞ

Le Pré Cadet starts its day as a lunchtime "local" for the banking and insurance company crowd, then turns into a meeting place for night owls in the evening. The place is always packed: one look at the blackboard of copious traditional dishes at friendly prices tells you why. House specialities include *tête de veau sauce gribiche* (calf's head in a vinaigrette sauce with chopped boiled eggs, gherkins, capers and herbs), *andouillette* (chitterling sausage) and *foie de veau* (calf's liver). The long list of espresso options promises an enjoyable taste of subtle fruit and caramel flavours.

Radis Roses

Traditional ✗

C1

68 r. Rodier ✉ 75009
✆ 01 48 78 03 20
e-mail radisroses@tele2.fr
www.radis-roses.com

Ⓜ Anvers
Closed 5-20 August,
Sunday and Monday – Pre-book

Menu (€27), €34

A/C

VISA

ⓂⒸ

A garden-theme sign, pistachio green façade and trendy contemporary setting. Contrary to appearances, this isn't a vegetarian restaurant, and the name refers to a pink radish soup recipe found in a Guy Martin book. But there are radishes on the menu – in the radish and beet tartare, and ginger-radish sorbet – which features updated specialities from the Drôme, in original combinations such as snail ravioli, honey-cinnamon preserved lamb with polenta and mangetout, quail in mango sauce, and root vegetable puree. Space is limited, so don't forget to book. Friendly service.

Sizin

Turkish ✗

B2

47 r. St-Georges ✉ 75009
✆ 01 44 63 02 28
e-mail ekilic@free.fr
www.sizin-restaurant.com

Ⓜ St-Georges
Closed August and Sunday

Carte €20/30

VISA

ⓂⒸ

One look at the thorough, bilingual menu and you will know this is the best Turkish restaurant in the whole 9th arrondissement. It is like taking a one-way trip to Istanbul and discovering new dishes at each meal, such as hummus, stuffed vine leaves (*yaprak sarma*), appetizing hot starters and a wide variety of grilled meats – with or without sauce – including leg of lamb kebabs (*sis*), veal cutlets stuffed with kasar cheese, mushrooms and pistachios (*dana sarma*). Last call for the attractive dining rooms with their old engravings, Iznic faience, Oriental lamps and background music! On board, you will have a very pleasant journey thanks to the friendly Kilics and their excellent suggestions.

Spring 😊

Traditional ✗

C2

28 r. Tour d'Auvergne ✉ 75009
✆ 01 45 96 05 72
e-mail freshsnail@free.fr
www.springparis.blogspot.com

Ⓜ Cadet
Closed two weeks in August, Christmas holidays,
Tuesday lunch, Wednesday lunch,
Saturday, Sunday and Monday
Number of covers limited, pre-book

Menu €32 (lunch), €35/39

A/C
VISA
Ⓜ©

All the ingredients for a successful *table d'hôte* have been combined right here – in the heart of Paris! That is the challenge brilliantly met by Daniel Rose, who came here from Chicago to study philosophy and fell in love with the idea of becoming a restaurateur. And he shares that passion with his diners, as they watch him prepare his delicious set menu, developed daily in the kitchen-dining area based on the market and his fancy. As for the wines, a group of handpicked wine-growers have selected their best bottles for you. Generosity by the score, a liberal dose of conviviality and just the right equation of talent. Please, sir, can we have some more?!

Villa Victoria

Contemporary ✗

C2

52 r. Lamartine ✉ 75009
✆ 01 48 78 60 05
Fax 01 48 78 60 05
e-mail victoria52@orange.fr

Ⓜ Notre-Dame-de-Lorette
Closed August and Sunday

Menu (€24), €32 – Carte approx. €40

A/C
VISA
Ⓜ©
AE

With dishes like razor clams in a herb vinaigrette with chunks of chorizo sausage, pan-fried scallops with *boudin noir* in a pomegranate emulsion, panna cotta in a trilogy of flavours, and *palet de chocolat* with vanilla ice cream, Villa Victoria is not the place to taste classic recipes. The chef here, who worked with "playful cuisine" advocate Gilles Choukroun, likes to give tradition a twist. Try one of her dishes – best when the inventiveness doesn't get too out of hand. Judge for yourself, while sitting in one of the two rooms at this warm neo-bistro with its wooden tables, exposed stonework and big blackboards on the walls.

Gare de l'Est · Gare du Nord · Canal St-Martin

The 10th arrondissement, an ethnically diverse district caught up in the world of fashion, has a multitude of facets. On one side, it remains working-class and off the main tourist tracks, while on the other, it has been snatched up by the bourgeois-bohemian wave that has awakened the sleepy banks of Canal St-Martin.

CANAL ST-MARTIN, A FALSE PICTURE POSTCARD

Little remains today of the mythical almost brash "atmosphere" of the canal St-Martin immortalised by Carné, Simenon, Doisneau and many others. The warehouses have been demolished and only the façade of the famous Hôtel du Nord, converted into a restaurant, remains. However, the "old-fashioned" charm of the canal's bridges, locks and barges continues to operate to the delight of the lovers of romantic Paris.

While it has no inclination to disown its picture postcard cinematographic past, the canal is also keen to keep up with fashion. A meeting-place for Parisian bourgeois-bohemians, the trendy cafés that line **quai de Valmy and quai de Jemmapes** are never empty. The terraces are inevitably so crowded, that people take their drinks across the street to the cobbled embankments. This is particularly true at the weekends when they become pedestrian and are very popular with families. Rue Beaurepaire is home to some of the capital's most avant-garde fashion stylists and also to highly specialised bookshop-galleries devoted to graphic arts and fashion. The capital's trendiest urbanites and up-and-coming artists are regulars to the district, if they aren't lucky enough to live in one of the workshop-lofts, rare in this district devoid of major museums. However the surrounding little streets can offer simple less crowded bistros.

DOORSTEP TO THE EAST

The ambience around the noisy, populous **gare de l'Est and gare du Nord** is in total contrast and resounds to the rhythm of the shops' cash registers and the hurried steps of travellers. However there is no need to take the Thalys to Amsterdam or the Eurostar to London to discover distant horizons. A world tour of savours from the most classical to the most exotic is just a stone's throw away. While the traditional flavour of Alsace continues to animate the hundred-year-old Art Deco brasseries, **porte de St-Martin and porte de St-Denis** are now an open door to the East and Africa. From authentic tandoori chicken and kebabs sold in tiny booths or colourful fragrant spices hawked from roadside stalls to the cheap hairdressing and barbers' salons, **rue**

S. Sauvignier / MICHELIN

du Faubourg St-Denis offers a cosmopolitan setting for the Turkish and Pakistani communities, while **boulevard de Strasbourg** for its part is the headquarters of the African population and the dilapidated **passage Brady and passage du Prado** have become a genuine Little India.

BUT THAT'S NOT ALL

The 10th arrondissement also offers a host of unique sites that are worth exploring. For example, the **couvent des Récollets**, a haven of peace and quiet and now the Maison de l'Architecture

and a popular meeting-place, the delightful village ambience of **place Ste-Marthe** or the pleasant garden of **St-Louis Hospital.** In terms of entertainment, the choice is vast from the mythical **New Morning** jazz club, the more eclectic **Point Ephémère** to countless theatres. If in search of a tempting treat, you could not do better than try the confectioner Furet's "Bonheur supreme" or the Verre volé bistro-wine cellar.

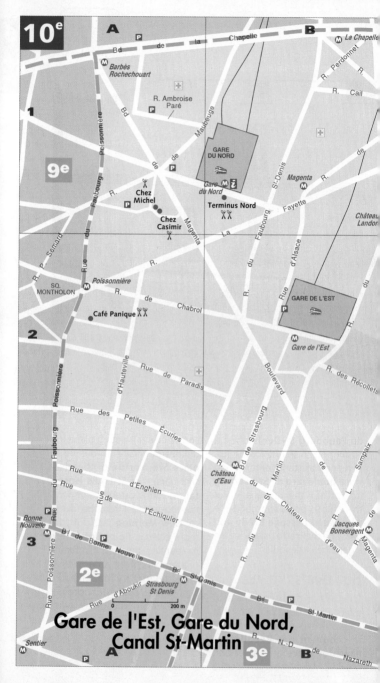

Gare de l'Est, Gare du Nord,
Canal St-Martin

224

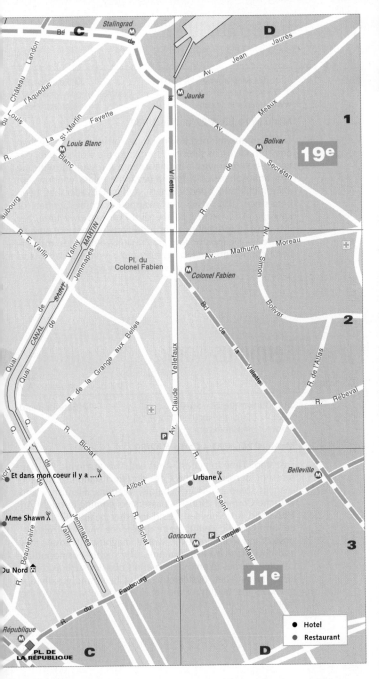

Café Panique 😊

Contemporary XX

A2

12 r. des Messageries ✉ 75010
☎ 01 47 70 06 84
www.cafepanique.com

Ⓜ Poissonnière
Closed August, February school holidays,
Saturday and Sunday

Menu (€ 20 bi), € 27 bi (lunch)/32

VISA
MC

Café Panique, hidden down a long corridor, has more than one surprise up its sleeve. A former textile workshop reconverted before it was fashionable into a restaurant with the airy atmosphere of a loft (mezzanine, glass window, art exhibitions and open kitchen). Odile Guyader has been here since 1992, when she swapped teaching German for cooking. And we're glad she did! Polished over time, her inventive, unpretentious and delicious recipes are sure to arouse your curiosity: foie gras ravioli with spices and verbena capuccino; *gâteau de veau aux pommes de terre*; and *mœlleux au chocolat, jus de vin rouge aux épices*.

Terminus Nord

Brasserie XX

B1

23 r. Dunkerque ✉ 75010
☎ 01 42 85 05 15 **Fax** 01 40 16 13 98
www.terminusnord.com

Ⓜ Gare du Nord

Menu (€ 24), € 31 – Carte € 32/80

VISA
MC

Last stop! Time to get off – and eat! This authentic Parisian brasserie across from the Gare du Nord station must have seen its share of Picards, Lillois, Wallons, Flemish – and with the Chunnel, British – passengers coming through! Art Deco and Art Nouveau blend together beautifully here in the atmospheric ceiling, period frescoes and high mirrors, posters and sculptures everywhere, magnificent mosaic tiles and chocolate leather furniture. The highly cosmopolitan clientele comes to enjoy the menu's classics such as *choucroute, andouillettes*, oysters and rib of beef, and greatly appreciates the quality of the service and the variety on the menu.

Chez Casimir

Bistro ✗

6 r. Belzunce ✉ 75010
✆ 01 48 78 28 80

Ⓜ Gare du Nord
Closed Saturday and Sunday

Menu (€22), €29

Chez Casimir, the annex of Chez Michel next door, shares the same qualities as its parent establishment, namely straightforward and tasty dishes prepared lovingly and without fuss, like its famous game specialities in season. Behind the façade is a congenial dining room with an bistro atmosphere – a little bar by the entrance, straw-coloured walls decorated with copperware and retro paintings, closely packed and simply set wooden tables, and brown imitation leather banquettes. The warm and convivial ambiance makes you feel like prolonging the meal. And don't think about skipping dessert – they're too inventive to pass up!

Chez Michel

Traditional ✗

10 r. Belzunce ✉ 75010
✆ 01 44 53 06 20

Ⓜ Gare du Nord
Closed 29 July-20 August, Monday lunch,
Saturday and Sunday

Menu €30 – Carte €45/65

OK, the place could use a bit of freshening up – especially the retro dining room and vaulted cellar decorated with Breton flags – but the informal and convivial atmosphere at this well-known establishment draws in local regulars and tourists from all over, overriding the issue of aesthetics. And you came here for Thierry Breton's cooking anyway, not the decor. His traditional menu with dishes from Brittany (where he hails from) is complemented by daily suggestions on the blackboard. There are no crêpes, but try the delicious and skilfully prepared dishes from the *terroir*, with a penchant for game – not to be missed when in season. Not to mention the authentic *kouign-amann* (sweet buttery pastry) – a delightful classic.

GARE DE L'EST • GARE DU NORD • CANAL ST-MARTIN

Et dans mon cœur il y a...

Bistro 🍴

56 r. Lancry ⌧ 75010   Ⓜ Jacques Bonsergent
℘ 01 42 38 07 37   Closed 25 December-1st January,
Fax 01 42 02 52 60   Saturday lunch and Sunday
e-mail reservation@etdansmoncoeur.com
www.etdansmoncoeur.com

Menu (€16 bi), €20 bi – Carte €37/49

Ⓐ/Ⓒ
Ⓥ𝗜𝗦𝗔
Ⓜ©
ⒶⒺ
Ⓞ

The dishes have catchy names – *"filet très mignon"*, *"véritable entrecôte pour connaisseurs"*, *quasi de veau* and *mœlleux au chocolat* – that reflect the straightforward, authentic and up-to-date cuisine at this bistro. A stone's throw from the Canal, it has a trendy look that blends old and modern with the vestiges of a Belle Epoque decor (superb spiral staircase and zinc bar), cosy purple velvet banquettes, neo-Baroque light fixtures and a bookcase. The closely-packed tables, warm wood panelling and soft lighting give it a charming, convivial air, and the service is very friendly. The perfect place for the neighbourhood Bobos (Bohemian bourgeois) and everyone else too!

Mme Shawn

Thai 🍴

34 r. Y. Toudic ⌧ 75010   Ⓜ Jacques Bonsergent
℘ 01 42 08 05 07   Closed 24 December-2 January
Fax 01 42 02 25 60
e-mail reservation@mmeshawn.com
www.mmeshawn.com

Menu (€12 bi), €17 bi – Carte €25/33

Ⓐ/Ⓒ
Ⓥ𝗜𝗦𝗔
Ⓜ©
ⒶⒺ
Ⓞ

Mme Shawn is a very trendy Thai restaurant! The tone is set right away by the discreet glass façade on a rather quiet street near the Canal Saint-Martin. Both chic and authentic, with none of the usual Asian restaurant clichés, it leaves a lasting impression. The dazzling decor features soft lighting, stone panels representing the Buddha, Thai objects, fine bamboo screens separating the relatively snug tables, attractive place settings with little enamel terracotta cups and wooden chopsticks. The cuisine offers a range of typical dishes full of flavour (with herbs, coconut, galangal, coriander, lemongrass and ginger).

Urbane 😊

Contemporary 🍴

D3

12 r. Arthur-Groussier ⊠ 75010
☏ 01 42 40 74 75
e-mail urbane.resto@gmail.com

Ⓜ Goncourt
Closed 3 weeks in August, Saturday lunch,
Sunday dinner and Monday

Menu (€15), €19 (weekday lunch)/29

VISA
Ⓜ©

Blue-grey façade, white interior with imitation leather banquettes and industrial lamps – here's a trendy place, run by Audrey, an Irish filmmaker, and her husband Olivier Maindroult. She has instilled the place with her urban spirit, while he takes care of the cooking, using fine ingredients in up-to-date dishes influenced by Gilles Choukroun. Trained as a pastry chef and baker, he is renowned for his pleasantly surprising desserts including a prune frangipane lollipop with gingerbread ice cream. Add to that the relaxed service, the magazines provided for your perusal, and an in-house DJ, and you're bound to have a good time.

1840, THE BIRTH OF THE PARISIAN BAGUETTE

The origin of the Parisian baguette is uncertain, but the most likely hypothesis is that it came from Vienna! It reached Paris in 1840, in a bakery at 92 rue de Richelieu owned by an Austrian who initiated Parisians into his country's traditions. In 1933 a decree was proclaimed regulating how traditional French bread was to be made (no additives or freezing), and the famous "tradi" was born. It has to be 70cm long and weigh between 250 and 300g. The golden crust must be grooved and crunchy, the inside fluffy, light and cream-coloured. The winner of the Grand Prix de la baguette, held every year by the Paris City Hall, supplies the Élysée Palace for one whole year.

Nation · Voltaire République

Encircled by place de la République, boulevard de Ménilmontant, boulevard de Charonne and rue du **faubourg Saint-Antoine,** the essentially residential 11th arrondissement is no less rich in history. It hosts two of the three squares that are still hotbeds of political unrest in the east of Paris, place de la République and place de la Nation. Synonymous with protest marches, rallies and demonstrations, these two squares alone symbolise two of the components held most sacred by the French people: democracy (République) and a community of fate (Nation). It may be the overpowering memory of some of France's most troubled moments that has contributed to the incessant, almost frenetic, activity of the 11th, visible in the jumble of markets, bars, nightclubs and restaurants that leave the walker in no doubt as to the district's amazing diversity.

NATION – RÉPUBLIQUE – THE ROAD TO ENLIGHTENMENT?

Both squares are linked by **boulevard Voltaire,** named after the satirist philosopher who is probably the figure that best represents the era of Enlightenment. In an amusing coincidence, the urban fabric along the boulevard reveals an immense variety of small booths and stalls, Haussmannian and dilapidated buildings and bars and restaurants of all sorts in a splendid illustration of what could be deemed to be the diverse nature of open-minded societies. The height of animation along the boulevard can be found at the crossroads with rue de Charonne. Here executives pressed for time rub shoulders with the fruit and vegetable vendors of **place de la Nation** and hard-up students, hence the range of restaurants for all budgets that cater to this vast socio-professional melting pot. The vicinity around place de la République is equally rich in **brasseries** and **large bistros,** which can be highly useful when an army of strikers require feeding during demos!

The atmosphere around Nation is both quieter and more marginal, with wide avenues almost entirely residential. **Rue de Charonne** runs from Bastille to Père-Lachaise cemetery, parallel with **rue de la Roquette** with which it shares more than one similarity. Both these long, narrow and sometimes winding streets are also increasingly popular with yuppies who are attracted by the district's lively character, range of leisure pursuits and social diversity.

TRENDSETTING BOHEMIA

The scenery changes as you reach the corner of **rue Saint-Maur** and **rue Oberkampf** to reveal a breeding ground of

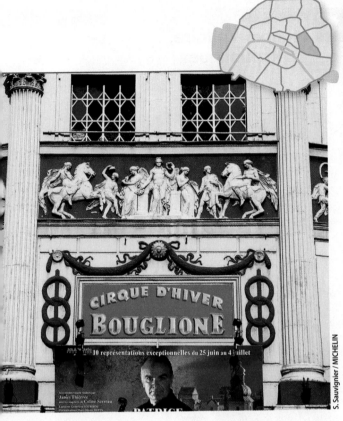

bourgeois-bohemian style festive effervescence. Formerly
deeply working-class, the district has been fundamentally
transformed under the impetus
of a generation of young trend-
setters in search of a certain
authenticity that can still be felt
in the countless **café-theatres
and concert halls,** small gastronomic (or otherwise) cafés
and picturesque unpretentious
eating houses frequented by an
ill-assorted clientele. The locals
sometimes mutter and curse
about being invaded in this way,
but those exploring the district
are overjoyed. Going down rue
Oberkampf towards boulevard
Richard Lenoir, look out for
the handsome **winter circus**
(formerly the "cirque Napoleon")
built by Hittorff on the model
of an antique coliseum. The
surrounding streets are extremely well equipped in bars and
restaurants of all types, although
not renowned for haute cuisine.

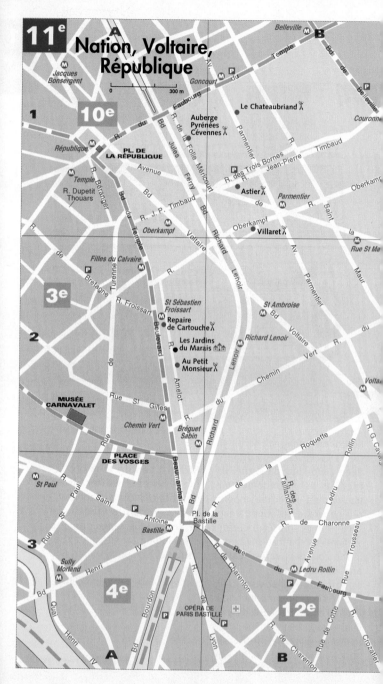

11e
Nation, Voltaire, République

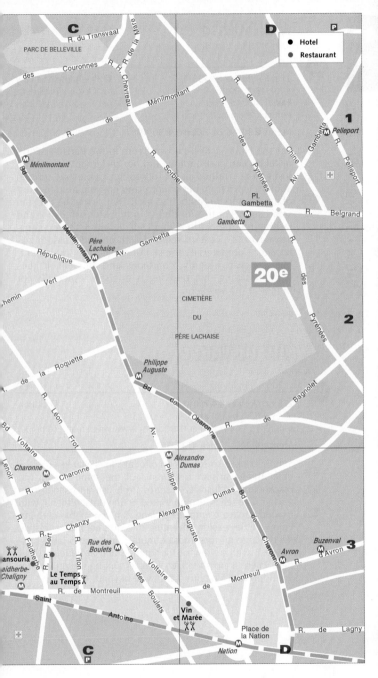

Mansouria 😊

C3

Moroccan 🍴🍴

11 r. Faidherbe ✉ 75011
✆ 01 43 71 00 16
Fax 01 40 24 21 97
e-mail lollisoraya@yahoo.fr

Ⓜ Faidherbe Chaligny
Closed 10-18 August, Monday lunch,
Tuesday lunch and Sunday

Menu €30/46 bi – Carte €30/49

🄰🄲
ⓥⒾⓢⓐ
Ⓜ🄲

Fatema Hal is a well-known figure in the Parisian world of Moroccan gastronomy, and her restaurant is quite an institution. Trained as an ethnologist, she has written about recipes from her country and has imparted the best of her roots to this authentic spot. That's why the Parisian smart set never tires of dining in this Moorish decor and tasting the true North African specialities – *tajines*, couscous, *pastillas*, custard scented with orange blossom water, etc. – prepared by the skilful cooks. The incomparable service is friendly, courteous and efficient. It goes without saying that booking is advised, especially for dinner at the weekend.

Vin et Marée

D3

Seafood 🍴🍴

276 bd Voltaire ✉ 75011
✆ 01 43 72 31 23 **Fax** 01 40 24 00 23
e-mail vmvoltaire@vin-et-maree.com **www.**vin-et-maree.com

Ⓜ Nation

Menu (€21) – Carte €32/58

🄰🄲
ⓥⒾⓢⓐ
Ⓜ🄲
🄰🄴

Simply cooked seafood is on offer at Vin et Marée – like the other three Parisian restaurants of the same name. The blackboard exclusively features fresh fish and shellfish in season. The sea is also honoured on the dessert menu, with roasted papaya *à la tahitienne* and Zanzibar baba au rhum. Enjoy a little seaside adventure in a discreet brasserie-style decor (large mirrors, mosaic murals and comfortable banquettes), with a view of the kitchen and an efficient wait staff. There is no shortage of takers among the crowds on the Boulevard Voltaire – and well beyond.

Astier

Bistro ✗

B1

44 r. J.-P. Timbaud ✉ 75011
✆ 01 43 57 16 35
e-mail restaurant.astier@wanadoo.fr

Ⓜ Parmentier
Pre-book

Menu (€20), €26 (lunch)/30

VISA
ⓂⒸ
🍇

The Astier recipe is unbeatable – an exceptionally well-stocked cellar and a traditional menu featuring simple food and good value for money. And its popularity never falters, because people never tire of its old bistro decor. The red-and-white checked tablecloths sporting the Astier monogram (like the tableware and waiters' aprons) and the tightly-packed, unpretentious tables tell you that you're in for an informal meal. The festivities start with *harengs pommes à l'huile*, moving on to baked monkfish or a *blanquette à l'ancienne*, topped off with a *crème caramel*, for example. Menus composed around one ingredient (rabbit, pork, lamb) are also available.

Auberge Pyrénées Cévennes 😊

Terroir ✗

A1

106 r. Folie-Méricourt ✉ 75011
✆ 01 43 57 33 78

Ⓜ République
Closed 30 July-20 August, Saturday lunch,
Sunday and public holidays

Menu €29 – Carte €28/69

A/C
VISA
ⓂⒸ
AE

The good humour in this establishment strikes you the minute you walk in the door. The jokes start flying and the proprietress gives you the warmest of welcomes. In the dining room where hams and sausages hang from the ceiling, the tables are snug. There's no doubt about it – diners here have a good time. The cuisine features dishes from the Pyrénées and the Cévennes, but doesn't neglect the other regions either. The recipes are authentic and generous, "plats canailles" and "lyonnaiseries", washed down with a very drinkable jug of Beaujolais, for example. This place has the charm of a regional inn at reasonable prices, and without any fuss. Wet blankets should stay at home!

NATION • VOLTAIRE • RÉPUBLIQUE

Au Petit Monsieur

A2

50 r. Amelot ✉ 75011
✆ 01 43 55 54 04
Fax 01 43 14 77 03
e-mail aupetitmonsieur@wanadoo.fr
www.aupetitmonsieur.fr

Ⓜ Chemin Vert
Closed August, Saturday lunch,
Sunday and Monday

Menu (€19), €26/35 – Carte €36/57

VISA
Ⓜ©
AE

The Petit Monsieur – formerly the C'Amelot – embodies the best of Parisian bistros. It has it all, from the snug tables and leatherette banquettes to the elegant table settings and very friendly service. That includes the pleasure of seeing and hearing what's being cooked up in the kitchen. Perhaps it will help you choose from among the daily suggestions and the very appetising dishes on the menu, including the fine cold meats (from Auvergne, Spain, Corsica and Italy) and a selection of delicious *bouchées fines* (tapas), available individually, as a tasting platter (a blend of all the items) or in your own combination.

Le Chateaubriand

B1

129 av. Parmentier ✉ 75011
✆ 01 43 57 45 95

Ⓜ Goncourt
Closed Saturday lunch, Sunday and Monday

Menu (€14), €19 (lunch)/40 (dinner) – Carte €28/36

VISA
Ⓜ©
AE

It looks just like a 1930s bistro, but plays on the neo-retro theme. While the decor is from the past, the culinary repertoire is up-to-date, and the well-trained staff right off a fashion catwalk. The "gorgeous guys" do a terrific waiting job, and that's the least they could do to present the dishes created by famous young Basque chef Inaki Aizpitarte. At lunchtime, clients on a tight schedule enjoy his straightforward and ultra-fresh creations. In the evening he caters to food-lovers who prefer to take their time, with more elaborate and simply delicious dishes – to the delight of his clientele, already won over.

Repaire de Cartouche

A2

Traditional ✗

99 r. Amelot ✉ 75011
☎ 01 47 00 25 86
Fax 01 43 38 85 91

Ⓜ St-Sébastien Froissart
Closed 1st-8 May, August,
Sunday and Monday

Menu (€14), €26 (weekday lunch) – Carte €35/48

VISA
ⓂⒸ
🐾

This restaurant seems to be cultivating its country inn look with its exposed beams, wood panelling, solid wood furniture, small-paned windows and frescoes to the glory of the impetuous Cartouche (who is said to have taken refuge here after he deserted the army in 1713). Could it be a nod to chef-owner Rodolphe Paquin's native Normandy? His traditional cuisine ignores trends which come in and out of fashion, sometimes borrowing from the bistro repertoire, and is fond of game in autumn. Needless to say, the well-stocked cellar – featuring numerous small producers and natural wines – has the perfect beverage for each of these dishes. The lunch formula and menu are offered at very reasonable prices.

NATION • VOLTAIRE • RÉPUBLIQUE

Le Temps au Temps

C3

Bistro ✗

13 r. Paul Bert ✉ 75011
☎ 01 43 79 63 40
Fax 01 43 79 63 40

Ⓜ Faidherbe Chaligny
Closed August, 24 December-1st January,
Sunday and Monday

Menu (€18), €30/38

VISA
ⓂⒸ
ⒶⒺ
🐾

This little neighbourhood bistro is run by a friendly and enthusiastic young couple who know everything there is to know about receiving guests. Take the time to check it out, and give in to its charming atmosphere. The lady of the house is in charge of the service and sustaining the convivial ambiance, while her talented husband creates streamlined recipes highlighting the freshest ingredients. The delicious and creative dishes include pan-fried cep mushrooms with foie gras, *poule au pot* with vegetables and wild flowers, and a lemon tart revised by the chef. The cleverly composed wine list prompts the same excitement. It's always full, so booking is advised.

Villaret

Bistro ✗

13 r. Ternaux ✉ 75011
✆ 01 43 57 75 56

Ⓜ Parmentier
Closed August, 24 December-2 January,
Saturday lunch and Sunday

Menu (€22), €27/50 (dinner) – Carte €33/49

VISA
Ⓜ
AE
⊗

Behind this discreet façade on the rue Ternaux is a really nice little establishment. Its motto is "do things well, in all simplicity". The pretty but unassuming bistro decor features a fine zinc bar of the kind one rarely sees anymore, exposed beams and wood everywhere. Looking over the menu, the "plats canailles" which the chef cooks his own way, are what stand out, although the market-inspired recipes look tempting too. As for the cellar, you dream of going down for a look at all those vintage bottles and other prestigious wines. Fans of Burgundy and Côtes-du-rhône will have lots of great ones to choose from!

"HAZAR DE LA FOURCHETTE" (POT LUCK)

Paris has always had working-class restaurants where people with no kitchen at home could get a hot meal. The number of gargotes (greasy spoons), taverns and guinguettes (open-air cafés) grew with the rural exodus in the first half of the 19C. The most modest of all were the "bijoux" vendors (so-called in Les Halles slang) who sold fries, sausages and soups on pushcarts near the markets. Their speciality was a large pot in which they cooked up a "harlequin", a mixture of table scraps from prosperous homes and restaurants which varied in quality from day to day. As a result, people called such places "hazar de la fourchette" (pot luck).

BISTROT

Bastille · Bercy
Gare de Lyon

A substantial slice of the city between Bastille, the Seine and the town of Vincennes, the 12th is one of those arrondissements where versatility is second nature. It would be fruitless to try and limit the area to its legendary square, the historic **Bastille,** now witness to the extravagant behaviour of the city's night-birds. It is of course a high spot of Parisian nightlife and the location of an international symphonic stage in harmony with the capital, but other districts a little further afield are also worth exploring. Along the Seine, pause and admire the titanic efforts deployed along the embankment, in particular on the former site of **Bercy's wine warehouses**. Near the ring road, the 12th reveals yet another facet, a quieter, greener and friendlier face as you approach Vincennes and its parks and woods.

To war!

The rifles and grenades of the great revolutionary struggles gave way to more festive and peaceful events. The Bastille is home to national celebrations (July 14) and also demonstrations. The district has changed immensely over the last 20 years, particularly with the construction of the Opera House and shops, cafés and restaurants have sprung up in a joyful and some-what chaotic mixture of styles and ambiences. Time-worn and freshly reno-vated buildings stand along-side modern edifices in what has become one of the capital's most attractive districts. The dock of the nearby **Arsenal** marina, shaded by plane trees and dotted with little harbour-side cafés, is extremely pleasant to stroll round.

A village
in the city

Apart from the imposing outline of the **Ministry of Finance,** Bercy used to be above all known for the grassy pyramid of its **Palais Omnisport,** whose immense hall, one of the largest in Paris, has given rise to a host of cafés, bars and grocery shops in the immediate vicinity that refuel the hungry music lovers on concert nights. Now however the rest of the embankment, which stretches as far as the ring road, has been treated to a major redevelopment plan including a landscaped floral park "à la française", the conversion of the old wine storehouses into restaurants, cafés and shopping malls, a new **cinema complex** and a long façade of neo-Haussmannian buildings, all of which has radically changed the appearance of this district. The area is alive and animated from morning until late into the night and **"Bercy-Village"** should not be missed.

S. Sauvignier / MICHELIN

LITTLE-KNOWN POINTS OF INTEREST

Two other areas are worth a detour, at least in gastronomic terms. First, **Gare de Lyon** and its surroundings, whose **traditional brasseries** that specialise in quick service make it a point of honour to cater to everyone at all times. Next, the district around the covered market of **place d'Alligre,** less well-known, even to Parisians, is now home to a friendly micro-district of "ordinary"

folk, where old-fashioned bistros welcome regulars and a few rare visitors with equal cordiality. Every weekend a flea market and African fruit and vegetables stalls add colour to the traditional market fare.

.

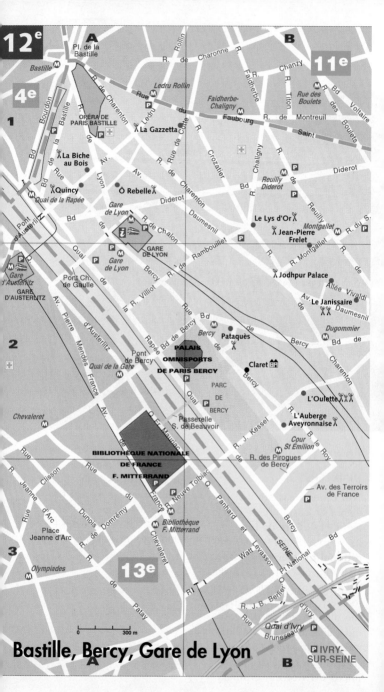

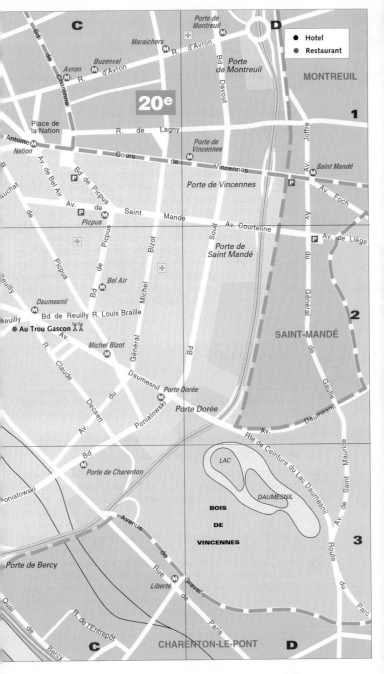

C

Bd de Charonne

Maraichers Ⓜ R. d'Avron

Porte de Montreuil ✚ Ⓜ

D

Porte de Montreuil

● Hotel
● Restaurant

Avron Ⓜ Buzenval R. d'Avron

MONTREUIL

20e

Place de la Nation

Antoine Ⓜ Nation

R. de Lagny

Cours de Vincennes

Porte de Vincennes Ⓜ

Av. Joffre

Av. Saint Mandé Ⓜ

1

Bd Davout

Av. de Bel Air

Bd de Picpus Ⓟ

Av. de Picpus Ⓟ Ⓜ Saint Mandé

Porte de Vincennes

Av. Courteline

Av. Foch

Av. de Liège Ⓟ

Porte de Saint Mandé

Soult

Av. du Général de Gaulle

Picpus

Bd de Picpus

Bizot

Michel

✚

✚

Bel Air

SAINT-MANDÉ

2

Daumesnil Ⓜ

Bd de Reuilly R. Louis Braille

Av. Daumesnil

● Au Trou Gascon ✗✗

Michel Bizot Ⓜ

Général

Daumesnil

Bd

Porte Dorée Ⓜ

Av. de Saint Maurice

R. Claude Decaen

Poniatowski

Parte Dorée

Av. Daumesnil

Rte de Ceinture du Lac Daumesnil

Bd

Porte de Charenton Ⓜ

LAC

DAUMESNIL

Av. de Saint Maurice

Poniatowski

BOIS

DE

Route

3

Porte de Bercy

Avenue de Gravelle

VINCENNES

Route du Parc

Quai de Bercy

R. de l'Entrepôt

Rue Liberté de

Ⓜ Paris

C

CHARENTON-LE-PONT

D

243

L'Oulette

🗶🗶🗶

B2

15 pl. Lachambeaudie ⊠ 75012
📞 01 40 02 02 12
Fax 01 40 02 04 77
e-mail info@l-oulette.com **www**.l-oulette.com

🅜 Cour St-Émilion
Closed Saturday and Sunday

Menu €45/90 bi – Carte €52/79

What is Marcel Baudis cooking up in his "Oulette", the Occitan name for a small pot? Specialities from the South-west, his native land, which he reinvents with talent. Among these flavourful dishes are his cream of artichoke soup with truffle cream, roasted codfish with a spice crust, braised oxtail, and the original *pain d'épice perdu à la coque* (gingerbread French toast). His ideas are drawn from areas such as Quercy, Corbières, Gascogne and the Cévennes. The ingredients and wines are expertly chosen (the cellar has about a hundred labels). As for the warm atmosphere in the discreetly contemporary, hushed dining room, it cheers up the "suit-and-tie" crowd at lunchtime. Special feature: the charming terrace shaded by thuja trees.

Le Janissaire

🗶🗶

B2

22 allée Vivaldi ⊠ 75012
📞 01 43 40 37 37
Fax 01 43 40 38 39
e-mail karamanmus@hotmail.com **www**.lejanissaire.fr

🅜 Daumesnil
Closed Saturday lunch and Sunday

Menu (€13), €23/42 – Carte €21/40

Le Janissaire offers an excellent overview of Turkey, authenticated by the entirely Turkish staff. The terrace invites you to take a seat here before even seeing the dining room, which is equally attractive with its Ottoman rugs, paintings and stained glass. In short, this is a fine environment in which to explore the gastronomic specialities from this land, such as *ezme* (spicy tomato purée), *borek* (cheese puff pastries), and *tavuk* (chicken brochettes). For dessert, try the rare and surprising *kabak tatlisi* and *yeniceri tatlisi* (pumpkin and aubergine preserves). While the regional wine is perfectly fine, if you want to try something really different, have the *ayran*, a drink made from salty yoghurt and lemon.

Au Trou Gascon ✿

South-west of France ✗✗

C2

40 r. Taine ⊠ 75012   **Ⓜ Daumesnil**
✆ 01 43 44 34 26   Closed August, Saturday and Sunday
Fax 01 43 07 80 55
e-mail trougascon@orange.fr **www**.autrougascon.fr

Menu €36 (lunch)/50 (dinner) – Carte €52/60

Au Trou Gascon

Alain Dutournier got his start here in 1973, gaining recognition in Paris for the Gascony terroir. Although he is now a starred chef who runs another fine establishment in a posh neighbourhood (the Carré des Feuillants), his old 1900s bistro is still a family affair. With his wife Nicole in charge and Jean-François Godiard in the kitchen, the Trou Gascon delights connoisseurs of southwestern specialities, specifically from Adour and the ocean, starting with the excellent *cassoulet*, game and *jambon au couteau* (hand-carved ham). In addition to these classics, the cuisine also has a creative and contemporary side. The terroir, honoured and reinterpreted here, and enhanced by a fabulous wine list (with over 1,000 different wines), has a very bright future indeed! The elegant grey and beige decor has a streamlined modern look offset by Empire mouldings and paintings. Service is friendly and attentive.

First Course
- Chipirons cuits à la plaque (summer).
- Gâteau de cèpes, copeaux de vieux jambon.

Main Course
- Cassoulet "Trou Gascon" aux haricots de maïs.
- Lièvre à la mode d'Aquitaine (autumn).

Dessert
- Poire pochée au miel d'arbousier, baba punché.
- Tourtière chaude et croustillante, glace caramel salé.

L'Auberge Aveyronnaise

B2

40 r. Lamé ✉ 75012
✆ 01 43 40 12 24 **Fax** 01 43 40 12 15
e-mail lesaubergistes@hotmail.fr

Ⓜ Cour St-Émilion
Closed 1st-15 August

Menu (€19), €25 – Carte €29/39

The name says it all: welcome to the Aveyron! More a brasserie than an inn, this establishment in the modern Bercy area is solidly rooted in the Rouergue terroir. The menu is filled with mouth-watering specialities: *tripoux* (sheep's offal and feet), *boudin* (blood sausage), shanks with lentils, stuffed cabbage, cold meats, *aligot, millefeuille à l'ancienne, flan à la louche*. The generous portions are made with the best of ingredients (Ségala veal, Aubrac beef, fresh Laguiole tome), and watered down with jugs of local wine. In addition to the neo-rustic rooms – with fireplace and checkered tablecloths naturally – you can enjoy the two terraces, on the street or in the private courtyard (only open at lunchtime in the summer).

La Biche au Bois

A1

45 av. Ledru-Rollin ✉ 75012
✆ 01 43 43 34 38

Ⓜ Gare de Lyon
Closed 20 July-20 August, 23 December-
2 January, Monday lunch, Saturday and Sunday

Menu €25 – Carte approx. €30

Fans of La Biche au Bois like this establishment for its quality and reasonable prices. The conscientious, dynamic owner takes pride in preserving tradition here, in the simple setting of a classic, convivial bistro with snug tables sporting tablecloths, fine silverware and old-style cooking. *Foie gras au torchon, terrine de campagne au poivre vert* (country terrine with green pepper sauce), *pavé de saumon sauce forestière* (salmon steak with mushroom and bacon sauce) are featured. Other dishes include game in season. For dessert, try the house *Opéra Biche* (a creamy cake with custard cream) or the fruit tart. In short, a menu with a strong flavour of the *terroir*, the reason for this establishment's success.

La Gazzetta

Fusion ✗

29 r. de Cotte ✉ 75012   Ⓜ Ledru Rollin
🕾 01 43 47 47 05   Closed August, Sunday and Monday
Fax 01 43 47 47 17
e-mail team@lagazzetta.fr **www**.lagazzetta.fr

Menu (€14), €19 (lunch), €34/45 – Carte €37/58

VISA
Ⓜ©
ⒶⒺ
🍇

The team from the China Club and the Fumoir has opened a third establishment, La Gazzetta, half cosy bistro and half modern brasserie. The all-in-one concept – restaurant, wine bar and cultural café (French and foreign-language press available) – has made this a trendy spot where the food has proved itself worthy on the menu featuring Mediterranean ingredients. After a hesitant start, La Gazzetta has hit its stride thanks to Petter Nilsson (ex-chef at Les Trois Salons in Uzès). A Swede, he is perfectly at home with Corsican, Italian and Spanish specialities, favouring simple flavours. The shoulder of lamb with honey and the *cassata* (chilled sweet Sicilian ricotta with candied fruit) are delicious, and the regional wines bursting with sun.

Jean-Pierre Frelet 😊

Traditional ✗

25 r. Montgallet ✉ 75012   Ⓜ Montgallet
🕾 01 43 43 76 65   Closed 28-26 August,
e-mail marie_rene. frelet@club-internet.fr   Saturday lunch and Sunday

Menu (€19), €27 (dinner) – Carte €39/46

A/C
VISA
Ⓜ©

The Frelets welcome you into their place like longstanding friends. Passionate about their profession, they work with the precision of true artisans. They form the perfect couple – she in the dining room and he in the kitchen – combining her warm reception with his know-how in cooking straightforward market-based cuisine with no false notes. The focus is on the ingredients here, freshly prepared in dishes that change by the day. That is the reason for the success of this little neighbourhood restaurant with a minimalist decor. Informed gourmets are inevitably drawn to the well-designed lunch menu, and consider themselves lucky to get in, as there are only twenty places per sitting. Book without delay.

Jodhpur Palace

B2

42 allée Vivaldi ✉ 75012   **Ⓜ** Daumesnil
☎ 01 43 40 72 46 **Fax** 01 43 40 17 02
e-mail jodhpur-palace@yahoo.fr **www.**jodhpurpalace.com

Menu € 16 bi (weekday lunch), € 25 bi/36 bi – Carte € 23/45

VISA

Ⓜ©

Indian cuisine, once scarce in the 12th arrondissement, has found a home in this spacious Oriental "palace" with its enticing red façade. Baldev Singh has chosen a quiet street near the Coulée Verte walkway for his second Parisian establishment. In this wonderful haven of peace (especially on the shady terrace) you will be transported to the land of saris and spices. The surprising decor blends traditional frescoes and mahogany wood panelling with the very modern-looking spotless white walls. This is a far cry from the usual atmosphere with subdued lighting (although it has that too, in a small alcove at the back). The menu features classic recipes from around the country, from Jodphur in the North all the way to the South of India.

Le Lys d'Or

B1

5 pl. Col-Bourgoin ✉ 75012   **Ⓜ** Reuilly Diderot
☎ 01 44 68 98 88 **Fax** 01 44 68 98 80
www.lysdorming.com

Menu (€ 12 bi), € 22/26 – Carte € 21/40

A/C

VISA

Ⓜ©

AE

Here you can enjoy all the gastronomic flavours of China in Paris, and in the setting of a luxurious palace where the colour red and greenery are the dominant notes (including an indoor garden with bamboo, streams and fountains). The award-winning Lys d'Or, which has been open for over 10 years, is an invitation to explore the underappreciated culinary art of the Middle Kingdom. The four regional cooking styles – Sechuan, Shanghai, Canton and Beijing – are surprisingly diverse and extremely refined. Although you will find the usual *dim sum* on the menu, try something different like the *gui fei* (grilled meat), tofu tartare with coriander, crab with crispy vegetables, or *gou fen* (Asian paella). The wine list has both Chinese and French wines.

Ô Rebelle

Innovative ✗

A1

24 r. Traversière ✉ 75012   Ⓜ Gare de Lyon
✆ 01 43 40 88 98   Closed 4-26 August, 24 December-1st January,
Fax 01 43 40 88 99   Saturday lunch and Sunday
e-mail info@o-rebelle.fr **www**.o-rebelle.fr

Menu € 24 (lunch)/57 – Carte € 42/62

VISA

ⓂⒸ

The name promises something revolutionary, but does the food really live up to it? The answer is yes, judging from the creative international cuisine cooked up by the Japanese chef. The dishes are a subtle blend of flavours: fricassee of squid in cuttlefish ink, tuna carpaccio with miso vinaigrette, snail pancakes on leek *croustillants* with vanilla, marshmallows with red berries. The cellar is equally exotic, featuring wines from the New World (Chile, Australia, California). The decor is less exuberant, preferring the current refined and tasteful look with beige banquettes, chairs covered in red canvas, leafy green walls and modern paintings. The perfect place for globe-trotting aesthetes!

Pataquès

Bistro ✗

B2

40 bd Bercy ✉ 75012   Ⓜ Bercy
✆ 01 43 07 37 75 **Fax** 01 43 07 36 64
e-mail pataquesbercy@aol.com **www**.pataques.fr

Menu € 30 – Carte € 33/47

A/C

VISA

ⓂⒸ

AE

This bistro-brasserie has become with time the "local" for the Ministry of Finance, just across the street. Its sunny decor suits the Mediterranean – and more specifically, Provençal – cuisine to a tee. The simply prepared dishes speak for themselves: tuna and eggplant *millefeuille,* codfish lasagna, *sauté de veau aux olives et citron* (veal with olives and lemon), and *patience d'Aix* served with nougat ice cream and a raspberry coulis. The flavours will transport you straight to the land of Cézanne. Furthermore, the contagious good cheer in the dining room, the attentive service and very attractive menu make Pataquès a very likable place.

Quincy

A1

Traditional ✗

28 av. Ledru-Rollin ✉ 75012
✆ 01 46 28 46 76
Fax 01 46 28 46 76
www.lequincy.fr

Ⓜ Gare de Lyon
Closed 15 August-15 September,
Saturday, Sunday and Monday

Carte €44/76

Although Paris is becoming more and more upscale, there are still some establishments outside the trends and fashions. The Quincy is one of them, and so much the better! Unchanged for the past thirty years, this rustic bistro like they don't make them anymore (watch out – they don't even take credit cards!) resembles its owner, Michel Bosshard, known as Bobosse. This generous, talkative bon vivant proposes dishes which are like him : 100% homemade and with influences from the Ardèche and Berry regions. Meat and cold meats are featured, as well as foie gras, *terrine fermière*, stuffed cabbage, *cassoulet*, and chocolate mousse. Better than a nostalgic *madeleine,* these recipes with their good old-fashioned flavours will bring you sheer delight.

IN VINO VERITAS

A stroll through Paris immediately brings to life its winemaking past – with names like Rues du Pressoir (Wine Press Street), des Vignes (Vine Street), des Vignobles (Vineyard Street), and Vineuse (Winey Street). Did you know that the name of the Goutte d'Or quarter comes from a wine so famous that it was given as a gift to kings? Or that the name guinguette (an open-air dance hall) comes from the "guinguet" grapes growing on the slopes of Belleville? There are still a few vineyards left in the city. The one in Montmartre is familiar to Parisians due to its Harvest Festival featuring bacchanalian brotherhoods, folklore groups and brass bands that come from all over France to take part in the parade and the village atmosphere. To be consumed without moderation!

Place d'Italie · Gare d'Austerlitz
Bibliothèque Nationale de France

As populous as it is vast, the 13th is one of the rare Parisian arrondissements to still show signs of demographic growth. In full boom since the rehabilitation of its embankments, this area of Paris is both a new rental bonanza and an attractive economic, commercial and cultural centre. Impressively enterprising, its multiple facets provide a surprising juxtaposition of scenery. From **Gare d'Austerlitz** and nearby Jardin des Plantes to **Place d'Italie** opening onto a more working-class and cosmopolitan district of the "left bank", the 13th is proud of its contrasts.

ASIA-ON-SEINE

The largest Asian community in Paris lives south of Place d'Italie, down the avenue of the same name, around the Olympiades, a vast complex of high-rise dwellings that watches over Chinatown. This pocket handkerchief of Asia is however a far cry from the suburbs of Peking and its population of Chinese, Vietnamese, Cambodians and Laotians has woven a tight net of combined linguistic, artistic and culinary influences. Visitors are invariably surprised by the ideograms of the illuminated shop signs that light up these tightly packed streets. Once the first surprise over, you cannot fail but be caught up in the spicy scents and the steam from the rice wafting out of the countless restaurants and which fill the air with the perfume of the East. Let yourself be tempted, or even better, venture into **Tang Frères,** a supermarket on avenue d'Ivry, whose shelves are piled high with unknown fruit and exotic spices, and see the produce first hand. If in the area at the beginning of the year, don't miss the **Chinese New Year** celebrations when red and gold dragons burst out of shops and tower blocks to wind their way through the traffic to the sound of beating drums.

PARIS YESTERDAY AND TODAY

The scenery and decor change radically in the new **"Paris Rive Gauche"** district that is being developed around the four "open books" of the **Bibliothèque Nationale de France** (referred to as the "BNF" by its regulars). Formerly the site of the mills of Paris, the sector is somewhat reminiscent of an architectural exhibition by its sundry assortment of buildings of all shapes, colours and materials. A testing ground for the most daring projects in smoked or printed glass, metal, brick, wood and most of all concrete.

S. Sauvignier / MICHELIN

PARIS VILLAGE

The neighbourhood around the **Butte aux Cailles** is no doubt more human and the townscape is comprised essentially of low-rise buildings and early 20C working-class houses. Its original village identity continues to prevail, despite its current appeal to the bourgeois-bohemians of Paris and the **bistros** continue to play a role in local life while negligently conjuring up the district's communard past. A similar if more floral picture can be seen around **Hénocque**

between Tolbiac and Maison Blanche whose colourful little ivy-clad houses definitely have a picture postcard appeal.

The district is not however home to the capital's top restaurants, but rather to authentic Parisian bistros with a warm family atmosphere. The final touch to this working-class heritage lies in the small triangle of the **cité florale** between **Montsouris Park** and the **Cité Universitaire,** a tiny world where time seems to have stood still.

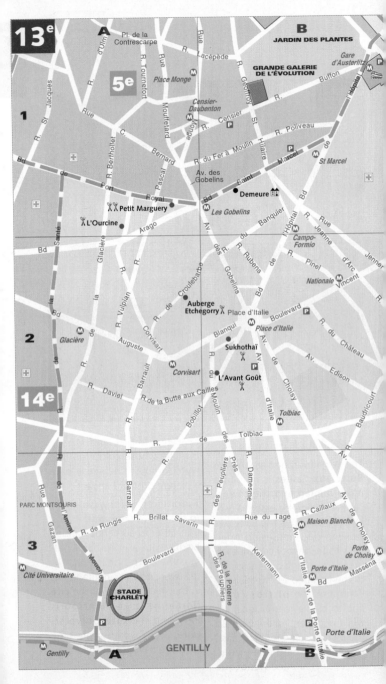

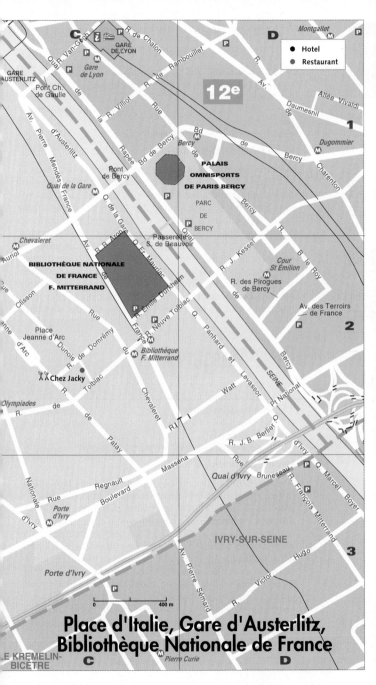

Place d'Italie, Gare d'Austerlitz,
Bibliothèque Nationale de France

Chez Jacky

Traditional 🍴🍴

109 r. du Dessous-
des-Berges ⊠ 75013
✆ 01 45 83 71 55
Fax 01 45 86 57 73
e-mail contact@chezjacky.fr **www**.chezjacky.fr

Ⓜ Bibliothèque F. Mitterrand
Closed August, 24 December-5 January,
Saturday, Sunday and public holidays

Menu €43 bi – Carte €47/79

A/C
VISA
MC

Venture into the quiet streets around the Bibliothèque F. Mitterrand to find this unusual inn, where time seems to have stopped its course. The recent change of management hasn't altered its spirit, and it still stands out in the urban landscape with its pleasantly old-fashioned country look. A rustic setting, warm atmosphere and cuisine featuring fine traditional French recipes such as duck foie gras, *tête de veau* (calf's head), and *cuisse de poularde* (chicken thighs). The service is equally flawless, both in technique (starters and desserts served from a trolley) and manner (attentive but not overly solicitous). Diners, take note: they take tradition seriously here, and Escoffier is still the standard!

Petit Marguery

Bistro 🍴🍴

9 bd Port-Royal ⊠ 75013
✆ 01 43 31 58 59
Fax 01 43 36 73 34
e-mail marguery@wanadoo.fr **www**.petitmarguery.fr

Ⓜ Les Gobelins
Closed Sunday and Monday

Menu €23 (lunch), €30/35

A/C
VISA
MC
AE

The reputation of the Petit Marguery is already well established. Apart from the arrival of chef Christophe Bisch – who has done a brilliant job taking over from the Cousin Brothers – nothing has changed within these august pink and burgundy walls, including the cooks at their posts, the waiters who wouldn't remove their classical black-and-white outfits for anything, and the spirit of the place, just as warm as ever. Regulars come back to taste the copious bistro dishes and game specialities, including th *lièvre à la royale* (hare). Others are cordially invited to try it. There's no doubt they will be won over by the food and Belle Epoque decor, fine enough to be a national monument. This is an institution that can never be brought down!

Auberge Etchegorry

Basque cuisine ✗

A2

41 r. Croulebarbe ✉ 75013   **Ⓜ** Les Gobelins
✆ 01 44 08 83 51 **Fax** 01 44 08 83 69   Closed Sunday and Monday
www.etchegorry.com

Menu € 22 bi (lunch)/55 bi – Carte € 36/58

It feels like Bayonne or St-Jean-Pied-de-Port, but this attractive red inn with a deeply Basque spirit is right in the 13th arrondissement. It's all there in the rustic dining room, from the sausages and hams to the *piments d'Espelette* (hot peppers) and *chisteras* hanging from the ceiling. The dishes, full of southwest tradition, are simple and generous. Connoisseurs will be delighted, and novices won over. The fine frescoes provide an unusual touch to admire between mouthfuls. Famous figures shown include Victor Hugo, Chateaubriand and singer Béranger, all regulars in the days when Madame Grégoire held her illustrious cabaret here. The façade still reflects those days.

L'Avant Goût

Contemporary ✗

B2

26 r. Bobillot ✉ 75013   **Ⓜ** Place d'Italie
✆ 01 53 80 24 00   Closed 3-26 August, Sunday and Monday
Fax 01 53 80 00 77   Number of covers limited, pre-book
www.lavangout.com

Menu € 31/41 – Carte € 36/48

The craze over this contemporary bistro on the Butte aux Cailles has not abated; on the contrary, it seems to be increasing by the year. As a result, it is always full – noon and night. So reservations are a must. Its success is due to Christophe Beaufront, who trained with Guérard and Savoy and is constantly inventing new associations of flavours, with a penchant for spices. In addition to the emblematic *pot-au-feu de cochon* (pork stew), try the *terrine de foie gras à la vanille*, the *dos de cabillaud* (cod) or the tiramisu strawberries. The menus change once a month – gourmets take note! Displayed on the blackboard, they are part of the pleasant and simple decor (with red banquettes and snug tables) which goes with the relaxed ambiance.

L'Ourcine

Bistro 🍽

A1

92 r. Broca ✉ 75013
☎ 01 47 07 13 65
Fax 01 47 07 18 48

Ⓜ **Les Gobelins**
Closed Sunday and Monday

Menu (€22), €30

VISA
ⓂⒸ
Quality and modesty are a fitting description of the spirit at l'Ourcine, a tasteful bistro which is always packed. It could be due to the eye-catching dark red façade that instantly tells you this is a place where they take food and wine seriously! Chef Sylvain Danière (who trained with Camdeborde) is passionate about authentic food. His pure market cuisine, changing daily and seasonally, uses only the freshest ingredients and flavours. The wines come from carefully chosen small winemaking estates. Booking is advised, as the number of place settings is deliberately limited.

Sukhothaï

Thai 🍽

B2

12 r. Père Guérin ✉ 75013
☎ 01 45 81 55 88

Ⓜ **Place d'Italie**
Closed 4-24 August,
Monday lunch and Sunday

Menu (€11,50 bi), €21/25 – Carte €20/30

VISA
ⓂⒸ
This authentic Thai local is a stone's throw from the Place d'Italie. It's less expensive than a direct flight to Bangkok, and is well worth the trip. The decor affords a change of scenery without going overboard, thus avoiding the pitfalls of affected folklore. A few sculpted buddhas, some engravings and flowers here and there suffice to create a pleasant hushed atmosphere. The service also exemplifies refinement and discretion. As for the cooking, prepared by the owner's wife, it is an explosion of flavours and spices. Beef, duck, pork and shellfish rub shoulders with lemon grass, basil, peppers and coconut milk. It's no wonder so many Thais come to Sukhothaï when they're in Paris. Booking is strongly advised.

Montparnasse Denfert Rochereau

The relatively extensive 14th arrondissement is quite representative of the large residential neighbourhoods of southern Paris. It too, like its neighbours the 13th and the 15th, has a village past that can still be felt in the structure of the streets and the variety of buildings and architectural trends, and a pleasantly provincial air continues to float around the 14th, annexed to Paris somewhat later than other arrondissements.

BOHEMIAN NIGHTS

There is however nothing "provincial" about **Montparnasse**. The district may well be named after the pleasure-loving gods of Olympus, but is now more well known as a high spot of Parisian night-life. Easy to find, the 200-metre high Montparnasse **Tower** can be seen from everywhere in Paris and its summit commands a grandiose panorama of the city (and the Eiffel Tower to boot). The surrounding streets literally swarm with typical Parisian **cafés, Irish pubs** and restaurants of every culinary tradition. **Rue de la Gaîté** is well known for its theatres and charms, while practically every high street chain and department store has a foothold on **rue de Rennes** that runs from the tower as far as Saint-Germain-des-Prés. The 300-metre long **rue du Mont-**

parnasse itself, that runs from Edgar Quinet to Notre-Dame-des-Champs, is the location of nearly twenty Breton pancake houses.

The atmosphere gradually changes as you leave the centre and head towards Montrouge. First stop, **Denfert-Rochereau** and its immense statue of the **Lion of Belfort,** built in memory of the soldiers of 1870-1871. Here the mood is both less audacious and more Bohemian and its network of narrow streets is packed with traditional bistros and small relaxed restaurants. The pedestrian **rue Daguerre,** two minutes from the metro station, provides a wide choice of food shops and delicatessens that pay homage to French produce. The locals do their daily shopping here, amidst holiday-makers and busy executives from avenue du Général Leclerc. On the other side of the square, between rue Froidevaux and rue Campagne Première, **Montparnasse cemetery** (the second largest in Paris) is an enclave and a world unto itself. It is here that Baudelaire, Camille Saint-Saëns, Jean-Paul Sartre and Serge Gainsbourg, among others, are buried. The paths, lined in splendid lime, cedar and sophora trees, are a perfect invitation to meditation.

X. Richer / MICHELIN

HILLS AND DALES

The last portion of the 14th around **Montsouris Park,** before the ring road, is well worth the visit. The garden itself is beautifully landscaped with artificial grottoes, waterfalls and a splendid ornamental lake. Practically uninhabited prior to 1860, the area was entirely reorganised by Napoleon III around the park created in his honour and which is the highest point of the left bank (at an altitude of 75 metres no less!). Highly popular on Sunday af-

ternoons, the neighbourhood is the perfect expression of the "village" character of the south of the arrondissement. George Braque, Salvador Dali and Henri Rousseau could be seen walking down the little streets to the west and their delightful houses and small apartment blocks continue to perpetuate the memory of those legendary years.

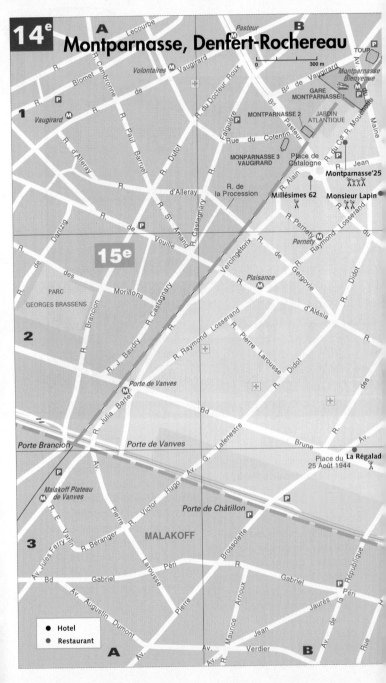

14ᵉ
Montparnasse, Denfert-Rochereau

A — Lecourbe — Pasteur — **B**

0 — 300 m

TOUR

Av. de Vaugirard

Montparnasse
Bienvenüe

Volontaires Ⓜ Vaugirard

R. Blomet
R. Cambronne

GARE
MONTPARNASSE 1

R. du Docteur Roux

MONTPARNASSE 2

JARDIN
ATLANTIQUE

1 Vaugirard Ⓜ

R. de

Pasteur

R. du Cdt R. Mouchotte

Maine

R. Paul Barruel

Rue du Cotentin

MONPARNASSE 3
VAUGIRARD

Place de
Catalogne

R. d'Alleray

R. Dutot

Jean

Montparnasse'25
🍴🍴🍴🍴

R. Alain

Millésimes 62 🍴

Monsieur Lapin 🍴🍴

R. St. Amand

d'Alleray

R. de
la Procession

R. Castagnary

R. de
Vouillé

R. Pernety Ⓜ
Pernety

Raymond Losserand

du

R. de Danzig

15ᵉ

Morillons

R. Castagnary

Vercingétorix

de

Gergovie

R. Didot

Plaisance
R.

des

PARC
GEORGES BRASSENS

R. Brancion

R. J. Baudry

R. Raymond Losserand

d'Alésia

2

R. Pierre Larousse

Didot

R.

R.

Porte de Vanves
Ⓜ

R. Julia Bartet

Bd

Lafenestre

des

Porte Brancion

Porte de Vanves

Brune

Av.

Porte de Vanves

La Régalad

Place du
25 Août 1944

🍴

Malakoff Plateau
Ⓜ de Vanves

Av.

R. Victor Hugo Av. G.

Porte de Châtillon

Pierre

3

Av. Jules Ferry

R. E. Varlin

R. Béranger

Larousse

Péri

Brossolette

R.

MALAKOFF

Gabriel

Gabriel

de la République

Bd

Gabriel

Péri

Arnoux

Jaurès

Av. Augustin Dumont

Pierre

Maurice

Jean

Av.

Verdier

A — **B**

●	Hotel
●	Restaurant

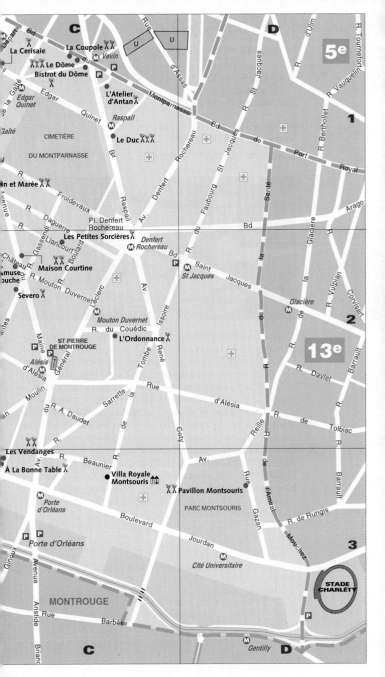

La Cerisaie
La Coupole ✕✕
Vavin
✕✕✕ Le Dôme
Bistrot du Dôme
L'Atelier
d'Antan ✕
Edgar
Quinet
Edgar
Quinet
Raspail
Gaîté
CIMETIÈRE
Le Duc ✕✕✕
DU MONTPARNASSE
in et Marée ✕✕
Froideveaux
Daguerre
Pl. Denfert
Rochereau
Les Petites Sorcières ✕
Denfert
Rochereau
Château
amuse
ouche
Maison Courtine
St Jacques
Saint
St Jacques
Jacques
Severo ✕
Mouton Duvernet
R. du Couédic
L'Ordonnance ✕
Glacière
Alésia
d'Alésia
ST PIERRE
DE MONTROUGE
Moulin
R. A. Daudet
Sarrette
Rue
d'Alésia
Les Vendanges
Beaunier
À La Bonne Table ✕
Villa Royale
Montsouris
Pavillon Montsouris ✕✕
Porte
d'Orléans
PARC MONTSOURIS
Porte d'Orléans
Boulevard
Jourdan
Cité Universitaire
STADE
CHARLÉTY
MONTROUGE
Barbès
Gentilly

5e

13e

1

2

3

C   D

263

Montparnasse'25 ❀

B1

MONTPARNASSE • DENFERT-ROCHEREAU

Hôtel Méridien
Montparnasse,
19 r. Cdt Mouchotte ✉ 75014
✆ 01 44 36 44 25 **Fax** 01 44 36 49 03
e-mail meridien.montparnasse@lemeridien.com
www.montparnasse.lemeridien.com

Ⓜ Montparnasse Bienvenüe
Closed 28 April-4 May, 14 July-31 August,
22 December-6 January, Saturday,
Sunday and public holidays

Menu €49 (lunch)/110 (dinner) – Carte €93/109

Montparnasse'25

The Montparnasse of the 1920s and 30s is gone, but Montparnasse'25 (on the first floor of the Méridien hotel) celebrates it through artists from the era – Modigliani in particular. The dining room is decorated with reproductions of his paintings, while the hotel lobby features silhouettes of Foujita and Sartre, other neighbourhood figures from those days. The restaurant exudes discreet luxury and intimacy: black-and-grey lacquer walls, soft light from artificial lighting and a huge picture window overlooking a garden. On the menu? Dishes created by Christian Moine that are up-to-date yet classic and masterfully prepared. The chef likes to highlight his fine ingredients, without any unnecessary extravagance, which just goes to show that great cuisine speaks for itself. Naturally. Needless to say, the service is up to the same standard.

First Course	*Main Course*	*Dessert*
• Langoustines royales poêlées au galanga.	• Saint-Pierre à l'huile de truffe aux blancs de poireaux.	• Allumette aux fruits de saison.
• Saint-Jaques dorées à la plancha (season).	• Canard laqué aux fruits tamarin.	• Tout chocolat.

Le Dôme

Seafood XXX

C1

108 bd Montparnasse ⊠ 75014   Ⓜ Vavin
📞 01 43 35 25 81   Closed Sunday and
Fax 01 42 79 01 19   Monday in July-August

Carte € 52/123

A/C
⟐
VISA
MC
AE
Ⓞ

In the Roaring Twenties, Le Dôme was a favourite hangout for the Bohemian artistic and literary crowd. This famous Montparnasse seafood brasserie with a unique, chic and lively atmosphere has been carefully preserved over the years. The fine Art Deco interior is a testimony to those glorious days, with period photographs and a fresco by painter Carzou, once a regular here. Every detail – the pervasive wood panelling, green and fauve banquettes, stained glass and soft lighting – contributes to the spirit of the place. The cuisine and service are of the same high quality. The ultra-fresh seafood is attractively presented in generous dishes, and served with well-paired wines.

Le Duc

Fish and shellfish XXX

C1

243 bd Raspail ⊠ 75014   Ⓜ Raspail
📞 01 43 20 96 30   Closed 1st-10 March, 2-24 August,
Fax 01 43 20 46 73   24 December-2 January, Saturday lunch,
     Sunday and Monday

Menu € 46 (lunch) – Carte € 48/144

A/C
⟐
VISA
MC
AE
Ⓞ

The blue and white colours and riveted sheet metal façade leave no doubt about Le Duc's maritime leitmotif. The plush decor (designed by Slavik) has the same marine look, faithfully reproducing the atmosphere of a yacht, complete with a mahogany ceiling, cabin lamps and shiny brass. The walls are decorated with giant stuffed tortoises and colourful illustrations, evoking a natural history museum. The cuisine naturally features a different kind of maritime fauna. High marks for the fish and raw shellfish composition – chef Pascal Hélard's favourite dish. The fresh seafood ingredients are delivered directly from France's fishing ports, ensuring the quality of Hélard's straightforward cuisine. No wonder his net has caught a large business clientele who have made this their "deluxe local", filling the place up at lunchtime.

La Coupole

Brasserie ✗✗

102 bd Montparnasse ✉ 75014   Ⓜ Vavin
✆ 01 43 20 14 20 **Fax** 01 43 35 46 14
e-mail jtosi@groupeflo.fr **www**.flobrasseries.com

Menu € 31 – Carte € 32/130

A/C

VISA

MC

AE

Ⓞ

Thanks to an expert facelift, the legendary Coupole has lost none of its original splendour. Built in 1927 by architects Barillet and Le Bouc, it was a hot spot for Parisian nightlife during the Roaring Twenties. Kessel, Picasso, Man Ray, Sartre, Giacometti and Hemingway are among the famous figures from the Montparnasse artistic and literary crowd who dined here. The new lighting (installed for its 80th birthday) has enhanced the superb Art Deco interior and 24 pillars decorated with artwork from the era. Add to that the remarkably courteous and efficient waiters, and a brasserie menu with a range of seafood platters and a renowned Indian-style lamb curry. Prepare to be charmed!

Monsieur Lapin

Traditional ✗✗

11 r. R. Losserand ✉ 75014   Ⓜ Gaîté
✆ 01 43 20 21 39   Closed August, Saturday lunch,
Fax 01 43 21 84 86   Sunday lunch and Monday
e-mail franck.enee@wanadoo.fr   Number of covers limited, pre-book
www.monsieur-lapin.fr

Menu € 35/45 – Carte € 47/65

A/C

VISA

MC

AE

There is only one celebrity here (in the decor and in the dishes), and that is Monsieur Lapin (Mr. Rabbit). Like the Mad Hatter in Alice in Wonderland, he is all over the place: on the shelves, in a framed photograph, on the fine pewter bar and in little niches. In the kitchen it is translated into *salade de Monsieur Lapin* (depending on the chef's inspiration), rabbit terrine in aspic with herbs from the *garrigue* or *croustillant de lapin* with dried fruit and wild mushrooms. But there is something for everyone on the menu, which also features quite up-to-date fish and meat dishes. Impatient diners can rest easy: if it involves a delicious meal, Lewis Carroll's famous hero is never late for such an important date!

Maison Courtine ✿

C2

157 av. Maine ✉ **75014**
✆ 01 45 43 08 04
Fax 01 45 45 91 35
e-mail yves.charles@wanadoo.fr

Ⓜ Mouton Duvernet
Closed 2 August-1st September,
23 December-2 January, Monday lunch,
Saturday lunch and Sunday

Menu €39/44

A/C
VISA
MC

MONTPARNASSE • DENFERT-ROCHEREAU

Maison Courtine

The Maison Courtine, in business for the past ten years, has not forsaken its origins. Yves Charles knew when he took over Lou Landès that it was a true ambassador of south-western French cooking (run by the emblematic Georgette Descat). To preserve its memory, he has continued to celebrate that distinctive cuisine, to the delight of his faithful customers. Encore! Cassoulet is still featured on the menu, which has retained its southern accent, honouring that tradition without reserve. The owner works with his chef, particularly in hunting down exceptional wines and ingredients, and in providing excellent advice about which great bottles to choose from small-scale wine-makers (in his well-stocked cellar).While the cuisine hasn't changed, the restaurant itself has been given a facelift. Like the façade that has brightened up the Parisian landscape, the decor is now airier, sporting a warm and classic look bathed in orange and yellow tones. Regulars enjoy the bar near the entrance.

First Course

- Escalopes de foie gras de canard poêlées aux raisins.
- Crémeux froid d'araignée de mer et croûtons au cumin.

Main Course

- Canette en deux services, filet rôti, cuisse confite.
- Médaillon de veau de lait et lentilles blondes de la Planèze.

Dessert

- Tourtière aux pommes caramélisées.
- Mœlleux de chocolat, coulis d'orange.

Pavillon Montsouris

D3

20 r. Gazan ✉ 75014
✆ 01 43 13 29 00
Fax 01 43 13 29 02
www.pavillon.montsouris.fr

Ⓜ Cité Universitaire
Closed February half-term holidays and
Sunday dinner from mid September to Easter

Menu € 40 – Carte € 56/87

An exceptional location in the Parc Montsouris gives this
establishment a special appeal. The superb Belle Epoque
pavilion offers diners the rare and enviable luxury of the
countryside in the heart of Paris. The smart colonial-style
decor (russet wood, plants, bronze lamps) and large glass
roof bathing the room with light make you instantly forget
the nearby hustle and bustle. The feeling of escaping it all
is even greater on the lovely terrace surrounded by vegetation – open as soon as the weather permits. Both are
charming and peaceful settings where you can enjoy the
authentic, up-to-date market cuisine proposed on the menu.
Private dining rooms are available.

Les Vendanges

C3

40 r. Friant ✉ 75014
✆ 01 45 39 59 98
Fax 01 45 39 74 13
e-mail guy.tardif@wanadoo.fr
www.lesvendanges-paris.com

Ⓜ Porte d'Orléans
Closed 4-31 August, 23 December-1st January,
Saturday except dinner from
November to January and Sunday

Menu (€ 25), € 35

The name (and the bunches of grapes on the façade) tip you
off. The "treasure" at this friendly restaurant is its well-
stocked and adventurous cellar. In addition to the multitude
of fine bottles from all of France's wine-growing regions,
you'll find some nice vintages from lesser known estates,
proposed at moderate prices. A godsend for those hoping
to learn about new wines from experienced professionals.
The same serious approach is evident in the menu, prepared
with fresh ingredients and renewed seasonally, with a wide
range of classic recipes and a few dishes from the South-
west. The friendly staff imbue the place with an extra dose
of charm.

14

Vin et Marée

Seafood ✗✗

108 av. Maine ✉ 75014   Ⓜ Gaîté
📞 01 43 20 29 50 **Fax** 01 43 27 84 11
e-mail vmmaine@vin-et-maree.com **www**.vin-et-maree.com

Menu (€21) – Carte €32/58

A/C

Looking for a taste of Brittany in Montparnasse? Head for Vin et Marée Maine! Fish, shellfish and crustaceans are the name of the game here, available according to the seasons and the whim of Neptune. Starters and desserts are in line with this Parisian chain's classics, including *huîtres spéciales perle blanche* (oysters) and *baba de Zanzibar* (rum baba). The discreet marine decor has a stylish personal touch (mahogany wood panelling, blue and white tones, ceramic tiles). The veranda side of the dining room makes the most of the daylight, while the upstairs room can be reserved for private dinners.

VISA
MC
AE

À La Bonne Table

Traditional ✗

42 r. Friant ✉ 75014   Ⓜ Porte d'Orléans
📞 01 45 39 74 91   Closed 13 July-3 August, 21 December-
Fax 01 45 43 66 92   4 January, Saturday lunch and Sunday

Menu €26 (lunch)/30 – Carte €29/46

A/C
VISA
MC
AE
①

Yoshitaka Kawamoto, the chef at À La Bonne Table, was trained in making traditional French food, and that's exactly what he does here. But connoisseurs will discern the special Japanese touch that makes all the difference in his recipes. Each dish has a unique character – in the choice of ingredients, their specific preparation and seasoning – leaving no doubt about the inspiration from the Land of the Rising Sun. That originality easily makes up for the rather retro decor (banquettes, ceiling mouldings and rustic furniture), especially when the prices are so reasonable.

L'Amuse Bouche

Soufflés X

186 r. Château ✉ 75014
☎ 01 43 35 31 61

Ⓜ Mouton Duvernet
Closed 1st-20 August, Sunday and Monday

Menu (€21 bi), €32

VISA
ⓂⒸ
Ⓞ

Only the façade remains of the butcher's shop once housed here. Soufflés are the speciality nowadays, featured on the menu in a wide variety to satisfy all tastes: sweet and savoury, as a starter, main course (flavourful creamy cheese soufflé) or dessert (try the delicious one made with Grand Marnier). We also like the more traditional dishes celebrating fresh ingredients, such as the *pavé de bœuf à la moutarde de Meaux* with a carrot and potato puree. The decor has a sweet look with little tables, wallpaper in orange tones and bouquets of flowers. A nice place for a romantic dinner or an evening among friends.

L'Atelier d'Antan

Traditional X

9 r. L-Robert ✉ 75014
☎ 01 43 21 36 19

Ⓜ Denfert-Rochereau
Closed August,
Saturday lunch and Sunday

Menu (€15), €18 (weekday lunch) – Carte €32/51

VISA
ⓂⒸ
AE

The Atelier d'Antan is a place for food-lovers, with a friendly, old-fashioned sepia-toned feel. The convivial atmosphere and bistro look have turned this simple and welcoming establishment into a meeting place for many local regulars. The food? Suffused in tradition, true to its name (*antan* = yesteryear). The menu by Molto Alvarez boasts the rich recipes and flavours of days gone by, from the home-made terrine, *salade de gésiers confits* (duck gizzards), *langue de bœuf sauce piquante* (tongue, prepared to perfection), and grouper stew in a red wine sauce, to seasonal fruit crumble, plum tart and coffee *crème brûlée*.

Bistrot du Dôme

Seafood ✗

C1

1 r. Delambre ✉ 75014   Ⓜ Vavin
✆ 01 43 35 32 00   Closed August, Sunday and Monday

Carte € 39/51

A/C

VISA

M/C

AE

This annexe is just next door to the Dôme, its prestigious "older brother". Given its classic bistro look (old counter, wood and pewter bar, waiters in black-and-white outfits), you might not see the family resemblance right away – unless you're looking at the menu with its wide choice of seafood dishes. The large blackboard features mouth-watering specials like haddock carpaccio, langoustine risotto and skate with capers. As the "baby" of the family, the Bistrot du Dôme has a more "well-behaved" side than its older sibling. The ambiance is more friendly and relaxed here than at the chic brasserie with its brisk and lively service. The large dining room with grape-leaf decorations on the ceiling is all the more enjoyable.

La Cerisaie

South-west of France ✗

C1

70 bd E. Quinet ✉ 75014   Ⓜ Edgar Quinet
✆ 01 43 20 98 98   Closed 1st-11 May, 28 July-25 August,
Fax 01 43 20 98 98   20 December-4 January,
          Saturday and Sunday – Pre-book

Menu (€ 23), € 32/39

VISA

M/C

You can try showing up here without booking, but Maryse Lalanne will just say: "It's (already) full!" in that charming way of hers. It's not really about the size of the restaurant – only 20 place settings. You'd get the same answer even if there was room for 30, 40 or 50. People love coming to this pocket restaurant for the blackboard specials: slowly simmered, market-inspired dishes reflecting the talent of a chef who worked in some of the finest establishments in Toulouse. The cellar has a good selection of regional wines, well-paired with the delicious food. La Cerisaie stands out as a first-rate representative of Southwestern cooking – in the heart of a "Breton" neighbourhood!

Millésimes 62

B1

Traditional ✗

13 pl. Catalogne ✉ 75014
📞 01 43 35 34 35
Fax 01 43 20 26 21
e-mail millesime62@wanadoo.fr
www.millesimes62.com

Ⓜ Gaîté
Closed 2-18 August,
Saturday lunch and Sunday

Menu (€ 20), € 25/28

VISA

Ⓜ©

ᴀᴇ

Millésimes 62 has all the elements of a fine little establishment, starting with its enviable location on a square designed by Ricardo Bofill, a stone's throw from the TGV (high-speed train) station, and major hotels and theatres in Montparnasse. The decor has the charm of a contemporary bistro in muted yellow and chocolate tones, completed by a terrace facing the fountain. Nothing extravagant, but all very pleasant. The menu offers tasty market cuisine and a fine selection of wines – also by the glass – chosen by oenologist Jacques Boudin. As you can well imagine, this place has become extremely popular. But don't worry – it hasn't pushed up the prices.

L'Ordonnance

C2

Contemporary ✗

51 r. Hallé ✉ 75014
📞 01 43 27 55 85
Fax 01 43 20 64 72
e-mail lestrapade2@wanadoo.fr

Ⓜ Mouton Duvernet
Closed August, Christmas holidays,
Saturday except dinner in winter and Sunday

Menu (€ 24), € 30

VISA

Ⓜ©

L'Ordonnance has now joined Chez Bruno and Au Petit Tonneau on this quiet little street in the 14th arrondissement. Patrick Liévin's new wave bistro blends two genres: Parisian and provincial inn. The three small and simply decorated rooms exude conviviality, sparking an immediate desire to begin your meal. The dishes come in a mixture of styles – home cooking, *terroir*, market-based, and seasonal – and all are copious and tasty, like the rabbit terrine with pickles, poached egg with pan-fried girolle mushrooms, and jar of rhubarb, whipped cream and strawberries. You can't go wrong here.

Les Petites Sorcières

Contemporary ✗

C2

12 r. Liancourt ✉ 75014
📞 01 43 21 95 68
Fax 01 43 21 95 68

Ⓜ Denfert Rochereau
Closed 12 July-16 August and
Sunday – Dinner only

Carte € 32/39

VISA
MC

Rest assured – these *sorcières* are very good little witches! Whether they are hanging from the ceiling, hiding in a corner or about to fly off on a broom, they are here to make your meal go smoothly. There is no magic formula, simply a very nice little establishment with a personalised decor in shades of red, attractively dressed little tables, an up-to-date and carefully prepared menu featuring excellent ingredients (green bean and haddock salad with sweet onions, fillet of cod with a broad bean ragout, pineapple and grape crumble with coconut sorbet), and prices that haven't skyrocketed!

La Régalade 😊

Traditional ✗

B3

49 av. J. Moulin ✉ 75014
📞 01 45 45 68 58
Fax 01 45 40 96 74
e-mail la_regalade@yahoo.fr

Ⓜ Porte d'Orléans
Closed 25 July-20 August,
1st-10 January, Monday lunch,
Saturday and Sunday – Pre-book

Menu € 32

A/C
VISA
MC
🍴

Who hasn't heard of La Régalade, the bistro with refined cuisine and reasonable prices that's always packed? Bruno Doucet, the chef with a brilliant pedigree (Gagnaire, Fouquet's, Apicius), took over from Yves Camdeborde in 2004. On the menu and daily blackboard, he serves up part *terroir*, part-market-based cuisine featuring generous and flavourful dishes, to the delight of gourmets and food-lovers of all persuasions. The authentic decor and flavours are matched by fine producer-bottled wines and particularly friendly staff. It's no wonder so many people have made it their "local" (be sure to book, or you may be sorely disappointed). Their one regret? They can only sample the treats at La Régalade during the week.

Severo

C2

8 r. Plantes ✉ 75014
✆ 01 45 40 40 91

◍ Mouton Duvernet
Closed 27 April-4 May,
26 July-24 August, 20-28 December,
Saturday and Sunday

Carte € 27/54

This excellent and unpretentious wine bistro has developed a fine reputation. And rightly so, since owner William Bernet puts a great deal into it as he whirls around the tables and shares his love of wine with diners. That passion is expressed on the large blackboards fixed to the walls, listing wines from all the different *terroirs* and for all budgets. This treasure trove is paired with a deliberately short, traditional menu honouring the Auvergne and Limousin regions. The dishes are cooked up with great care; the owner, a former butcher, ages the meat himself, and the chef still makes home-made French fries!

MONTPARNASSE • DENFERT-ROCHEREAU

A CHOCOLATIER WHO OPENED HIS PARIS SHOP IN **1659**

While the Pre-Colombians were the first to have a soft spot for chocolate, they were soon joined by the Spanish in the 16C, then by the French in 1615 when Louis XIII married the Infanta Anne of Austria. On 28 May 1659, Louis XIV granted David Chaillou the exclusive right to sell hot chocolate on the rue de l'Arbre sec in Paris. Today the city of gourmets has more treats than ever for chocolate-lovers. Chocolatiers make vintage, organic and fair-trade ganaches, truffles, pralines and bars. And despite the European directive allowing 5 % vegetable fat, the sweets are still made with 100 % cocoa butter!

Porte de Versailles
Vaugirard · Beaugrenelle

The most densely populated arrondissement of Paris is also one of its least well known. Its impressive dimensions conceal a dual heritage that is typical of both western and southern Paris; bourgeois and opulent in areas, but also deeply marked by its former "village" past, prior to being annexed to the rest of Paris. The variety of the streets, architecture and populations make it difficult to define its identity and the locals claim that it takes a whole lifetime to discover its secret nooks and crannies.

INTERNATIONAL PARIS

A genuine town within a town, the Porte de Versailles **exhibition centre** attracts millions of visitors from all over the world every year. It is the site of the most awaited (and the most visited) shows such as the **automobile show, agricultural show** and the famous **Paris Fair** and its Lépine invention competition. The area can become frankly overpopulated during some of these international events, rendering the road network almost impracticable and pushing the bus and metro system to its limits. There are however bonuses to this inconvenience and the area is chock-full of brasseries, small bistros and even restaurants with gastronomic claims, all at reasonable prices to attract the crowds of visitors.

VILLAGERS AT HEART

The real heart of the arrondissement, where the genuine locals live, lies between the **Vaugirard** and Grenelle districts. These former suburbs were annexed to Paris at a relatively late date and today represent a tightly woven mesh of typically Parisian mini-districts. Convention and George Brassens to the south, **La Motte Piquet** and Commerce to the north, they are made up of tiny squares and crossroads that are frequently adorned with gardens, music stands, unassuming little churches or the statue of some long forgotten war hero. Extremely well endowed in terms of neighbourhood shops, these havens of village life in the heart of Paris continue to nurture a genteel way of life, made up of discreet sociability and long-standing customs. Far from the frantic pace of the rest of Paris or the denser, and if the truth be known, less intimate, living conditions of the central arrondissements, these islands of quiet tranquillity reveal a little-known and relatively affluent side of Paris. Book lovers should not miss the **book market** every Sunday on rue Brancion, two minutes from the lawns and gardens of **Georges Brassens Park**.

K. Blackwell / MICHELIN

MANHATTAN-PARIS

The contrast afforded by **Beaugrenelle,** a shopping and financial centre built on the embankment of the former Javel district, couldn't be more marked. The sheer height of these tower blocks, built out of smoked glass, steel and concrete, is such that the skyline seems more akin to that of a North American city than to Paris, an impression that is even more pronounced from the hill on the other side of the river in the 16th. If you can manage to ignore the cruelly out-of-date architectural style, you will enjoy the district's several lounge bars and trendy restaurants, some of which command stunning views of the Seine.

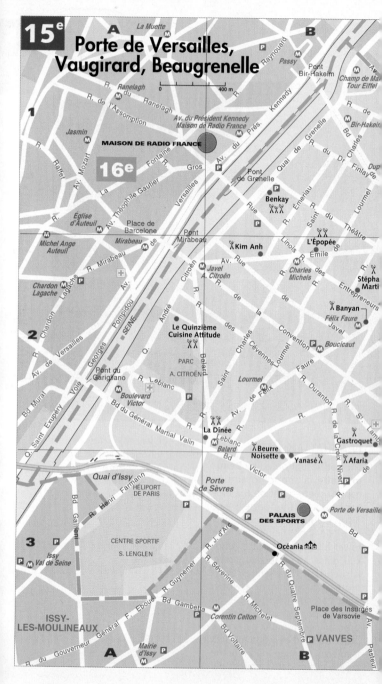

15e
Porte de Versailles, Vaugirard, Beaugrenelle

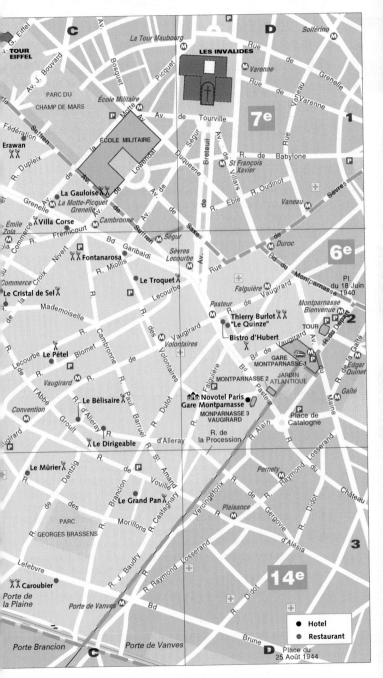

Benkay

B1

Novotel Paris Tour Eiffel,
61 quai de Grenelle ⊠ 75015　　　　　**Ⓜ** Bir-Hakeim
☎ 01 40 58 21 26 **Fax** 01 40 58 21 30
e-mail h3546@accor.com **www**.novotel.com

Ⓐⓒ

Menu € 30 (lunch), € 75/125 – Carte € 42/131

Located on the top floor of a small building next to the
Novotel (the former Hotel Nikko), this comfortable Japanese restaurant is in a choice setting with a pretty view of
the Seine and the Maison de la Radio. The spare, Zen-like
decor features clean lines, light-coloured marble, dark
wood, and spacious, traditional Japanese tables. The food
focuses on quality ingredients and beautiful presentation:
fillet of beef seared on a hotplate at the tableside, sautéed
calamari, spectacular and delicious *crêpes flambées* served
on dry ice. An exciting culinary experience for those in
search of something a bit exotic.

Caroubier 😊

C3

82 bd Lefebvre ⊠ 75015　　　　　　**Ⓜ** Porte de Vanves
☎ 01 40 43 16 12　　　　Closed 19 July-25 August and Monday
Fax 01 40 43 16 12

Menu € 19 (weekday lunch)/28 – Carte € 28/47

A real North African oasis, a short distance from the Parc
des Expositions, the Caroubier has embodied the best of
Moroccan cuisine for 30 years. This family restaurant proposes tasty traditional food prepared with just the right
touch, in a contemporary setting decorated with rugs, photographs and objects from North Africa. All the great classics are made flawlessly and served in copious portions,
including generous couscous dishes, *tajines* with subtle and
candid flavours, and *pastillas* full of the Atlas sun. With the
thoughtful staff, quick and efficient service and reasonable
prices, you should leave this place feeling very satisfied

La Dînée

Contemporary 🍴🍴

B2

85 r. Leblanc ✉ 75015   Ⓜ Balard
☎ 01 45 54 20 49 **Fax** 01 40 60 73 76   Closed Saturday and Sunday
e-mail contact@restaurant-ladinee.com
www.restaurant-ladinee.com

Menu € 36/39

VISA

Ⓜ©

ⒶⒺ

⓪

This little seafood restaurant with a discreet blue façade is located on a street near Balard. It has developed a blue-chip reputation in the neighbourhood by using fresh, quality ingredients in simple, well-balanced dishes. The long dining room has a pleasant contemporary decor with pastel walls and banquettes, abstract paintings and soft lighting. Well-prepared dishes from the sea include pan-fried squid with lemon, scallop and whelk tartare, and braised Cajun-style salmon. There are plenty of treats for game- and poultry-lovers too.

L'Épopée

Traditional 🍴🍴

B2

89 av. É. Zola ✉ 75015   Ⓜ Charles Michels
☎ 01 45 77 71 37   Closed 26 July-20 August, 24 December-
Fax 01 45 77 71 37   3 January, Saturday lunch and Sunday

Menu (€ 29), € 35

A/C

VISA

Ⓜ©

ⒶⒺ

🍇

A meal at l'Epopée (read "Epic") can easily turn into an adventure, especially when the proprietor communicates his passion about wines. The dishes share a similar talent for lyricism and hyperbole. The plush interior with light parquet floors, watercolours on the walls and comfortably spaced tables creates a relaxed, low-key atmosphere. Regulars come back for the refined and rather copious traditional cuisine, in addition to the well-stocked cellar. The fresh, carefully prepared ingredients and excellent service make this a truly epic experience!

PORTE DE VERSAILLES • VAUGIRARD • BEAUGRENELLE

Erawan

C1

Thai XX

76 r. Fédération
✉ 75015
✆ 01 47 83 55 67 **Fax** 01 47 34 85 98

Ⓜ La Motte Picquet Grenelle
Closed 5-25 August and Sunday

Menu € 13,50 bi (weekday lunch), € 30/45 – Carte € 20/29

A/C
VISA
Ⓜ©
A/E

In Thai mythology, Erawan was a three-headed elephant with an uncommon appetite. No doubt it would have felt quite at home in this pleasant Thai restaurant hidden behind a rather all-purpose Asian façade. The dining room boasts traditional art work, wood panelling, tantric bas-reliefs and soft lighting– a decor that evokes the minimalist mystique of Southeast Asian culture. A father-and-son team handles the service and prepares the characteristic light and fragrant cuisine. The mouth-watering dishes are flavoured with coconut, lemongrass and curcuma.

Fontanarosa

C2

Italian XX

28 bd Garibaldi ✉ 75015
✆ 01 45 66 97 84 **Fax** 01 47 83 96 30
e-mail contact@fontanarosa-ristorante.eu
www.fontanarosa-ristorante.eu

Ⓜ Cambronne

Menu (€ 17), € 21 (weekday lunch)/30 – Carte € 32/69

This friendly trattoria is aptly located on the boulevard Garibaldi, named after the father of Italian unity. An ambassador of Sardinian culinary traditions, it was an immediate success in the heart of the Grenelle district. The refined, flavourful and copious Italian specialities are served in a distinctive setting boasting a pretty pink façade, sheltered green terrace and an interior in pastel tones. Various seasonal antipasti, gnocchi with the frank flavours of the Italian sun and a Milanese-style risotto provide a delicious sample of this great culinary tradition. The well-stocked wine list covers all the different regions in the country.

La Gauloise

Traditional XX

C1

59 av. La Motte-Picquet   **Ⓜ** La Motte Picquet Grenelle
✉ 75015
✆ 01 47 34 11 64 **Fax** 01 40 61 09 70

Menu (€25) – Carte €33/52

Judging from the number of signed photographs proudly displayed on the walls, La Gauloise must have hosted a fair number of political and media figures over the course of its long history. The turn-of-the-century decor – old banquettes, venerable mirrors and cascading chandeliers – evokes the golden age of the Parisian brasserie. The simple and well-prepared traditional dishes on offer include onion soup, preserved duck and rib-eye steak. Also worth noting are the pleasant terrace in summer, and the small private dining room.

Le Quinzième Cuisine Attitude

Contemporary XX

A2

14 r. Cauchy ✉ 75015   **Ⓜ** Javel
✆ 01 45 54 43 43   Closed 10-20 August, Monday lunch,
Fax 01 45 57 22 96   Saturday lunch and Sunday
e-mail resa@lequinzieme.com
www.restaurantlequinzieme.com

Menu €40 (weekday lunch), €105/150 – Carte €46/100

The talented Cyril Lignac, the French Jamie Oliver, opened this elegant restaurant a short distance from the Parc André Citroën. The place is a lot like its creator, which he is the first to admit. The chic contemporary setting features wood, glass and ceramics, and the furniture in sober tones emphasises the open, light and comfortable feel of the space. Quality and innovation are also present in the kitchen, where the inventive dishes combine choice ingredients and tried-and-true recipes. Sweet-and-savoury tastes and crispy-creamy textures create contrasts and surprises. A view of the kitchen through a large picture window allows diners at the "chef's table" to admire Lignac at work.

Thierry Burlot "Le Quinze" 🐷

Contemporary ✗✗

8 r. Nicolas Charlet ✉ 75015   Ⓜ Pasteur
✆ 01 42 19 08 59   Closed 15 July-15 August, 22-28 December,
Fax 01 45 67 09 13   Saturday and Sunday

Menu (€29), €35/59 – Carte €40/52

A/C
VISA
Ⓜ©
AE

This Pasteur neighbourhood institution, a few hundred metres from the Paris-Montparnasse station, is well-loved for its intimate atmosphere. The decor is discreetly contemporary and cosy, with lacquered wood panelling, smoked glass partitions, soft lighting and comfortable armchairs. The black-and-white photographs – the owner's hobby – and the soothing jazzy ambiance are other distinctive features. Thierry Burlot has earned a solid reputation in this arrondissement and beyond. The light and inventive dishes include prawn dumplings with kafir lime and *rougail* (a spicy relish from Reunion Island); scallops, shiitake mushrooms and chestnut shards, and a new take on rum baba. Refined and delicious

Afaria 🐷

South-west of France ✗

15 r. Desnouettes ✉ 75015   Ⓜ Convention
✆ 01 48 56 15 36   Closed 24-30 December, 3-24 August,
Fax 01 48 56 15 36   Sunday and Monday lunch

Menu (€21), €27 (lunch) – Carte €30/49

VISA
Ⓜ©

In the Basque language, Afaria means "Dinner is served". How could you resist such an invitation from Julien Duboué, the talented chef formerly at the Carré des Feuillants, Daniel Boulud's (New York) and Drouant, who opened this southwestern-style bistro with his wife Céline? For pre-dinner drinks, a table d'hôte features delicious local tapas. When you get to the dining room, the menu has more tempting surprises in store for you. Try the boudin en croûte de *moutarde et pommes* (black pudding with mustard and apples), the superb pollack with bouillabaisse, and top it off with apple pie and prune-armagnac ice cream. Washed down with an Ermitage de Chasse Spleen, it will have you looking on the bright side in no time.

Banyan

Thai ✗

B2

24 pl. E. Pernet ⊠ 75015
℘ 01 40 60 09 31 **Fax** 01 40 60 09 20
e-mail lebanyan@noos.fr **www**.lebanyan.com

Ⓜ Félix Faure
Closed 11-24 August

Menu (€20), €25 (weekday lunch), €35/55 – Carte €33/52

Ⓐ/Ⓒ
VISA
Ⓜ©
ⒶⒺ

Don't be put off by the ordinary-looking façade. The Banyan is a genuine piece of Thailand right in Paris. Oth Sombath, the talented young chef who started out at the Blue Elephant, creates his own tasty and inventive version of Thai food. His skilful recipes have the sweet smell of Bangkok's gardens, flavoured with curcuma and galangal, scented with basil and the powerful aromas of lemongrass and curry. Meals are served on simple wooden tables in the low-key dining room decorated with traditional etchings. Takeaway dishes are also available.

Le Bélisaire 😊

Bistro ✗

C2

2 r. Marmontel ⊠ 75015
℘ 01 48 28 62 24
Fax 01 48 28 62 24

Ⓜ Vaugirard
Closed 21-27 April, 4-24 August,
22-28 December, Saturday lunch and Sunday

Menu (€17), €20 (weekday lunch), €30/37

VISA
Ⓜ©

This restaurant, named after the eponymous novel by Marmontel, has little in common with the Byzantine general. The atmosphere is calm, and the up-to-date cuisine tasty – a far cry from the rigours of military life at any rate. While it may look like an unassuming café, this establishment has built up a solid reputation among local gourmets thanks to its young chef, Mathieu Garrel. The carefully prepared, market-based dishes vary according to the seasons. Try the game in autumn – the excellent venison stew for example – or the vegetable starters in the spring. Efficient service in the two pleasant dining rooms with a country bistro feel.

Beurre Noisette 😊

Contemporary ✗

B3

68 r. Vasco de Gama ✉ 75015
✆ 01 48 56 82 49
Fax 01 48 28 59 38

Ⓜ Lourmel
Closed 1st-24 August, 1st-7 January,
Sunday and Monday

Menu (€ 20), € 24 (weekday lunch)/32 – Carte € 29/36

VISA
ⓂⒸ
ⒶⒺ
Ⓞ

If you think the name of this restaurant (which translates as "nut-brown butter") is enticing, wait until you try the truly mouth-watering dishes. The two dining rooms with warm colours and soft lighting make you feel right at home, the staff are welcoming, and the ambiance pleasantly convivial. The chef, who has worked at some of the finest establishments in Paris, lovingly cooks up delicious contemporary food, with market-inspired dishes featured on the blackboard. At lunchtime, the menu is a touch less ambitious. Nice selection of wines by the glass.

Bistro d'Hubert

Contemporary ✗

D2

41 bd Pasteur ✉ 75015
✆ 01 47 34 15 50
Fax 01 45 67 03 09
e-mail message@bistrodhubert.com
www.bistrodhubert.com

Ⓜ Pasteur
Closed Monday lunch, Saturday lunch,
Sunday and public holidays

Menu € 34 – Carte € 38/79

VISA
ⓂⒸ
ⒶⒺ
Ⓞ

The setting at this restaurant on the boulevard Pasteur, a stone's throw from Montparnasse Station, is very attractive. The dining room looks like an inn from the Landes region with its light wood walls and ceiling, its rustic tables and shelves filled with bottles and jars from the *terroir*. The legendary Hubert is no longer in the kitchen, but his daughter has inherited his passion for the good things in life. Updated traditional recipes are proposed in the bistrot, using fine and carefully selected ingredients. If you are tempted by a choice after-dinner liqueur or a good cigar, the proprietress will be glad to share her excellent recommendations.

Le Cristal de Sel

Contemporary ✗

C2

13 r. Mademoiselle ✉ 75015
✆ 01 42 50 35 29
Fax 01 42 50 35 29

Ⓜ Commerce
Closed August, Christmas holidays,
Sunday and Monday

Carte €34/50

VISA
Ⓜ©

With its immaculate decor of whitewashed walls and beams, giant blackboards and updated bistro furniture, "The Salt Crystal") is aptly named. Run by two highly professional young men (Karil Lopez in the kitchen and Damien Crépu in the dining room, both formerly at the Hôtel Bristol), this new establishment puts the accent on excellent fresh ingredients: John Dory with asparagus and girolle mushrooms, *viennoise de veau aux câpres* (veal coated in egg, breaded and fried) and sardines Ramon Penas (sardines on an open sandwich with seaweed butter). Each dish is more appetizing than the last! As for the desserts, we loved the *financier à l'abricot* (small apricot cake) served warm with a scoop of vanilla ice cream.

Le Dirigeable ☺

Bistro ✗

C2

37 r. d'Alleray ✉ 75015
✆ 01 45 32 01 54

Ⓜ Vaugirard
Closed 1st-24 August, 24-31 December,
Sunday and Monday

Menu (€19), €22 (lunch) – Carte €30/52

VISA
Ⓜ©
AE

Take a culinary cruise on this discreetly charming airship just a few minutes from the Vaugirard metro station. Chocolate banquettes, wooden furniture and light-coloured walls with large mirrors form the simple, laid-back decor at this friendly neighbourhood restaurant. The well-prepared traditional cuisine uses the most carefully selected ingredients, with an attractive lunchtime menu chalked on the blackboard and a more daring repertoire in the evening. A large clientele of regulars has built up over the years thanks to the high-quality dishes, convivial ambiance and pleasant staff.

Gastroquet

B2

10 r. Desnouettes ✉ 75015
✆ 01 48 28 60 91
Fax 01 45 33 23 70

Ⓜ Convention
Closed August, 1st-10 January,
Saturday dinner in summer and Sunday

Menu € 22/29 – Carte € 49/59

VISA
MC
AE

This authentic gastronomic *troquet* (small cafe) a short distance from the Parc des Expositions is not without charm. The dining room – comfortable in a understated way – has a wide, curtained picture window giving onto a narrow street. The place is masterfully run by an energetic couple with an enduring passion for fine ingredients, attracting neighbourhood gourmets as well as occasional passers-by. The traditional, market-based cuisine is simple and often copious, while the friendly family atmosphere delights customers. Good choice of wines by the glass.

Le Grand Pan

C3

20 r. Rosenwald ✉ 75015
✆ 01 42 50 02 50
Fax 01 42 50 02 66

Ⓜ Plaisance
Closed 1st-24 August, Christmas holidays,
Saturday and Sunday

Menu (€ 20), € 28/32

VISA
MC

Counter top, wooden chairs and tables, dishes of the day chalked up on blackboards...you get the picture. This is the kind of neighbourhood bistro made for the likes of singer-songwriter Georges Brassens, who lived nearby (and wrote the song that gave the restaurant its name). After working for years with Christian Etchebest at Le Troquet, Benoît Gauthier has been going it alone here since the spring of 2007. The appetising dishes include soups as starters for lunch and, for dinner, fabulous grilled meats for two – Ibaïona pork chops and rib of Aquitaine Mauléon beef. Desserts like the creamy rice pudding with rhubarb compote are sure to bring back fond childhood memories.

FROM WHATEVER ANGLE WE LOOK
AT THE QUESTION, THERE IS NO
BETTER ANSWER THAN TGV
FOR TRAVEL IN FRANCE.

TGV is indeed the fast and simple solution to discover France.
Once comfortably seated on board, all you'll have to do is relax
and enjoy a safe and high-speed ride to your chosen destination.
Travelling with TGV is merely common sense. **START ORGANISING
YOUR STAY IN FRANCE STRAIGHT AWAY BY VISITING TGV.COM**

**PRICE STARTING
FROM
22 EUROS***

Prenez le temps d'aller vite

What is Jenny doing?

a) She's looking for a new MP3 player for her husband

b) She's choosing a video game for her son's birthday

c) She's buying a digital camera for her younger sister

d) She's using her VIPix loyalty card and taking advantage of loads of special offers to spruce up her home!

The answer is: a, b, c and d

At PIXmania.com, Jenny can take advantage of great services and the lowest prices on a huge selection of products!

13 shops • 45,000 products • 6 million customers • 26 European countries

Kim Anh

Vietnamese 🍴

B2

51 av. Emile Zola ✉ 75015
📞 01 45 79 40 96
Fax 01 40 59 49 78

Ⓜ Charles Michels
Closed Easter holidays, 11-25 August and
Monday – Dinner only

Menu €37 – Carte €43/71

AC
VISA
MC

This establishment serving appetising and authentic Vietnamese specialities is sheltered from busy avenue Émile Zola by a wall of shrubbery. You are here for the food, so don't worry about the plain façade and unassuming interior decor. The menu features the whole gamut of spicy and sweet Tonkin flavours, including delicious caramelised langoustines and grilled tripe seasoned with garlic, hot peppers, sugar and lemon. You are about to embark on a memorable cruise on the Mekong to explore the culinary marvels of southern Vietnam, with a nice French wine to boot.

Le Mûrier

Traditional 🍴

C3

42 r. Olivier de Serres ✉ 75015
📞 01 45 32 81 88
e-mail lepimpecmartin@yahoo.fr

Ⓜ Convention
Closed 11-17 August,
Saturday and Sunday

Menu €24/29

VISA
MC

The atmosphere is peaceful and friendly, and the prices reasonable at this low-key establishment on a quiet street near the Convention metro station. Behind the unassuming façade, a long dining room in shades of yellow is simply arranged and decorated with turn-of-the-century posters giving it an "old café" look. Little touches of blue and bits of greenery here and there brighten up the room. The cuisine thrives on tradition and – like the decor – is skilfully put together. Classics include the fine grilled steak, veal kidneys with mustard and home-made terrines. The service is efficient and unpretentious.

Le Pétel

C2

4 r. Pétel ✉ 75015
📞 01 45 32 58 76
Fax 01 45 32 58 76
www.lepetel.com

🚇 **Vaugirard**
Closed 25 July-15 August,
Sunday and Monday

Menu (€18), €31

A/C
VISA
MC
AE
①

We love this warm and friendly neighbourhood bistro
where you feel right at home the minute you walk in. The
ambiance is distinctive – zinc bar, fabric-covered banquettes, patinaed wood panelling, net curtains, tablecloths,
candles and photographs on the walls. As for the cooking,
chef Michel Marie's dishes of the day are featured on a
blackboard, or you can pick from the menu with its unfussy
take on traditional cuisine. His tasty recipes include a *galette*
of fresh sardines, duck breast with honey and ginger, gingerbread *nougat glacé*. To top it off, a nice selection of wines
and attentive service. When you're feeling a bit down, head
for Le Pétel and you're sure to perk right up!

Stéphane Martin

B2

67 r. Entrepreneurs ✉ 75015
📞 01 45 79 03 31
Fax 01 45 79 44 69
e-mail resto.stephanemartin@free.fr

🚇 **Charles Michels**
Closed 3 weeks in August,
Christmas holidays and Easter holidays,
Sunday and Monday

Menu (€17), €22 (weekday lunch)/35 – Carte €38/49

A/C
VISA
MC

Stéphane Martin is a very popular place, and not just with
locals. This pleasant establishment has earned an enviable
reputation with food-lovers from all over the Left Bank. The
setting is cosy and tasteful, with a bordeaux and caramel
colour scheme, dark wood furniture and a fresco of an
ancient library. The cuisine features appetising up-to-date
recipes that are skilfully prepared with carefully selected
ingredients. Try the *émincé* of duck foie gras or the ham
hocks braised in honey – ideal blends of inventiveness and
quality.

Le Troquet 😊

Terroir ✗

C2

21 r. F. Bonvin ✉ 75015
📞 01 45 66 89 00
Fax 01 45 66 89 83

Ⓜ Cambronne
Closed 2-10 May, 1st-24 August, 24 December-
1st January, Sunday and Monday

Menu (€24), €28 (weekday lunch), €30/40

VISA

MC

This is the quintessential troquet with its timeworn bistro decor of leatherette banquettes, mirrors and the closely-packed tables that create a feeling of conviviality. People come here mainly for the food – from the terroir – and the ambiance, which wouldn't be the same without Christian Etchebest, the voluble owner from the South West. His generous recipes, including Basque specialities, vary with the market. Superb ingredients, flavourful dishes presented on a blackboard (lamb stew the way his grandmother used to make it, stuffed shoulder of suckling pig, *millefeuille* etc.) and very reasonable prices – what more could you ask for?

Villa Corse

Corsican cuisine ✗

C1

164 bd Grenelle
✉ 75015
📞 01 53 86 70 81 **Fax** 01 53 86 90 73
e-mail lavillacorse@wanadoo.fr **www.**lavillacorse.com

Ⓜ La Motte Picquet Grenelle
Closed Sunday

Menu €25 (lunch)/60 – Carte €44/58

A/C

☞

VISA

MC

AE

Dreaming of Corsica in Paris? This elegant restaurant in the Cambronne neighbourhood takes the island's gastronomic delights to new heights, proposing food with the powerful flavours of the *maquis* (scrubland). The place amazingly evokes a Corsican villa, with vaulted arcades, wrought-iron balustrades and lithographs illustrating the Isle of Beauty. The three dining rooms, decorated in different styles, have something to please everyone: library, bar-lounge or terrace. The dishes are proud to show off their origins, featuring cold meats with character, local herbs with strong aromas, and robust local wines – a vigorous and noble cuisine with all it takes to captivate the *pinsu*.

Yanasé

B3

PORTE DE VERSAILLES • VAUGIRARD • BEAUGRENELLE

75 r. Vasco-de-Gamma ✉ 75015
✆ 01 42 50 07 20
Fax 01 42 50 07 90
e-mail yanase@orange.fr

Ⓜ Lourmel
Closed 2-25 August, 24 December-2 January,
Saturday lunch and Sunday

Menu €19 bi (weekday lunch), €38/58

A/C

VISA

Ⓜ Ⓒ

Japanophiles will love this place, the first restaurant in Paris with "robata" cuisine (literally, "around the fire"). Yanasé (a cedar tree from southern Japan) has a charcoal grill placed in the centre of the room, framed by a counter top. Meat and fish are grilled in front of you and served using a wooden paddle. The blend of tradition and modernity is another distinctive feature here, where the waiters dressed in kimonos move around the peaceful, ultra-contemporary space. The surprisingly delicate dishes are the work of three Japanese chefs specialising in Japanese, French and Italian cuisine. So, why not give that green tea pannacotta a try?

THE OPERA'S BEES

Can you guess what the Opéra Bastille, the Palais Garnier and the Eiffel Park Hotel have in common? They all have bee hives on their roofs! The idea has come a long way since it was first tried out in 1982, when the person in charge of props secretly set up a colony on top of the Opéra Bastille. A few days later, he found his frames dripping with richly scented honey. Nowadays this sweet nectar, still grown in these unusual spots, is sold at the Opera shop and fought over at Fauchon's. Not to mention the harvest from the hundred-year-old hives at the Luxembourg Gardens, which is sold out in a matter of days!

Étoile · Trocadéro · Passy Bois de Boulogne

The 16th is so vast that it has two postal codes, an exception in Paris, and indeed the differences between the north and south sectors of the arrondissement extend far beyond a mere digit. From the luxury and opulence around **place de l'Étoile** to the peaceful lawns of the **bois de Boulogne,** without forgetting the splendid vista from the **palais de Chaillot,** this arrondissement, in which it is said that nothing ever happens, in fact has much to offer visitors. Bordered by the Seine, avenue Marceau and the Bois de Boulogne, it has far more to recommend it than well-heeled streets and luxury boutiques.

TRIUMPHAL

On the main road into the west of Paris, the Étoile has conquered more than one visitor in its time. Is it because of the grandiose symbolism of the **triumphal arch** built by Napoleon to celebrate his victories? Or is it because of the memory of the unknown soldier, whose tomb is the culminating point of an annual military parade? More prosaically though, it is most probably the nightlife and shops that explain its constant popularity with tourists. By day its tightly-packed shopping malls and luxury boutiques, and come sunset, its nightclubs,

among the most exclusive of the capital, never empty. It is also home to some of the capital's finest restaurants, providing of course that you are prepared to foot the bill.

A PARISIAN OASIS

To the southwest of the Étoile, the climate progressively mellows as the presence of shops grows rarer and we can only urge visitors to take advantage of this break from the urban bustle to explore the Bois de Boulogne and its neighbourhood. A survivor of the forest of Rouvray that bordered Paris in the Middle Ages, this gigantic wood is two and a half times larger than Central Park. Lakes and waterfalls add interest to the dozens of kilometres of roads and paths through the wood, as do several of the capital's most beautifully located gastronomic restaurants. Several portions of the wood are in fact parks in their own right, such as the **Jardin d'Acclimatation,** an immense playground with a zoo and theme park, the **Jardins de Bagatelle,** laid out in an "Anglo-Chinese" style and the **Pré-Catelan,** landscaped gardens inspired by the works of Shakespeare. Even though the "bois", as the Parisians affectionately refer to it, can hardly be called unspoilt countryside, it is

S. Sauvignier / MICHELIN

sufficiently varied to appeal to everyone!

BOURGEOIS AND VILLAGERS

Few areas of Paris have retained their village-like features in the same way as **Passy and Auteuil;** formerly towns on the outskirts of Paris, they were annexed to the capital under Napoleon III but continue to display their original charm. Bourgeois, even select, they are the epitome of carefree, unchanging Paris. Rue de Passy for example is lined with all sorts of shops, in particular clothing, while around Auteuil are some of the capital's best gourmet establishments where each café, delicatessen and restaurant has its own speciality. East of Passy don't forget to pause on **place du Trocadéro** and savour the splendid view of the Tour Eiffel before branching out into the surrounding streets to sample the fare of the smart bistros and trendy restaurants.

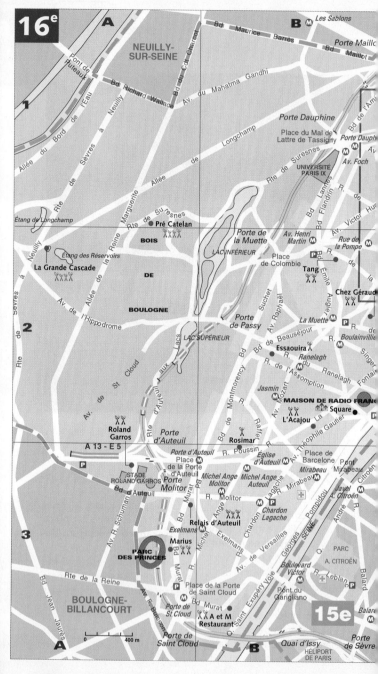

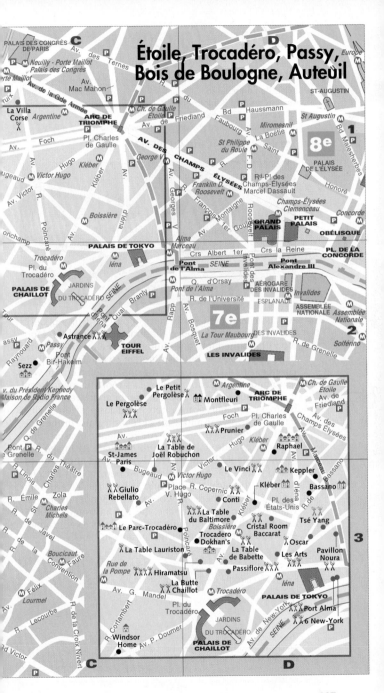

Étoile, Trocadéro, Passy, Bois de Boulogne, Auteuil

La Grande Cascade ❀

A2   Contemporary XXXX

allée de Longchamp   Closed 20 February-10 March
(in the bois de Boulogne) ✉ 75016
☎ 01 45 27 33 51 **Fax** 01 42 88 99 06
e-mail grandecascade@wanadoo.fr **www**.lagrandecascade.fr

Menu €75/177 – Carte €130/200

J.C. AMIEL

A classic and deliciously retro look is still in vogue in this former hunting lodge that once belonged to Napoleon III. Turned into a restaurant for the Exposition Universelle of 1900, it blends different styles (Empire, Belle Époque, Art Nouveau), exuding unparalleled charm with its rotunda dining room, huge glass roof and magnificent terrace – booked up at the first sign of good weather. The business clientele comes here for a taste of the stylish Paris of yesteryear and a bit of "country air" in the Bois de Boulogne. Georges and André Menut treasure their Grande Cascade, taking care to cultivate its image as a "grande dame". But they have also kept up with the times. The proof? They hired Frédéric Robert, a brilliant chef who was formerly at the Grand Véfour, the Vivarois and Lucas Carton (where he worked with Senderens for ten years). Given carte blanche, he has invented a subtle cuisine with strong flavours and raised this establishment among the finest gourmet restaurants in Paris.

First Course	*Main Course*	*Dessert*
• Fleurs de courgette ivres de girolles, couteaux à l'huile d'olive.	• Thon rouge croustillant poivre et sel, graines de sésame et coriandre en condiment.	• Variation sur le café.
• Grosses langoustines snackées et huître en cromesqui, chou vert croquant et nage réduite au beurre iodé.	• Pomme de ris de veau cuite lentement, olives, câpres et croutons frits, herbes à tortue comme au Moyen-Âge.	• Soufflé Grand Marnier "Cuvée du Centenaire".

Pré Catelan ❀❀❀

Innovative XXXX

A1

rte Suresnes ✉ 75016
✆ 01 44 14 41 14
Fax 01 45 24 43 25
e-mail leprecatelan-restaurant@lenotre.fr **www**.lenotre.fr

Closed 3-25 August, 27 October-3 November,
February school holidays, Sunday and Monday

Menu €85 (weekday lunch), €180/230 – Carte €180/224

Pré Catelan

With its magnificent setting full of history, the Pré Catelan is a truly delightful getaway in the heart of the Bois de Boulogne. This enchanting place with its gardens and shady terrace – wonderful in fine weather – boasts a beautiful Napoleon III pavilion with a listed decor (Belle Époque style, Caran d'Ache ceiling frieze, warm and soft tones). The delicious and inventive cuisine here has been prepared in recent years by Frédéric Anton. This talented award-winning chef (Meilleur Ouvrier de France) has created a menu combining balance, harmony and generosity. He strives for perfection in every dish, down to the graphic effects. The precision and quality of execution he learned from his mentors (including Robuchon) are his signature, as well as a talent for creating unusual associations and highlighting the essence of his ingredients. Add to that an impressive cellar, impeccable reception and traditional service – just a few of the arguments in favour of this noble establishment that has reached the heights.

First Course	Main Course	Dessert
• L'étrille.	• Le pigeonneau.	• Le café "expresso".
• La tomate.	• Le ris de veau.	• La pomme.

Hiramatsu ✿

Innovative ✕✕✕✕

D3

52 r. Longchamp ✉ 75116
✆ 01 56 81 08 80
Fax 01 56 81 08 81
e-mail paris@hiramatsu.co.jp
www.hiratamatsu.co.jp

Ⓜ Trocadéro
Closed 2-31 August, 29 December-6 January, Saturday and Sunday
Number of covers limited, pre-book

Menu €48 (lunch), €95/130 – Carte €104/140

A/C · ⊡ · ☞ · VISA · MC · AE · Ⓓ · ✿

Hiramatsu

A Japanese restaurant on the Rue de Longchamp in the 16th arrondissement? Well, yes and no. The Asian-sounding name comes from the owner, Hiroyuki Hiramatsu, who is indeed from Japan. But the establishment, which once belonged to Henri Faugeron, an ardent defender of a certain culinary classicism, has remained an ambassador of traditional French cuisine. Hiramatsu has no cause to feel embarrassed anymore – after his initial rejection at this very address when he came to France in the late 1970s to learn his craft. Whether through a twist of fate or a fortunate coincidence, he now runs the place, with a contemporary touch of class and a dash of sophistication. This is a blend of Japanese rigour in the decor (an elegant dining room as restrained and Zen-like as a temple) and well-balanced French flavours. The extreme refinement is matched by the discreet but attentive service.

First Course

- Fricassée de ris de veau et écrevisses aux jeunes légumes, sauce vin jaune.
- Foie gras de canard aux choux frisés, jus de truffe.

Main Course

- Fines lamelles d'agneau, compotée d'oignons blancs, jus de truffe.
- Feuilleté de homard aux parfums de truffes, jus d'estragon.

Dessert

- Cassonade brûlée de café corsé, sabayon à la cannelle.
- Gâteau au chocolat "Hiramatsu".

Astrance ✿✿✿

Innovative 🗙🗙🗙

C2

4 r. Beethoven ✉ 75016 Ⓜ Passy
☎ 01 40 50 84 40

Menu €70 (lunch), €190/290 bi

Closed 1st-9 March, August, autumn half-term holidays, Saturday, Sunday and Monday
Number of covers limited, pre-book

A/C
VISA
Ⓜ©
AE
①
🍇

Astrance

Thrills are "in" these days, and Astrance is one. This is a unique place that preserves its surprise effect. First, you have to book months in advance, so your frustration evolves into delightful anticipation of an outstanding dinner. Second, you have to enjoy jumping into unknown territory because the food here is reinvented every day – and that's not a figure of speech. You have no idea beforehand what you're going to eat. Is it improvisation? There's a bit of that in the surprise menu created every morning, based on market ingredients and mood. But this is no beginner's operation. Christophe Rohat and Pascal Barbot (formerly with Alain Passard) had the necessary experience to launch the slightly crazy project of this unconventional restaurant in the year 2000. Located near Trocadéro, the intimate contemporary dining room only holds 25 diners. That's 25 lucky people who – in going along with the house rules – get to taste the expertly crafted cuisine open to the world and new ideas. It combines the exotic with the *terroir*, has a wine list of the same high quality, and is subtle and inventive. How many more epithets are there?

First Course	Main Course	Dessert
• Foie gras, agrumes et fleurs sauvages.	• Cabillaud, racine de persil.	• Jasmin, châtaigne.
• Cèpes, langoustine.	• Cochon, radis noir.	• Croustillant chocolat blanc-gingembre, glace thé vert.

ÉTOILE • TROCADÉRO • PASSY • BOIS DE BOULOGNE

Les Arts

Traditional XXX

D3

9 bis av. d'Iéna ⊠ 75116
𝒞 01 40 69 27 53
Fax 01 40 69 27 08
e-mail restaurant.am@sodexho-prestige.fr
www.sodexho-prestige.fr

Ⓜ Iéna
Closed 28 July-28 August,
23 December-2 January, Saturday,
Sunday and public holidays

Menu €38 – Carte €57/79

The magnificent Hôtel d'Iéna is the prestigious setting for this elegant classical restaurant. Since 1925 this building has been the headquarters of the Société des Ingénieurs des Arts et Métiers, for which this establishment was named. The splendid ornamental opulence of the main dining room features a high ceiling decorated with mouldings, Doric columns and copies of masterpieces. A classic cuisine mainly strives to please the clientele of engineers and businessmen. In summer, book a table on the terrace with its superb garden.

Port Alma

Seafood XXX

D3

10 av. New York ⊠ 75116
𝒞 01 47 23 75 11 **Fax** 01 47 20 42 92
e-mail restaurantportalma@wanadoo.fr

Ⓜ Alma Marceau
Closed Sunday and Monday

Menu (€25), €29/39 (dinner) – Carte €28/90

The Port Alma, a mecca for Parisian seafood-lovers, is located on the quayside of the Left Bank a short distance from the Pont de l'Alma. You can't go wrong at this port of call. The menu features high-quality ingredients in refined dishes such as sole and scallop fricassee, roasted langoustines with preserved tomatoes, and grilled line-caught sea bass. The decor is a perfect match for the cuisine with its classic-looking dining room featuring a veranda, exposed beams, ultramarine velvet armchairs, and many other elements evoking the deep blue sea. Now you know where to go when in need a breath of fresh sea air.

Passiflore ✿

Contemporary XXX

33 r. Longchamp ⊠ 75016
📞 01 47 04 96 81
Fax 01 47 04 32 27
e-mail passiflore@club-internet.fr
www.restaurantpassiflore.com

Ⓜ **Trocadéro**
Closed 20 July-20 August,
Saturday lunch and Sunday

Menu €35 (lunch), €45/54 (dinner) – Carte €64/100

AC
VISA
MC
AE

Passiflore

ÉTOILE • TROCADÉRO • PASSY • BOIS DE BOULOGNE

Roland Durand is a forerunner. This genuine Auvergnat – a Meilleur Ouvrier de France award-winner and avid traveller – was blending a noble rustic quality with foreign tastes (especially from Asia) well before anyone else and before "world food" and "fusion" were ever invented. It's more than a passion, it's a fundamental belief. In 2001 Durand took over the Passiflore, a Chinese restaurant until then (Asia was already in the air), and turned it into an ode to the exotic. First, in the decor, with its striking Zen ambiance in a warm and refined setting dotted with objets d'art from far-away places. Then in the cooking, a reinterpretation of traditional dishes featuring seasonal ingredients and herbs and spices from the Orient. The chef's calm, precise, classical approach is enhanced by the interesting twists he adds. He also likes to develop dishes on a theme (such as rice, soups, mushrooms, etc). In short, a menu in perpetual motion and a fine selection of wines without borders.

First Course
- Ravioles de homard en mulligatowny.
- Foie gras de canard poêlé, marmelade d'orange.

Main Course
- Riz noir et langoustines en saté au citron vert.
- Tournedos de pied de cochon, grenailles de rattes dorées au beurre salé.

Dessert
- Quatre sorbets verts pimentés.
- Gâteau chaud au chocolat grand cru, sorbet cacao.

Le Pergolèse ✿

Classic XXX

40 r. Pergolèse ✉ 75116   **Ⓜ Porte Maillot**
✆ 01 45 00 21 40   Closed August, Saturday and Sunday
Fax 01 45 00 81 31
e-mail le-pergolese@wanadoo.fr **www.**lepergolese.com

Menu €42 (lunch)/90 – Carte €73/107

Le Pergolèse

It only took Stéphane Gaborieau two years to create his own style and turn the Pergolèse into a "beautiful place to receive diners, as if it were my own home." It seemed like a risky bet taking over from the high-profile Albert Corre, whose clients were extremely faithful. But this chef from Lyon, a winner of the Meilleur Ouvrier de France award, soon settled in, with help from his wife Chantal in the dining room. Together they succeeded in transporting the "spirit of the countryside" to the chic 16th arrondissement, creating a blend of conviviality, good taste and top-quality flavours. Although his cooking honours his origins, a classical base and fine ingredients, it also exhibits a typically Mediterranean verve. It's not surprising, since Gaborieau trained in southern France. The colourful, sun-drenched dishes are served in a warm and plush atmosphere featuring soft tones and lighting, bronze statuettes and paintings dotting the room. The wine list has some fine bottles. A place well worth trying.

First Course

- Ravioli de langoustines, duxelles de champignons, émulsion de crustacés au foie gras.
- Mœlleux de filets de sardines mariné aux épices, fondue de poivron.

Main Course

- Aiguillette de Saint-Pierre dorée, cannelloni farcis aux multi-saveurs.
- Carré d'agneau au cumin, sucrine au jus, financier à l'échalote grise.

Dessert

- Traditionnel soufflé framboises, sorbet framboise et soupe.
- Tarte crémeuse au chocolat, sorbet cacao pur Caraïbe.

Prunier

Seafood XXX

D2

16 av. Victor-Hugo
✉ 75116
✆ 01 44 17 35 85 **Fax** 01 44 17 90 10
e-mail prunier@maison-prunier.fr

Ⓜ Charles de Gaulle-Étoile
Closed August and Sunday

Menu € 59/155 – Carte € 68/122

Prunier, an institution that appeared to be stuck in a time warp, now has a new lease on life and is poised to recapture the interest of the sharpest palates. Chef Eric Coisel has a lot to do with it, bringing the sparkle back to this venerable establishment (1925) whose motto remains "everything from the sea". It still features the finest seafood – caviar and salmon (Balik, Tsar Nikolaj) – and a *banc d'écailler* (oyster bar) in the entrance, complemented by new dishes that are frequently updated. Thanks to the high-quality cuisine and the exceptional setting – with fine workmanship by top mosaicists, engravers and sculptors from the Art Deco period – this deluxe brasserie has joined the 21st century.

Tsé Yang

Chinese XX

D3

25 av. Pierre 1er de Serbie ✉ 75016
✆ 01 47 20 70 22 **Fax** 01 47 20 75 34
www.tseyang.fr

Ⓜ Iéna

Menu € 49/59 – Carte € 35/133

This elegant Chinese restaurant located just behind Trocadéro will transport you to the halls of the Forbidden City the minute you walk through the door. The decor redesigned by James Tinel and Emmanuel Benet taps into the hidden sources of the Middle Kingdom, with monumental jade lions at the entrance, a rich interior with dark fabrics and a gilded ceiling, and black wood furniture with sculpted motifs. The classic Chinese cuisine features traditional spicy soups, dim sum, Peking duck and beef sautéed with soy sprouts, prepared with a talented twist by the inventive young chef. This establishment should appeal to even the most unaccustomed Western palates!

Relais d'Auteuil ✿

A3

Classic XXX

31 bd. Murat ✉ 75016
☎ 01 46 51 09 54
Fax 01 40 71 05 03
e-mail pignol.p@wanadoo.fr

Ⓜ Michel-Ange Molitor
Closed August, Christmas holidays,
Monday lunchtime,
Saturday lunchtime and Sunday

Menu € 58 (lunch), € 119/149 – Carte € 116/171

A/C

VISA

Ⓜ Ⓒ

Ⓐ Ⓔ

Ⓞ

Christophe Biche

Patrick Pignol makes people feel completely at home in this plush establishment. A chic and faithful clientele has been coming here in a steady stream ever since it opened in 1984, and diners always return for more of the hedonistic, convivial atmosphere. The discreet service with a personal touch provided by Laurence Pignol and the refined flower-filled dining room with a contemporary decor create the ideal conditions for enjoying a delicious meal. Trendy gourmets may not like it, but the generous and up-to-date bourgeois cooking isn't trying to be spectacular or visually daring. The chef is a fan of game – the restaurant looks like a hunting lodge when it's in season – and enjoys highlighting subtle flavours and ingredients from the terroir. And while the menu professes to be simple, you could get dizzy just reading the wine list, which has some particularly fine vintages.

First Course

- Amandine de foie gras de canard des Landes et son lobe poêlé.
- Langoustines croustillantes infusées au citron et parfum de coriandre.

Main Course

- Grosse sole de ligne dorée entière sur l'arête.
- Gibier.

Dessert

- Madeleine cuites "minute" au miel de bruyère, glace au miel et noix.
- Soufflé citron vert dans sa coque, coulis au poivre maniguette et vodka.

La Table de Joël Robuchon ✿ ✿

C3

Contemporary 𝖃𝖃𝖃

16 av. Bugeaud ⊠ 75116　　　　　Ⓜ Victor Hugo
✆ 01 56 28 16 16 **Fax** 01 56 28 16 78
e-mail latabledejoelrobuchon@wanadoo.fr

Menu €55 bi (lunch)/150 – Carte €55/145

AC

VISA

MC

La Table de Joël Robuchon

Joël Robuchon's name is known far beyond the borders of France, where it is increasingly seen as an international symbol of French cuisine that is both classic and visionary. This peerless chef has created a number of branches around the world, from Las Vegas and Tokyo to London, Macao and Hong-Kong. In Paris, he has two establishments. At l'Atelier, he provides 21st century cuisine with a playful touch and a kitchen that opens onto a bar with a deluxe tapas and teppanyaki feel. La Table, although it looks more conventional with a streamlined minimalist look that is both intimate and refined, boasts equally stunning flavours. The attractive menu highlights ingredients prepared in a traditional spirit, featuring original choices of small (or large) portions for a lively and varied gourmet experience. The masterfully balanced no-nonsense cuisine is well worth the trip. Dining here is always a pleasure, given the quality of the meals, the attractive prices on the daily set menu, and the excellent service.

First Course

- La langoustine en papillotes croustillantes au basilic.
- Le thon au fromage de chèvre et cannelloni d'aubergine confite.

Main Course

- La caille au foie gras et caramélisée avec une pomme purée truffée.
- Le cabillaud en pavé, nage de petits pois à la sarriette.

Dessert

- Le "chocolat sensation" crème onctueuse au chocolat araguani, glace chocolat au biscuit oréo.
- Punch "retour d'un voyage des îles" au rhum ambré.

La Table du Baltimore ❀

Contemporary XXX

Hôtel Sofitel Baltimore,
1 r. Léo Delibes ⊠ 75016
✆ 01 44 34 54 34 **Fax** 01 44 34 54 44
e-mail h2789-fb@accor.com **www**.sofitel.com

Ⓜ Boissière
Closed August,
Saturday and Sunday

Menu € 48 bi (lunch)/50 – Carte € 54/71

G.Corbic/MICHELIN

"Enjoyable food", the leitmotiv of the chef here, conjures up an image of authentic cooking with a personal touch – both stimulating and colourful. Jean-Philippe Pérol, who has run the Sofitel's Baltimore restaurant since 2001, worked hard to create an evolving menu inspired by the changing seasons and the freshest ingredients. The chef is a classicist who has worked in a number of fine establishments, including the Pré Catelan and the Meurice, and cares about giving good value for money. He has done his utmost to win over any food-lovers who may still feel hesitant about dining at a hotel, inviting them to simply come and enjoy it. The dining room provides a pleasant and comfortable environment for a meal, with old photographs of the city of Baltimore (thus the name), mirrors that create the illusion of a bigger space, pretty table settings and old wood panelling offsetting the contemporary furniture. The stage is set, now the only thing missing are the principal characters – you.

First Course
- Tomate confite entière, mozzarella au thym, crémeux d'avocat aux olives.
- Langoustine cuite en feuille de bananier, risotto noir, sauce citronnelle gingembre.

Main Course
- Seiche juste saisie à la plancha, tiges de blettes au jus, feuilles froissées.
- Râble de lapin à la cannelle, cuisses en pastilla, courgettes juste sautées.

Dessert
- Abricot en mousseline, croustillant au cacao amer, glace romarin.
- Ananas confit, sirop parfumé au kirsch et croustille à la noix de coco.

L'Acajou

Contemporary ✗✗

B2

35 bis r. La Fontaine ✉ 75016 — ⓜ Jasmin
✆ 01 42 88 04 47 **Fax** 01 42 88 95 12 — Closed August,
www.l-acajou.com — Saturday lunch and Sunday

Menu (€ 28), € 35/40 bi – Carte € 53/68

A/C
VISA
MC
AE

Jean Imbert is a promising and talented young chef with the kind of savoir-faire acquired from training with Bocuse, Rostang and Westermann. The short menu says it all: crunchy tandoori-style Dublin Bay prawns with a courgette-feta-red pepper cream sauce, roast free-range pork with pineapple and creamy polenta, chocolate soufflé, *financier aux agrumes*. And the list is far from complete, as the chef enjoys changing the menu at his restaurant, located between the Maison de la Radio and the Eglise d'Auteuil. The decor is quiet and tasteful, featuring mahogany furniture and contemporary art work, and the family atmosphere combines conviviality and professionalism.

A et M Restaurant 😊

Contemporary ✗✗

B3

136 bd Murat ✉ 75016 — ⓜ Porte de St-Cloud
✆ 01 45 27 39 60 — Closed August,
Fax 01 45 27 69 71 — Saturday lunch and Sunday
e-mail am-bistrot-16@wanadoo.fr

Menu (€ 23), € 30 – Carte € 35/48

A/C
VISA
MC
AE
①

The A and M refer to Apicius and Marius, two famous gourmet restaurants in Paris whose owners founded this chef's bistro. Chic and relaxed are the words for this establishment offering high-quality food, reasonable prices and a convivial atmosphere, with dishes of the day and wines of the month featured on the blackboard. The Japanese chef cooks up delicious up-to-date recipes that are discreet yet inventive. His warm goat cheese tart with salad and honey vinaigrette, hazelnut and rosemary-crusted *suprême de poulet fermier*, and *millefeuille aux fraises* celebrate authentic and well-balanced flavours. With its cream and tobacco tones and soft lighting, the contemporary decor reflects the same feeling of harmony.

ÉTOILE • TROCADÉRO • PASSY • BOIS DE BOULOGNE

La Butte Chaillot

Contemporary XX

D3

110 bis av. Kléber ✉ 75116 **Ⓜ** Trocadéro
✆ 01 47 27 88 88 Closed 3 weeks in August and Saturday lunch
Fax 01 47 27 41 46
e-mail buttechaillot@guysavoy.com **www**.buttechaillot.com

Menu € 33/50 – Carte € 37/56

A/C
⬚
VISA
ⓂⒸ
AE
Ⓓ

This annex of the Guy Savoy empire is just a few minutes from the Place du Trocadéro. Its pleasant and modern 21st century bistro look was designed by the chef's favourite architect, Jean-Michel Wilmotte. The airy, streamlined space is done in copper-coloured tones, with contemporary artwork around the comfortable tables and deep armchairs. The dining rooms provide a more private experience – ideal for enjoying the flavourful cuisine blending tradition and current tastes. The free-range spit-roasted poultry with thyme and potato purée – a longstanding favourite – is still on the menu, which also features some enticing new dishes.

Chez Géraud

Bistro XX

B2

31 r. Vital ✉ 75016 **Ⓜ** La Muette
✆ 01 45 20 33 00 Closed 1st August-1st September,
Fax 01 45 20 46 60 23 December-5 January, Saturday and Sunday

Menu € 32 – Carte € 48/71

VISA
ⓂⒸ

With its welcoming traditional bistro decor this restaurant has a reputation that reaches far beyond its quiet neighbourhood. The painted façade with Longwy faience evokes the fine old establishments of yesteryear, hinting at the equally delightful interior with its large ceramic fresco and matching plates on rather rustic, attractively laid-out tables. The clientele of businessmen from the 16th arrondissement love the chic look. In the kitchen, the chef proves that tradition can be a good thing, with classic dishes such as *pot-au-feu* (stew), rib steak and home-made terrines, along with tasty game specialities in season. You are sure to leave this smart and reasonably priced place with a smile on your face!

Conti

D3

Italian ✗✗

72 r. Lauriston ✉ 75116   **Ⓜ** Boissière
✆ 01 47 27 74 67   Closed 4-24 August, 25 December-1st January,
Fax 01 47 27 37 66   Saturday, Sunday and public holidays

Menu €33 (lunch) – Carte €41/65

ⒶⒸ
ⓋⒾⓈⒶ
ⓂⒸ
ⒶⒺ
Ⓞ
🕸

Stendhal would certainly have enjoyed this restaurant where his beloved Italy is celebrated in the cuisine, and his two emblematic colours – red and black – are featured in the decor (velvet, tapestries, wood panelling, Murano glass chandeliers). This chic and refined establishment is run by two Frenchmen in love with food from across the Alps. Their Italian recipes with a twist have a contemporary touch blending influences from France and Italy. The resulting dishes are subtle and finely crafted, using the finest ingredients. The seafood is top-quality, the fresh pasta irresistible, the tiramisu fabulous, and the (Franco-Italian) wine list remarkable.

Cristal Room Baccarat

D3

Innovative ✗✗

11 pl. des États-Unis ✉ 75116   **Ⓜ** Boissière
✆ 01 40 22 11 10 **Fax** 01 40 22 11 99   Closed Sunday – Pre-book
e-mail cristalroom@baccarat.fr

Menu €59 (lunch), €92/200 bi – Carte €90/123

ⒶⒸ
ⓋⒾⓈⒶ
ⓂⒸ
ⒶⒺ

In addition to the restaurant, this splendid townhouse also houses the headquarters of the Baccarat crystalworks, as well as a shop and museum. Like the brand, the setting is exceptional with its Empire decor completely redesigned by Philippe Starck, preserving the original marble, parquet floors and exposed beams, offset by the boldly modern look. The decor only serves to enhance the high-quality menu with tasty, up-to-date food including marinades, meat and fish *à la plancha*, spit-roasted poultry and simmered casserole dishes.

Giulio Rebellato

C3

Italian ✗✗

136 r. Pompe ✉ 75116
☎ 01 47 27 50 26

Ⓜ **Victor Hugo**
Closed August

Carte € 36/66

A/C
VISA
MC
AE

Sumptuous fabrics, old engravings and sparkling, finely worked mirrors are part of the smart decor at this comfortable restaurant – designed by Garcia and inspired by the golden age of Venice – where you can enjoy Italian specialities. This place has attracted a demanding clientele from the Rue de la Pompe for years, and built up a solid reputation for its quality ingredients and generous cuisine. The ample menu is a superb tribute to Italian gastronomy, featuring dishes such as the lovingly baked lasagna, copious ravioli, delicious risottos and delicate and light Italian desserts.

Marius

A3

Seafood ✗✗

82 bd Murat ✉ 75016
☎ 01 46 51 67 80
Fax 01 40 71 83 75
e-mail restaurant.marius@orange.fr

Ⓜ **Porte de St-Cloud**
Closed August,
Saturday lunch and Sunday

Carte € 43/68

VISA
MC

Marius, a real institution in the Porte de Saint-Cloud neighbourhood, is a place for those who love seafood (from Provence here). The menu spotlights the finest catch of the sea. Impeccably fresh fish and shellfish are featured in well-prepared dishes and a few specialities including their delicious bouillabaisse. The chef's suggestions change daily, ranging from crab salad with herbs one day to sea bream in a salt crust the next, as well as a host of other dishes that are sure to bring you back. Comfortable decor (light-coloured walls, mirrors and wooden blinds) and shady summer terrace.

Pavillon Noura

D3

Lebanese XX

21 av. Marceau ✉ 75116   **M** Alma Marceau
✆ 01 47 20 33 33 **Fax** 01 47 20 60 31
e-mail noura@noura.fr

Menu €36 (weekday lunch), €56/64 – Carte €37/54

A/C

VISA

M/C

AE

D

This temple of Lebanese cuisine, on one of the smartest avenues in the city, boasts a sumptuous Middle Eastern decor with Levantine frescoes decorating the walls, chairs upholstered in ultramarine velvet and beautiful table settings. Dining at Noura's is a true gastronomic journey to the Land of Cedars and an exploration of Phoenician flavours. The tasty meat and vegetarian *mezzes* are complemented by the spectacular variety on the pastry trolley, where semolina, honey and almonds are combined in a thousand different ways. A fine selection of Lebanese wines – often with spicy aromas – and traditional Arak liqueur.

Roland Garros

A3

Contemporary XX

2 bis av. Gordon Bennett   **M** Porte d'Auteuil
✉ 75016
✆ 01 47 43 49 56
Fax 01 40 71 83 24

Closed 31 July-25 August, 24 December-5 January,
Saturday and Sunday from October to March and
Sunday dinner from April to September

Menu (€42), €52 – Carte €51/87

VISA

M/C

AE

The ambiance is airy and pleasantly country-like at this terrace restaurant – one of the finest in the city – located inside the Porte d'Auteuil complex, with its contemporary furniture, comfortable light velvet banquettes, lovely wood veranda and sunny terrace planted with grass. Marc Veyrat assists in composing the up-to-date menu, which evolves with the market and the seasons. The ingredients are fresh, and the poultry roasted in the impressive rotisserie is mouthwatering. The beautiful setting nearly puts the high-quality food in the background. Tennis fans will enjoy it here.

6 New-York

D3

6 av. New-York ✉ 75016
℘ 01 40 70 03 30
Fax 01 40 70 04 77
e-mail 6newyork@wanadoo.fr

Ⓜ Alma Marceau
Closed August,
Saturday lunch and Sunday

Menu (€ 28), € 30 (lunch) – Carte € 48/62

AC
VISA
MC
AE
DC

This fashionable establishment is not North American, but the address is n° 6 Avenue de New York, on the banks of the Seine, with a view of the Eiffel Tower. The location attracts a chic and well-heeled clientele and tourists in search of a fine eatery. The contemporary decor is the image of a tasteful and trendy restaurant. The cuisine is up-to-date, with a healthy, subtly inventive touch. The owner has excellent advice to offer if you can't choose between the cep mushroom salad with rocket, basil and foie gras, cod with girolle mushrooms, and strawberry soup with ginger and preserved lemons. The well-trained waitstaff provides the kind of classic service you expect.

La Table de Babette

D3

32 r. Longchamp ✉ 75016
℘ 01 45 53 00 07
Fax 01 45 53 00 15
e-mail tabledebabette@wanadoo.fr
www.tabledebabette.com

Ⓜ Trocadéro
Closed Saturday lunch,
Sunday and lunch on public holidays

Menu (€ 28), € 38 – Carte € 45/77

AC
VISA
MC
AE

La Table de Babette – a delicious journey to the sunny isles in the heart of the 16th arrondissement – has earned a solid reputation with neighbourhood gourmets and Caribbean food-lovers from all over Paris. You have to admit the proprietress of this haven of colourful flavours and spicy aromas knows what she's doing. The traditional Caribbean dishes served here are subtly reinterpreted with a playful touch. The warm and cosy decor evokes a tropical bijou flat with its exotic wood furniture, luxuriant plants and flowery carpet. The music appropriately draws on beguine classics, creating an atmosphere that is both hushed and happy.

Tang

Chinese ✗✗

B2

125 r. de la Tour ✉ 75116   Ⓜ Rue de la Pompe
✆ 01 45 04 35 35   Closed August, 21-29 December,
Fax 01 45 04 58 19   Monday lunch and Sunday
e-mail charlytang16@yahoo.fr

Menu €39 (weekday lunch), €85/108 – Carte €65/149

A/C

VISA

MC

Paris now has three different Chinatowns! This huge restaurant on a discreet and rather forlorn street in the chic 16th arrondissement is indeed a true institution in the city. The Chinese food here is straightforward and authentic – a nice change from the usual spring rolls. Creation is ever present at Tang, where excellent ingredients are used to prepare the reinvented traditional dishes, including spring salad with langoustine tails and fresh pasta, spicy Peking duck *croustillant* with green pepper sauce, thin crepes and chive julienne – bold and delicious! The setting does credit to both tips of Eurasia with its subtle fusion of French elegance and traditional elements.

Le Vinci

Italian ✗✗

D3

23 r. P. Valéry ✉ 75116   Ⓜ Victor Hugo
✆ 01 45 01 68 18   Closed 2-24 August,
Fax 01 45 01 60 37   Saturday and Sunday
e-mail levinci@wanadoo.fr

Carte €39/68

A/C

VISA

MC

AE

This ristorante on a quiet street near the Avenue Victor Hugo is a little gem of Italian gastronomy. To get you right in the mood, the classic and colourful decor (with Murano glass chandeliers) has the lovely scent of the *mezzogiorno*. Sitting comfortably at your table, get out your menu and start reading about all the wonderful Italian specialities. It's hard to choose among the various kinds of gnocchi, polenta with cured ham, risottos, osso buccos, and veal piccata, not to mention the delicious vanilla and triple coulis panna cotta – familiar recipes that are perfectly prepared and subtly reinterpreted here. A very popular establishment.

ÉTOILE • TROCADÉRO • PASSY • BOIS DE BOULOGNE

Essaouira

Moroccan ✕

B2

135 r. Ranelagh ✉ 75016
✆ 01 45 27 99 93
Fax 01 45 27 56 36

Ⓜ Ranelagh
Closed August,
Monday lunch and Sunday

Menu (€16) – Carte €32/55

VISA
ⓂⒸ

Walking into this Moroccan restaurant is like plunging into an exotic and colourful world – a large wooden door, rugs displayed on the walls, lovely mosaic fountain, warm tones and mirrors. But there's nothing over the top about it, and the décor is in the best of taste. Speaking of tastes, the chef is serious about carrying on his country's culinary traditions, celebrating all the great classics such as pigeon pastille, harira (minestrone with chickpeas, lentils and vermicelli), salads, chicken tajine with carrots, preserved lemons and olives, couscous, baklava, *cornes de gazelle* pastries, etc. The fine selection of wines and the pleasant service are a plus.

Oscar

Traditional ✕

D3

6 r. Chaillot ✉ 75016
✆ 01 47 20 26 92
Fax 01 47 20 27 93
e-mail fredmartinod@orange.fr

Ⓜ Iéna
Closed 5-20 August,
Saturday lunch and Sunday

Menu €22 – Carte €32/47

VISA
ⓂⒸ
ᴀᴇ

Behind its discreet glass façade, on a quiet street in the smart 16th arrondissement, this authentic neighbourhood bistro is a rare species in Paris – a bastion of gourmet tradition with reasonable prices. Run by two experienced associates, it has become a big success – with a reputation far beyond the area. The simple and unassuming setting is not exactly eye-catching with its snug tables, stainless steel cutlery and paper tablecloths. But the food is truly a delight, featuring straightforward and generous dishes such as the home-made terrine, classic rib steak cooked to perfection and the daily blackboard suggestions. Copious and delightful!

Le Petit Pergolèse

Traditional ✗

C2

38 r. Pergolèse ⊠ 75016
☎ 01 45 00 23 66
Fax 01 45 00 44 03

Ⓜ Porte Maillot
Closed August, Saturday and Sunday

Carte €31/59

A/C

VISA

MC

As its name indicates, this restaurant is an annexe of the famous Pergolèse located a short distance away on the same street. In short, this is a chef's bistro which strives for quality through simplicity. The contemporary decor of the dining room, the unpretentious layout with snug tables and spirited atmosphere create a lively and functional setting which attracts a wide clientele of hurried and demanding businessmen. Judiciously updated and flavoursome cuisine features simple and well-prepared dishes. The blackboard changes according to the market, like the chef's daily specialities, announced out loud.

Rosimar

Spanish ✗

B3

26 r. Poussin ⊠ 75016
☎ 01 45 27 74 91
Fax 01 45 20 75 05

Ⓜ Michel-Ange Auteuil
Closed 2 August-2 September, 24-31 December,
Saturday, Sunday and public holidays
Lunch only except Friday

Menu €36 bi – Carte €36/55

A/C

VISA

MC

AE

With its numerous mirrors and pink tablecloths, this "kitsch as can be" restaurant could be the set for an Almodovar film. Paella is just one of the many specialities at this family-run Spanish enclave, also famous for its delicious black rice dishes (with cuttlefish for example), fish (codfish salad, monkfish sautéed with figs) and shellfish. Not to mention the powerfully flavoured Spanish cold meats (*lomo* with tomato-rubbed bread). Everything is very satisfying and well-prepared. Quality and authenticity are obviously the motto of this establishment. As for the delightful wines, there's only one thing to add: *Salud*!

La Table Lauriston

Traditional ✗

129 r. Lauriston ✉ 75016
✆ 01 47 27 00 07
Fax 01 47 27 00 07

Ⓜ Trocadéro
Closed 3-24 August, 24 December-2 January,
Saturday lunch and Sunday

Menu (€ 25) – Carte € 40/61

A/C
VISA
MC
AE

This is where to go for a change from the chic and cushy atmosphere in many of the gourmet restaurants in this area. The Table Lauriston is a typical convivial Parisian bistro, a stone's throw from rue de Longchamp and Avenue Poincaré. Food-lovers are sure to enjoy its satisfying, well prepared and authentic bistro cuisine. Take a look at the blackboard and dive in without delay. All the seasonal classics are featured there in an assortment of straightforward and comforting flavours – calf's liver tournedos in vinegar, choice rib steak, *harengs pommes à l'huile*, and *baba au rhum*. The fine selection of wines by the glass is an added bonus.

La Villa Corse

Corsican cuisine ✗

141 av. Malakoff ✉ 75016
✆ 01 40 67 18 44
Fax 01 40 67 18 19
e-mail lavillacorserivedroite@wanadoo.fr www.lavillacorse.com

Ⓜ Porte Maillot
Closed Sunday

Menu (€ 25 bi) – Carte € 42/60

🍴
A/C
👆
VISA
MC
AE

The Villa Corse in the 15th arrondissement now has a branch on the Right Bank. The concept is the same: a distinctive, somewhat "exotic" atmosphere in which to discover the terroir of the Island of Beauty. The huge dining room, topped by a mezzanine, is decorated with ochre patinas, Murano chandeliers and deep armchairs, while the library-salon has a fireplace. The overall effect is a trendy lounge look. The menu features all the great Corsican classics – some of them updated – including cold meats, *stufatu de veau tigré aux olives* (veal with olives), *civet de sanglier et son ravioli à la châtaigne* (wild boar stew with chestnut ravioli), and *fiadone aux écorces d'agrumes* (Corsican flan with citrus zest). Not to mention the wines from Arena and Leccia, Patrimonio's "stars".

Palais des Congrès · Wagram Ternes · Batignolles

Appreciated for its tranquillity, the 17th is nonetheless an arrondissement unlike others. Wedged in between avenue de Saint-Ouen and avenue de la Grande Armée, this formerly very rural sector was annexed to Paris in 1860. Most of the buildings date from the 1860-1920 period, making it an homogenous monument of Haussmannian architecture, and its graceful facades of dressed stone bourgeois buildings and flawlessly straight wide avenues create a picture of ordered, if unsurprising, urban planning. Practically devoid of parks or gardens, such was the need for housing at the time it was annexed. With the exception of the very exclusive Monceau Park and a few railway lines running out of Saint-Lazare station, almost all the arrondissement has been developed. Three distinct districts are nonetheless worth taking the time to explore. Near Étoile, the **Ternes-Wagram** sector with its **cabarets** and shows is in fact more characteristic of the 8th than the quiet 17th. Next, towards the ring road and **porte Maillot** stands the **Palais des Congrès,** a major shopping and tourist attraction. Lastly, towards the 18th, just before **place de Clichy,** the walker will enjoy the typically Parisian "village" spirit of the Batignolles area, a rarity in the arrondissement.

IMPERIAL SHOW TIMES

A stone's throw from place de l'Étoile, the area between avenue des Ternes and avenue de Wa-gram combines the bourgeois appeal of its Haussmannian architecture with intense commercial and leisure activity. The famous salle Wagram, built in 1865 on the site of a former dance hall and two minutes from the former Empire Theatre, has been a high spot of entertainment for almost 150 years. Ever at the forefront of modernity, it was the first to host new cultural forms that emerged in the 20C. The scene of the first Paris automobile show, it also staged boxing fights at the time of Al Brown and Marcel Cerdan and some of the greatest post-War jazz musicians from Bud Powell to Duke Ellington played here. No doubt this glorious past is partly the reason for the abundance of relatively upmarket restaurants and brasseries. Heading down towards place des Ternes, the district becomes livelier and also more commercial: the **Ternes Fnac** music and bookshop is still the largest in Paris and the flower market (everyday except Mondays) on place des Ternes is a genuine institution in the neighbourhood. A few more or less exclusive nightclubs provide a pleasant setting for a late night drink.

CULTURAL EXCEPTION

Heading eastwards along boulevard de Courcelles, make sure you stop at Parc Monceau, the only garden worthy of the name in the arrondissement, and admire the

H. Legac / MICHELIN

splendid landscaping à la française and elegant perspectives as you stroll past manicured lawns in a relaxing break from the frantic pace of the city. The surrounding buildings overlooking the park are among the most sought after of the capital because of their calm location and elegant Haussmannian architecture.

The real soul of the 17th lies just a short distance away further east. Batignolles village, a genuine exception in the arrondissement, rises like a refreshing island from the mists of a monotonous ocean of dressed stone. Cosy restaurants serving fine cuisine at reasonable prices, friendly bistros and gourmet grocery stores line the narrow streets up towards square des Batignolles and its adjoining church, endowing the village with a delightfully provincial feel. To such an extent, that it has caught the fancy of a population of stylish yuppies and bourgeois-bohemians, who could hardly be qualified as needy, attracted by the charm and authenticity of a small suburban town, without the inconvenience.

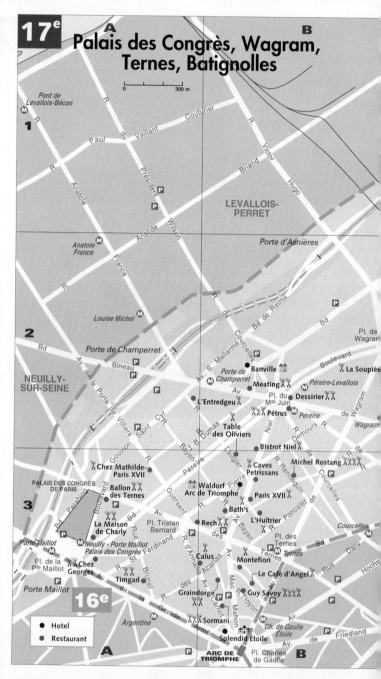

17e Palais des Congrès, Wagram, Ternes, Batignolles

Pont de Levallois-Bécon

Coutier

LEVALLOIS-PERRET

Porte d'Asnières

Anatole France

Louise Michel

Porte de Champerret

NEUILLY-SUR-SEINE

Bineau

Pl. de Wagram

Bd de Reims

Boulevard

● Banville 🏨   ✗ La Soupiè

Porte de Champerret

Meating ✗✗   Péreire-Levallois

● Dessirier ✗✗

Av.   Pl. du Mal Juin

✗ L'Entredgeu ✗   ● Pétrus

✗✗✗ Pétrus   Péreire

Table des Oliviers   de Wagran

● Bistrot Niel ✗

✗ Chez Mathilde-Paris XVII   ✗ Caves Petrissans   Michel Rostang ✗✗✗✗

🏨 Waldorf Arc de Triomphe

PALAIS DES CONGRÈS DE PARIS

Ballon ✗✗ des Ternes   Paris XVII ✗

● Bath's

La Maison de Charly ✗✗   ● Rech ✗✗   L'Huîtrier ✗

Pl. Tristan Bernard

Neuilly - Porte Maillot Palais des Congrès   Pl. des Ternes

Porte Maillot

Caïus ✗

Pl. de la Pte Maillot   ✗✗ Chez Georges   ● Montefiori

Courcelles

Porte Maillot   Timgad ✗✗   ● Le Cafe d'Angel ✗

Graindorge ✗✗   ● Guy Savoy ✗✗✗✗

16e

✗✗✗ Sormani

● Hotel   Ch. de Gaulle Étoile

● Restaurant   Splendid Étoile

Argentine

ARC DE TRIOMPHE   Pl. Charles de Gaulle

322

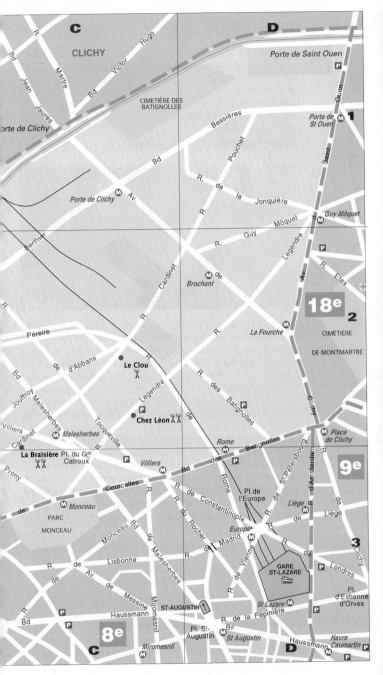

Guy Savoy ❀❀❀

B3

Innovative 𝕏𝕏𝕏𝕏

18 r. Troyon ✉ 75017
✆ 01 43 80 40 61
Fax 01 46 22 43 09
e-mail reserv@guysavoy.com
www.guysavoy.com

Ⓜ **Charles de Gaulle-Étoile**
Closed August, 24 December-2 January,
Saturday lunchtime, Sunday and Monday

Menu €245/295 – Carte €134/267

A/C
VISA
MC
AE

Guy Savoy

Starred chef Guy Savoy has mastered his art, and he owns this restaurant in a prestigious neighbourhood along with several other equally chic establishments, but it hasn't changed anything. The great chef still calls himself an "inn-keeper" – in all simplicity. His 21st century inn, redesigned by Jean-Michel Wilmotte in the year 2000, is generous and welcoming, with an extremely attentive staff. The setting is discreet and refined, uncluttered and warm all at once. The space can be moved around thanks to sliding partitions, thus transforming the highly intimate dining areas upon request. Paintings and African sculptures evoke some of Guy Savoy's other passions in life, although gastronomy remains his raison de vivre, in his own words "a celebration of joy and poetry". Refined, authentic and inventive without excess, his fine cuisine works wonders, highlighting the most emblematic ingredients from the terroir.

First Course

- Soupe d'artichaut à la truffe noire, brioche feuilletée aux champignons et truffes.
- Suprême de volaille de Bresse, foie gras et artichaut.

Main Course

- Bar en écailles grillées aux épices douces.
- Ris de veau rissolés, "petits chaussons" de pommes de terre et truffes.

Dessert

- Figues en trois préparations.
- Fondant chocolat au pralin feuilleté et crème chicorée.

Michel Rostang ✿ ✿

B3

20 r. Rennequin ✉ 75017
✆ 01 47 63 40 77
Fax 01 47 63 82 75
e-mail rostang@relaischateaux.com
www.michelrostang.com

Ⓜ Ternes
Closed 3-25 August, Monday lunch,
Saturday lunch and Sunday

Menu €78 (lunch), €185/285 – Carte €125/210

A/C

VISA

MC

AE

Michel Rostang

PALAIS DES CONGRÈS • WAGRAM • TERNES • BATIGNOLLES

Michel Rostang's path was clearly cut out for him – that of a chef in the purest classical French tradition. Like his father, his grandfather, and even farther back. Indeed, gastronomy has been a family business for five generations. After years of training (in particular at Lasserre, Lucas-Carton and Pierre Laporte), he opened his eponymous Parisian restaurant. His cooking comes from a long and noble tradition that is based above all on the terroir. Michel Rostang, who allows himself a few contemporary touches, celebrates the Dauphiné and Lyonnais regions. The magnificent ingredients follow the seasons (game in autumn, truffles in winter), and the wines are of the same high quality (especially the Côtes du Rhône). In short, nothing but the best food and wine here. The same impression emerges from the warm decor in a variety of styles – from the Art Nouveau and Lalique rooms to the Robj room affording a view of the kitchen and the collection of artwork (César, Arman, porcelain statuettes). An aesthetic as well as a gourmet experience.

First Course
- Carte "truffes".
- Quenelle de brochet soufflée à la crème de homard.

Main Course
- Grosse sole de ligne "cuisson meunière", marinière de coquillages au curry mauricien.
- Canette au sang en deux services.

Dessert
- Soufflé chaud au caramel beurre salé.
- Tarte mœlleuse au chocolat amer, sauce café.

Pétrus

B2

Traditional XXX

12 pl. Mar. Juin ✉ 75017
☎ 01 43 80 15 95 **Fax** 01 47 66 49 86

Ⓜ Pereire
Closed 5-23August

Carte €40/80

All that remains from the former fish restaurant is the name and the comfortable atmosphere, as Pétrus forges ahead with its new team. The changes have given the place a new lease of life, but in a spirit of continuity. It is still a deluxe brasserie boasting the same elegance and attention to detail. The modernised décor is more streamlined and contemporary, while the menu blends tradition and reinvented classics (melon, watermelon and Serrano ham *glacé*, scallops *à la plancha* with girolle mushrooms, *sablé* with raspberries). The restaurant's regular customers haven't forgotten the way. In summer, enjoy the pleasant terrace across from the Place du Maréchal Juin.

Sormani

B3

Italian XXX

4 r. Gén. Lanrezac
✉ 75017
☎ 01 43 80 13 91 **Fax** 01 40 55 07 37
e-mail sasormani@wanadoo.fr

Ⓜ Charles de Gaulle-Étoile
Closed 1st-25 August, Saturday,
Sunday and public holidays

Carte €50/114

All the charms of baroque Italy are evoked – with restraint – in the plush dining rooms of this comfortable restaurant with its red colours, majestic Murano glass chandeliers, elegant place settings, mirrors and mouldings. Pascal Fayet's cuisine naturally follows this *dolce vita* theme in his resolutely Italian menu, half of which is devoted (in season) to the rare truffle. The wine cellar goes by the same refrain with its superb labels from the finest winemaking areas in Italy. Regulars at this chic establishment include a large clientele of businessmen, who enjoy the privacy of the lounge on the ground floor.

Chez Léon

Traditional 🍴🍴

C2

32 r. Legendre ✉ 75017
☎ 01 42 27 06 82
Fax 01 46 22 63 67
e-mail chezleon32@wanadoo.fr

Ⓜ Villiers
Closed 26 July-24 August, 24 December-4 January,
Saturday, Sunday and public holidays

Menu (€24), €32 (lunch)/34 (dinner) – Carte €42/52

Chez Léon, they don't toy with tradition. This 1950s bistro is proud of its strong identity, with a simple setting that is appealing precisely because of its retro Parisian quality. Most of the "ambasssadors" of timeless French gastronomy are present on the menu – from chicken liver terrine and Burgundy snails for starters, to turbot in a *beurre blanc*, andouillette sausages, *jambon persillé*, veal kidneys, sole meunière, and salmon with sorrel sauce, before ending with the homemade profiteroles or lukewarm pear soup with blackcurrants. The tasty recipes are well-prepared and served with speed and a smile. Guaranteed conviviality at this excellent little establishment – a place to remember.

Dessirier

Seafood 🍴🍴

B2

9 pl. Mar. Juin ✉ 75017
☎ 01 42 27 82 14
Fax 01 47 66 82 07
e-mail dessirier@michelrostang.com
www.michelrostang.com

Ⓜ Pereire
Closed 10-17 August,
Saturday and Sunday in July-August

Menu €38 – Carte €53/87

An appetising oyster bar tips you off immediately – people come here to enjoy the fine seafood specialities. The delicious roasted line-caught sea bass for two is one of the best dishes of the house. But the kitchen produces a multitude of other enticing seafood dishes prepared with ingredients selected with great care by Michel Rostang, proprietor of five other bistros. The elegant and unfussy decor is worthy of the great Parisian brasseries with its banquettes and upholstered armchairs, wood panelling, engravings and pretty painted plates. This lively place is mainly frequented by a business clientele at lunchtime.

Graindorge ☺

Flemish cuisine ✕✕

15 r. Arc de Triomphe
✉ 75017
☎ 01 47 54 00 28
e-mail le.graindorge@wanadoo.fr

Ⓜ Charles de Gaulle-Étoile
Closed 1st-15 August,
Saturday lunch and Sunday

Menu (€ 24), € 28 (weekday lunch)/34 – Carte € 42/56

VISA
ⓂⒸ
Æ

If you've never sampled Flemish cuisine, Graindorge is the place to try it. Chef-owner Bernard Broux has succeeded in bringing a piece of northern France to the capital, near Place de l'Étoile. His plush Art Deco restaurant is the perfect place to enjoy the straightforward flavours from the chef's terroir, including *potjevleesch*, *bintje* stuffed with a *brandade de morue*, seafood *waterzoï* with Ostende shrimp, and grilled Boulogne kippers with fried onions. The generous recipes are complemented by market specialities. There are wines to go with them, naturally, and an excellent selection of local beer from across the Quiévrain (Angélus, Moinette Blonde).

La Maison de Charly

A3

Moroccan ✕✕

97 bd Gouvion-St-Cyr ✉ 75017
☎ 01 45 74 34 62 **Fax** 01 55 37 90 21
www.lamaisondecharly.com

Ⓜ Porte Maillot
Closed August and Monday

Menu € 29 (weekday lunch)/33

A/C
VISA
ⓂⒸ
Æ
Ⓞ

The two olive trees are like a landmark in front of the dark ochre façade. When you walk into La Maison de Charly, you can tell right away that this is not one of those Moroccan restaurants loaded with flashy stucco and gold decorations. There's nothing kitsch about the Moorish decor here, which has discreet and elegant contemporary touches. But the lovely ambiance has a definite North African flavour, with flowers and trees all over, fine materials, sculpted doors and even a palm tree under the large glass roof. The traditional couscous-tajines-pastillas trio is doubly delicious; and specialities such as *tanjia* (baby lamb preserved with spices) will have you hurrying back for more.

Ballon des Ternes

A3

Brasserie ✗✗

103 av. Ternes ✉ 75017   Ⓜ Porte Maillot
✆ 01 45 74 17 98 **Fax** 01 45 72 18 84
e-mail leballondesternes@fr.oleane.com

Carte €35/60

If you want to show your colleagues from across the Atlantic an authentic 1900s brasserie, then look no further. Take them to the Ballon des Ternes between conventions at the Palais des Congrès. It has it all, from the red velvet banquettes and bistro chairs to the little lamps, ceiling *fixé sous verre*, furniture from the Champagne region and mirrors on all the walls; not to mention the smiling waiters zooming around the tables and the impressive menu featuring seafood and traditional dishes. For the "French Touch", don't forget to point out the upside down table painted on the ceiling!

Chez Georges

A3

Brasserie ✗✗

273 bd Pereire ✉ 75017   Ⓜ Porte Maillot
✆ 01 45 74 31 00 **Fax** 01 45 72 18 84
e-mail chez-georges@hotmail.fr

Carte €40/67

This brasserie at the Porte Maillot has been an institution since 1926 and is still going strong! The decor exudes the kind of Parisian atmosphere people love: banquettes in imitation leather, white tablecloths, mirrors, retro lamps and bouquets of flowers. The menu features classic bistro cuisine: *foie gras des Landes*, *jambon persillé* (cooked ham in jelly), *tartare de bœuf coupé au couteau* (beef tartare) with home-made French fries, *sole meunière*, *quenelles de brochet sauce Nantua* (pike dumplings), and for dessert, a vanilla *millefeuille* or *baba au rhum*. A word of advice to food-lovers: try the famous leg of lamb, carved at the table and served with flageolet beans – a delight.

La Braisière ✿

54 r. Cardinet ✉ 75017
✆ 01 47 63 40 37
Fax 01 47 63 04 76
e-mail labraisiere@free.fr

🄼 Malesherbes
Closed August, 1st-8 January,
Saturday and Sunday

Menu € 38 (lunch) – Carte € 51/67

A/C
VISA
MC
AE
D

La Braisière

You didn't think it was possible to bring a bit of the country-side to Paris? Well that is exactly what has been done with great verve by Jacques Faussat, a proud native of the Gers. His restaurant in the Ternes area makes no bones about its authentic and unfussy market-based southwestern cuisine. The chef likes nothing better than the simple tradition inspired by his roots and his childhood. That simplicity was also a legacy of his training with Michel Guérard and particularly with Alain Dutournier. His experience working with this passionate chef, who shares the same origins, was a determining factor in his career, starting with the ten years he spent in the kitchen at the Trou Gascon. His inventive menu follows the seasons while reinterpreting the classics. The discreet contemporary decor at La Braisière exudes calmness and conviviality – thanks to the kindness of the lady of the house, in charge of welcoming diners, and the service. This is the kind of place that feels almost like home.

First Course

- Gâteau de pommes de terre au foie gras et aux girolles.
- Salade de homard bleu et œuf lucullus, crème d'oursin en homardine.

Main Course

- Gibier (October-January).
- Parmentier façon Braisière.

Dessert

- Tarte mirliton aux fruits de saison.
- Soufflé aux poires au poivre de Séchuan.

Meating

B2

Meat specialities ✗✗

122 av. de Villiers ✉ 75017　　　　　　　　　　ⓂPereire
☎ 01 43 80 10 10 **Fax** 01 43 80 31 42　　Closed Sunday and Monday
e-mail chezmichelpereire@wanadoo.fr

Menu €28/37 – Carte €48/72

VISA
ⓂⒸ
ⒶⒺ
⓪

Yes, the pun is intended – i.e. a place to meet and to eat meat. This chic and unique neighbourhood steakhouse is the latest fashion concept, and carries it off well. The talented chef selects the finest meats, carefully checks their origins, and cooks them "to within a degree" (likewise for the fish). The key to its success? The trendy décor in dark tones, catering to a hip clientele of carnivores who have become regulars. Simple as pie? But they thought of it first, and had the nerve to open a place where l'Apicius once stood. Could we have a rare rib steak over here, please?!

Rech

A3

Traditional ✗✗

62 av. des Ternes ✉ 75017　　　　　　　　　　ⓂTernes
☎ 01 45 72 29 47 **Fax** 01 45 72 41 60　　Closed August,
www.alain-ducasse.com　　　　　　　　Sunday and Monday

Menu €34/53 – Carte €46/74

Ⓐ/Ⓒ
VISA
ⓂⒸ
ⒶⒺ

A minor revolution has taken place at Rech, now part of the Ducasse group. This elegant seafood bistro, created by Alsatian August Rech in 1925, has undergone a complete overhaul and is once again showing off its elegant Art Deco-inspired setting (mirrors, wall sconces, period mosaics, wood panelling, cream and grey tones, and Hungarian oak floors). In the kitchen, chef Baptiste Peupion has stuck to the house rule of "putting the produce first". The classics are still there too (*l'aile de raie* and extra-large coffee or chocolate eclairs), and the presentation has flair – like the sardine fillets marinated with preserved lemons and tomatoes, served "straight from the tin".

Timgad

A3

21 r. Brunel ✉ 75017   Ⓜ Argentine
☎ 01 45 74 23 70 **Fax** 01 40 68 76 46
e-mail contact@timgad.fr **www**.timgad.fr

Menu €45/60 bi – Carte €38/71

[A/C]
☞☝
VISA
Ⓜ©
ÆE
Ⓞ

Welcome to the days when Timgad reigned supreme! This little corner of North Africa, with a name that refers to an ancient city, is well worth it just for the decor: gilded chandeliers, Moorish furniture and – to top it off – the superb, finely worked stucco sculpted by Moroccan crafts-men, which took over a year to finish! The menu is equally impressive with its rich selection of couscous (the semolina is extremely delicate), *tajines* and *pastillas* enjoyed for their generosity and thousand and one flavours. After that, what could be finer than prolonging your meal in the lovely hushed salon with a murmuring fountain? A guaranteed change of scenery!

Bistrot Niel

B2

75 av. Niel ✉ 75017   Ⓜ Pereire
☎ 01 42 27 88 44   Closed Saturday lunch and Sunday
Fax 01 42 27 32 12
e-mail gensdarmesb@aol.com

Menu €32 (lunch) – Carte €37/49

☂
☞☝
VISA
Ⓜ©
ÆE

A chic but relaxed bistro, rather like Bruno Gensdarmes himself, now alone at the helm of this fine ship after fifteen years with Guy Savoy. This experienced chef cooks up typical bistro dishes in his own special way, with flavours from here, ingredients from there – Argentine rib steak in mustard butter, warm leeks and "Arrosagarai" salt-cured ham –, well-dosed condiments and spices; then his creativ-ity takes care of the rest. The short and original menu has no chance of falling into a routine since it changes every two months. In summer, the deliciously shady terrace is a real favourite.

Bath's ✿

B3

Contemporary ✕

25 r. Bayen ✉ **75017**
✆ 01 45 74 74 74
Fax 01 45 74 71 15
e-mail contact@baths.fr
www.baths.fr

Ⓜ Ternes
Closed 2 August-1st September,
22-28 December, Saturday lunch,
Monday lunch, Sunday and public holidays

Menu €25 (lunch)/42 – Carte €50/64

A/C
VISA
MC
AE

Bath's

The new Bath method? A streamlined bistro look in tune with
the times, a simplicity that's deceptively difficult, and sun-
drenched cuisine. Goodbye to that golden triangle ambiance
with its ultra-refined establishments, and hello to the latest
restaurant run by Jean-Yves Bath and his son Stéphane, which
has jettisoned some sophistication but gained in modernity
in moving from the 8th to the 17th arrondissement. The
slightly eclectic setting has a very personal touch (sculptures
by the owner and paintings by ex-rugby player Jean-Pierre
Rives) with a blue neon sign outside, soft lighting, black
lacquer tables, orange walls, a bar overlooking the dining
room, and Bellota hams hung from the ceiling. The decor is
somewhat reminiscent of Asia, but the food boasts broad
allusions in the dishes of the Basque country and even further
south (Spain, Italy). The secret of the consistent quality here
lies in the marriage of two or three discreetly and simply
presented ingredients of irreproachable freshness and quality.

First Course
- Cassolette d'œufs brouillés.
- Sushi de saumon au chèvre frais.

Main Course
- Encornets juste sautés, riz paëlla, sauce chorizo.
- Filet de bœuf de Salers aux épices douces.

Dessert
- Riz au lait, compotée d'ananas.
- Soufflé au citron.

Le Café d'Angel

B3

16 r. Brey ✉ 75017
✆ 01 47 54 03 33
Fax 01 47 54 03 33

Ⓜ Charles de Gaulle-Étoile
Closed 28 July-18 August, 24 December-6 January,
Saturday, Sunday and public holidays

Menu € 25/45 – Carte € 38/45

A/C

VISA

Ⓜ©

This is a really pretty café with plenty of appeal – imitation leather banquettes, faience on the walls and little square tables with paper placemats. Not to mention the highly friendly and communicative ambiance, which you can already see through the glass façade before even stepping in. This is a place for people who feel nostalgic for the Parisian bistros of yesteryear. The food is exactly what you would expect in a restaurant like this, with good, 100% homemade traditional recipes. They change every day, so just have a look at the blackboard while strolling by. There's a good chance that, without even realizing it, the Café d'Angel will become your favourite local establishment! This place was surely born under a lucky star.

Caïus

B3

6 r. d'Armaillé ✉ 75017
✆ 01 42 27 19 20
Fax 01 40 55 00 93

Ⓜ Charles de Gaulle-Étoile
Closed August, Saturday and Sunday

Menu (€ 23), € 39

A/C

VISA

Ⓜ©

AE

Hidden behind the unassuming façade and traditional neighbourhood bistro look is a rather chic establishment. And what inventive food! Jean-Marc Notelet's cuisine is full of originality. His secret? Spices and rare ingredients. He has a knack for transforming ordinary recipes into trendy dishes with a pinch of vanilla and a dash of argan oil. Bursting with new ideas, he changes the listings on the huge blackboard every day. As a result, one never tires of the food, nor of the atmosphere in the little modern dining room with clean lines, light wood panelling and photographs of precious condiments. This is a place where all the senses are celebrated.

Caves Petrissans

B3

Traditional ✗

30 bis av. Niel ✉ 75017   Ⓜ Pereire
☎ 01 42 27 52 03   Closed 1st-11 May, 25 July-25 August, Saturday,
Fax 01 40 54 87 56   Sunday and public holidays – Pre-book
e-mail cavespetrissans@noos.fr

Menu (€29), €35 – Carte €38/55

The regulars at this hundred-year-old cellar are legion. And delightful Marie-Christine Allemoz – the fourth generation! – greets newcomers with the same warm welcome, seating you in a flash at one of the tables where Céline, Abel Gance or Roland Dorgelès may have eaten in their day. Follow the proprietors' excellent advice on which wine to choose. They will find the best bottle for you from their amazing adjoining shop, taking the homemade terrine, *tête de veau sauce ravigote* or one of the numerous bistro classics – all delicious! – to a whole new level. There is a more private room in the back and a terrace covered with Virgina creeper.

Chez Mathilde-Paris XVII

B3

Bistro ✗

41 r. Guersant ✉ 75017   Ⓜ Porte Maillot
☎ 01 45 74 75 27   Closed 26 July-26 August, 24 December-
www.chezmathilde.fr   1st January, Saturday and Sunday

Carte €22/31

Tradition has a bright future at this pleasant restaurant, both in the sunny décor featuring paintings and a rustic sideboard, and in the cuisine that will never go out of fashion. So who's complaining? Have a look at the blackboard for the day's market specialities, including delicious traditional and *canaille* bistro food. How about a marinated octopus salad, a *feuilleté* of lamb sweetbreads, *blanquette de veau*, or a *sauté* of Guinea fowl with prunes and linguini, and a *mœlleux au chocolat* for dessert? Granted, it's not revolutionary, but the well-prepared dishes are worth it, and you will really enjoy them in this cheerfully snug space with its charming atmosphere.

PALAIS DES CONGRÈS • WAGRAM • TERNES • BATIGNOLLES

Le Clou

C2

132 r. Cardinet ⊠ 75017
⃞ 01 42 27 36 78
Fax 01 42 27 89 96
e-mail le.clou@wanadoo.fr **www**.restaurant-leclou.fr

Ⓜ Malesherbes
Closed 11-24 August and Sunday

Menu € 22/33 – Carte € 38/50

VISA
MC
AE
O

The pretty painted wood façade, old posters, blackboard, wood panelling, snug and simply laid tables tell you that you are in a typical neighbourhood bistro. And yet, there is valet parking at lunch and dinner, and great vintages (Petrus, Château Margaux) to accompany your meal. Who said conviviality and refinement couldn't go together? Certainly not Christian Leclou, the chef-proprietor of this restaurant, as evidenced by his dishes. Going by traditional names, they clearly demonstrate his skill as he follows the seasons and highlights fine ingredients from the *terroir*, in particular from Poitou, the chef's native region.

L'Entredgeu 😊

A2

83 r. Laugier ⊠ 75017
⃞ 01 40 54 97 24
Fax 01 40 54 96 62

Ⓜ Porte de Champerret
Closed 25 April-5 May, 5-25 August,
20-27 December, Sunday and Monday

Menu € 22 (weekday lunch)/30

VISA
MC

The ambiance in this place is amazing! You'd think the entire 17th arrondissement had made it their "local" – and with reason. Philippe Tredgeu (the chef-proprietor) and his wife Pénélope know how to please gourmet diners. With fine market ingredients, perfectly mastered traditional recipes and restrained prices, their formula is a hit and has already developed a large clientele of regulars. Furthermore, the warm welcome extended by the proprietress makes it even more enjoyable! Due to this great success, it is often booked and the service is sometimes a bit rushed. But the friendly atmosphere makes you forgive and forget. After all, what would this place with a touch of the southwest be without all the banter and clinking glasses?

L'Huîtrier

Seafood ✗

B3

16 r. Saussier-Leroy ✉ 75017
℘ 01 40 54 83 44
Fax 01 40 54 83 86

Ⓜ Ternes
Closed August, Sunday from May to
September and Monday

Carte €31/65

A/C
VISA
Ⓜⓒ
AE

It's no mystery that people come here for the oysters, which is clear from the name and the attractive oyster bar at the entrance. But there are other fish and seafood on the generous blackboard besides these famous shellfish. Watch it carefully, to catch the appetizing seasonal and tide-based novelties. The dishes are simply prepared to highlight the extremely fresh ingredients delivered constantly throughout the year. Enjoy them in the warm and discreetly contemporary setting.

Montefiori

Italian ✗

B3

19 r. de l'Étoile
✉ 75017
℘ 01 55 37 90 00
e-mail montesiori@wanadoo.fr

Ⓜ Charles de Gaulle-Étoile
Closed 4-23 August, 24 December-2 January,
Saturday lunch, Monday dinner and Sunday

Menu (€17), €22 – Carte €31/65

A/C
VISA
Ⓜⓒ
AE

If you like Italian cuisine, preferably in a trendy restaurant, this establishment with a beautiful façade is the place for you (a former bakery, it is now a historic monument). The Montefiori has a clientele of regulars from the neighbourhood and a rather "fashion-conscious" red-and-green decor (Italy's colours) with clean lines and a few objects with a Baroque touch (chandeliers, statues) which give it a well-designed personal style. Tradition is also the main theme in the kitchen, where they don't fool around with the great Italian classics such as veal Milanese, tiramisu – although the chef sometimes adds his own twist here – linguine with clams, peach and champagne sorbet.

PALAIS DES CONGRÈS • WAGRAM • TERNES • BATIGNOLLES

La Soupière 😊

B2

154 av. de Wagram ✉ 75017
📞 01 42 27 00 73
Fax 01 46 22 27 09
e-mail cthuillart@yahoo.fr
www.lasoupiere.fr

Ⓜ Wagram
Closed 1st-24 August,
Saturday lunch and Sunday

Menu €35/58

[A/C]
[VISA]
[MC]
[AE]

You feel like lifting the lid of the *Soupière* (soup tureen) just to taste Christian Thuillart's one-of-a-kind Wild or Spring Mushroom Menus. In season, this passionate chef concocts meals celebrating the delicate flavours of these precious mycelia. The menu also features traditional dishes with tasty, carefully selected and skilfully prepared ingredients. The setting includes a fine trompe-l'œil garden and colonnade, giving the hushed little dining room (with 30 place settings) a mock-Tuscan look. Warm reception.

Table des Oliviers

B3

38 r. Laugier ✉ 75017
📞 01 47 63 85 51
Fax 01 47 63 85 81
e-mail latabledesoliviers@wanadoo.fr
www.latabledesoliviers.fr

Ⓜ Pereire
Closed in August, Monday lunch,
Saturday lunch and Sunday

Menu (€22), €30 – Carte €49/55

[A/C]
[📺]
[VISA]
[MC]
[AE]

Mr. and Mrs. Olivier decide to a restaurant. What should they call it? La Table des Oliviers, naturally. And what is on the menu? Specialities from Provence, of course! Apart from that, everything depends on when you dine here. The Niçois like to sample their *socca* (crepes) on Thursday, while the Marseillais prefer to have their *bouillabaisse* on Friday or Saturday. Every day has its particular dish, but Sunday – as the chef explains on the blackboard – is a day for relaxation! During the rest of the week, you can enjoy the homemade olive oil bread, the dishes seasoned with thyme and basil, and the very pleasant southern French decor. You can almost hear the cicadas chirping.

Montmartre · Pigalle

Montmartre is famous for its artists, its tourists, its basilica unique in the world and its steep streets. The portrait is clearly that of Paris, but how can we describe Pigalle with its frilly cabarets, Can-can girls and neon lights that never sleep? At times it seems as if the 18th embodies all on its own the entire fantastical dimension of Paris. This is however unsurprising when one thinks of the sheer size of this arrondissement, bordered by boulevard de Rochechouart, avenue de Saint-Ouen and the ring road. The range of ambiences and panoramas is as broad as it is unexpected, from festive, almost brazen in Pigalle, picturesque and more bohemian around Montmartre to distinctly cosmopolitan at the Goutte d'Or.

PARIS BY NIGHT

Considered broadly, **Pigalle** is made up of several distinct sectors: first of all, place Pigalle itself, at the meeting point of avenue de Clichy and boulevard de Rochechouart, then rue Pigalle that goes down towards the 9th and finally the informal jumble of lanes at the foot of the hill of Montmartre. It would be pointless to try and pretend that Pigalle is not known first and foremost for its nightlife; it is home to some of the capital's most famous **cabarets,** such as the **Moulin Rouge,** a multitude of bars and discos and a growing number of pubs with dance floors in answer to the fun-loving demands of a new

generation of party-goers. What the visitor should however also know is that the area is literally crammed with tiny restaurants, gourmet cafés and friendly eateries serving every imaginable type of cuisine from Indian and Chinese to Basque, Auvergne, African and even Balkan. Apart from Montmartre (see below), another area branching off from Pigalle is worth exploring. Head directly north towards the town of Saint-Ouen along the street of the same name and the famous **flea market of Clignancourt,** located on several hectares of land and paradise for lovers of bric-a-brac and antiques.

PICTURE POSTCARD MONTMARTRE

Clichés are often long-lived but that of **Montmartre** remains fully justified: picturesque narrow cobbled streets and long flights of steps with wrought-iron railings paint this picture postcard portrait of Paris, crowned by the basilica of the **Sacré-Cœur** and its stunning view of the city. Formerly the haunt of artists of all kinds, tourism is gradually overtaking the hillock, with its good and bad side effects. Bar a few notable exceptions, it is dotted with restaurants that the Parisians somewhat sneeringly refer to as "tourist traps", meaning that they are expensive and uninteresting. However the district still has a

K. Blackwell / MICHELIN

few genuine locals and aficionados who meet up for a drink in one of the many authentic bistros that continue to survive. Nor should one forget that the **artistic tradition** of Montmartre has far from said its last word as is proven by the aptly named Montmartre-aux-artistes on rue Ordener that provides workshops and housing for painters, sculptors and creators of all kinds.

Finally, it would be unthinkable to leave without mentioning the **Goutte d'Or** area around Barbès. The district vibrates in permanence to the rhythm of its international communities speaking languages from around the world, offering a unique picture in Paris. Lovers of exotic food, from fruit to spices, are sure to find what they're looking for in the district's countless specialised shops or, even better, on market days (Wednesday and Saturday).

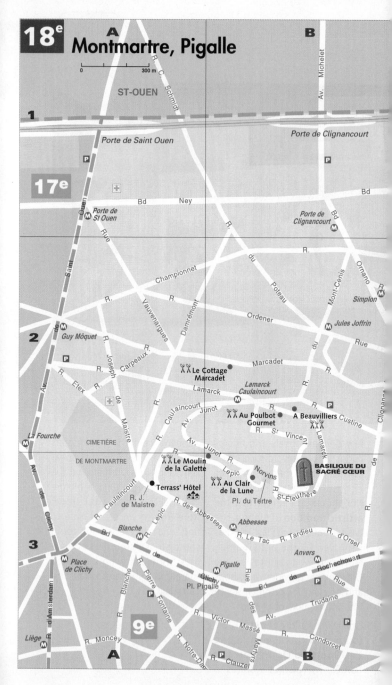

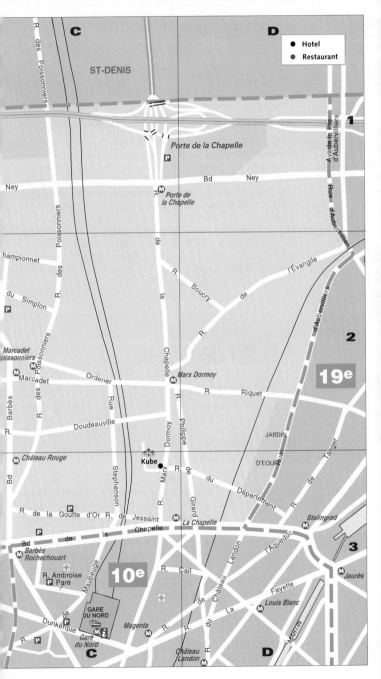

A Beauvilliers

Contemporary ✗✗✗

52 r. Lamarck ✉ 75018
✆ 01 42 55 05 42
www.abeauvilliers.com

Ⓜ Lamarck Caulaincourt
Closed 10-20 August,
Sunday dinner and Monday

Menu (€ 25), € 35 (lunch), € 45/68 – Carte € 71/83

Yohan Paran has been the chef for several years now at this Montmartre institution and has remained faithful to its past while adding a personal touch. He kept the name honouring Antoine de Beauvilliers, a famous chef who worked for the Comte de Provence, and modernised the three comfortable and intimate dining rooms (velvet banquettes, cream tones, mouldings and mirrors). But in the kitchen, the talented Yohan creates his own up-to-date dishes such as foie gras in hibiscus aspic, and rack of lamb with crispy citrus fruit. In summer, ask for a table on the flower-decked terrace that is pleasant and shady.

Au Clair de la Lune

Traditional ✗✗

9 r. Poulbot ✉ 75018
✆ 01 42 58 97 03
Fax 01 42 55 64 74
www.auclairdelalune.fr

Ⓜ Abbesses
Closed 18 August-15 September,
Monday lunch and Sunday

Menu € 32 – Carte € 37/69

The affable Jerfauts brothers, twins who have run this establishment for over fifteen years, will welcome you into their inn located just behind the Place du Tertre. One is in the dining room and the other in the kitchen, forming the perfect duo for pampering diners and serving up classic dishes celebrating traditional French cuisine. The pleasant atmosphere is quite charming with its murals of the Butte in earlier times, Louis-Philippe furniture and convivial ambiance. Welcome to the heart of Jean-Pierre Jeunet's Montmartre.

Au Poulbot Gourmet

Traditional XX

39 r. Lamarck ✉ 75018
✆ 01 46 06 86 00
e-mail renaud1973@hotmail.com

Ⓜ Lamarck Caulaincourt
Closed 3-24 August, Sunday and Monday

Menu (€19), €38 – Carte €41/55

VISA
MC

This authentic Montmartre bistro was named for Poulbot, the poster designer famous for his unforgettable street urchins scuffling around the neighbourhood in their clodhoppers. Inside, the padded black banquettes, white tablecloths and the collection of old posters evoke a friendly "village" ambiance. Regulars can't get enough of the place and its signature dish, *cassoulet*. The rest of the menu is in the same spirit – simple and with ingredients from the terroir cooked with savoir-faire, such as the *croustillant au magret de canard et foie gras*, and baked cod. Desserts include little gems like the *tarte bourdaloue sauce caramel* (hot poached fruit tart).

Le Cottage Marcadet

Contemporary XX

151 bis r. Marcadet
✉ 75018
✆ 01 42 57 71 22 **Fax** 01 42 57 71 24
e-mail contact@cottagemarcadet.com
www.cottagemarcadet.com

Ⓜ Lamarck Caulaincourt
Closed Spring school holidays,
August, Sunday and Monday

Menu (€28), €35 – Carte €64/96

A/C
VISA
MC
①

The decor at this elegant restaurant at the foot of the Butte is comprised of yellow and salmon tones, Louis XVI-style furniture, paintings by local artists and smart table settings. The soft lighting creates a hushed ambiance which offsets the up-to-date seasonal cuisine on the attractively priced set menus. The à la carte menu features various dishes including sardine fillets with onion compote, caramelized sea bream with sweet spices, and a caramel bavarois with salted butter. Drawn by the setting, the chef's touch and the professional service, the local business clientele has made it one of their preferred restaurants. Remember to book, as there are less than thirty place settings.

Le Moulin de la Galette

B3

Contemporary ✕✕

83 r. Lepic ✉ 75018   Ⓜ Abbesses
℘ 01 46 06 84 77 **Fax** 01 46 06 84 78
e-mail moulindelagalette@yahoo.fr **www**.lemoulindelagalette.fr

Menu (€ 17), € 25 (lunch)/42 (dinner) – Carte € 50/78

In the mood for a slice of old Paris? Try the Moulin de la Galette. This establishment on rue Lepic (since 1622) has recently been taken over by Antoine Heerah and Jérôme Bodereau, the expert Franco-Mauritian duo from the former Chamarré. They have been a godsend for this restaurant immortalized by Renoir and Toulouse-Lautrec, which had become a bit of a tourist trap. Less folklore and more authenticity – that's what our two fellows are aiming for with their simple more-bistro-then-fusion dishes and the new facelift (red ochre walls, streamlined dining room, and verdant terrace). For the time being, the Moulin is still getting into its stride. Stay tuned.

RESTORATIVE AND REINVIGORATING!

Restaurants weren't always as we know them today. In fact, before taking on the current meaning (in the 2nd half of the 18C), the term simply referred to a kind of reinvigorating and fortifying broth used to strengthen the weakest and poorest people. Those from the upper echelons of society were not in the habit of frequenting common inns, guest houses or taverns. A turning point came in 1765 when Mathurin Roze de Chantoiseau opened a particularly smart place where a wide choice of broths and a variety of other dishes were served at all hours. The first restaurant was born, and it was an immediate success with intellectuals, aristocrats and artists.

La Villette-Cité des Sciences Buttes Chaumont

Typical of sprawling northeastern Paris, the 19th arrondissement covers a vast area between place de Stalingrad, rue de Belleville and the ring road. The result of the annexation of the former towns of Belleville, Villette and parts of Pantin and Aubervilliers, traces of its multiple and composite past can still be seen. It is impossible to reduce the 19th to a single definition due to the many changes and evolutions brought about by the massive urban development programmes implemented by the city of Paris and the French government. As a result, the distinctive futurist quality of the Villette district has little in common with the steep narrow lanes of the Buttes Chaumont, all of which ensure that a stroll through the 19th will afford surprises that are both aesthetic and culinary.

OLD AND NEW

A 19C fruit and vegetable vendor would indeed be hard put to recognise his old district around the **Villette** today because the entire sector has been developed to make way for the **Cité des Sciences et de l'Industrie,** the **Cité de la Musique** and immense expanses of lawn. The old abattoirs, no longer in use, were pulled down, as were the fruit and vegetable stalls, and replaced with immense esplanades, manicured lawns and footbridges spanning the canals of the **Ourcq** and **Saint-Denis,** creating what is now an urban zone that is both modern and luminous and highly popular with walkers. The sector is home to several cinemas, including the famous **Géode** and its amazing 360° screen, and to the **Zénith** concert hall, a genuine institution in Paris. The outlying areas, particularly towards Pantin, have retained their former charm, but it is not here that you will taste fine cuisine. The area is home to a tightly meshed network of little restaurants of every imaginable culture. Further west, you will encounter rue de Flandre that cuts across the entire north segment of the arrondissement as far as Stalingrad. Relatively opulent (and bourgeois-bohemian) towards the canal, it occasionally evokes a Haussmannian boulevard, but is more populous and working-class on the other bank, where it features some of the most daring, if not always the most attractive, examples of residential housing in Paris.

THE DISCREET CHARM OF THE BUTTES CHAUMONT

Buttes Chaumont Park, another of Napoleon III's ambitious projects, is one of the capital's largest parks and the centre of tiny districts of sometimes unexpected charm. The park itself is worth a trip for its landscaped splendid mineral formations, several artificial grottoes and a temple of Greek inspiration that dominates the site. Around the park you

R. Visage / SUNSET

will discover another surprisingly green facet of the 19th. Towards the ring road lies the **Mouzaïa district,** an unspoilt steep island of greenery; built on former gypsum quarries, none of its comfortable little houses with gardens are over two storeys high giving the overall impression of a sleepy residential suburb of a small provincial town.

Southwest of the park, towards rue Simon Bolivar, a few minutes' walk suffices to climb up the Bergeyre mound to a district, also seemingly forgotten by time, of small 1920's working-class houses

lining staircase streets interspersed with flower-decked gardens. The view over **Belleville** is outstanding, giving the impression of flying over the city, while to the west you will have no difficulty in picking out the details of the Sacré-Coeur. The district, devoid of fancy restaurants and gourmet halts, is rather home to lively neighbourhood bars steeped in history, where the locals will happily wax lyrical on the merits of their beloved district.

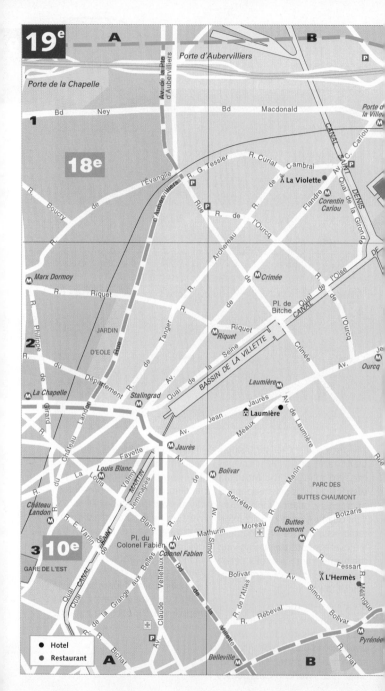

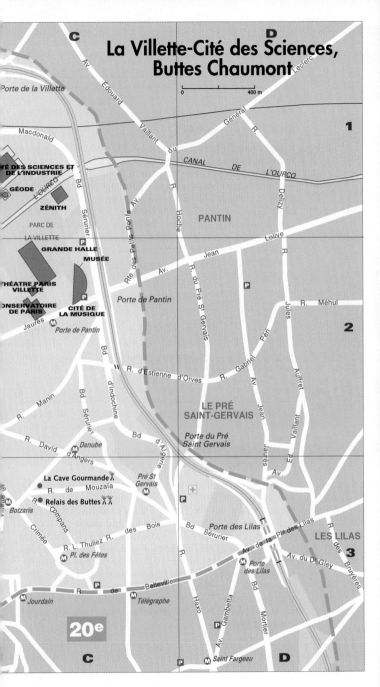

La Villette-Cité des Sciences, Buttes Chaumont

C **D**

Porte de la Villette

Macdonald

Av. Édouard Vaillant

Leclerc

Général

R.

1

CANAL DE L'OURCQ

CITÉ DES SCIENCES ET DE L'INDUSTRIE

GÉODE

L'OURCQ

Bd Sérurier

Rte des Petits Ponts

Av.

R. Hoche

Delizy

PANTIN

ZÉNITH

PARC DE LA VILLETTE

GRANDE HALLE

MUSÉE

Lolive

Jean

Av.

R. du Pré St Gervais

R. Méhul

THÉÂTRE PARIS VILLETTE

CONSERVATOIRE DE PARIS

CITÉ DE LA MUSIQUE

Porte de Pantin

R. Jules

2

Ⓜ Jaurès

Porte de Pantin

R. Gabriel Péri

Av. Jean

Autfret

Bd d'Indochine

R. d'Estienne d'Orves

LE PRÉ SAINT-GERVAIS

Av. Ed. Vaillant

R. Manin

Bd Sérurier

Porte du Pré Saint Gervais

R. David

Bd d'Algérie

Jaurès

Av.

Ⓜ Danube

d'Angers

La Cave Gourmande ✕

R. de Mouzaïa

Pré St Gervais Ⓜ

Relais des Buttes ✕✕

Porte des Lilas

LES LILAS

R. des Bruyères

3

Ⓜ Botzaris

Compans

R. L. Thuliez R. des Bois

Bd Sérurier

Porte des Lilas

Av. du Dr Gley

Crimée

Ⓜ Pl. des Fêtes

R.

Av. de la Pte des Lilas

Ⓜ Porte des Lilas

Haxo

Av. Gambetta

Bd Mortier

Ⓜ Jourdain

R. de Belleville

Ⓜ Télégraphe

20e

Ⓜ Saint Fargeau

C **D**

0 400 m

Relais des Buttes

C3

86 r. Compans ☒ 75019   **Ⓜ** Botzaris
✆ 01 42 08 24 70   Closed August, 24 December-3 January,
Fax 01 42 03 20 44   Saturday lunch and Sunday

Menu € 34 – Carte € 43/57

Escape from the hustle and bustle of Paris and recharge your batteries in this peaceful restaurant which has the look of a country house. In winter you can sit by the fire in the dining room decorated with colourful paintings. In fine weather, trade in the warm fireplace for the warm sun on the delicious flowery patio. Throughout the year you will enjoy the classic cuisine prepared by chef Marc Gautron, including fine seafood specialities (oyster and scallop timbale with Bourbon, fillet of red mullet). You couldn't dream of a better place to enjoy a meal in a little country inn – on the hills of the Buttes-Chaumont.

La Cave Gourmande

C3

10 r. Gén. Brunet ☒ 75019   **Ⓜ** Botzaris
✆ 01 40 40 03 30   Closed 1st-24 August, February school holidays,
Fax 01 40 40 03 30   Saturday lunch and Sunday
e-mail lacavegourmande@wanadoo.fr

Menu € 31/36

This pleasant establishment has everything going for it. The key to its success? Undoubtedly, the little touch of inventiveness which the chef sprinkles in all his dishes, carefully prepared with fresh seasonal and market-based ingredients. Or could it be the warm ambiance? The first room - with a view of the kitchen - has a bistro look (wooden tables, bottle racks, mirrors), while the second is simpler. One thing is for sure; the gracious hospitality of the proprietors has won them a clientele of regulars, who like to treat themselves to a well-deserved meal here - after walking up and down the paths of the largest and steepest public garden in Paris!

L'Hermès

Bistro ✗

B3

23 r. Mélingue ✉ 75019
☎ 01 42 39 94 70
e-mail lhermes@wanadoo.fr

Ⓜ **Pyrénées**
Closed Easter holidays, August,
February school holidays,
Wednesday lunch, Sunday and Monday

Menu €16/30 – Carte €33/82

VISA
ⓂⒸ

You have to go all the way to the end of the rue Mélingue to find this establishment, which is somewhat hidden but worth hunting for. It is easier to find at night with its string of fairy lights (on the painted wood façade) indicating the road to l'Hermès – better than a compass – and giving it the look of a *guinguette* (open-air café). Inside, the rustic dining room has a deliciously country charm with its old sideboard, ochre tones, wood furniture, lace curtains, colourful paintings and plaid tablecloths. This is the kind of place that just makes you feel good. The menu features bistro dishes presented on the blackboard, ingredients from the *terroir*, and a cellar with some pleasant surprises.

La Violette

Contemporary ✗

B1

11 av. Corentin Cariou
✉ 75019
☎ 01 40 35 20 45
e-mail restolaviolette@free.fr
www.restaurant-laviolette.com

Ⓜ **Corentin Cariou**
Closed 9-24 August, 20 December-4 January,
Saturday and Sunday
Number of covers limited, pre-book

Carte €35/47

VISA
ⓂⒸ
AE

There is only one exception in the radically black-and-white decor at this restaurant : a purple banquette! It runs the length of this room exclusively in wood and marble (on the bar, tables, and walls), where the atmosphere evokes the 1930s. Photographs of the city and a wine-growing theme – wine crates, racks and brass plaques engraved with names of vintages – give the place a style that is both hip and cosy. It is smart, like the cuisine featuring tasty and up-to-date little dishes enjoyed by the clientele of businessmen, with whom it is very popular at lunchtime. Remember to book (there are less than thirty place settings), and request the smaller room for more privacy.

Père Lachaise · Belleville

Composed of the former town of Belleville and the Père-Lachaise district, the 20th sports relatively ample dimensions within its immense tangle of lanes and passageways. It is no doubt due to the rural and working-class past of Belleville that this part of the capital has continued to exhibit such a propensity for diversity since its annexation. Formerly a zone of vineyards and slopes, it first became a working-class district of immigrants, before it evolved into a hunting ground for Parisians in search of more reasonably priced housing. Nowadays the district is a genuine melting pot of constantly changing influences and populations from all over the world, bohemian artists in search of authenticity or inspiration and occasional walkers who pass each other without always mixing, making the 20th a district of contrasts.

DIVERSITY

An enthusiastic enterprising spirit seems to characterise the Belleville district. You only have to take a walk round the market (every Tuesday and Friday) to discover the tastes and smells of five continents with produce from all over France in addition to West Indian, African and Asian spices and craftwork from nearly everywhere. The housing and shops of the district reflect this variety of cultures, as do the dozens of tiny restaurants that proudly represent every culinary tradition in the world.

The scenery changes radically as you head further south, around the Buzenval, Alexandre Dumas and porte de Montreuil metro stations. Here the bourgeois-bohemians are progressively settling areas formerly abandoned. As a result **Buzenval** has become the favourite haunt of artists in search of space and also of more or less legal squats wedged in between waste ground and buildings to be demolished. Those in search of authenticity will however adore the area and will no doubt want to stop in one of the many nearby popular cafés for a well-earned pastis.

BETWEEN TWO WORLDS

A visit to **Père-Lachaise cemetery** also offers the chance to take a walk through the history of France (and the world) and the list of its famous residents is seemingly endless from Oscar Wilde to Jim Morrison and from Auguste Comte to Marcel Proust. The necropolis, set on 45 hectares of land and home to some 70 000 graves, is a real town within a town with avenues lined in

S. Sauvignier / MICHELIN

neo-Byzantine mausoleums and imposing burial vaults.

The surrounding quiet residential streets make a welcome break from the effervescence of the nearby **Ménilmontant** district. Here, exotic restaurants, trendy cafés and old-fashioned bistros joyfully cohabit in a tangled web of steep streets and shaded squares. Then, heading down towards **place de la Nation,** the district becomes surreptitiously bourgeois: Asian influences are gradually supplanting the former North African and African communities, and many of the restaurants and delicatessens are well worth a pause.

In the opposite direction, towards **place de Bagnolet** and its high-rise council flats, don't miss the chance for a quick walk in the village referred to as "the countryside in Paris", a delightful 1910 estate perched on a hill and dotted with terraced gardens; almost Montmartre in the heart of the 20th!

Père Lachaise, Belleville

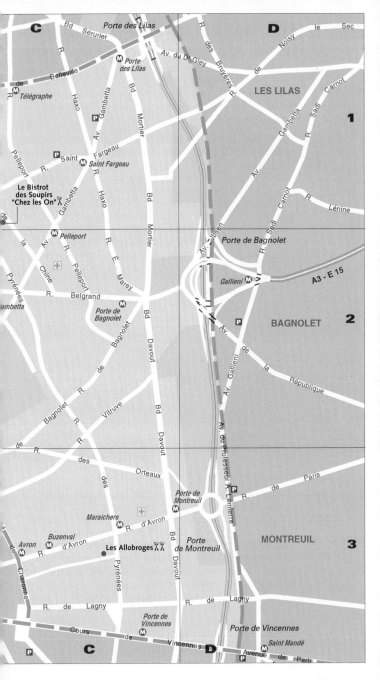

357

Les Allobroges 🏵

C3

71 r. Grands-Champs ✉ 75020
✆ 01 43 73 40 00
Fax 01 40 09 23 22

Ⓜ Maraîchers
Closed 3-27 August,
Sunday dinner and Monday

Menu € 20/34

VISA
Ⓜ©

The owners and chef have changed, but not the convivial spirit at Les Allobroges, still enchanting them in the 20th arrondissement and well beyond! The veteran restaurateurs, established in eastern Paris for thirty years, have upheld the success of this popular place. Their secret? Market-based food that is simple and satisfying. The menu speaks for itself: *tatin d'endive au parmesan*, stuffed cabbage with *gésiers* and foie gras, roasted lamb shanks with preserved garlic, *financier crème praliné*, and French toast with *fromage blanc* ice cream. The warm and stylish décor and charming welcome create a delightful ambiance. So, are you ready to try out a new area now?

Le Bistrot des Soupirs "Chez les On"

C1

49 r. Chine ✉ 75020
✆ 01 44 62 93 31
Fax 01 44 62 77 83

Ⓜ Gambetta
Closed 1st-10 May, 5-25 August,
25 December-1st January, Sunday and Monday

Menu € 16 (lunch), € 35/50 – Carte € 28/43

VISA
Ⓜ©

This fine establishment in the 20th arrondissement falls in the bistro category. Although small in size, it is larger-than-life in terms of its atmosphere, which is distinct and always fun. The decor has an authentic and unpretentious charm with its fine oak counter, wood everywhere and carefully preserved 1930s ambiance. Regulars never tire of its "country" appeal and blackboards with their delicious specials such as homemade terrines, generous *canaille* and bistro dishes (snails, homemade foie gras, *andouillettes*), and seasonal game. The generous and well-prepared food is paired with an interesting selection of proprietors' wines. Unbeatable value for money.

Where **to stay**

Hotels from A to Z

▶ *HOW TO USE THIS GUIDE...*

Hotels are classified according to comfort, from 5 to 1 house(s), then in alphabetical order within each category.

🏠🏠 *Red houses indicate our favourites.*

Where to stay

Le Bristol

112 r. Fg St-Honoré ✉ 75008   Ⓜ Miromesnil
✆ 01 53 43 43 00 **Fax** 01 53 43 43 01
e-mail resa@lebristolparis.com **www**.lebristolparis.com

124 rm – ✝€610/630 ✝✝€710/1160, ⌁ €53 – **38 suites**
🍴 *Le Bristol* (see restaurant index)

Le Bristol

For its guests, this superb hotel, built in 1925 around a magnificent garden, remains the symbol of a certain kind of luxury, with the accent on comfort and well-being. With its Louis XVI furniture and masterpieces, the décor in the rooms and suites, some of which have terrace gardens, plays on soft nuances highlighted by rare wood panelling and precious fabrics. The marble bathrooms are comfortably sized. The reception and concierge area have been remodelled; and the fitness centre and beauty salon were also reorganised. Food-lovers will enjoy the winter and summer restaurants, while the amazing barge-like pool on the top floor, surrounded by teak and glass, gives onto a solarium with a view over the whole of Paris. Although time seems to have stopped in this haven of calm and luxury, 2007 was a real turning point. In acquiring a new building on the corner of the rue du faubourg Saint-Honoré and Avenue Matignon, the hotel added thirty more rooms and a new restaurant grill.

Crillon

10 pl. Concorde ✉ 75008
✆ 01 44 71 15 00 **Fax** 01 44 71 15 02
e-mail crillon@crillon.com **www**.crillon.com

119 rm – ♦€695/750 ♦♦€765/830, ⊿ €47 – **28 suites**
⍩⎔ **Les Ambassadeurs** (see restaurant index)

● Concorde

Crillon

"Here, all is order and beauty, luxury, calm, and delight."
Baudelaire's L'Invitation au voyage is a fitting description
of this luxury hotel à la française, ideally located a stone's
throw from the rue du faubourg Saint-Honoré, the Champs-
Élysées and the Louvre. Overlooking the Place de la Concorde, with which is shares a rich history, this majestic
building is an 18th century masterpiece designed by Jac-
ques-Ange Gabriel (architect of the Petit Trianon at Versailles).

Without rejecting this prestigious past, Sonia Rykiel and
Sybille de Margerie have redesigned the rooms and suites,
blending a personal touch with the sumptuous antique
furniture. Luxurious apartments look out over the square,
while the Bernstein and Louis XV suites on the top floor
have terraces with a view of Paris.

Parisian chic is in evidence everywhere, from the receptions
rooms to the bar. At Les Ambassadeurs, the gastronomic
restaurant, one of the best chefs of his generation has put
together a classic yet innovative French menu. Sheer bliss.

▶ **Plan page 167**

CHAMPS-ÉLYSÉES • CONCORDE • MADELEINE

8

Four Seasons George V

31 av. George V ✉ 75008   **Ⓜ** George V
℘ 01 49 52 70 00 **Fax** 01 49 52 70 10
e-mail par.lecinq@fourseasons.com **www**.fourseasons.com

197 rm – ♦€700/1350 ♦♦€730/1350, ⌁ €38 – **48 suites**
⅋○ **Le Cinq** (see restaurant index)

Four Seasons George V

The legendary George V has been "the" luxury hotel in Paris ever since it opened in 1928. Walking past the porch and awning, one is immediately struck by the majesty of the huge marble lobby, followed by the lobby-gallery and a succession of lounge areas where brunch is served. White marble and gilt work are everywhere, illuminated by magnificent floral arrangements. The light in the grand dining room, with its Louis XVI decor worthy of a palace, comes from an inner courtyard – an oasis of greenery designed as a hanging garden. The food is extremely refined, and the superb wine list makes it even more appealing. The two stylish private dining rooms can be booked in advance. The same 18C spirit pervades the guestrooms, decorated with old engravings. All the rooms have a terrace or balcony on the upper floors, where the same floral exuberance is on display. The hushed ambiance and absolute comfort make this the quintessential Parisian luxury hotel, and one of the most sought after by the international jet set.

Intercontinental Le Grand

2 r. Scribe ✉ 75009   Ⓜ Opéra
✆ 01 40 07 32 32 **Fax** 01 42 66 12 51
e-mail legrand@ihg.com **www**.paris.intercontinental.com
442 rm – †€650/830 ††€650/830, ⌂€38 – 28 suites
▯O *Café de la Paix* (see restaurant index)

G.Corbic/MICHELIN

▲ **Plan page 210**

1862 and 2003 are two historic dates for the Grand Hôtel. The first marks the inauguration of this establishment a stone's throw from the Opéra Garnier. The second is when this monumental Napoleon III style building was reopened after a complete facelift.

Rooms and suites are decorated in a Second Empire style with a range of blues, reds and gold. Luxury and comfort are the watchwords here, where the classical décor of varnished mahogany furniture, refined prints and raised beds with elegant plaid covers blends in perfectly with the state-of-the-art facilities.

The restaurant, which has had its moments of glory, is well up to the challenge. Since the spring of 2006, Laurent Delarbre (Meilleur Ouvrier de France 2004) has been in charge of the kitchen at the Café de la Paix. Meals are served continuously here, from breakfast to late-night dinner, under the period frescoes in this listed historic monument.

Opéra • Grands Boulevards

9

Le Meurice

ⒽⒶⒽ

228 r. Rivoli ✉ 75001   Ⓜ Tuileries
☎ 01 44 58 10 10 **Fax** 01 44 58 10 15
e-mail reservations@lemeurice.com **www**.lemeurice.com

137 rm – †€ 520/620 ††€ 680/2100, ⌣ €48 – 23 suites
🍽 *Le Meurice* (see restaurant index)

🍽
Ⓢⓟⓐ
ㄥ♿
🛗
♿
Ⓐ/Ⓒ
✂
☎))
ⓢⒶⓣ
♨

Ⓥⓘⓢⓐ
Ⓜⓒ
ⒶⒺ
Ⓓ

Le Meurice

The Meurice, the legendary luxury hotel at 228 rue de Rivoli, is a stone's throw from the Tuileries Gardens, near Place de la Concorde. Formerly located at 223 rue Saint-Honoré, it was moved here in 1835 by the owner, Augustin Meurice. He was so successful in his attempt to attract a clientele from across the Channel that an advertisement from those days boasted: "no other hotel in Paris offers so many advantages to English travellers". Perfection was already the ideal then, constantly sought after – and now achieved. In 1935, when the hotel was completely renovated (except for the listed façades), the poet Léon-Paul Fargue said there were three kinds of guests in Parisian hotels: "bad ones, good ones, and those at the Meurice", including celebrities and crowned heads. Today, after the facelift undertaken in 1998 (lasting two years), the Meurice is dazzling them once again. Philippe Starck recently redesigned the reception area in warm golden tones. The service is everything one could wish for from such a prestigious establishment, the perfect match for Yannick Alleno's sublime cuisine.

Park Hyatt

5 r. Paix ✉ 75002   Ⓜ Opéra
☎ 01 58 71 12 34 **Fax** 01 58 71 12 35
e-mail vendome@hyattintl.com **www**.paris.vendome.hyatt.com

167 rm – †€600/810 ††€600/810,⌑€40 – 22 suites
🍴 *Le Pur' Grill* (see restaurant index)

Park Hyatt

Art-lover and architect Ed Tuttle had been living in Paris for years – and had already designed several dream hotels around the world – when Hyatt chose him to renovate its five Haussmann buildings on Rue de la Paix. His idea? To create a place where artwork would be prominently featured in the decor. While highlighting a certain French classicism, he reworked traditional styles and materials in a contemporary way, designing all the furniture and subtly blending various periods from Louis XVI to the thirties.When the "elegant, sophisticated and very Parisian" Park Hyatt Paris-Vendôme opened its doors on 20 August 2002, it was clear that he had achieved his goal. Jean-François Rouquette, previously at several starred establishments, runs the kitchen in both restaurants: les Orchidées, with its glass conservatory and open-air courtyard, and the more low-key Pur'Grill. A fine challenge for him too.

BOURSE ▶ Plan page 64

2

Plaza Athénée

B3

25 av. Montaigne ✉ 75008   Ⓜ Alma Marceau
📞 01 53 67 66 65 **Fax** 01 53 67 66 66
e-mail reservations@plaza-athenee-paris.com
www.plaza-athenee-paris.com

146 rm – 🛏€720/740 🛏🛏€820/840, 🍽€48 – **45 suites**

🍴 *Alain Ducasse au Plaza Athénée* and *Le Relais Plaza*
(see restaurant index)

Plaza Athénée

This legendary Parisian hotel, where the watchwords are luxury, elegance and refinement, is the epitome of excellence. Since its inauguration in 1911, the Plaza has attracted the most illustrious figures in business, entertainment and politics. Past the majestic lobby, the eye is drawn to the colours of the Cour Jardin and Galerie des Gobelins. Flowers, marble, gilt work and famous paintings adorn every room, creating an impression of absolute comfort, enhanced by the extremely attentive service.

The grand tradition reigns in the rooms on the first six floors of the hotel, which give onto the garden or the avenue Montaigne, featuring traditional Louis XV, Louis XVI and Regency-style furnishings offset with light tones.

The suites celebrate an Art Deco ambiance. Some are duplexes with sauna, fitness facilities and a view of the Eiffel Tower. The 500 square metre Royal suite is the largest in Paris, offering a truly spectacular view of the city. This is the stuff that dreams are made of.

CHAMPS-ÉLYSÉES • CONCORDE • MADELEINE ▶ Plan page 166

Raphael

🏠🏠🏠🏠

17 av. Kléber ✉ 75116   Ⓜ Kléber
✆ 01 53 64 32 00 **Fax** 01 53 64 32 01
e-mail reservation@raphael-hotel.com **www.**raphael-hotel.com

48 rm – 🛉€345/490 🛉🛉€345/570, ☕€38 – 37 suites

With its portrait by Raphael in the grand lobby, a Turner painting, wood panelling, gilt and 15th century English furniture, the Hôtel Raphaël, in the heart of the prestigious Golden Triangle Parisian business district, is a must. This valiant centenarian offers its guests the slightly old-fashioned but ever-so-reassuring charm of the luxury hotels of the Belle Époque. The lift takes you up to the Grand Siècle rooms and apartments, as well as to the Jardins Plein Ciel featuring seasonal-based dining with a 360° panoramic view of the capital. Traditional food is also served in the dining room and at the Bar Anglais. As the owners of the Regina and Majestic hotels too, Léonard Tauber and Constant Baverez would be proud of the Raphaël, which they originally opened in the spring of 1925. Eighty years later, after a long period of renovation work and of integrating the latest technological innovations, it remains an independent, family-oriented, private place – unheard of in Paris.

▶ Plan page 297

ÉTOILE • TROCADÉRO • PASSY • BOIS DE BOULOGNE

16

369

Ritz

B1

15 pl. Vendôme ✉ 75001 Ⓜ Opéra
✆ 01 43 16 30 30 **Fax** 01 43 16 36 68
e-mail resa@ritzparis.com **www**.ritzparis.com

124 rm – 🚹€710/810 🚹🚹€710/810, ☕ €36 – 37 suites
🍴 ***L'Espadon*** (see restaurant index)

Ritz

After training as a sommelier in his native Switzerland, César Ritz studied in the finest establishments in Europe. Imagining an ideal residence that would offer "all the refinements a prince could want in his own home", he began to "dream of a house he would be proud to associate his name with". A sumptuous 18th century building was for sale at 15 Place Vendôme in Paris, and on 1st June 1898, the former townhouse of the Duke de Lauzun became the Ritz.

After serving as a temporary hospital for soldiers in the First World War, the hotel regained its former magnificence in the Roaring Twenties. In 1944 a soldier named Ernest Hemingway, later a regular here, helped remove the Germans occupying it: "Whenever I dream of paradise and the beyond, I find myself transported to the Ritz in Paris", he wrote.

In 1979 the Ritz family sold the establishment to Mohamed Al Fayed. After nine years of restoration work and a great deal of investment, the Ritz got back its glamour, and the legend goes on.

Balzac

6 r. Balzac ✉ 75008   Ⓜ George V
✆ 01 44 35 18 00 **Fax** 01 44 35 18 05
e-mail reservation-balzac@jjwhotels.com **www**.hotelbalzac.com

69 rm – ♦€420/470 ♦♦€470/550, ⌐€38 – 13 suites

Balzac

Behind this elegant Haussmann façade near the Champs-Élysées is a delightful hotel that reopened in the summer of 2007 after a facelift costing 11 million euros. Vibrant colours, wall hangings and carpets decorate the majestic lobby giving onto a cosy-comfy lounge and bar. Luxury and refinement are also on display upstairs. The very comfortable rooms are quite large for Paris and charmingly decorated with Murano lamps, superb fabrics, elegant period furniture and marble bathrooms, combining an attractive French art de vivre with high-tech facilities (wide plasma TV screens, CD and DVD players, high-speed Wifi internet connection). Discreet elements here and there evoke the memory of Honoré de Balzac, the famous writer for whom the street and the hotel were named. A 24-hour butler and concierge service ensures the well-being of the hotel's guests. Food-lovers have a treat in store for them at the hotel's Pierre Gagnaire restaurant.

CHAMPS-ÉLYSÉES • CONCORDE • MADELEINE ▶ Plan page 166

8

371

Costes

A1

239 r. St-Honoré ✉ 75001   Ⓜ Concorde
℘ 01 42 44 50 00 **Fax** 01 42 44 50 01
www.hotelcostes.com

82 rm – ♦€ 400 ♦♦€ 550, ⌒ € 30 – **3 suites**

A solid, Napoleon III style building near the Place Vendôme with a discreet façade sporting the name, and a unique atmosphere the moment you walk in. That's the Costes – located a few blocks from what was once the Hotel Meurice in the 19th century.

The reception and lounges give onto a gorgeous Italian courtyard decorated with antique statues, a delightful place to dine at the first sign of good weather, while nooks with pear wood love seats and tub armchairs are perfect for intimate conversations.

The purple and gold bedrooms, decorated with refinement and attention to detail, incorporate harmonious colours, stylish furniture and monogrammed linens, creating a Baroque touch. There is also a swimming pool, a fitness centre, and a bar designed by Jacques Garcia.

Très Costes, as in the restaurant, a temple of the "hip lounge" trend.

De Vendôme

B1

1 pl. Vendôme ✉ 75001   Ⓜ Opéra
☎ 01 55 04 55 00 **Fax** 01 49 27 97 89
e-mail reservations@hoteldevendome.com
www.hoteldevendome.com

29 rm – ♦€450/660 ♦♦€535/855, ⌐€30 – 10 suites

De Vendôme

This former 18th century townhouse, truly a gem, is fitted out in the finest tradition of French decorative arts. The reception boasts pilasters with gilt capitals, inlaid polychrome marble floors and a desk made of precious wood.

The spacious rooms come in sparkling or more pastel colours, all with elegant draperies, as well as antique and period furniture. The discreet atmosphere in the bar recalls that of an English club, and your imagination can easily fly across the Channel as you sip a glass of Scotch surrounded by the subdued lighting, mahogany furniture and Chesterfield armchairs. Meanwhile, the chef is in the kitchen cooking delicious meals.

The presidential suite, which can be used for private parties, is on the top floor of the hotel, with a vast lounge and terrace. This is your chance to have a breathtaking view over the rooftops of Paris. In short, a charming and magical place.

PALAIS-ROYAL • LOUVRE • TUILERIES • LES HALLES ▶ Plan page 44

1

Fouquet's Barrière

A2

46 av. Georges V ⊠ 75008   Ⓜ George V
📞 01 40 69 60 00 **Fax** 01 40 69 60 05
e-mail hotelfouquets@lucienbarriere.com
www.fouquets-barriere.com

67 rm – †€690/910 ††€690/910,⊑€35 – 40 suites, 1 du-plex

🍽️ **Fouquet's** (see restaurant index)

Véronique Mati

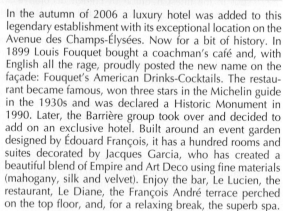

In the autumn of 2006 a luxury hotel was added to this legendary establishment with its exceptional location on the Avenue des Champs-Élysées. Now for a bit of history. In 1899 Louis Fouquet bought a coachman's café and, with English all the rage, proudly posted the new name on the façade: Fouquet's American Drinks-Cocktails. The restaurant became famous, won three stars in the Michelin guide in the 1930s and was declared a Historic Monument in 1990. Later, the Barrière group took over and decided to add on an exclusive hotel. Built around an event garden designed by Édouard François, it has a hundred rooms and suites decorated by Jacques Garcia, who has created a beautiful blend of Empire and Art Deco using fine materials (mahogany, silk and velvet). Enjoy the bar, Le Lucien, the restaurant, Le Diane, the François André terrace perched on the top floor, and, for a relaxing break, the superb spa.

8

Lutetia

▶ Plan page 112

45 bd Raspail ✉ 75006   Ⓜ Sèvres Babylone
✆ 01 49 54 46 46 **Fax** 01 49 54 46 00
e-mail lutetia-paris@lutetia-paris.com **www**.lutetia-paris.com

231 rm – ✝€ 250/950 ✝✝€ 250/950, ⌑ €27 – **11 suites**
🍽 *Paris* (see restaurant index)

Affirmatif

This exceptional historic establishment was the first Art
Deco hotel in Paris, built in 1910 by the owners of the Bon
Marché department store. A stone's throw from the government ministries and Saint-Germain-des-Prés, it is easy to
spot with its sumptuous façade celebrating the Bacchanalia
and nature. Inside, the reception and lobby illustrate the Rykiel era, with works by Philippe Hiquily, Arman, César and
Chemiakin – a reminder of the cultural effervescence here.
Numerous paintings and lithographs decorate the rooms,
all in the spirit of the Roaring Twenties. The well-equipped
marble bathrooms are truly luxurious in the suites and
junior suites. The pure Art Deco style is also on display at
Le Paris, serving excellent food in a warm setting with wood
panelling, elegant oval tables and colourful tableware, directly inspired by the ocean liner, Le Normandie. The Brasserie Lutetia has the same marine accent, with a menu
devoted to seafood. There is live jazz music at the bar in
the evenings from Wednesday to Saturday.

ST-GERMAIN-DES-PRÉS • QUARTIER LATIN • LUXEMBOURG

6

Murano

13 bd du Temple ✉ 75003   Ⓜ Filles du Calvaire
☎ 01 42 71 20 00 **Fax** 01 42 71 21 01
e-mail paris@muranoresort.com **www**.muranoresort.com

49 rm – ♦€ 360/650 ♦♦€ 440/1850, ⌸ €32 **– 2 suites**

Murano

The eye-catching façade combines classicism and modernity. The upper floors of the building are true to their 19th century origins, while the ground floor is all steel and frosted glass. The Murano Urban Resort, in one of the oldest neighbourhoods in Paris, is a holiday destination of a completely new kind.

The phenomenal renovations included two years of reflection, five hundred architectural plans and fifteen months of construction work, transforming this hotel into a totally unique and spacious setting. The Murano opens onto a gallery of white marble decorated by flowing organdie drapes, with glass sculptures lining the passageway. Luminous cubes, precision lighting, modern paintings and contemporary furniture create an immaculate, airy decor without walls. The ingenious design gives you a sense of freedom while preserving the feeling of intimacy.

The light and comfortable guestrooms are decorated in contrasting colours – from sky blue, lilac and sunshine yellow to emerald green and turquoise – for a variety of moods. The hotel also features modular suites and a central lounge with fireplace. The height of modern refinement.

Napoléon

▶ Plan page 166

40 av. Friedland   Ⓜ Charles de Gaulle-Étoile
✉ 75008
✆ 01 56 68 43 21 **Fax** 01 47 66 82 33
e-mail napoleon@hotelnapoleon.com
www.hotelnapoleonparis.com

101 rm – ♦€ 440/630 ♦♦€ 440/690,⌑ €26

Napoléon

Step off the plane from New York, and the minute you walk into the Napoléon, it's like stepping back into the early 19th century Paris of the emperor himself.

Better than a museum, this establishment created in 1928 is the living embodiment of a time in French history that exemplified splendour and magnificence. Here you can experience life as it was in those days while enjoying all the modern comforts. Consider the plush Empire and Directoire decor with its fine collection of paintings, autographs and figurines to the glory of Napoleon, wood panelling and warm tones, soft lighting and thick curtains creating a quiet and tasteful atmosphere.

Every inch of the hotel exudes refinement and elegance – a delight for tourists and Parisians fond of all things chic and authentic. This is a truly exceptional place – due to its Arc de Triomphe location, and to its clientele of legendary figures like Josephine Baker and Errol Flynn, for whom it was quite simply "The Place to be"!

CHAMPS-ÉLYSÉES • CONCORDE • MADELEINE

8

Le Parc-Trocadéro

C3

55 av. R. Poincaré ⊠ 75116   Ⓜ Victor Hugo
☎ 01 44 05 66 66 **Fax** 01 44 05 66 00
e-mail corinne.leponner@renaissancehotels.com
www.marriott.com

112 rm – ♦€195/450 ♦♦€245/950, ⌑ €27 – **4 suites**

LIEGOIS

In the autumn of 2007 the Sofitel Le Parc changed hands
and was renamed as the Parc-Trocadéro. Pending renovations, the reception, lounges and rooms still feature the
same resolutely British look – as cosy as can be with lovely
print fabrics cleverly hiding the state-of-the-art facilities. For
true peace and quiet, most of the rooms are located around
the terrace garden. At the cocktail hour, head for the library-
lounge with its plaid motifs or the chocolate-and-rust-col-
oured bar, where the space has an elegant look highlighted
by the Arman sculptures (also in the reception area). Breakfast features a "hunting" ambiance in a room decorated with
trophies. The terrace of the Relais du Parc restaurant is in a
verdant cobblestone courtyard, the perfect place to enjoy
up-to-date French cuisine in a quiet environment.

16

Pavillon de la Reine

28 pl. Vosges ⊠ 75003 — **Ⓜ** Bastille
☎ 01 40 29 19 19 **Fax** 01 40 29 19 20
e-mail contact@pavillon-de-la-reine.com
www.pavillon-de-la-reine.com

41 rm – ♦€370/460 ♦♦€430/460,⌕ €25 – 15 suites

Pavillon de la Reine

The Place Royale (now Place des Vosges) was built at the initiative of "good King" Henri IV and inaugurated in 1612, two years after his assassination. The square soon turned the Marais district into a mecca for high society, frequented by writers such as the Marquise de Sévigné, Racine, La Fontaine and Molière.

These days art galleries and antique dealers fill its arcades, where strolling around and window shopping are a terrific way to soak up the special ambiance in this soulful neighbourhood.

In the heart of historic Paris, the Pavillon de la Reine is in a unique location, close to the bubbling Place de la Bastille, the Marais' prestigious townhouses-turned-museums, and the captivating Jewish quarter. Rooms are available on the courtyard or garden side. Its flowered courtyards and luxurious accommodations (part 17th century) are hidden from sight, giving it the look of a charming pied-à-terre.

LE MARAIS • BEAUBOURG ▶ Plan page 77

3

St-James Paris

C3

43 av. Bugeaud ✉ 75116   **Ⓜ** Porte Dauphine
☎ 01 44 05 81 81 **Fax** 01 44 05 81 82
e-mail contact@saint-james-paris.com **www**.saint-james-paris.com

38 rm – 🛏€380/630 🛏🛏€490/630, ⊑ €28 **– 10 suites**

St-James Paris

The Saint James is quite unique in that it is the only château-hotel in Paris and is also one of the few with a huge private garden. Its story is quite fascinating.

Born in Marseille in 1797, Adolphe Thiers, a former minister in the government of Louis-Philippe who opposed Napoleon III, was for two years the first president of the 3rd Republic. A large townhouse was built in his memory in 1892 on the site of the first Parisian aerodrome for hot-air balloons.

Long a special place reserved for France's best students, it was bought by the English in 1986 and became a typical London club; six years later, it changed hands again and was turned into a luxurious hotel residence. According to tradition in this vast home, access to the lovely oval dining room is reserved for residents and members of the club, who are the only ones permitted to dine there.

16

Daniel

8 r. Frédéric Bastiat   Ⓜ St-Philippe du Roule
✉ 75008
✆ 01 42 56 17 00 **Fax** 01 42 56 17 01
e-mail danielparis@relaischateaux.com **www.**hoteldanielparis.com

22 rm – ♦€350/490 ♦♦€410/490,⬛€32 – 4 suites

Daniel

The intimate and elegant Daniel has the charm of a town-house ideally located between the Champs-Élysées and rue du Faubourg Saint-Honoré. Since reopening in September 2004, after a facelift from Tarfa Salam, it feels a bit like entering Ali Baba's cave. Here, Eastern and Western aesthetics are happily combined in a well-conceived blend of styles – a cosmopolitan marriage of motifs and materials. The owners are said to be real antique buffs, which is quite clear from the decoration mixing carpets from Kazakhstan, vases from Asia, Chinese wallpaper, toile de Jouy fabrics, English sofas with lots of cushions, ebony furniture from Lebanon, Moroccan ceramics (in the bathrooms), Syrian chairs and silver platters from Turkey. You can savour this soothing and exotic atmosphere in a corner of the lounge under the glass roof. Comfortably settled in, you will forget all about time and dream of journeys to distant places.

CHAMPS-ÉLYSÉES • CONCORDE • MADELEINE ▶ Plan page 166

8

D'Aubusson

D1

33 r. Dauphine ✉ 75006 Ⓜ Odéon
✆ 01 43 29 43 43 **Fax** 01 43 29 12 62
e-mail reservations@hoteldaubusson.com
www.hoteldaubusson.com

49 rm – ♦€310/470 ♦♦€310/470,⌒€23

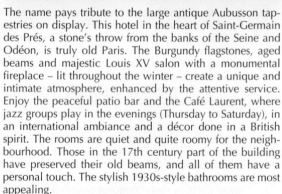

The name pays tribute to the large antique Aubusson tapestries on display. This hotel in the heart of Saint-Germain des Prés, a stone's throw from the banks of the Seine and Odéon, is truly old Paris. The Burgundy flagstones, aged beams and majestic Louis XV salon with a monumental fireplace – lit throughout the winter – create a unique and intimate atmosphere, enhanced by the attentive service. Enjoy the peaceful patio bar and the Café Laurent, where jazz groups play in the evenings (Thursday to Saturday), in an international ambiance and a décor done in a British spirit. The rooms are quiet and quite roomy for the neighbourhood. Those in the 17th century part of the building have preserved their old beams, and all of them have a personal touch. The stylish 1930s-style bathrooms are most appealing.

ST-GERMAIN-DES-PRÉS • QUARTIER LATIN • LUXEMBOURG ▶ Plan page 113

6

De Sers

41 av. Pierre 1er de Serbie ⊠ 75008   Ⓜ George V
✆ 01 53 23 75 75 **Fax** 01 53 23 75 76
e-mail contact@hoteldesers.com **www.**hoteldesers.com

49 rm – †€480/550 ††€550/900, ⤳€29 – 3 suites

De Sers

Architect Thomas Vidalenc describes his approach in redesigning the Hôtel de Sers as trying to create "a home
where time is experienced in a different way, articulating
a feeling of contemporary melancholy". To achieve that
soothing effect, he has opted for a design with clean lines,
matching fabrics and airy, clutter-free spaces. Comfort,
aestheticism and modernity are the key concepts in the
rooms, expressed with restraint and refinement in the parquet floors, sumptuous beds, bathrooms with light Italian
marble and white ceramics, grey, beige and violet tones,
and designer furniture. The building has retained a few
traces of its origins (once home of the Marquis de Sers, then
a health care establishment, and since 1935, a hotel) such
as the monumental staircase visible from the reception. The
garden has also been converted into a lovely patio-terrace where breakfast is served in summer. Leisure facilities
include a gym, a sauna and hammam, massage and a
"bath menu" with a variety of relaxing options
available upon request.

CHAMPS-ÉLYSÉES • CONCORDE • MADELEINE ▶ **Plan page 166**

8

Duc de St-Simon

14 r. St-Simon ✉ **75007**   ⓜ Rue du Bac
☎ 01 44 39 20 20 **Fax** 01 45 48 68 25
e-mail duc.de.saint.simon@wanadoo.fr
www.hotelducdesaintsimon.com

34 rm – ♦€225/290 ♦♦€225/395, ☕€15

Duc de Saint-Simon

Curiously, although the Duc de Saint-Simon had several residences in the area, he never lived on the street that bears his name. Thus the well-known 17th century French memoirist never lived in this hotel either. Never mind! This fine establishment near Les Deux Magots and Le Flore, the two most famous cafés in the historic neighbourhood of Saint-Germain-des-Près, is a haven of comfort and tranquillity – just like being at home. Past the courtyard with its climbing wisteria, a cosy salon with a warm and elegant decor awaits you. Each of the rooms is individually styled, with an overall unity in the furniture and matching colours. A lift takes you down to the bar in the cleverly designed 17th century cellar. The shady flower-decked courtyard is an added touch for guests to enjoy in fine weather.

7

Esprit Saint-Germain

22 r. Saint-Sulpice ✉ 75006   **Ⓜ** Mabillon
☎ 01 53 10 55 55 **Fax** 01 53 10 55 56
e-mail contact@espritsaintgermain.com
www.espritsaintgermain.com

28 rm – †€310/550 ††€310/550, ☕€26 – **5 suites**

Esprit Saint-Germain

"Just like home" is how the owners describe this charming hotel in the heart of the 6th arrondissement between the Luxembourg Gardens and boulevard Saint-Germain. Nothing distinguishes the façade from the neighbouring buildings, apart from its discreetly highlighted name. But once inside, you can feel the subtle differences at play here, where all is elegance, conviviality, comfort and refinement. In decorating her "house", owner Laurence Taffanel created a warm atmosphere with verdigris partitions in the lobby, neo-Romantic figurative paintings on the walls, and jam-packed bookcases. After thirty months of renovations, she transformed this typical 17th century building into "an historic hotel with a modern infrastructure". The relaxation area with a view over the rooftops of Paris is an added bonus.

ST-GERMAIN-DES-PRÉS • QUARTIER LATIN • LUXEMBOURG ► Plan page 113

6

François 1er

7 r. Magellan ✉ 75008   Ⓜ George V
☎ 01 47 23 44 04 **Fax** 01 47 23 93 43
e-mail hotel@hotel-francois1er.fr **www.**the-paris-hotel.com

40 rm – †€300/780 ††€350/1000,⌴€22 – 2 suites

Fabrice Rambert

Blending old-style elegance with contemporary comforts seems to have been Pierre-Yves Rochon's leitmotiv when redesigning the François 1er at the dawn of the year 2000. And he clearly succeeded. The proof is in the luxurious and charming rooms cleverly combining canopies, thick curtains, Toile de Jouy, plush carpeting, old lithographs, mouldings and antique furniture. In the bathrooms, Italian marble and modern designer fittings create a very smart retro look. The stylish details further enhance the charm of the place. The result is a soothing and rather comforting "stately home" feel, exemplified by the cosy lounge with fireplace, and the winter garden with flowers in all seasons, or the antiques, elegant armchairs and precious marble decorating every nook and cranny. In short, the height of refinement, as well as a model of hospitality with its discreet, pleasant and friendly staff.

8

L'Hôtel

13 r. des Beaux Arts   Ⓜ St-Germain-des-Prés
✉ 75006
☎ 01 44 41 99 00 **Fax** 01 43 25 64 81
e-mail stay@l-hotel.com **www**.l-hotel.com

16 rm – ♦€255/640 ♦♦€280/640,⬚ €18 – 4 suites
🍴○ **Le Restaurant** (see restaurant index)

L'Hôtel

ST-GERMAIN-DES-PRÉS • QUARTIER LATIN • LUXEMBOURG ▶ Plan page 113

The restrained façade is a striking contrast to the inside with its absolutely Baroque blend of genres! This hotel built in 1816 was given a facelift by Jacques Garcia, and it is one of his finest accomplishments. First, there is the Empire spirit faithfully reproduced in the dizzying central shaft and skylight overlooking the reception, and the row of little lounges with marbled red and green colonnades. The atmosphere is intimate and cosy despite this lofty elegance. The rooms range from scrupulously historical to freer reconstructions in different styles, including Pondichéry, Coti, Charles X, Roi de Naples and "Merteuil" - all with marble bathrooms. Not to mention the sumptuous suite that was the last dwelling place of Oscar Wilde, which inspired him to say: "I am dying beyond my means!". The cosy restaurant topped by a large glass roof resembles a winter garden with its heavy fabrics and plush armchairs and sofas. The earthly nourishment is in the classic genre, prepared by a young and ambitious team.

6

Les Jardins du Marais

A2

74 r. Amelot ✉ 75011   Ⓜ St-Sébastien Froissart
✆ 01 40 21 20 00 **Fax** 01 47 00 82 40
e-mail resabastille@homeplazza.com **www.**homeplazza.com

201 rm – ♦€350 ♦♦€370,⌐€32 – 64 suites

Bruno Delessard

This hotel is in a great location on the edge of the Marais. On foot or by bike (thanks to Vélib'), you can taste the charms of the Place des Vosges, the pretty nearby shops (especially on rue des Francs-Bourgeois), and the Carnavalet (no charge) and Picasso Museums. People enjoy the peace and quiet at this hotel, where the buildings all give onto a former cul-de-sac with lovely trees, flowers and small private terraces. Some of them date from the 16th and 17th centuries, while others were designed by Gustave Eiffel. The lobby is an original blend of red velvet armchairs, Art Deco-style light fixtures and Philippe Starck chairs. The rooms, renovated between 2001 and 2004, have a 1930s décor with furniture in maple and dark inlaid wood, elegant lighting, and warm net curtains and fabrics. Now just pick the room that matches your mood and budget.

11

Keppler

C1

10 r. Keppler ⊠ 75016   Ⓜ George V
☎ 01 47 20 65 05 **Fax** 01 47 23 02 29
e-mail hotel@keppler.fr **www**.keppler.fr

34 rm – ♦€300/350 ♦♦€420/490, ☐€22 – 5 suites

Two real professionals came together to create this delightful hotel, a perfect blend of luxury and refinement. The owners, who already have several high-quality establishments in Paris, fell in love with this building, ideally located on a quiet street a stone's throw from the Champs-Élysées and the Arc de Triomphe. The project was entrusted to famous interior architect Pierre-Yves Rochon, who has designed and renovated hotels and restaurants all over the world. The results are up to his reputation. Lounges in soft pastel colours, pretty furniture, decorated mantelpiece, beautiful mouldings, airy glass roof, bookshelves and original carpets create a highly elegant atmosphere. The rooms offer the same pleasant feeling of harmony thanks to the skilful blend of attractively updated classic furniture, along with some contemporary touches and carefully chosen colours. The steam room, sauna and fitness room add an extra touch to this prestigious establishment.

ÉTOILE • TROCADÉRO • PASSY • BOIS DE BOULOGNE ▶ Plan page 297

16

K+K Hotel Cayré

4 bd Raspail ✉ 75007   Ⓜ Rue du Bac
☎ 01 45 44 38 88 **Fax** 01 45 44 98 13
e-mail reservations@kkhotels.fr **www**.kkhotels.com/cayre

125 rm – ♦€320/412 ♦♦€348/680,⌐ €25

K-K Hotel Cayré

K + K, as in Koller, Josef and Helmut, brothers who created their hotel group in 1961, with 10 establishments in Europe. You'll find the same initials and the same identity in London, Munich, Salzburg, Vienna, Budapest, Prague and Bucharest. In Paris too, of course, where the writer George Bernanos and the musician Pablo Casals were regulars at the Hôtel Cayré.Set in an area known for its fashion and art connections, the hotel has been entirely renovated in a decisively modern spirit. The contrast is striking between the Haussmannian façade overlooking the Boulevard Raspail and the contemporary design in the rooms with their soft, clean lines. Pastel and vivid colours blend together seamlessly in the hall and reception, as well as in the bar and bistro. The business lounge is an ideal setting for confidential meetings. Not to mention the gym and sauna, ideal for getting in shape and eliminating stress.

7

Kube

1 passage Ruelle ✉ 75018 ⓜ La Chapelle
☎ 01 42 05 20 00 **Fax** 01 42 05 21 01
e-mail paris@kubehotel.com **www**.kubehotel.com

41 rm – ♦€250 ♦♦€300/750,☕€25

Laurent Pons

The building – with a listed façade – is located in a calm little street far from the hustle and bustle of the city. Inside, it is both private and provocative. The concept is strikingly high-tech and playful.Fans of new technology will love this hotel, with its forty rooms and suites. Novelty seekers will enjoy the huge lounge bar with its armchairs covered in synthetic fur, cubic chairs and tables, mirrors and plasma screens covering the walls. Original and baroque, like the extraordinary Ice Kube bar engulfed in 20 tons of ice – an unreal decor where the temperature goes down to minus 5 degrees Centigrade! Black lights, dark walls and fluorescent figures create a different kind of atmosphere in the luminous and contrasting rooms, with all the modern comforts. And after staying here once, you will find that "Kubism" is a state of mind.

MONTMARTRE • PIGALLE ▶ **Plan page 343**

18

Océania

52 r. Oradour sur Glane   Ⓜ Porte de Versailles
✉ 75015
✆ 01 56 09 09 09 **Fax** 01 56 09 09 19
e-mail oceania.paris@oceaniahotels.com **www**.oceaniahotels.com

232 rm – ♦€160/270 ♦♦€175/285, ⌿ €15 – 18 suites

This hotel is perfect for anyone looking for accommodation in a modern style. The large, recent building (2005) boasts a vast, decidedly contemporary lobby, a terrace and a garden with exotic plants. The spa area, a rarity in this type of establishment, is well-equipped and most welcome after a day of work or exploring the streets of Paris, including a pool with a glass roof, steam room, fitness room (with numerous workout machines), massage rooms and a jacuzzi. Comfort and relaxation are also the watchwords in the rooms, decorated with streamlined furniture, dark and light wood panelling, flat screens with 60 channels and a video system on demand, internet access and functional bathrooms. The effective double glazing keeps out the noise from the ring road that runs between the hotel and the Parc des Expositions at the Porte de Versailles.

PORTE DE VERSAILLES • VAUGIRARD • BEAUGRENELLE ▶ Plan page 278

15

Pont Royal

7 r. Montalembert ✉ 75007   Ⓜ Rue du Bac
☎ 01 42 84 70 00 **Fax** 01 42 84 71 00
e-mail hpr@hotel-pont-royal.com **www**.hotel-pont-royal.com

65 rm – ♦€395/455 ♦♦€395/455,⌑€27 – 10 suites

Pont Royal

The Pont Royal is considered one of the very chic places on Paris' Left Bank, a refined literary hotel once frequented by Apollinaire and Gide where writers enjoy meeting at the elegant and cosy bar. The place still echoes with the voices of F. Scott and Zelda Fitzgerald, who were fond of staying here. You can easily imagine them running into André Malraux (who is said to have been happy to introduce his conquests to the first American cocktails). Steeped in history yet decidedly modern, this is a hotel that has kept up with the times.It is perhaps no accident that Joël Robuchon, whose team takes care of breakfasts and room service, chose this place to set up the first of his *Ateliers*, now a worldwide brand.

Tour Eiffel • École Militaire • Invalides ▶ Plan page 133

7

Relais St-Germain

9 carrefour de l'Odéon ✉ 75006   **Ⓜ Odéon**
✆ 01 43 29 12 05 **Fax** 01 46 33 45 30
e-mail hotelrsg@wanadoo.fr

22 rm ☕ – **†€165/220 ††€205/440**

🍽 **Le Comptoir** (see restaurant index)

Denis Clément

As a child in his native Béarn, Yves Camdeborde dreamt of playing rugby and had no idea that one day he would have his own restaurant – the Relais St-Germain –in the heart of the Odéon quarter of Paris. After confirming his passion for cooking with Christian Constant at the Ritz, then at the Crillon, he opened his own place in 1992, and the Régalade (a "must" in the 14th arrondissement) instantly became the leader of the "neo-bistro" vogue. With his wife Claudine, who also supervised the decoration here, Yves Camdeborde is now the owner of this charming hotel with twenty rooms next door to their restaurant, the Comptoir.The hotel exudes 17th century elegance and authenticity. The rooms – huge and all different – are cosy and decorated with great attention to detail, from the original beams to the luxurious fabrics, furniture and antique objects. The suite with terrace was designed with intimacy and comfort in mind. The copious and amazing breakfast is the perfect way to start your day on the right foot!

Sezz

C2

6 av. Frémiet ✉ 75016   **Ⓜ** Passy
✆ 01 56 75 26 26 **Fax** 01 56 75 26 16
e-mail mail@hotelsezz.com **www**.hotelsezz.com

22 rm – ♦€280/335 ♦♦€330/460,⌑€25 – 5 suites

Combining an ultramodern concept with a touch of real class is what Christophe Pillet has pulled off after remodelling this fine establishment. It took 18 months of renovations to transform a simple hotel, a magnificent example of Haussmanian architecture, into a temple of chic and functional design. The luxurious grey-toned decor is a minimalist symbiosis with clean lines and seductive curves that puts the grey Portuguese stone in its best light. The rooms are sublime spaces for the enhancement of one's well-being, outrageously comfortable and decorated with a monotony-banishing eye to detail with bold contemporary furniture, glass-partitioned open bathrooms, paintings and photographs picked up at the FIAC show, and sophisticated plasma screens. Two small lounges, a bar area, jacuzzis and steam rooms are also provided for guests. The ultimate luxury: the massages given upon request in a private room.

▶ **Plan page 297**

ÉTOILE • TROCADÉRO • PASSY • BOIS DE BOULOGNE

16

Splendid Étoile

B3

1 bis av. Carnot
✉ 75017
✆ 01 45 72 72 00 **Fax** 01 45 72 72 01
e-mail hotel@hsplendid.com **www**.hsplendid.com

Ⓜ Charles de Gaulle-Étoile

50 rm – €295 €295, €23 – 7 suites

A/C SAT VISA AE

Splendid Étoile

This fine Haussmann building in an exceptional location just across from the Arc de Triomphe offers all the charm of a traditional hotel in the heart of Paris. Some rooms even have a pretty view of the famous Parisian monument, built during the reign of Napoleon in the early19th century. A climb up to the top will afford you an exceptional panorama of the Champs-Élysées and the eleven other avenues that flow into Place de l'Étoile.The hotel, run by the same family since 1976, enjoys a quiet and tasteful atmosphere featuring cosy lounges and a congenial English bar. The rooms, upstairs, are decorated in the same spirit: Louis XV-style furniture, chandeliers with pendants, carpets, old engravings, discreet wallpaper, light wood panelling and marble bathrooms. The soundproofed façade works wonders.

▶ Plan page 322

Square

3 r. Boulainvilliers ✉ 75016   Ⓜ Mirabeau
✆ 01 44 14 91 90 **Fax** 01 44 14 91 99
e-mail reservation@hotelsquare.com

20 rm – †€300/480 ††€300/480, ☕€22 – 2 suites

G.Corbic/MICHELIN

Le Square, an amazing hotel built in 1995, looks like a modern ocean liner moored across from the Seine. The lobby envelops you in its curves, and the setting captivates you from the start with its warm contemporary style. The inspiration for the décor? A blend of minimalist purity, abstract art and ethnic touches like the zebra pattern featured throughout the hotel and its restaurant, appropriately named Zébra Square, where the (plainly displayed) motto is: "Our pleasure lies in pleasing others". The pleasure is both gastronomic (in the up-to-date cuisine) and visual – in the dining room softly lit with Chinese lanterns. The bar-lounge offers a cosy night-owl atmosphere in dark blue and brown tones (velvet fabrics, Chesterfield sofas). The comfortable rooms are designed in shades of pearl grey, beige and chocolate, procuring a feeling of peace and serenity.

16

Terrass'Hôtel

12 r. J. de Maistre ✉ 75018   Ⓜ Place de Clichy
℘ 01 46 06 72 85 **Fax** 01 44 92 34 30
e-mail reservation@terrass-hotel.com **www**.terrass-hotel.com

85 rm – †€270/290 ††€320/345, ☕€18 – 15 suites

Terrass'Hôtel

How does that old saying go: location is everything? Well, the Terrass'Hôtel has it – in an environment that is both picturesque (at the foot of Sacré-Cœur) and romantic (Montmartre cemetery). And the rooftop terrace at Le Diapason, its restaurant, is an "eagle's nest" with a view over the whole of Paris – from May to September. The rest of the year, you can sample the updated traditional food in the contemporary dining room with clean lines and soft shades of grey – before climbing up the steps to the famous basilica.

The light and spacious rooms are elegant – with tasteful furniture offsetting bright, silky fabrics – and offer a range of styles for all tastes, from discreetly classical to more decisively modern.

This charming hotel in an unusual location is just a stone's throw from many retro, " roguish " and nostalgia-filled spots that have figured prominently in the city's history.

Trocadero Dokhan's

D3

117 r. Lauriston ⊠ 75116　　　　　　　　Ⓜ Trocadéro
𝒞 01 53 65 66 99 **Fax** 01 53 65 66 88
e-mail reservation@dokhans.com **www**.dokhans-sofitel-paris.com

45 rm – †€430/460 ††€430/460,⊑€27 – 4 suites

Trocadero Dokhan's

The challenge was to create a luxurious – yet not ostenta-tious – establishment that would discreetly combine mod-ernity and classic tradition. Mission accomplished at this stylish but absolutely up-to-date hotel a stone's throw from the Place de Trocadéro. The fine 19th century freestone façade is covered in ivy, while sculpted box trees frame the outside steps, shaded by a broad black-and-white stri-ped awning. Inside, it has the charm and elegance of a private mansion, with a circular lobby. The neo-Classical decor – with restored gold-leaf wood panelling – sets the tone of complete freedom in the decor. To create an im-pression of greater space, the niches were fitted with mir-rors in which the round tables, velvet armchairs and warm parquet floors are reflected. In designing the rooms, the decorator also used contrasting tones and materials. For the ultimate in luxury, try the suite conceived as a romantic private pied-à-terre, inviting you to prolong your stay.

ÉTOILE • TROCADÉRO • PASSY • BOIS DE BOULOGNE ▶ **Plan page 297**

16

Villa Panthéon

41 r. des Écoles ✉ 75005   Ⓜ Maubert Mutualité
✆ 01 53 10 95 95 **Fax** 01 53 10 95 96
e-mail pantheon@leshotelsdeparis.com
www.leshotelsdeparis.com

59 rm – ♦€160/350 ♦♦€160/350, ☕€18

Bruno Delessard

This hotel is in an ideal place for a stay in the heart of the Latin Quarter. Many famous sites are within easy walking distance, including the Sorbonne, the Pantheon, the Luxembourg Gardens, the lively streets around Saint-Michel and even Notre-Dame Cathedral. Back at number 41 rue des Écoles, you will appreciate the delicious, cosy atmosphere all the more. The lobby and rooms have a British look, with parquet floors, colourful wall hangings, exotic wood furniture and Liberty-style lamps. The bathrooms are pretty and well-equipped. Whisky fans will enjoy listening to the barman's excellent advice while sitting in a comfortable Chesterfield armchair and sipping their cocktail (in moderation) or fruit juice at the bar. The footbridge linking the hotel's two buildings overlooks a patio where you can relax in fine weather. Breakfast is served in a pleasant, colourful room.

Le A

4 r. d'Artois ✉ 75008   Ⓜ St-Philippe du Roule
☎ 01 42 56 99 99 **Fax** 01 42 56 99 90
e-mail hotel-le-a@wanadoo.fr **www**.paris-hotel-a.com

16 rm – ♦€355/485 ♦♦€355/485, ☕€23 – 10 suites

Le A

The essence of this recently opened contemporary hotel can
be summed up in two words: "A" as in atypical and artistic.
Designed by architect Frédéric Méchiche as a private house
illustrating the latest in modernism, the A, hidden behind a
classical Haussmann façade, features a highly graphic and
totally black-and-white decor. The indoor/outdoor contrast
is striking. Far from monotonous, this two-toned environment is dotted with Buren-like stripes (on some of the walls
and carpets), designer wengue furniture, comfortable armchairs, orchids placed in slender vases, and stylized lamps.
Artist Fabrice Hyber has also invented creative designs for
the rooms, the bar and the lounge-library. Luxury and refinement blend together here without ostentation, creating
a feeling of discreet elegance. This original venue near the
Champs-Élysées was designed for the kind of guest who
enjoys staying in cosy and peaceful places with a different
touch.

8

Banville

166 bd Berthier ✉ 75017   Ⓜ Porte de Champerret
☎ 01 42 67 70 16 **Fax** 01 44 40 42 77
e-mail info@hotelbanville.fr **www.**hotelbanville.fr

38 rm – ♦€ 280/400 ♦♦€ 280/400, ☞€18

G.Corbic/MICHELIN

This building dating from 1926, near the Porte de Champerret and just a few minutes from the Place de Étoile, houses one of the most charming hotels in Paris. Here, elegance and comfort are the watchwords, and there is a sense of total harmony the minute you enter the lobby, with its grand piano, fireplace and comfortable armchairs. The light and spacious feeling also pervades the rooms, all decorated with a personal touch. "Préludes" and "Pastourelles", the latest rooms, are particularly appealing. The "Appartement de Marie" and the "Chambre d'Amélie" on the eighth (and top) floor boast a terrace with a breathtaking view of Paris. "It's nice to come to a place where you feel comfortable", confided one frequent guest. "Everything here is so easy and relaxing. This is a real Parisian neighbourhood where you can rub shoulders with the local inhabitants, and adopt their lifestyle and customs", added another guest. Room service, air conditioning, soundproofing, relaxing massages and beauty treatments are some of the features available in the rooms.

Bassano

D3

15 r. Bassano ✉ 75116   Ⓜ George V
📞 01 47 23 78 23 **Fax** 01 47 20 41 22
e-mail info@hotel-bassano.com **www**.hotel-bassano.com

28 rm – ♦€175/290 ♦♦€195/310,⌕ €18 – 3 suites

G.Corbic/MICHELIN

The Bassanos, a dynasty of painters in the Italian Renaissance, gave their name to this street and the freestone hotel on a corner, strategically located a stone's throw from the Champs-Élysées. The Mediterranean influence is evident from the minute you walk into the hotel, where Provençal colours prevail over Parisian greys. The cosy atmosphere is enhanced by a harmonious blend of colours – with discreet tones in the wood panelling and cerused wood furniture, and brighter shades in the fabrics and cosy armchairs – and the rooms are true havens of peace and quiet. Wrought-iron furnishings adorn the bright and roomy reception area, while the dining room is decorated with large pale wood panels and wall paintings representing bowls full of vegetation. Enjoy a copious breakfast there before heading off to the luxury boutiques and admiring the view from on top of the Arc de Triomphe, or wandering around the immense Petit Palais and Grand Palais Garnier.

ÉTOILE • TROCADÉRO • PASSY • BOIS DE BOULOGNE ▶ **Plan page 297**

16

Le Bellechasse

D1

8 r. de Bellechasse ✉ 75007   Ⓜ Solférino
✆ 01 45 50 22 31 **Fax** 01 45 51 52 36
e-mail info@lebellechasse.com **www**.lebellechasse.com

34 rm – ♦€290/440 ♦♦€320/490,⌐ €25

Le Bellechasse

It's baroque, romantic, "arty", contemporary and neo-classical. Christian Lacroix has crafted a lovely blend of genres in the décor for the Bellechasse, after creating the Petit Moulin in the 3rd arrondissement. The fashion designer from Arles, known for his rich and colourful style, was given a free hand in designing the personalised spaces combining patterns, fabrics, forms and eras. Multiple influences, references to art and architecture, and no less than seven different worlds evoke his personal interpretation of Paris: Patchwork, Saint-Germain, Tuileries, Avengers, Mousquetaire, Quai d'Orsay and Jeu de Paume. It gives you an idea of the special charm of this hotel, with its discreet exterior and classical façade. The surprise element is guaranteed when you walk inside and see the mix of Left bank artistocratic elegance and Bohemian spirit. A sensual, dreamy and artistic "journey within a journey".

7

Bourg Tibourg

19 r. Bourg Tibourg ✉ 75004   Ⓜ Hôtel de Ville
☎ 01 42 78 47 39 **Fax** 01 40 29 07 00
e-mail hotel@bourgtibourg.com **www**.hotelbourgtibourg.com

30 rm – †€180 ††€230/360,⌷€16

Bourg Tibourg

This charming little Costes hotel nestled in the heart of the Marais gallantly displays its chic exuberance behind a rather discreet façade. Blending as always "high style and simple ways, the high life and the simple life", and eager to create a "thrilling place", superstar designer Jacques Garcia composed an environment here which is both unique and profuse. The rooms and their astonishing variety of styles reflect the multiple influences which blend into a kaleidoscope of colours and shapes – from Romantic and Baroque to Eastern and neo-Venetian, plunging guests into a world of comfortable exoticism with soft, subtle lighting. Don't expect huge spaces as the ambiance here is decidedly intimate, featuring small, luxuriously furnished rooms with molten-glass mosaics in the bathrooms, wide, flat TV screens and numerous other colourful touches. The hotel lounge is plush and attractive. Don't miss the splendid interior garden designed by Camille Muller.

ÎLE DE LA CITÉ • ÎLE ST-LOUIS • ST-PAUL ▶ **Plan page 84**

4

Caron de Beaumarchais

B2

12 r. Vieille-du-Temple ✉ 75004 🖂 **Hôtel de Ville**
📞 01 42 72 34 12 **Fax** 01 42 72 34 63
e-mail hotel@carondebeaumarchais.com
www.carondebeaumarchais.com

19 rm – ♦€125/162 ♦♦€125/162, ☕€12

Caron de Beaumarchais

The author of the Barber of Seville and the Marriage of Figaro has lent his name to this amazing haven of aristocratic charm. Being a guest here is more like taking a trip into the past than merely staying at a hotel, for one is transported into an era of pomp and luxury when France's language and culture reigned in Europe (and the rest of the world). The establishment honours the memory of those blessed times with its spectacular 17C interior featuring rooms in noble materials including wood, stone and velvet, Gustavian-style period furniture and really fine exposed beams. Its perfection can be seen in the refinement of details, in the superb prints, old documents on the walls or on a Louis XV writing desk, and in the personalised linens. Most of the rooms give onto a pretty inner courtyard, and the smaller ones on the top floor have a magnificent view of the Right Bank. An exceptional place for an absolutely unforgettable experience.

4

Le 123

C2

123 r. du Faubourg St-Honoré ✉ 75008
🄼 St-Philippe-du-Roule
✆ 01 53 89 01 23 **Fax** 01 45 61 09 07
e-mail hotel.le123@astotel.com **www.**astotel.com

41 rm – 🛏€269/420 🛏🛏€309/450, ⌑ €24

Le 123

In an area known for its famous fashion designers, it was inevitable that the decor here at 123, created by Philippe Maidenberg, would play up the haute couture card. This architect and designer had fun putting together an original display of materials. Grained leather sits side by side with chain mail, while silk blends with velvet, and the wooden bar stools mix in well with the restaurant's leather tables. Your gaze is irresistibly drawn to the monumental chandelier, composed of 3000 Swarovski crystals, while the red crystal sconces create a magical feeling. The staircase, decorated in typical London red brick, leads up to the rooms and suites designed in a contemporary style. Some rooms have cut stone, others have four-poster beds; several of the bathrooms have light oak parquet floors, a view of the starry sky above their zinc roofs, warm Cordovan leather, English wallpaper and tiles, creating a very well-designed blend of styles.

CHAMPS-ÉLYSÉES • CONCORDE • MADELEINE ▸ Plan page 167

8

Chambiges Élysées

8 r. Chambiges ✉ 75008
                  Ⓜ Alma Marceau
𝒸 01 44 31 83 83 **Fax** 01 40 70 95 51
e-mail reservation@hotelchambiges.com
www.hotelchambiges.com

32 rm ☞ – **♦€270/310 ♦♦€270/390 – 2 suites**

Chambiges Élysées

Luxurious fabrics, antique consoles and original paintings are all part of the refined decor at the Chambiges Élysées, where the attention to detail, warm colours and comfortable surroundings create a charming and cosy atmosphere.

Facilities include three categories of elegant rooms – Standard, Deluxe (with a small sitting room, in red, raspberry, yellow or blue) and Suites (caramel, yellow or green tones) – and a superb 45m^2 apartment on the top floor. Each of the rooms has its own personality: Toile de Jouy wallpaper, old lithographs, large mirrors and period furniture.

Not to mention the "special touches", like the buffet breakfast served in a plush setting (shades of red and yellow), bathed in light from the stylish winter garden. In the afternoon, you can relax in the tea room over a cup of tea and a delicious pastry – or get some work done (high-speed wireless connection).

8

Claret

Bruno Delessard

B2

44 bd Bercy ⊠ 75012

Ⓜ Bercy

📞 01 46 28 41 31 **Fax** 01 49 28 09 29

e-mail reservation@hotel-claret.com **www**.hotel-claret.com

52 rm – ♦€95/115 ♦♦€105/149, ☕€10

The name of this hotel pays tribute to the original vocation of the Bercy quarter, once devoted entirely to the wine business. The sports arena, gardens, cinemas, shops and restaurants of today have replaced the former wine warehouses and wine stores. The hotel caters to businessmen and tourists in a warm and pleasantly rustic setting located across from the Ministry of Finance. Exposed beams, a remnant from the hotel's past as a coaching inn, add a charming note to the rooms decorated in contemporary furniture and discreet furnishings embellished by touches of colour; the top floor has garret rooms. Guests bothered by the hustle and bustle of the city should ask for a room at the back. The suggestively named Bouchon Bistro restaurant proposes French cuisine with a daily menu featured on a large blackboard. Opt for the terrace facing a row of tall trees in fine weather.

BASTILLE • BERCY • GARE DE LYON ▶ Plan page 242

12

Demeure

51 bd St-Marcel ⊠ 75013 **Ⓜ** Les Gobelins
℘ 01 43 37 81 25 **Fax** 01 45 87 05 03
e-mail la_demeure@netcourrier.com
www.hotelparislademeure.com

37 rm – ♦€165 ♦♦€203,⌣€13 – 6 suites

La Demeure has a doubly interesting location – near the Jardin des Plantes, the Natural History Museum, and the picturesque rue Mouffetard. The building was built in 1903; the well-appointed rooms are discreetly decorated in a contemporary spirit (streamlined furniture in a range of shades), while double glazing protects them from the traffic noise. The comfortable and pleasant ground floor lobby is decorated in warm tones, dark wood furniture and old photographs of Paris. Breakfast is served buffet-style because everyone has his own way of starting the day. The atmosphere here is friendly and family-oriented. The father and son owners and their staff take pride in giving all their guests special treatment.

Des Académies et des Arts

15 r. de la Grande Chaumière ✉ 75006   Ⓜ Vavin
📞 01 43 26 66 44 **Fax** 01 40 46 86 85
e-mail reservation@hoteldesacademies.com
www.hoteldesacademies.com

20 rm – ♦€ 220/285 ♦♦€ 220/285, ⬛ €16

Des Académies et des Arts

This hotel on a quiet street where Modigliani once lived
(across from the Académie de la Grande Chaumière art
school) harks back to the old Montparnasse of the Roaring
Twenties. The owners hired interior architect Vincent Bastie
for the décor, which spotlights contemporary artwork. The
impeccable façade sets the tone with a white silhouette by
Jérôme Mesnager against a dark red background. Inside, his
figures decorate the walls, offset by white acrobats sculpted
by Sophie de Watrigant – even on the staircase. For your
enjoyment, a screening room is available to watch art vid-
eos. The cosy lounge with fireplace and the library are
bathed in light from the large windows giving onto the
street. Upstairs, the rooms feature various styles ranging
from Art Deco to trendy – and all chic. This is a warm and
rather atypical place with a very fitting name.

St-Germain-des-Prés • Quartier Latin • Luxembourg ▶ Plan page 112

6

411

Du Petit Moulin

29 r. du Poitou ✉ 75003   Ⓜ St-Sébastien Froissart
✆ 01 42 74 10 10 **Fax** 01 42 74 10 97
e-mail contact@hoteldupetitmoulin.com
www.hoteldupetitmoulin.com

17 rm – †€190/350 ††€190/350,☕€15

CH. BIELSA

My first is a building with a 1900s listed façade, home to a bakery not so long ago. It was said to be the oldest bakery in Paris, dating back to Henri IV, where Victor Hugo used to buy his bread.

My second is a plain apartment block on the corner of Rue de Poitou and Rue de Saintonge, joined to the former bakery and redesigned by the Bastie architectural practice.

My third is a famous *couturier* who draws divinely and who has fulfilled a childhood dream – crafting a decor, day by day "in the spirit of the times, creating an ambiance with volumes and colours, not merely on paper or through fashion collections."

The riddle is solved at the Hôtel du Petit Moulin, where Christian Lacroix, who admits he immediately liked the slightly off-kilter perspectives and the maze-like design of the floors, designed seventeen different styles for the seventeen rooms – like seventeen ways of experiencing the Marais!

3

Élysées Céramic

34 av. Wagram ✉ 75008   Ⓜ Ternes
✆ 01 42 27 20 30 **Fax** 01 46 22 95 83
e-mail info@elysees-ceramic.com **www**.elysees-ceramic.com

57 rm – ♦€175/195 ♦♦€210/230,⊑€12

Élysées Céramic

The Belle Epoque era attempted to bring art into even the smallest aspects of everyday life; and that is the spirit in which one should contemplate the façade of the Élysées Céramic and its organic architecture with intertwining forms, glazed stoneware and sculpted stone created by Lavirotte in 1904 – a pure example of the modern style at its most exuberant. The "show" continues into the lobby and lounge area, all in wood, with ceiling mouldings, a fireplace decorated with ceramics, and heavy draperies. The rooms are done in the same Art Nouveau style, but in a more understated way – with silvery lotus flower prints, and furniture and lighting that fit in – to create a restful environment. The modern bathrooms are cleverly laid out. The buffet breakfast is served in a winter garden setting. After that, you have your choice of the shops on the Avenue des Ternes, the Théâtre de l'Empire, sightseeing on the Champs-Élysées or the peace and quiet of the Parc Monceau.

CHAMPS-ÉLYSÉES • CONCORDE • MADELEINE ▶ Plan page 166

8

413

Grands Hommes

17 pl. Panthéon ✉ 75005   ⓜ Luxembourg
✆ 01 46 34 19 60 **Fax** 01 43 26 67 32
e-mail reservation@hoteldesgrandshommes.com
www.hoteldesgrandshommes.com

31 rm – ♦€80/310 ♦♦€90/430, ☲€12

Jérome D'ALMEIDA

This beautiful 18C building is ideally located across from the Pantheon, near the Luxembourg Gardens and the Sorbonne. It is far from anonymous, and has a distinctive name. André Breton, the father of Surrealism, lived here while writing his manifesto, *Les champs magnétiques*; and it was here that he invented automatic writing with his associate Philippe Soupault. Staying across from the Pantheon, visible from all the best rooms, reminds you of all the famous people resting in peace under the dome, including Alexandre Dumas, Victor Hugo, Pierre and Marie Curie, André Malraux and Jean Jaurès. The rooms, not large but all renovated in 2002, are elegant and stylishly comfortable, with refined furniture, a Directoire atmosphere (a tribute to Napoleon) and wall hangings in shimmering colours. The rooms on the upper floors have small balconies overlooking the rooftops of Paris and Sacré-Cœur in the distance.

5

Kléber

7 r. Belloy ✉ 75116   **Ⓜ** Boissière
☎ 01 47 23 80 22 **Fax** 01 49 52 07 20
e-mail kleberhotel@wanadoo.fr **www**.kleberhotel.com

23 rm – ♗€99/299, ♗♗€99/299, ⌸€14 – **1 suite**

G.Corbic/MICHELIN

The intimate family-oriented Kléber owes its personality to its owners, who are passionate antique hunters. The décor reflects their varied tastes: wrought-iron consoles, laquerware commodes, coffee tables with porphyry tops, medallion armchairs, fine marquetry in precious wood, velvet draperies, sideboards covered with motifs, exposed stone walls, Oriental rugs, luxurious tapestries, old paintings, mirrors, and painted ceramic lamps. The rich and flamboyant setting offers various types of atmosphere and recalls the baroque spirit of the 18th and 19th centuries. Trompe-l'œil frescoes evoking the Commedia dell'Arte add to the already abundant and eclectic charm. The rooms have fine parquet floors and personal touches along the same lines. The bathrooms, decorated with mosaics, boast spa baths, hydrojets and jacuzzis.

ÉTOILE • TROCADÉRO • PASSY • BOIS DE BOULOGNE ▶ **Plan page 297**

16

Noailles

9 r. Michodière ✉ 75002   Ⓜ Quatre Septembre
✆ 01 47 42 92 90 **Fax** 01 49 24 92 71
e-mail goldentulip.denoailles@wanadoo.fr
www.hoteldenoailles.com

59 rm – ♦€180/255 ♦♦€200/345, ☞€15 – 2 suites

Noailles

This is the kind of French hotel with a wonderful personal touch. A classical façade offsets the cutting-edge interior design, part of a recent facelift that has transformed the establishment. A luminous patio-terrace is the "centre of gravity" for this new look. Enhanced by cascading vegetation, it is a lovely breakfast setting and a source of light for the library and side lounges, with their clean-lined leather furnishings. The jazz cocktail hour on Thursday evenings livens things up around the fireplace in the bar. The pared-down, contemporary rooms (also arranged around the patio) have a Japanese look, with a mineral style in the bathrooms. Additional features include a sauna and fitness facilities. With the welcoming, enthusiastic staff and attentive service, you are guaranteed to have a really enjoyable stay.

2

Pershing Hall

B3

49 r. P. Charon ✉ 75008   Ⓜ George V
📞 01 58 36 58 00 **Fax** 01 58 36 58 01
e-mail info@pershinghall.com **www**.pershinghall.com

26 rm – ♦€312/420 ♦♦€420/500,⌑€26 – 6 suites

Pershing Hall

One of the most unusual gardens in Paris is hidden here, where the names of John Pershing and Andrée Putman are closely linked. The former, commander of American forces in France, used this townhouse as his residence during the First World War. The latter, a designer, created the decor when it was turned into a charming hotel.The Empire-style façade remains intact. But, inside, the building has been considerably altered over the years. Andrée Putman took on the task of designing the space and the furniture on the five floors of rooms. From the patio, you can enjoy the amazing open-air garden with its hundreds of varieties of plants, an ideal place for relaxing. The elegant and cosy rooms exemplify luxury with clean lines, lighting effects, and a blend of noble materials and colours. The bathrooms are decorated with mosaic tiles, and the rooms and corridors are filled with artwork by a number of contemporary artists.

CHAMPS-ÉLYSÉES • CONCORDE • MADELEINE ▶ Plan page 166

8

Villa Royale Montsouris

144 r. Tombe-Issoire ⊠ 75014 Ⓜ Porte d'Orléans
☎ 01 56 53 89 89 **Fax** 01 56 53 89 80
e-mail montsouris@leshotelsdeparis.com
www.leshotelsdeparis.com

36 rm – ♦€85/230 ♦♦€95/370, ☲€18

Bruno Delessard

It's hard to imagine this luxury hotel and its "Thousand and One Nights" décor behind the unassuming, typically Parisian white façade. But once inside, with all the Mediterranean colours, wrought-iron furniture, plaited wicker sofas, carpets, net curtains and knick-knacks, it seems like some exotic place far away from Paris. The same Arab-Andalusian atmosphere pervades the rooms, decorated in vivid tones, multi-coloured curtains and cushions, rare objects, stained-glass lamps and finely worked metal bedheads. The bathrooms have an original style too, with blue and ochre tiles in enamelled lava. Every room is named after a Moroccan city, highlighting the *riad* style: Marrakech, Essaouira, etc. Breakfast is another strong point at this establishment, with carefully selected products including fresh fruit, *viennoiseries*, rolls and jam. Before rushing back into the city, enjoy a walk in the nearby Parc Montsouris.

Waldorf Arc de Triomphe

36 r. Pierre Demours ✉ 75017   Ⓜ Ternes
℘ 01 47 64 67 67 **Fax** 01 40 53 91 34
e-mail arc@hotelswaldorfparis.com **www**.hotelswaldorfparis.com

44 rm – ♦ € 340/460 ♦♦ € 370/460, ⌣ € 20

Waldorf Arc de Triomphe

This prestigious chain has inaugurated its third Parisian hotel after extensive renovations, and the result is very appealing. Located at a reasonable distance from the Place de l'Étoile, it has even preserved a certain peace and quiet far from the hustle and bustle of the Champs Élysées. The range of standard, superior and deluxe rooms in neutral, pleasantly restful tones is elegant and contemporary. The personalized furniture, refined fittings and exquisite taste, down to the tiniest details, go along with the establishment's seamless luxury status. The diligent service and quality of the breakfast, taken in the comfortable cream-coloured dining room, come as no surprise. Everything here has been done to make the guests feel comfortable, including the sauna and steam room awaiting you downstairs where you can unwind after a long day. The height of luxury – the small indoor swimming pool and fitness room are a pleasant alternative to television. Impeccable.

PALAIS DES CONGRÈS • WAGRAM • TERNES • BATIGNOLLES ▶ Plan page 322

17

Du Nord

C3

47 r. Albert Thomas   Ⓜ Jacques Bonsergent
✉ 75010
☎ 01 42 01 66 00 **Fax** 01 42 01 92 10
e-mail contact@hoteldunord-leparivelo.com
www.hoteldunord-leparivelo.com

24 rm – †€68/79 ††€68/79,⌣€7,50

Du Nord

This area between Place de la République and the Canal Saint-Martin is quite low-key despite the arrival in recent years of a "lite" Bobo crowd (bohemian bourgeois). There's nothing luxurious about the rooms in this small hotel, but they are all decorated in bright colours that add a personal touch and a fresh and cheerful note to the rustic look of the establishment. Breakfast is served in a vaulted room where the exposed stonework creates the atmosphere of an old Parisian residence. You won't have to break the piggybank with the reasonable rates here, so why not enjoy an evening at one of the theatres on the Grands Boulevards. The hotel encouraged guests to bike around town well before the high-profile Vélib' programme set up in the summer of 2007, and has 10 bicycles available for guests free of charge. Now's your chance!

10

Laumière

4 r. Petit ✉ 75019   Ⓜ Laumière
☎ 01 42 06 10 77 **Fax** 01 42 06 72 50
e-mail lelaumiere@wanadoo.fr **www**.hotel-lelaumiere.com

54 rm – ♦€58/70 ♦♦€59/78, ⊑ €8

Laumière

This little establishment run by the same family since 1931 makes up for its distance from the main Parisian tourist sites by being near the Parc des Buttes-Chaumont, the Canal de l'Ourcq, the Parc de La Villette and the Cité des Sciences et de l'Industrie. A metro station just next to the hotel (Laumière) will take you into the centre of town.The small and discreetly furnished rooms are decorated in a subtle contemporary style. Some have a little balcony giving onto a garden with trees – these are the ones to request if you prefer a quieter room. Breakfast is served overlooking the greenery, where tables are set up as soon as the weather permits, to the delight of regulars and new guests. The rates – very reasonable for Paris – are another strong point at this hotel.

LA VILLETTE-CITÉ DES SCIENCES • BUTTES CHAUMONT ▶ **Plan page 350**

19

Notes

NOTES

Index of plans

Index of **plans**

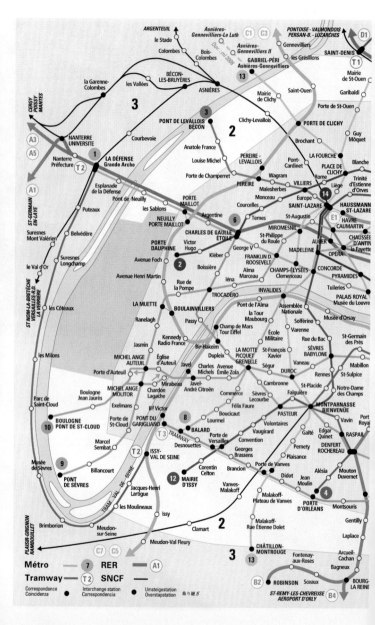

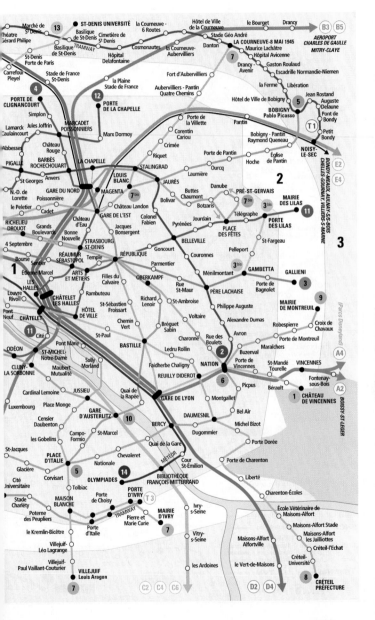

429

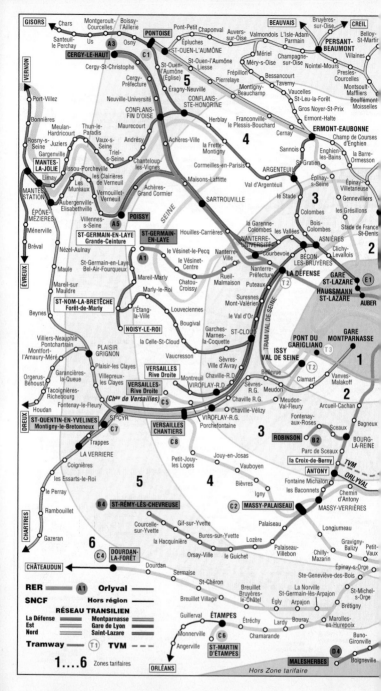